REBELLIOUS PARENTS

REBELLIOUS PARENTS

Parental Movements in Central-Eastern Europe and Russia

Edited by
KATALIN FÁBIÁN
and
ELŻBIETA KOROLCZUK

INDIANA UNIVERSITY PRESS
Bloomington and Indianapolis

This book is a publication of

Indiana University Press
Office of Scholarly Publishing
Herman B Wells Library 350
1320 East 10th Street
Bloomington, Indiana 47405 USA

iupress.indiana.edu

The paper used in this publication meets the minimum requirements of the American National Standard for Information Sciences—Permanence of Paper for Printed Library Materials, ANSI Z39.48–1992.

Manufactured in the United States of America

Library of Congress Cataloging-in-Publication Data

Names: Fábián, Katalin, editor. | Korolczuk, Elżbieta, editor.
Title: Rebellious parents : parental movements in Central-Eastern Europe and Russia / edited by Katalin Fabian and Elzbieta Korolczuk.
Description: Bloomington : Indiana University Press, 2017. | Includes bibliographical references and index.
Identifiers: LCCN 2017017971 (print) | LCCN 2017002957 (ebook) | ISBN 9780253026736 (e-book) | ISBN 9780253026262 (cloth : alk. paper) | ISBN 9780253026675 (pbk. : alk. paper)
Subjects: LCSH: Parents—Poltical activity—Europe, Eastern. | Parents—Poltical activity—Europe, Central. | Parents—Political activity—Russia (Federation)
Classification: LCC HQ755.8 (print) | LCC HQ755.8 .R395 2017 (ebook) | DDC 306.874094—dc23
LC record available at https://lccn.loc.gov/2017017971

1 2 3 4 5 22 21 20 19 18 17

In grateful memory of the loving care and ever-patient, gentle support of my mother, Éva, who died just as the book was being completed. Her honest, humble, and always pragmatic approach as well as beautiful spirit always faithfully guided me. KF

Contents

Acknowledgments

We wish to thank several people and institutions for supporting our work and helping us to transition this book from an idea to a reality. Both Södertörn University, home to researchers focusing on Eastern Europe and the Baltic Sea region, and the University of Gothenburg, which specializes in the study of social movements, provided excellent infrastructural and intellectual support for our work. We were greatly assisted by the Swedish Research Council-funded research project, "Institutional Constraints and Creative Solutions: Civil Society in Poland in Comparative Perspective" (grant 421–2010–1706), and we extend our sincere thanks to them. We are especially grateful to Professor Kerstin Jacobsson, who in her capacity as a project leader steadfastly supported our efforts both intellectually and organizationally. Thanks are also due to Lafayette College for supporting Katalin Fábián's research and providing funding for Devon Clifton and Andrew Keck.

We would also like to thank the Centre for Baltic and East European Studies (CBEES) for their generous support; the contributing authors of this book presented their findings at the international workshop, "Parental Movements: The Politicization of Motherhood and Fatherhood in Central and Eastern Europe and the Post-Soviet Region," organized in May 2014 at Södertörn University, Stockholm, Sweden. The participants were invited to discuss their chapters to encourage the dialogue across different disciplines and theoretical interpretations. We wish to thank the reviewers and all the scholars who offered comments on our work and gave us constructive criticism both during the workshop at CBEES and at the seminar held at the University of Gothenburg, where we presented the main findings. We are also grateful to Agnieszka Graff, Kerstin Jacobsson, Janet Elise Johnson, and Katarzyna Wojnicka for their insightful comments. Any mistakes are, of course, ours. Elżbieta Korolczuk also wishes to express her gratitude to Renata E. Hryciuk, who introduced her to the theme of motherist movements and with whom she studied mothers' and fathers' groups in Poland. Their collaboration provided significant inspiration for this book.

We wish to thank Janice Frisch and Raina Nadine Polivka of Indiana University Press, for their careful attention and help along the way, and Robert J. Sloan, then Editor-in-Chief of Indiana University Press, for his enthusiastic support of our project. We are indebted to Lesley Cameron and Andrew Kortyna, who both offered excellent suggestions and provided generous support. We would like to acknowledge Devon Clifton and Andrew Keck for helping us to proofread and format the text. Last but not least, we are grateful to all the contributing authors of this book for their cooperative approach to this project.

REBELLIOUS PARENTS

Introduction: Rebellious Parents in Central-Eastern Europe and Russia

Katalin Fábián and Elżbieta Korolczuk

Introduction

This volume focuses on a broad range of parental movements that have emerged in contemporary Central-Eastern Europe and Russia over the past two decades. Examples of such movements include social mobilizations of conservative parental groups against legal and discursive changes that would affect gender equality in Ukraine and Russia, Czech parents opposing mandatory vaccination of children, and fathers' groups in Poland and the Czech Republic focusing on custody rights. Parental activism is increasingly visible and influential, but it has been the subject of relatively little research to date (e.g., Caiazza 2002; Fábián 2013; Hryciuk and Korolczuk 2013; Jagudina 2009; Kok 2002; Wojnicka 2013). We aim to rectify this by analyzing what we have identified as representative cases of parental movements in Central-Eastern Europe and Russia. We hope to enrich and explain the current interpretations of social activism and civil society in the postcommunist region, which is often associated with a low level of social engagement and weak civil society, and to offer new conceptualization of mothers' and fathers' activism that may be applicable in other geographical contexts.

Our collection of essays aims to fill a gap in the scholarship on civil society and social movements that is both empirical and theoretical, presenting an entirely new set of observations on the developments in contemporary parental activism in Central-Eastern Europe and Russia and proposing new conceptualizations of civic activism and civil society. The authors address the following questions:

1. How have mothers, fathers, and those thinking of becoming parents responded to contemporary political, social, cultural, and economic challenges on a collective level? Under which conditions do parental movements emerge in the region?
2. If and how do the legacies of different forms of existing communism as well as the effects of contemporary neoliberal influences, globalization, and a recent nationalist-conservative turn affect the emergence, trajectory, and activities of parental movements in the respective countries?
3. Which strategies have activists used? What kind of identities and frameworks do they construct? What are the effects of parental mobilizations?

The essays in this book address these questions by examining interactions between the political sphere, everyday lives and practices, and social activism of parents and close kin. The up-to-date empirical studies included demonstrate that the identities, frames, and strategies applied by these movements are embedded both in local ideals of parenthood and gender and in the context of local civil society and citizenship, while simultaneously building on various, often conflicting, transnational ideologies and practices.

Parental Movements: Definitions and Main Themes of the Book

Parental movements include formal organizations such as non-governmental organizations (NGOs), as well as informal networks, and online platforms that mobilize people on the basis of their identities and experiences as parents; their goal is to introduce political and social changes pertaining not only to families, but to society in general. These movements' claims to represent the whole nuclear or extended heterosexual family, rather than just mothers or fathers, reflect the anti-individualistic ideological stance of most parental activists.[1] Such claims also fit with the parental activists' stated appreciation for informal, community, and grassroots organizing.

We used the term "parental movements" because in contrast to parents' movements, which concentrate mostly on legal changes concerning custody, welfare, and health care, the movements examined in this book have broader agendas. They address a range of social and political issues, such as national identity, citizens' relationship to the state, and the gender order, and they often engage other family members, such as siblings and grandparents.

This book focuses on three main themes in parental mobilization: (1) conservative nationalist trends and reemerging traditionalism, (2) changes concerning the status and social perception of fatherhood and gender equality, and (3) shifts in health-related social policies. Parental movements may incorporate more than one of these themes in their repertoires. For example, Ukrainian parental movements combine nationalism with fatherhood, and Bulgarian parental movements combine nationalism with a demand for state support for reproductive technologies. We are also aware of parental mobilizations in the postcommunist region that point beyond these three main themes, for example, nascent groups that address the issue of nonheteronormative parenting. However, we decided to narrow the thematic focus in this book to show how similar trends, such as conservative and nationalist tendencies, have developed differently in specific national sociopolitical contexts. We also decided to have a separate section on fathers' activism, rather than on mothers' movements, for two main reasons. First, gender and feminist scholars tend to focus on women and their activism, and we argue that there is a need to explore the emerging social activism of men and fathers in the region in more detail. Second, while there is a growing number of studies on mothers' mobilizations in the region (e.g., Fábián 2009, 2010; Hrycak 2002; Hryciuk 2012; Hryciuk and Korolczuk 2013; Jagudina 2009), fathers' activism remains relatively unexplored (Wojnicka 2013; Rodin and Åberg 2013).

This three-pronged thematic focus also allows us to highlight the amalgamation of both long-term and more recent developments, as well as local and global trends in the region. Cultural, political, and economic changes have forced people in the postcommunist countries to reformulate and reimagine their identities as practiced in the family and as members of the broader political community. In other historical and geographic contexts, such renegotiations and often fundamental changes in family life and corresponding social and cultural tensions have led to the emergence of social mobilizations based on parental, usually maternal, identities (cf. Jaquette 1994; Molyneux 1985). However, little is known of how mothers and fathers in the postcommunist region collectively respond to similar trends.[2]

The case studies in this book highlight that parental movements emerge from and uncannily reflect at least three sets of ambiguities that indicate how local, transnational, long-term, and contemporary sociopolitical and cultural trends interact in the region. These interactions perhaps also apply to other regional and thematic contexts of civil society and social movements.

The set of ambiguities concerns the activists' relationship to the following: (1) the state (as the source of regulations influencing family life and children, including mandatory vaccination or sex education), (2) what they perceive as the "West," with its individualist focus and recognition of new family arrangements (LGBTQ families, marriage equality, and new family configurations resulting from the use of reproductive technologies), and (3) gender equality as fostered by the European Union (EU), the United Nations (UN), or the state. The attitudes of the parental mobilizations toward these entities and concepts are often ambivalent and also subject to change. In their flexibility and adaptability, these attitudes can offer strategic potential. As we demonstrate in the conclusions (chapter 12), where we present the regional and theoretical lessons resulting from the analyses included in this volume, parental movements can at times influence local environments and use local and transnational political opportunity structures to their benefit by flexibly relying on these three main sets of ambiguities.

This book showcases parent-driven movements that can be conservative or progressive in orientation. From this broad spectrum, we highlight many of the notable organizations that do not fit neatly into the commonly used ideological categories of left/right and progressive/conservative. Rather, many represent a yet undefined, hybrid ideology, closest perhaps to a version of populism focusing on the perceived conflict between the elite/experts and "the people," and on valorization of community, the local, and what they call authentic values. Activists in several parental movements oppose the social acceptance of certain changes in family models, such as the recognition of lesbian, gay, bisexual, transgender, and queer (LGBTQ) families and the increasing number of divorces and extramarital births. A key part of their specific form of conservatism is based on the rejection of what the activists see as "rampant individualism" of the modern world. While rejecting the modern emphasis on individualism, these movements also raise a voice against the consumerism and neoliberalism embodied in such trends as the privatization of the healthcare sector and the reduction of state support for families, linking neoconservative trends with opposition toward neoliberalism.

The rise of parental activism, especially with a conservative orientation, is not specific to postcommunist countries; it is a transnational phenomenon. Movements opposing alternative family arrangements, gender equality, and sexual and reproductive rights are active not only in the postcommunist region, but also in North and Latin America, and some parts of

Africa (Bob 2012; Case 2011). Such conservative trends are also on the rise in Europe, with over 490 organizations and networks working in 32 European countries today (Datta 2013). Occasionally, their activists and supporters mobilize on a mass scale. In 2013, for example, hundreds of thousands of protesters, many of them parents with young children, took to the streets of Paris to oppose the legalization of marriage for homosexual couples and to defend what they called the "natural family" (Fassin 2014). In 2014, in the south and west regions of Baden-Württemberg and Cologne, Germany, an alliance called *Besorgte Eltern* (Concerned Parents) organized a series of protest marches to voice their opposition to the new sex education curriculum initiated by the coalition of *Bündnis 90/Die Grünen* (the Green Party) and *Sozialdemokratische Partei Deutschlands* (SDP, the Social Democratic Party of Germany). They marched with slogans such as "Marriage and Family! Stop gender ideology and sexualization of our children!" (Blum 2015, 47–48).

Most of the existing organizations involved in such actions are faith-based (Catholic, Protestant, and Orthodox Christian) and many religious groups mobilize parents. Still, other such opposition groups pose as parental groups for strategic reasons, claiming to represent the interests of parents and children and to defend "family values" (Graff and Korolczuk 2017; Hodžic and Bijelić 2014). Thus, the question remains as to whether recent mass mobilizations in France and Germany are initiated by concerned parents or by conservative groups disguising themselves as such in order to achieve wide social impact. The answer will probably vary depending on the context, but the cases included in this volume demonstrate that conservative parental movements in Central-Eastern Europe and Russia are often grassroots initiatives of mothers and fathers.

Despite the apparent anti-Western stance of some parental groups in the region, there are tangible links between activists from Western Europe, the United States, and local groups in the postcommunist countries. In fact, the Central-East European and Russian conservative parental movements draw on both sets of material and cultural resources: a historically rooted, local, anti-Western tradition and a contemporary global social conservative context, as Höjdestrand, Strelnyk, and Dimitrova point out in chapters 1, 2, and 3. The global flow of ideas and strategies includes opposition not only to gender equality but also to other values and themes that are considered modern or postmodern, such as vaccination or same-sex marriage (Fassin 2014; Hasmanová Marhánková in this volume). As a result, a new type of "patriotic" civil society has emerged in Central-Eastern Europe and Russia that links nationalist rhetoric with an illiberal ideological stance (see, for example, Höjdestrand, Dimitrova, and Korolczuk and Hryciuk in chapters 1, 3, and 4).

It should be noted, however, that while some parental movements tend to be conservative, others are open to new ideas and embrace social change, and thus can be termed progressive. As the analysis of the Polish fathers' mobilization shows in chapter 4, even within the same country some organizations subscribe to nationalist discourse while others do not. Thus, we propose to interpret the conservative stance of many parental activists in the region not as local specificity, but as an inherent part of contemporary political shifts taking place on both national and transnational levels. Interweaving cultural and political aspects into their agendas, the conservative parental movements in countries such as Russia or Poland reflect transnational conservative trends while also embodying regional specificity. The rejection of the gender equality agenda associated with the former communist regime is one such example. These movements are likewise deeply embedded in their respective national contexts.

Lessons for Civil Society Studies

The chapters in this book show that earlier scholars may have underestimated the dynamic nature of civil society in the region. Parental activism confirms this dynamic, even in contexts such as Russia, where civil society has been weakened significantly in recent years.

Our intended theoretical contribution to scholarship on civil society and social movements pertains to challenging both (a) the idealized model of civil society ingrained in many studies on social activism in the postcommunist region and (b) the transposition of Western-centric ideals onto the postcommunist experience of social activism, which in turn appears as a failure or as deficient. While the renewed interest in civil society originated in Central-Eastern Europe, we agree with scholars such as Chris Hann, who asserts that civil society studies have been "too narrowly circumscribed by modern western models of liberal individualism" and argues that analyses of civil society require more attention to "a range of informal interpersonal practices" (Hann 1996, 3). Other scholars point to the fact that studies of civil society in the region tend to be based on an ideal functioning civil society measured by how many people volunteer, the membership of organizations, or the number of people who have signed petitions (Ekiert and Kubik 2014). Most existing studies focus on formal organizations and take for granted the functional division between service providers and lobbyists, as well as the ideological division between progressive and conservative groups (Jacobsson and Saxonberg 2013).

These trends may help to explain why parental movements have rarely appeared in the literature on the postcommunist European region, despite their growing visibility and international connections. Arguably, this omission could be explained by their relative novelty. Many parental movements are relatively new, such as conservative parental networks in Ukraine and Russia, parents' mobilization around reproductive technologies in Bulgaria, and the antivaccination movement in the Czech Republic. However, other parental movements were already visible in the early 1990s. Such examples include the home-birth movements in the Czech Republic and Hungary, fathers' groups in Poland, and organizations of parents with children with disabilities in Baltic states (Fábián 2013; Sumskiene 2014; Wojnicka 2013). We argue that in addition to the relatively recent appearance of parental movements, there are also conceptual and theoretical limitations on the existing models of civil society and civic activism that may explain these movements' seeming absence from the literature thus far.

First, parental mobilizations are generally grassroots in nature and may not necessarily have been formalized as, for example, an NGO. These groups often distance themselves from politics, stressing that their goals are practical issues connected to everyday life rather than systemic changes. Scholarship on non-NGO, grassroots-based, low-key types of social activism in the region and beyond has noted how likely it is that such activities will be missed entirely from analyses of civil society and political protest (e.g., Bilić and Stubbs 2015; Jacobsson 2015; Jacobsson and Korolczuk 2017; Lichterman and Eliasoph 2014). Because parental mobilizations in Central-Eastern Europe and Russia tend to organize locally and over a long period of time, often focusing on self-help and service provision, they are not visible in the same way as other social movements. Additionally, for ideological reasons, some parental groups and networks do not ask for or receive state support or foreign funding. Refraining from such funding may limit their resources, organizational capacity, and visibility even further.

Second, these movements rebel against what they perceive as unjust state control and resist some authorities such as gender equality experts, medical authorities, and judicial or international institutions. However, the activists rarely organize series of major protests events, which are the main staple of contentious activism and also the principal mechanism leading to news coverage and scholarly interest. Their strategies depend strongly on the local context. In some countries activists avoid open contestation and protests, and in others they combine service provision with advocacy and occasional, usually small-scale, protests. If and when political opportunities become relatively open, as was the case for parents with children with disabilities in the Baltic states, the activists focus on finding ways to collaborate with the state. However, under major duress, parental groups can overcome organizational and financial constraints and organize highly disruptive and visible protests; as in the case of fathers' groups in Poland (chapter 4), mobilization of home-birth activists in Hungary (chapter 11), or the 2014 Warsaw protest in which parents of disabled children occupied the office of the prime minister (Kubicki 2015).

Third, unlike other notable social movements, such as women's and feminist movements, some parental mobilizations in Central-Eastern Europe and Russia do not fit the liberal vision of civil society, which many scholars define as a specific type of societal action that is based on the recognition of plurality, difference, and equality between individuals (e.g., Kocka 2006). In contrast, many parental movements tend to be conservative in the sense that they oppose a focus on the individual and value hierarchy over equality, especially in the area of gender and parent-child relations. While parental movements may not reflect the liberal definition of civil society due to their ideological orientation and values, neither do they represent "uncivil society" (Kopecký and Mudde 2003), because they rarely employ disruptive strategies to reach their aims.

Consequently, we argue that a new, locally embedded conceptualization of civil society is needed to explain these mobilizations—one that would enable us to see the richness and heterogeneity of existing forms of activism (c.f. Dunn and Hann 1996; Jacobsson 2015; Jacobsson and Korolczuk 2017). As we discuss in detail in the conclusions (chapter 12), contributions to this volume highlight the fluid, flexible, and context-dependent aspects of civic engagement. Parental activists employ a set of flexible and adaptable ambiguities in their relationship to the state, to what they interpret as the West, and to gender equality. We interpret this flexible ambiguity as a highly adaptable approach to engage in political activism while simultaneously challenging and redefining what politics and civic engagement mean in the postcommunist context. While elements of these trends had already emerged in different countries, similar developments, labeled "disavowal," characterize segments of US civil society (Bennett et al. 2014; Johnson and Robinson 2006), the combination of these ambiguities appears highly visible in contemporary parental movements in Central-Eastern Europe and Russia.

Parental Movements: The Intersection of Disciplines, Theories, and Concepts

In this study of parental movements, we have applied interdisciplinary dialogue by using the methodologies and theories of sociology, anthropology, political science, and gender studies. All the contributing authors, trained in varied academic fields in the social sciences, have made disciplinary incursions into the theories of civil society and social movements that form central elements of this book. Building on these theoretical strands, the contributions refer to the most relevant literature on gendered aspects of various types of social change, including gendered nationalism, and the impact of social policy changes and reactions to such changes. Moreover, the authors are all long-term observers and inhabitants of the countries that they report on, thus they combine a bird's-eye view with careful depictions of social movement activities on the ground.

This book is in dialogue with four main schools of literature linking civil society with the changes in gendered practices and ideologies of parenting, and shifts in social policies. First, it challenges the depiction of civil society and social movements in the postcommunist region as tendentiously falling short of expectations; that is, described as weak, bureaucratized, and demobilized (e.g., Howard 2003; Mendelson and Glenn 2002). As such, this book adds to the growing body of literature showing that there is a significant potential for social activism and social movements in the region, but they are not necessarily of a kind that are highly visible or easily empirically accessible (Jacobsson 2015; Jacobsson and Saxonberg 2013; Jacobsson and Korolczuk 2017; Kubik and Linch 2013). Our contribution to this growing scholarly body of literature is the incorporation of parental activism since there is currently no book (edited or single-authored) exploring parental activism in Central-Eastern Europe and Russia. The chapters show that the "lack of"/"deficient in" perspective needs to be more nuanced; when grassroots parental activism is accounted for, civil society appears to thrive (or at least exist) in the same context.

Second, this volume contributes to the growing body of literature that examines the intersections between civil society, the family, and gender (Hagemann, Michel, and Budde 2008; Howell 2005; Kok 2002; Korolczuk 2013; Nautz et al. 2013). To date, anthropologists and sociologists interested in family and kinship systems have seldom discussed the question of civic engagement; conversely, most scholars interested in civil society have focused on associations, leaving out "the most powerful and complex association of all—the family" (Ginsborg 2013, 18) and the gendered consequences of the divide between the public and the private spheres (Okin 1998; Scott and Keates 2004). Jude Howell (2005) observes that studies interrogating the relationship between gender, family, and civil society are badly needed given the centrality of civil society as a space of contestation by feminists and women in general (engaged in self-help groups, faith-based organizations, and mothers' groups). As the chapters in this volume aptly show, family members—both men and women—politicize their gendered identities and practices related to the family. This book explores the collective (de)gendered identities that parental movements promulgate and the frames they employ, along with the corresponding local understandings of civil society and political engagements that are reflected in this type of activism.

Third, we aim to contribute to the significant body of scholarship on mothers' mobilizations in different cultural contexts, which has maintained an especially notable focus on Latin America and the United States (e.g., DiQuinzio 2006; Jaquette 1994; Molyneux 1985; Naples 1998; Werbner 1999). We also aim to enhance the literature on fathers' activism, which has been limited mostly to the otherwise wide-ranging Anglo-Saxon context and Western Europe (e.g., Bertoia and Drakich 1993; Crowley 2008; Flood 2012; Collier and Sheldon 2006). Scholars have rarely discussed the question of how women and men in Central-Eastern Europe and Russia organize as mothers and fathers. Moreover, existing research on the region focuses on a few specific cases such as the Soldiers' Mothers in Russia, mothers fighting for welfare provisions, and fathers' groups in Poland, as well as the home-birth movement in Hungary (e.g., Fábián 2013; Hrycak 2002; Hryciuk 2012; Hryciuk and Korolczuk 2013; Jagudina 2009; Wojnicka 2013). Some of these movements are part of the present book, but our aim is to offer a broader view of contemporary parental mobilizations in the postcommunist Eurasian region and situate this phenomenon in the scholarly literature on social movements and civil society.

Finally, some chapters in this book engage with the scholarship on current demographic, socioeconomic, and political changes in the context of shifts in the dominant ideologies and practices of gender and parenthood (Björnberg 1992; Carlbäck et al. 2012; Glass and Fodor 2007; Michel 2012; Mätzke and Ostner 2010). Scholars studying fundamental sociodemographic changes that have taken place over the past century in Europe show how shifts in the composition of households and in relationships within families (e.g., increasing individualization and diversity of relationship practices) influence and are influenced by social policy. Since the mid-1990s, family-related social policies have gained immense public attention, and the changes that began with increasing neoliberal pressure to reduce expenses in Western welfare states later extended to other regions, such as postcommunist Europe.

The intense public attention to the relationship between demographics and social policy also includes Central-Eastern Europe and Russia, which went through the transition toward smaller, "thinner," and "non-co-resident families" at a different, slightly faster pace (Hantrais 2006, quoted in Carlbäck et al. 2012, 3). The focus of academics has been on how these socioeconomic and political changes impact social policies, and how they affect practices and ideologies of parenting and care work (e.g., Carlbäck et al. 2012; Glass and Fodor 2007; Fodor et al. 2002; Szelewa and Polakowski 2008). Scholars focusing on Central-Eastern Europe and the post-Soviet states showed also that political-economic processes of postcommunist transformation have been deeply gendered. These works have highlighted that states and markets regulate gender relations in line with local and transnational trends (Funk and Mueller 1993; Gal and Kligman 2000; Johnson and Robinson 2006; Mahon and Williams 2007; Lukić, Regulska, and Zaviršek 2006). While this literature discusses the changes in social policies and the practices and norms concerning gender, family, and parenthood in the region, this book looks at how parental activism responds to and influences these historical, social and policy changes.

In addition to linking different strands of research on civil society, social movements, family, and gender, our volume highlights also temporal intersections. The authors have adopted an implicitly comparative angle regarding temporal change. Thus, while most authors highlight the lasting legacy of differently experienced communist systems, some also readily acknowledge that many of the trends discussed in this book have relatively long historical roots (see Åberg and Rodin in chapter 5, Höjdestrand in chapter 1, and Hrešanová in chapter 10 of this book). The pronatalist orientation and fears concerning depopulation and the prospects of national future have been firmly in the political agenda as a matter of concern since the nineteenth century. In many countries, debates on the best governmental response to the threat of demographic decline became a social and cultural focal point as early as the late 1930s and the first half of the 1940s, as shown by Ina Dimitrova in the case of Bulgaria (chapter 3). Contemporarily, population policy and fears of demographic decline appear not only as part of national welfare policy, as was the case in the twentieth century, but also as an element of nationalist revival and as a rationale behind applying biotechnology to human reproduction.

Finally, this volume examines the responses to the changes that emerged due to the fall of communism. Contemporary parental movements may appear as phenomena rooted in recent demographic shifts, migration, and changes in values and practices, as well as social policies pertaining to parenthood of the transformation era (Carlbäck et al. 2012). During the last two decades the region has been a major testing ground for globalization and its contemporary political and economic lieutenants of democratization, privatization, and associated transnational ideological currents, such as neoliberalism. The postcommunist transformation in many countries brought about significant cuts in family allowances and the decline in female employment, which substantially changed the economic situation of families (Saxonberg and Sirovatka 2006; Szelewa and Polakowski 2008). At the same time, as the cases of parental mobilization in the Baltic states, the Czech Republic, and Hungary demonstrate, these movements give voice to new norms concerning not only parenthood and health care, but also the market and the media (Carlbäck et al. 2012). International organizations and institutions may also promulgate these norms that can include new cultural ideals of motherhood; for example, "intensive motherhood" and "engaged fatherhood" as described in the US context (Dowd 2000; Hays 1996). The parental movements discussed in this book often address different aspects of these normative and economic changes simultaneously. For example, the case of Bulgarian mobilization around reproductive technologies links the long-simmering fear of depopulation with new neoliberal ideals of "deserving" parents (chapter 3), while the Czech antivaccination activists redefine parental engagement in terms of their opposition to the bio-power of the state (chapter 8).

Alongside and partially in reaction to liberalism, conservative and nationalist tendencies have also emerged in the region (Gal and Kligman 2000; Graff 2009; Kováts and Põim 2015). Parental activists have frequently become carriers of such conservative messages, often highlighting that their goal is the wellbeing not only of the family and children, but also of the larger national community. As Höjdestrand's analysis of the parents' movement in contemporary Russia (chapter 1) aptly shows, some parental groups have emerged in reaction to and as a result of partial democratization, neoliberal-inspired transformations in the economy, and the newly reconfigured social functions of the postcommunist state.

From Mothers' and Fathers' to Parental Movements? (De)Gendering Social Activism

Parental movements are hardly new phenomena. However, they have often been subsumed under such increasingly recognized foci of social movements as protests for welfare provisions, gender equality, nationalist revival, and environmental sustainability. Family members have actively participated in these movements on behalf of their own interests and in the name of future generations (Molyneux 1985). In addition to mobilizations in trade unions and other formal institutions, recent labor histories have also unearthed numerous case studies that show families adding collective action to their strategies for economic survival (Kok 2002). The emotional and economic ties that families represent have provided an ample basis for information exchange, awareness raising, and collective action of members. The generational location and socially prescribed provider responsibility of parents make them a group who would most likely rebel against certain state-endorsed policies and demand attention to their plight by initiating collective action. Social movements of parents, usually mothers, have long-established roots as parts of revolutions and as initiators of major social reforms.

In using the phrase "parental movements," we follow the self-definition of activists, some of whom avoid gendered representations of parenthood. They define themselves as parents rather than as mothers or fathers and stress that they fight on behalf of the family. In practice, the intent to appear gender-neutral, in other words, "parental," can camouflage an empirical reality of relatively small membership. Depending on context, it may also serve to obscure the fact that activists are nearly all men (as fathers) or nearly exclusively female (as mothers or those who wish to be mothers).[3] The claim of parental mobilizations to represent parents in a gender-neutral form and advocate on behalf of the family as an important social unit can also satisfy multiple politically expedient messages. One such message concerns the demographic downturn, and parents use terms such as "demographic winter" to strengthen their position vis-à-vis the state (Dimitrova in chapter 3 in this volume). Moreover, due to the social transition in late modernity, men and women increasingly share childcare and related responsibilities. Corresponding with this demographic and social transition, some parental movements wish to capitalize on gender neutrality and speak on behalf of all families, which is evident in "daddy schools" in Russia (Åberg and Rodin in chapter 5 of this book). Finally, in some cases, projecting a gender-neutral image is an effective strategy to invite, include, and mobilize men as activists in support of specific claims, as in the case of mostly female infertility patients in Poland (Korolczuk 2015).

Historically, the earliest parental movements were mothers' movements. They developed in various geographical and cultural contexts, often triggered by deteriorating living conditions or changes in social policy that have accompanied sociopolitical, economic, and cultural changes. Mobilizations of women in their capacity as mothers ignited, escalated, and profoundly affected revolutions and reforms such as the French Revolution, the collapse of the Argentine military junta, and the democratization of the former Soviet Union (Caiazza 2002; Jagudina 2009; O'Reilly 2010). The activists often used essentialist notions of motherhood based on the vision of the mother as symbolically reproducing the nation in order to legitimize their claims and avoid repression, especially under authoritarian rule (Jaquette 1994; Mazurek 2010; Werbner 1999). However, there are political movements by and on behalf of mothers that are feminist in their ideological orientation (e.g., DiQuinzio 2006; Hryciuk and Korolczuk 2015; Korolczuk 2013).

While mothers' movements have increasingly been reintegrated as part of both scholarship and politics as important contributors to social change, feminist scholars and activists continue to discuss whether women should use their role as mothers on behalf of their children and, by extension, advocate for society at large. Motherhood is a contested terrain—not only as a set of practices but also as a social and political concept that arouses strong emotions (Nakano Glenn 1994). One powerful argument in support of politicizing motherhood is that it remains an empowering political role and a culturally resonant symbol

(Jaquette 1994; Werbner 1999). The opposing argument is that the role of motherhood is reductionist and essentialist, replacing the broad spectrum of what women's role in society entails, thus creating a trap that keeps women in reproductive roles and allows them to advocate only on behalf of others. These debates have surfaced substantially in the postcommunist context as well, and they are exemplified by the Hungarian home-birth movement's insistence on a parental stance and the waves of mobilizations of Polish mothers, some of which also opted for the gender-neutral identity of a parent rather than a mother (Fábián 2013; Hryciuk and Korolczuk 2013; Korolczuk 2017).

Women's movements in general, and motherist movements in particular, have aptly shown that the activists' relationship with the state is often ambiguous and that the arrow of contestation may go both ways. Some mothers' movements demand that the state pulls back from engaging in what activists consider private terrain. In many other cases, however, they demand that the state and its broad disciplinary apparatus (laws, courts, police, the military, schools, health care, food security, etc.) engage more actively in what had previously been considered a private matter. Of course, the agenda of social movements greatly depends on the local political and cultural context. The fact that many of the movements discussed in this book that consist mostly of women opted for the gender-neutral identity of "parents" is highly significant. It suggests that while traditionally mothers' movements advocated from the position of relative political powerlessness combined with strong symbolic significance, today the symbolic significance of motherhood may be weaker than expected, especially if mothers' rights are framed as social and economic rights. Previous research has shown in both Poland and Hungary that activists who frame their rights as civil or human rights of parents are more likely to gain support than those who fight for the social rights of mothers (Fábián 2014; Hryciuk and Korolczuk 2013).

Fathers' movements very seldom apply the strategy of appearing gender neutral (Korolczuk and Hryciuk in chapter 4, and Saxonberg in chapter 7 in this volume). Fathers' groups and networks have emerged in Austria, Canada, Germany, Spain, the United Kingdom, and the United States, as well as in Central-Eastern Europe, which has also resulted in increased scholarly interest (e.g., Bergmann, Scambor and Wojnicka 2014; Bertoia and Drakich 1993; Crowley 2008; Flood 2012; Municio-Larsson and Algans 2002). As the cases of fathers' groups in Ukraine, Poland, and the Czech Republic show, even those fathers' movements that stress the need for more gender equality simultaneously claim distinct gender-specific capacities for men and women that complement each other in what they interpret as "traditional" families and societies (Karzabi, Korolczuk and Hryciuk, Saxonberg, and Strelnyk in this book). Gender equality remains a contested concept, and even the activists who promote "engaged fatherhood" may not necessarily coincide with support for equality understood more broadly (e.g., equal share of care-related work).

At the same time, even if most fathers' groups focus on the rights of men in their capacity as parents (Flood 2012), they often stress their aim to fight for the well-being of children and in the name of the family and the nation. This claim has important theoretical and practical implications. Such declarations point to a redefinition of civic activism that emerges from local and everyday conditions. Claiming to represent the whole family—whether in their capacity as fathers or as parents—corresponds with the anti-individualistic ideological stance of many parental activists. Finally, the focus of social movement activists on the family and on people's needs and experiences as parents blurs the division between private and public realms.

Diversity and Intersectionality: A Comparative View on Parental Movements in Central-Eastern Europe and Russia[4]

This edited volume examines various kinds of parental activism in contemporary Central-Eastern Europe and Russia with a specific focus on Bulgaria, the Czech Republic, Estonia, Hungary, Latvia, Lithuania, Poland, Russia, and Ukraine. We aimed to balance the diverse set of empirical cases by highlighting width, depth, and intersectionality while respecting thematic and analytical coherence. Two or more chapters focus on the Czech Republic, Russia, and Ukraine, giving the reader access to a deeper social and political context with the presentation of more than one author's perspective. We chose to deepen the analysis on Russia and Ukraine for highly relevant reasons, including these countries' large and fundamental effects on peace and prosperity in contemporary Europe and beyond. While the war between Ukraine and Russia pits these populations against one another, the chapters in this book highlight many similarities between their respective societies, if investigated from the perspective of parental movements. Seemingly on the opposite side, namely the peaceful development of civil society, are the three chapters on Czech Republic that show this country also trying to balance the heritage of communist-era gender equality policies and the many effects of contemporary globalization, neoliberalism, and conservative trends.

By including only one case study each on Bulgaria, Estonia, Hungary, Latvia, Lithuania, and Poland, we offer a more broadly comparative framework for those countries. The contributions highlight the interaction of various kinds of social and political determinants of mobilization, thus offering an active application of the concept of intersectionality. The chapters analyze parental movements against a backdrop of gender, age, economic class, religion, ethnicity, political value orientations, and spatial distributions. We also examine the considerable influence of international norms and actors, especially that of neoliberalism and the EU, that directly affect the case study countries. Only Ukraine and Russia are not members of the EU, and both have a very strong and contradictory relationship with it (Morozov 2015).

Parental movements in the region are highly diverse, but they all react to the state's recent history and are engaged in intense dialogue with global trends. References to the past form an essential part of parental movements' rhetoric. Indeed, the movements' interpretations of national and regional history are part of this collection as well. Several of the case studies have extensive ideational and organizational roots dating back to the late communist period, such as the Hungarian home-birth movement and Polish fathers' mobilization. The case studies presented in this book stem from the more recent past and the contemporary period without delving into parental practices or the paucity of parental movements during the communist period (c.f. Björnberg 1992; Carlbäck et al. 2012, Pascall and Kwak 2005).

Similarly to mothers' movements in other regions (e.g., Naples 1998) and contemporary anti-austerity movements in Europe and beyond, parental mobilizations in postcommunist Europe often oppose the influence of global neoliberalism and the corresponding reductions in welfare provisions and privatization of healthcare and childcare sectors. International financial organizations, such as the International Monetary Fund (IMF) and World Bank, mandated or strongly encouraged such changes as far back as the early 1990s, leading to protests and social mobilizations already in the early postcommunist period (Fábián 2009; Hryciuk and Korolczuk 2013; Kubicki 2015; and Sumskiene, Karzabi in this volume).[5] Some scholars argue that in the postcommunist context characterized by underdeveloped conventional political institutions, organized collective protest became a legitimate and relatively effective strategy for conducting state-society dialogue and for inducing policy change (Ekiert and Kubik 1999).

Many parental movements in postcommunist countries subscribe to conservative and nationalist ideas, but neither the region nor the parental movements are homogenous in their ideological orientation. Some Bulgarian, Polish, Russian, and Ukrainian parental mobilizations are eager to collaborate with broader national community-building projects, while no such willingness appears in the Czech case. Recognizing this diversity, nationalism and conservatism in parental movements do not appear to be determined by a local "culture" or characteristic of Central-Eastern European "mentality." Rather, they appear as reactions to the uneven and contested integration of Central-Eastern Europe and Russia, reflecting their ambiguous position as the "first" world's semi-periphery (Kubik and Linch 2013; Morozov 2015).

Outline of the Chapters

In order to create thematic cohesion, we focus on three main strands of parental mobilizations: conservative/nationalist mobilizations, the activism of fathers' groups, and various social movements coalescing around health-related concerns, such as disability and new reproductive technologies. The book is organized into three sections that reflect these themes.

The first thematic section offers analyses of parents' organizations and groups that can be seen as part of a broader wave of conservative mobilization in the region that includes a transcontinental outlook. The authors discuss how issues concerned with children's welfare and parenthood are intertwined with gendered nationalism and anti-colonial discourses. In the chapter on the Russian grassroots parents' movement, Tova Höjdestrand discusses conservative grassroots mobilizations exploring how concepts such as "civil society" and "civic activism" are translated and operationalized in the contemporary Russian sociopolitical context. This chapter shows that even though the Russian Parents' Movement mobilizes against a presumed Western cultural attack on Russian traditions and sovereignty, it also uses the notion of civil society in order to construct itself as an authentic voice of the people. While the activists reject Western conceptions of liberal democracy and favor President Putin's vision of a patriotic civil society, they also criticize specific government policies and reject the state administration as corrupt. This ambivalent attitude toward the contemporary state sets apart the Russian parental mobilization from that of Ukraine, as presented by Olena Strelnyk in following chapter.

Like its Russian counterpart, the Parents' Committee of Ukraine also focused on what its members see as the need to protect children from homosexuality, pedophilia, "gender," and sexual education in schools. At the same time, rather than stressing their independence from the then ruling political elite, the activists cooperated with the state and transnational institutions, for example, in the campaign against EU accession. Strelnyk shows that the idea of "child protection" plays a central role in the spread of moral panic and consequent popular mobilization. What is really at stake is not only the model of family and gender relations, but also the geopolitical orientation of Ukraine toward the EU or the Eurasian Customs Union.

The last chapter in this section is also concerned with nationalist discourse used by the organization of people who would like to become parents by using reproductive technologies in Bulgaria. Ina Dimitrova argues that the activists employ a strategy of "reactionary techno-progressivism." They successfully combine the reactionary-nationalist discourse with strong confidence in technological progress in medicine and neoliberal discourse to gain public support—both symbolic and financial. The Bulgarian case study demonstrates that the nationalist and traditionalist discourses may be effectively combined with neoliberalism, influencing citizenship in a way that develops and attempts to legitimate an exclusionary practice of population management.

The book's second section concerns fathers' activism in Poland, Russia, Ukraine, and the Czech Republic in the context of gender relations and perspectives on gender equality. The first chapter of the section focuses on how Polish activists frame their claims and state the expected outcomes. Elżbieta Korolczuk and Renata Hryciuk's analysis shows that although the Polish case bears some resemblance to conservative fathers' movements in other countries, especially the United Kingdom, the United States, and Canada, in their common focus on custody and strong antifeminist rhetoric, there are also significant differences reflecting the local context. For example, Polish activists strongly renounce fathers' financial responsibility for children after divorce and do not stress the social ills of fatherlessness. Their main mobilization frames appear as a response to the local construction of fathering, influenced by the communist model of state-dominated fatherhood, and the contemporary backlash against gender equality and the rights of sexual minorities.

In the second chapter on fathers' activism, Pelle Åberg and Johnny Rodin examine fathers' movements in the context of the social and political borderlands between civil society, the state, and the family in Russia. They show that the "daddy-schools" (*papa shkoly*), voluntary seminars that train fathers to be more involved with their children, have created an arena for fathers-to-be to discuss masculinity and male parenting. This study shows also that civil society organizations, especially in increasingly authoritarian contexts such as contemporary Russia, can have a political impact by framing their issues in a way that legitimizes them as service providers. This strategy can provide further opportunities for them to fill the role of advocate.

A similar dynamic can be observed in Iman Karzabi's analysis of the Ukrainian context. Promotion of fathers' involvement in childcare and family life could be interpreted as a new stage in advancing gender equality both at home and in the wider Ukrainian society. Karzabi shows, however, that whereas the activists defend the principle of equality of rights, they simultaneously view the father's position as complementary to and different from the role of the mother, failing to challenge gender stereotypes concerning the division of care work.

Contestation over the interpretation of gender equality is also one of the main themes in the final chapter in this section. Steven Saxonberg's analysis of the fathers' rights activism in the contemporary Czech Republic highlights the injustice frames used in the Czech fathers' online forum. The fathers blame feminism for turning the legal system against them and accuse women of breaking up families. Applying theories of masculinity and the sociology of emotions, Saxonberg argues that the fathers' discourse abandons the careful and tolerant ideals of the hegemonic masculinity, taking on the more aggressive tone associated with marginalized masculinity.

The third and the last section of the book focuses on parental activism concerning health-related parents' rights. It shows how changes in parenting ideals and shifts concerning health care and the development of medicine both affect and are affected by parents' activism. In the case of the movement against mandatory vaccination in the Czech Republic, Hasmanová Marhánková shows changing attitudes toward medicine and vaccination. The author discusses how the debates concerning vaccination have given rise to new subjectivities among parents who claim specific rights based on shared definitions of risk, create an oppositional stance toward medicine, and apply notions of individual responsibility toward one's own health.

Egle Sumskiene's chapter on parents' advocacy for children with intellectual disabilities analyzes the development of organizations established by parents raising children with intellectual disabilities in the three Baltic countries. The author portrays the complexity of parental mobilization from different geographical-chronological and individual-organizational perspectives, demonstrating that parent organizations can balance establishing comprehensive links to political and social elites and maintaining political independence. Ema Hrešanová's chapter on the natural childbirth movement in the Czech Republic discusses activism that challenges both the existing medical model and the regulations of state authorities in order to improve the current birth care system. As in Hungary and Poland, the issue of natural or undisturbed childbirth has recently become a headline in the Czech Republic. This chapter maps the trajectory of the natural childbirth movement to examine the forces that have shaped its emergence and impact. Hrešanová argues that in the Czech cultural context, the traditionally powerful position of doctors, the high regard for medicine, and their related "scientization" (i.e., unquestioned authority) in society are major obstacles to the movement's success as they prevent midwives and women from becoming partners in negotiations with medical and state authorities.

Finally, the chapter on parental activism in the Hungarian home-birth movement investigates how parents organized domestically and internationally to raise awareness about the benefits of alternative birth practices. The Hungarian home-birth movement reacted to the persecution of Dr. Geréb, a practitioner of alternative homebirths, with a series of transnational protests that eventually led to the recognition of independent midwifery in Hungary. In addition to generating more support domestically by presenting their arguments with powerful images, the movement also sparked an international wave of protests that in turn became a source of political pressure on the Hungarian authorities.

Based on the cases included in this volume, we would like to suggest future directions for research in the area of civil society and social movements in and beyond the Central and Eastern European and Russian contexts. First, there are many evolving types of parents' activism in the region, such as motherist movements, nascent LGBTQ groups, and feminist organizations focusing on motherhood and fatherhood, which deserve more scholarly attention. Second, much of existing scholarship on parental movements worldwide, including the studies of this volume, tends to be based on single-country studies. There is a need for more systematic comparisons across countries and an analysis of different movements in the same national context to consider in more detail how the emergence, choice of tactics and strategies, and effects of such activism depend on local and transnational sociopolitical and cultural environments. Third, while the authors of the present volume employed a wide variety of analytical tools to examine parental activism, we would like to encourage future studies to apply different theoretical perspectives to the study of parents' mobilizations. Options may include a more detailed analysis of the role of political and discursive opportunity structures, the specific organizational aspects of parental activism, the role emotions play in parental movements, or the influences of both local and transnational institutions. Hopefully, this volume will strengthen and encourage further research on parental activism in the region and beyond.

Katalin Fábián, Professor, Department of Government and Law, Lafayette College, Easton, PA, USA

Katalin Fábián studies the intersection of gender and globalization as they influence various policy processes of emerging democracies. She edited *Globalization: Perspectives from Central and Eastern Europe* (Elsevier, 2007) and served as the editor of a special issue of *Canadian-American Slavic Studies* that focuses on the changing international relations of Central and Eastern Europe. Her book, *Contemporary Women's Movements in Hungary: Globalization, Democracy, and Gender Equality* (Johns Hopkins University Press, 2009), analyzes the emergence and political significance of women's activism in Hungary. She conducted research among government officials and activists of NGOs that support victims of domestic violence in the post-Soviet Baltic countries, the Czech Republic, Hungary, Poland, Slovenia, and Slovakia. This research led her to contribute chapters to and edit *Domestic Violence in Postcommunist States: Local Activism, National Policies, and Global Forces* (Indiana University Press, 2010), which focuses on the transnational connections between the various European and Eurasian postcommunist movements against domestic violence.

Elżbieta Korolczuk, researcher, School of Culture and Education, Södertörn University, Sweden; and Lecturer of Gender Studies at Warsaw University, Poland

Elżbieta Korolczuk, PhD, is a sociologist working at Södertörn University in Sweden. She also teaches at the Gender Studies Centre at Warsaw University in Poland. Her research interests include social movements, civil society, and gender (especially motherhood/fatherhood, assisted reproductive technologies, and feminism). Recently, she conducted research on parental activism and social and legal implications of assisted reproduction in Poland, and on gender and political cultures of knowledge. She coedited (with Renata E. Hryciuk) two volumes (in Polish): *Farewell to the Polish Mother? Discourses, Practices and Representations of Motherhood in Contemporary Poland* (2012), which explores ideologies and practices of motherhood in Poland, and *Dangerous Liaisons: Motherhood, Fatherhood and Politics* (2015), which focuses on the intersection between motherhood, fatherhood and politics in Poland and Russia. Her most recent publication is an edited volume (with Kerstin Jacobsson): *Civil Society Revisited: Lessons from Poland*, published by Berghahn Books in April 2017.

Notes

1. Parental activists usually define the family narrowly, as a group determined by birth and marriage. However, in some cases social activism can coalesce around broadening the very definition of family, for example, to include nonheteronormative families.

2. The emergence and increasing capacity of parental movements worldwide stem also from developments in new information and communication technologies. Following Benedict Anderson's (1983) analysis of reading circles in the early days of the printing press, we can conceptualize some online groups as contemporary imagined political communities. Information dissemination via online social networking appeals especially to parents who usually have little free time (Christensen 2009; DiQuinzio 2006). Due to relative anonymity online, people can feel more at ease to address sensitive or taboo issues, such as infertility, perceived discrimination, or marginalization in a public space (Korolczuk 2014; Norris 2002), even though active engagement online does not necessarily turn into mobilization and numerous possible important drawbacks of online mobilization (for example, state surveillance) can also limit such mobilizations' reach (Morozov 2012; Myers 2000).

3. Such a strategy has been adopted also in other cultural contexts, for example, by the US-based National Parents Organization, which represents mostly divorced fathers but opts for the gender-neutral term "parents" in its name. See (last accessed June 29, 2015) https://www.nationalparentsorganization.org.

4. Although the label we opted to use for the region is undoubtedly long, we had to navigate signifiers that keep changing their meanings. While "Eastern Europe" has traditionally included Russia, in the past two decades the term "Central-Eastern Europe" has come to refer to the postcommunist European states without including Russia. We opted for following this recently established trend, while remaining keenly aware of the deep connections (both friendly and antagonistic) between histories and cultures and noting the political connotations of each new seemingly geographic label and the contorted meanings of this historically contested region.

5. We use the term "postcommunist" to indicate the collective experience of one-party rule after the end of World War Two in these countries, even though we recognize that its applicability to Central-Eastern Europe and Russia two-and-a half decades after the regime change is debatable (Bernhard and Jasiewicz 2015) and that the communist system varied considerably during the forty years of its existence and its national practice differed greatly.

Works Cited

Anderson, Benedict. 1983. *Imagined Communities: Reflections on the Origin and Spread of Nationalism*. London: Verso.

Baiocchi, Gianpaolo, Elizabeth A. Bennett, Alissa Cordner, Peter Taylor Klein, and Stephanie Savell. 2014. *The Civic Imagination: Making a Difference in American Political Life*. Boulder, CO: Paradigm.

Bennett, Elizabeth A., Alissa Cordner, Peter Taylor Klein, Stephanie Savell, and Gianpaolo Baiocchi. 2013. "Disavowing Politics: Civic Engagement in an Era of Political Skepticism." *American Journal of Sociology* 119 (2):518–548.

Bergmann, Nadja, Elli Scambor, and Katarzyna Wojnicka. 2014. "Framing the Involvement of Men in Gender Equality in Europe: Between Institutionalised and Non-Institutionalised Politics." *Masculinities and Social Change* 3 (1):62–82.

Bernhard, Michael, and Krzysztof Jasiewicz. 2015. "Whither Eastern Europe? Changing Approaches and Perspectives on the Region in Political Science." *East European Politics and Societies* 29 (22):311–322.

Bertoia, Carl, and Janice Drakich. 1993. "The Fathers' Rights Movement." *Journal of Family Issues* 14 (4):592–615.

Bilić, Bojan, and Paul Stubbs. 2015. "Unsettling 'the Urban' in Post-Yugoslav Activisms: Right to the City and Pride Parades in Serbia and Croatia." In *Urban Grassroots Movements in Central and Eastern Europe*, edited by Kerstin Jacobsson, 119–138. Aldershot, UK: Ashgate.

Björnberg, Ulla, ed. 1992. *European Parents in the 1990s: Contradictions and Comparisons*. New Brunswick, NJ: Transaction.

Blum, Alice. 2015. "Germany." In *Gender as Symbolic Glue: The Position and Role of Conservative and Far Right Parties in the Anti-Gender Mobilizations in Europe*, edited by Eszter Kováts and Maari Põim. http://www.feps-europe.eu/assets/cae464d2-f4ca-468c-a93e-5d0dad365a83/feps-gender-as-symbolic-glue-wwwpdf.pdf.

Bob, Clifford. 2012. *Global Right Wing and Clash World Politics*. New York: Cambridge University Press.

Caiazza, Amy. 2002. *Mothers and Soldiers: Gender, Citizenship, and Civil Society in Contemporary Russia*. New York and London: Routledge.

Case, Mary Ann. 2011. "After Gender the Destruction of Man: The Vatican's Nightmare Vision of the 'Gender Agenda' for Law." *Pace Law Review* 31:802–817.

Carlbäck, Helene, Yulia Gradskova, and Zhanna Kravchenko, eds. 2012. *And They Lived Happily Ever After?* Budapest: Central European University.

Christensen, Wendy M. 2009. "Technological Boundaries: Defining the Personal and the Political in Military Mothers' Online Support Forms." *Women's Studies Quarterly* 37 (1–2):146–166.

Collier, Richard, and Sally Sheldon, eds. 2006. *Fathers' Rights Activism and Law Reform in Comparative Perspective*. Oxford and Portland: Hart.

Crowley, Jocelyn Elise. 2008. *Defiant Dads: Fathers' Rights Activists in America*. Ithaca: Cornell University Press.

Datta, Neil. 2013. "Keeping It All in the Family: Europe's Anti-Choice Movement." *Conscience* 24 (2):22–27.

DiQuinzio, Patricia. 2006. "The Politics of the Mothers' Movement in the United States." *Journal of the Association for Research on Mothering* 8 (1–2):55–70.

Dowd, Nancy. 2000. *Redefining Fatherhood.* New York: New York University Press.

Ekiert, Grzegorz, and Roberto Foa. 2012. "The Weakness of Post-Communist Civil Societies Reassessed." *CES Papers—Open Forum 11.* Harvard University: Center for European Studies.

Ekiert, Grzegorz, and Jan Kubik. 2014. "Myths and Realities of Civil Society." *Journal of Democracy* 25 (1):46–58.

Fábián, Katalin. 2014. "Disciplining the 'Second World': The Relationship between Transnational and Local Forces in Contemporary Hungarian Women's Social Movements." *East European Politics* 30 (1):1–20.

———. 2013. "Overcoming Disempowerment: The Home-Birth Movement in Hungary." In *Beyond NGO-ization: The Development of Social Movements in Central and Eastern Europe*, edited by Kerstin Jacobsson and Steven Saxonberg, 71–95. Aldershot, UK: Ashgate.

———. 2010. *Domestic Violence in Postcommunist States: Local Activism, National Policies, and Global Forces.* Bloomington, IN: Indiana University Press.

———. 2009. *Contemporary Women's Movements in Hungary: Globalization, Democracy, and Gender Equality.* Washington, DC: Woodrow Wilson Center Press and Johns Hopkins University Press.

Fassin, Éric. 2014. "Same-Sex Marriage, Nation, and Race: French Political Logics and Rhetorics." *Contemporary French Civilization* 39 (3):281–301.

Flood, Michel. 2012. "Separated Fathers and the 'Fathers' Rights Movement." *Journal of Family Studies* 18 (2–3):235–245.

Fodor, Éva, Christy Glass, Janette Kawachi, and Livia Popescu. 2002. "Family Policies and Gender in Hungary, Poland and Romania." *Communist and Post-Communist Studies* 35:475–490.

Funk, Nanette, and Magda Mueller, eds. 1993. *Gender Politics and Post-Communism: Reflections from Eastern Europe and the Former Soviet Union.* New York: Routledge.

Gal, Susan, and Kligman Gal, eds. 2000. *Reproducing Gender. Politics, Publics and Everyday Life after Socialism.* Princeton, NJ: Princeton University Press.

Ginsborg, Paul. 2013. "Uncharted Territories: Individuals, Families, Civil Society and the Democratic State." In *The Golden Chain: Family, Civil Society and the State*, edited by Jurgen Nautz, Paul Ginsborg, and Ton Nijhuis, 17–42. New York and Oxford: Berghahn Books.

Glass, Christy, and Éva Fodor. 2007. "From Public to Private Maternalism? Gender and Welfare in Poland and Hungary after 1989." *Social Politics: International Studies in Gender, State and Society* 14 (3):323–350.

Graff, Agnieszka. 2009. "Gender and Nation, Here and Now: Reflections on the Gendered and Sexualized Aspects of Contemporary Polish Nationalism." In *Intimate Citizenships: Gender, Sexualities, Politics*, edited by Elżbieta H. Oleksy, 133–146. London: Routledge.

Graff, Agnieszka, and Elżbieta Korolczuk. 2017. "Worse than Communism and Nazism Put Together: War on Gender in Poland." In *Anti-Gender Campaigns in Europe*

Mobilizing against Equality, edited by Roman Kuhar and David Paternotte, 175–194. London: Rowman & Littlefield International.
Hagemann, Karen, Sonya Michel, and Gunilla Budde. 2008. *Civil Society and Gender Justice. Historical and Comparative Perspectives*. New York, Oxford: Berghahn Books.
Hann, Chris. 1996. "Introduction: Political Society and Civil Anthropology." In *Civil Society: Challenging Western Models*, edited by Chris Hann and Elizabeth Dunn, 1–27. London: Routledge.
Hann, Chris, and Elizabeth Dunn, eds. 1996. *Civil Society: Challenging Western Models*. London: Routledge.
Hantrais, Linda. 2006. "Living as a Family in Europe." In *Policy Implications of Changing Family Formation: Study Prepared for the European Population Conference 2005*, edited by Linda Hantrais, Dimiter Philipov, and Francesco C. Billari. Population Studies, No. 49, Strasbourg: Council of Europe Publishing.
Hays, Sharon. 1996. *The Cultural Contradictions of Motherhood*. New Haven and London: Yale University Press.
Hodžic, Amir, and Nataša Bijelić. 2014. "Neo-Conservative Threats to Sexual and Reproductive Rights in the European Union" *CESI*. http://www.cesi.hr/attach/_n/neo-conservative_threats_to_srhr_in_eu.pdf.
Howard, Marc Morjé. 2003. *The Weakness of Civil Society in Post-Communist Europe*. Cambridge: Cambridge University Press.
Howell, Jude. 2005. "Gender and Civil Society." In *Global Civil Society*, edited by Helmut K. Anheier, Mary Kaldor, and Marlies Glasius, 38–63. London: SAGE.
Hryciuk, Renata E. 2012. "O znikającej matce. Upolitycznione macierzyństwo w Ameryce Łacińskiej i w Polsce" [On Disappearing Mother. Politicized Motherhood in Latin America and Poland]. In *Pożegnanie z Matką Polką? Dyskursy, praktyki i reprezentacje macierzyństwa we współczesnej Polsce* [*Farewell to the Polish Mother*], edited by Renata E. Hryciuk and Elżbieta Korolczuk, 267–288. Warszawa: Warsaw University Press.
Hryciuk, Renata E., and Elżbieta Korolczuk. 2013. "At the Intersection of Gender and Class: Social Mobilization Around Mothers' Rights in Poland." In *Beyond NGO-ization: The Development of Social Movements in Central and Eastern Europe*, edited by Kerstin Jacobsson and Steven Saxonberg, 49–70. Farnham: Ashgate.
———. 2015. "Konteksty upolitycznienie macierzyństwa i ojcostwa we współczesnej Polsce" [Politicizing Mothering and Fathering in Contemporary Poland]. In *Niebezpieczne związki. Macierzyństwo, ojcostwo i polityka* [*Dangerous Liaisons: Motherhood, Fatherhood and Politics*], edited by Renata E. Hryciuk and Elżbieta Korolczuk, 11–44. Warszawa: Warsaw University Press.
Hrycak, Alexandra. 2002. "From Mothers' Rights to Equal Rights: Post-Soviet Grassroots Women's Associations." In *Women's Community Activism and Globalization: Linking the Local and Global for Social Change*, edited by N. Naples and M. K. Desai, 62–79. London and New York: Routledge.
Jacobsson, Kerstin, and Steven Saxonberg, eds. 2013. *Beyond NGO-ization. The Development of Social Movements in Central and Eastern Europe*. Farnham: Ashgate.

Jacobsson, Kerstin, ed. 2015. *Urban Grassroots Movements in Central and Eastern Europe*. Farnham: Ashgate.

Jacobsson, Kerstin, and Elżbieta Korolczuk. 2017. *Civil Society Revisited: Lessons from Poland*. New York and Oxford: Berghahn Books.

Jagudina, Zaira. 2009. *Social Movements and Gender in Post-Soviet Russia: The Case of the Soldiers' Mothers NGOs*. Göteborg Studies in Sociology, Department of Sociology: University of Gothenburg.

Jaquette, Jane S. 1994. "Conclusion: Women's Political Participation and the Prospects for Democracy." In *The Women's Movements in Latin America: Participation and Democracy*, edited by Jane S. Jaquette, 223–257. Boulder, San Francisco, Oxford: Westview Press.

Johnson, Elise Janet, and Jean C. Robinson, eds. 2006. *Living Gender after Communism*. Bloomington: Indiana University Press.

Kocka, Jurgen. 2006. "Civil Society from a Historical Perspective." In *Civil Society: Berlin Perspectives*, edited by John Keane, 37–50. New York and Oxford: Berghahn Books.

Kok, Jan, ed. 2002. *Rebellious Families: Household Strategies and Collective Action in the Nineteenth and Twentieth Centuries*. New York and Oxford: Berghahn Books.

Kopecký, Petr, and Cas Mudde. 2003. *Uncivil Society? Contentious Politics in Post-Communist Europe*. London: Routledge.

Korolczuk, Elżbieta. 2017. "When Parents Become Activists. Exploring the Intersection of Civil Society and Family." In *Civil Society Revisited: Lessons from Poland*, edited by Kerstin Jacobsson and Elżbieta Korolczuk, 129–152. New York and Oxford: Berghahn Books.

———. 2015. "'Those Who Are Full Can Never Understand the Hungry': Challenging the Meaning of Infertility in Poland." In *The Identity Dilemma*, edited by Aidan McGarry and James Jasper, 170–191. Philadelphia: Temple Press.

———. 2014. "Terms of Engagement. Re-Defining Identity and Infertility On-line." *Culture Unbound: Journal of Current Cultural Research* 6 (22):431–449.

———. 2013. "Gendered Boundaries between the State, Family and Civil Society—The Case of Poland after 1989." In *The Golden Chain: Family, Civil Society and the State*, edited by Jurgen Nautz, Paul Ginsborg, and Ton Nijhuis, 240–259. New York and Oxford: Berghahn Books.

Kováts, Eszter, and Maari Põim, eds. 2015. *Gender as Symbolic Glue: The Position and Role of Conservative and Far Right Parties in the Anti-Gender Mobilizations in Europe*. http://www.feps-europe.eu/assets/cae464d2-f4ca-468c-a93e-5d0dad365a83/feps-gender-as-symbolic-glue-wwwpdf.pdf.

Kubicki, Paweł. 2015. "Rodzice dzieci z niepełnosprawnością. Analiza polityk publicznych we współczesnej Polsce" [Parents with Children with Disabilities. Analysis of Social Policies in Contemporary Poland]. In *Niebezpieczne związki. Macierzyństwo, ojcostwo i poliyka* [*Dangerous Liaisons: Motherhood, Fatherhood and Politics*], edited by Renata E. Hryciuk and Elżbieta Korolczuk, 133–159. Warszawa: Warsaw University Press.

Kubik, Jan, and Amy Linch, eds. 2013. *Post-Communism from Within: Social Justice, Mobilization, and Hegemony*. New York: New York University Press.

Lichterman, Paul, and Nina Eliasoph. 2014. "Civic Action." *American Journal of Sociology* 210 (3):798–863.

Ljubownikow, Sergej, Jo Crotty, and Peter W. Rogers. 2013. "The State and Civil Society in Post-Soviet Russia: The Development of a Russian Style Civil Society." *Progress in Development Studies* 13 (2):153–166.

Lukić, Jasmina, Joanna Regulska, and Darja Zaviršek, eds. 2006. *Women and Citizenship in Central and Eastern Europe*. Aldershot, UK: Ashgate.

Mätzke, Margitta, and Ilona Ostner. 2010. "Explaining Recent Shifts in Family Policy." *Journal of European Social Policy*. Special Issue 20 (5):388–398.

Mazurek, Małgorzata. 2010. *Społeczeństwo kolejki. O doświadczeniach niedoboru 1945–1989 [Queuing Society: On the Experience of Shortages 1945–1989]*. Warsaw: TRIO Publishers.

McAdam, Doug, John D. McCarthy, and Mayer N. Zald. 1996. *Comparative Perspectives on Social Movements*. Cambridge: Cambridge University Press.

Mendelson, Sarah E., and John K. Glenn, eds. 2002. *The Power and Limits of NGOs: A Critical Look at Building Democracy in Eastern Europe and Eurasia*. New York: Columbia University Press.

Michel, Sonya. 2012. "Maternalism and Beyond." In *Maternalism Reconsidered: Motherhood, Welfare and Social Policy in the Twentieth Century*, edited by Marian van der Klein, Rebecca Joe Plant, Nicole Sanders, and Lori R. Weintrob, 22–37. New York, Oxford: Berghahn Books.

Molyneux, Maxine. 1985. "Mobilization without Emancipation? Women's Interests, the State and Revolution in Nicaragua." *Feminist Studies* 11 (2):227–254.

Morozov, Viatcheslav. 2015. *Subaltern Empire in a Eurocentric World*. London: Palgrave Macmillan.

Municio-Larsson, Ingegerd, and Carmen Pujol Algans. 2002. "Making Sense of Fatherhood: The Non-Payment of Child Support in Spain" In *Making Men into Fathers,* edited by Barbara Hobson, 191–212. Cambridge: Cambridge University Press.

Myers, D. J. 2000. "Communication Technology and Social Movements: Contributions of Computer Networks to Activism." *Social Science Computer Review* 12:125–160.

Nakano Glenn, Evelyn. 1994. "Social Constructions of Mothering. A Thematic Overview." In *Mothering: Ideology, Experience and Agency*, edited by Evelyn N. Glenn, Grace Chang, and Linda Forcey, 1–32. New York: Routledge.

Naples, Nancy A. 1998. *Grassroots Warriors: Activist Mothering, Community Work, and the War on Poverty*. New York and London: Routledge.

Nautz, Jurgen, Paul Ginsborg, and Ton Nijhuis, eds. 2013. *The Golden Chain: Family, Civil Society and the State*. New York and Oxford: Berghahn Books.

Norris, Pippa. 2002. "The Bridging and Bonding Role of Online Communities." *The Harvard International Journal of Press and Politics* 7 (3):3–13.

Okin, Moller Susan. 1998. "Gender, the Public and the Private." In *Feminism and Politics*, edited by Anne Philips, 116–141. Oxford, New York: Oxford University Press.

O'Reilly, Andrea, ed. 2010. *Twenty-First Century Motherhood: Experience, Identity, Policy, Agency*. New York: Columbia University Press.

Pascall, Gillian, and Anna Kwak. 2005. "Introduction: Gender and the Family under Communism and After." In *Gender Regimes in Transition in Central and Eastern Europe*, edited by Gillian Pascal and Anna Kwak, 1–30. Bristol: Policy Press.

Saxonberg, Steven, and Tomáš Sirovátka. 2006. "Failing Family Policy in Post-Communist Central Europe." *Journal of Comparative Policy Analysis: Research and Practice* 8 (2):185–202.

Scott, Joan W., and Diane Keates, eds. 2004. *Going Public: Feminism and the Shifting Boundaries of the Private Sphere*. Urbana and Champaign: University of Illinois Press.

Sumskiene, Egle. 2014. "Psichikos sveikatos priežiūros deinstitucionalizacija Lietuvoje: minimalū spokyčiai 'maksimalistinėse' organizacijose" [Deinstitutionalization of Mental Health Care in Lithuania: Minimal Reforms in "Maximalist" Organizations]. *STEPP: socialinė teorija, empirija, politika i praktika* [*STEPP: Social Theory, Empirics, Policy and Practice*] 8:89–99. Vilnius University.

Szelewa, Dorota, and Michał P. Polakowski. 2008. "Who Cares? Changing Patterns of Childcare in Central and Eastern Europe." *Journal of European Social Policy* 18 (2):115–131.

Werbner, Pnina. 1999. "Political Motherhood and the Feminization of Citizenship: Women's Activism and the Transformation of Public Sphere." In *Women, Citizenship and Difference*, edited by Nina Yuval-Davis and Pnina Werbner, 221–246. London and New York: Zed Books.

Wojnicka, Katarzyna. 2013. "Męskie ruchy społeczne we współczesnej Polsce: Wybrane ustalenia i wnioski" [Men's Social Movements in Contemporary Poland: Selected Findings and Conclusions]. *Acta Universitatis Lodziensis Folia Sociologica* 47:87–103.

1

Nationalism and Civicness in Russia: Grassroots Mobilization in Defense of "Family Values"

Tova Höjdestrand

Introduction

> On behalf of the parental community and the civil society of Russia, we appeal to the representatives of the state power of the Russian Federation, who, in accordance to the Constitution of our country, are obliged to defend family, motherhood, and childhood. We demand that further pressure from representatives of international political organizations on Russia should not be tolerated, or their involvement in domestic concerns of our country or in Russian legislation and lawmaking, since they result in the destruction of Russian families, of traditional culture, of family life and upbringing of children, and in the intensification of demographic problems that will result in the extinction of our people.[1]

Thus begins the Saint Petersburg Resolution, an open protest letter against a draft recommendation by the European Council on children's rights and parental responsibilities.[2] It was signed in October 2011 by eighty Russian nonstate organizations, most of them being relatively new grassroots groups, and was published on a broad range of nationalist and conservative religious Orthodox websites. The Parents' Movement (*roditel'skoe dvizhenie*), as these grassroots define themselves, is a nationwide mobilization in the defense of Russian traditional family values. The Resolution is but one in a long series of petitions and open letters since 2010 in which the movement rejects foreign involvement in Russian affairs, and it (as stated later in the text) expresses deep anxieties about transnational treaties challenging parental authority or equating homosexual relationships with heterosexual marriage.

This chapter will explore the agenda and the emergence of the Parents' Movement, with a primary focus on the very first words of the Resolution, "on behalf of the parental community and the civil society." In documents and discussions in the "parental cyberspace," the word *grazhdanskiy* (civil/civic; derived from citizen, *grazhdan*) appears frequently and in various contexts, be it concerning action, resistance, community, or society. Such phrasings are not self-evident in conservative Russian discourse. Intrinsic to the idea of Western liberal democracy, the concept "civic" has previously been associated with non-governmental organizations (NGOs) created in the 1990s, largely with Western funding, for the very purpose to promote democracy and civil society in the formerly authoritarian East. Nationalists relate to this NGO sector with outright hostility, which the Resolution makes very clear: "We are seriously concerned about the activities of some relatively small groups proclaiming their ideals in the name of the entire civil society, while in reality their objectives contradict the authentic interests of sovereign peoples." Human rights in general (which will be discussed later) and children's rights in particular, tolerance, anti-discrimination, and so forth are, according to parental activists, only decoys for Western imperialism in its attempts to eliminate Russia as a civilization.

Nonetheless, the notion of civicness appeals to the Parents' Movement because it aims to establish a dialogue between grassroots and the Russian state administration, which is considered to be not only corrupt and abusive, but also treacherous to Russian sovereignty and tradition by not being patriotic enough. Parental grassroots organizations articulate their own notion of what civicness implies, because neither the organizational forms nor the "moral coordinates," as they would phrase it, of the former liberal guardians of the "civic concepts" match their own ideas about what active and ethically acceptable citizenship implies.

Here, I make no pretensions to new theoretical insights of what "civil society," "civic action," etc. actually are—it is the normativity and Eurocentrism of these concepts that make them malleable and, thereby, rewarding subjects for negotiation and reshaping (Hann and Dunn 1996). Rather, my aim is to show how emic conceptions about civil society and civicness are instrumental for a collective identity in Melucci's (1989) sense: a continuous and highly emotionally charged negotiation of shared aims, means, and fields of action, articulated through interaction by a common language and common sets of practices. This identity also involves antiliberalism, patriotism, and a religious worldview—ideological scaffolds that are relatively stable. Civicness, in contrast, the understanding of how to be and act as a subject in civil society, is perpetually negotiated as the Parents' Movement itself transforms and develops.

After a comment on the methods of this study, I will first contextualize the emergence of conservative profamily discourse and activism in relation to Soviet anti-Western discourse and to post-Soviet global ideological flows. Secondly, I will situate the Parents' Movement in the context of the general development of civic organizations and grassroots activism in Russia from the 1990s onward. After outlining the organizational principles of parental organizations and their cautious relationship (to say the least) to power, I will discuss the movement's agenda and its most prioritized item—the struggle against a legal implementation of the UN Convention of the Rights of the Child that led to the rapid proliferation of the movement in recent years. Success poses new challenges, however, so I will lastly discuss how recent options to influence power have challenged the previously prevalent ideas among parental activists about civicness and, thereby, also the movement's collective identity as a whole.

Field and Method

"The Parents' Movement," *roditel'skoe dvizhenie*, is a term that activists use in a self-evident manner without further definitions. It refers to anything from a seemingly narrow selection of Orthodox extreme nationalist networks to any supporter of the movement's main objectives. (Since the term is quite general, it appeals also to other parental initiatives, but search machines and media archives reveal few, if any, competitors.) Many groups, including a number of the signatories of the Saint Petersburg Resolution, simply call themselves *roditel'skiy komitet*, "the Parents Committee," of a particular place (the term is usually applied to the parental committees of schools and kindergartens). Others mix different buzzwords in reference to their agendas: "Family, Love, Fatherland," or "In Defense of Family, Childhood, and Morality." So far, I have counted 300 such parental groups, although not all of them advertise regular activities and some seem to be created for the sole purpose of signing resolutions and petitions. Also, it is not possible to determine the number of participants in these groups since, as I was told by a respondent, "it depends on what you count: me and the other guy who in practice are doing all the work, another 50 who turn up now and then, or the 300 who've joined us at *vkontakte*."

Vkontakte ("In Touch") is a Russian equivalent to Facebook that is my main source of information, together with a wide array of virtual communities, social networking sites, blogs, websites of "real life" organizations; Orthodox patriotic internet journals and news websites; and mainstream media archives (Integrum, in particular). From March 2012, I have followed two main websites that have served as points of departure to further trace significant issues, concepts, actors, and events.[3]

I have also conducted twelve interviews with activists and leaders of local parental groups in Moscow and Saint Petersburg in 2012, in addition to talking to several professionals experienced with the policies and projects of concern to the Parents' Movement. All respondents are anonymized: the professionals because many of them spoke off the record, and parental leaders because their decision to meet me, (as two told me), might compromise them in the eyes of other activists. It was evident in 2012 that these respondents positioned me as a potential enemy, both as an academic and as a Westerner, and the ongoing conflict in Ukraine has hardly ameliorated this animosity. Many of those whom I contacted never replied, so I have decided to not include the names of the ones who nonetheless did; I am just very grateful that they agreed to talk to me at all.

Maleficent Modernity and Western Warfare: The Emergence of a Moral Conservative Opposition

The Russian Parents' Movement dates back to the mid-2000s, but its critical stance toward Western ideologies and culture has considerably older roots. Messianic ideas about "the Third Rome" and "Holy Rus'" have, for at least five centuries, pitted Russia against an allegedly degenerated Western adversary. In the Soviet period most social problems were glossed over as results of capitalist ideological contagion. A core trope in today's anti-Western rhetoric is Russia's demographic decline, which was already proclaimed a major social threat in the 1980s. Socioeconomic explanations were not ignored, but many politicians and leading intellectuals preferred purportedly Western scapegoats such as feminism and licentious sexual behavior (Attwood 1990).

Birthrates and "cultural influence theories" remained central tropes to nationalist discourse throughout the drastic demographic decline of the 1990s. By the end of the decade, Russian nationalists picked up a moral crusade against sexualized mass media and Western-funded educational projects on reproductive health and sexuality (cf. Kon 1999). Initiated by ultranationalist Orthodox clerics and intellectuals, this debate was not a social movement inasmuch as a battle fought in mass media. Nonetheless, by the turn of the millennium a handful of grassroots groups of "concerned parents" appeared, from which the Parents' Movement would emerge nearly ten years later.

This nascent conservative opposition stems from a historically rooted local anti-Western tradition while simultaneously tapping into a contemporary global social conservative ideoscape (Appadurai 1996), in which the Russian "anti-sex rhetoric" (Fine 1988) differs little from others of its kind. Russian sexologist Igor Kon (1999) has even suggested that US missionaries initiated the Russian campaign. Whether or not he is right (I lack other sources), discourses and ideological currents tend to travel in less intentional ways. Today, parental activists worldwide are immersed in a global cyberspace with endless options to pick from each other's repertoires. US sources are particularly rewarding since they, being among the oldest, provide the largest amounts of text, moreover in English, which is today's major lingua franca.

The cross-fertilization between domestic and foreign elements is particularly conspicuous in the narratives of moral warfare and conspiracy from which the Russian anti-sex rhetoric departs. Conspiracy theory as such has century-old roots in Russia, but it became, for obvious reasons, a commonplace facet of Cold War propaganda in both the East and the West. In Russia, an endless number of mutations have developed rapidly in the post-Soviet period (Ortmann and Heathershaw 2012), many of which are heavily inspired by a burgeoning US supply of similar narratives. In the Russian "sexualized" narrative, the formerly near-obligatory Jewish plot is replaced by a mafia of gays and/or liberals, and anti-Communist elements are re-wrought to fit the prevalent Soviet nostalgia of Russian nationalists. It borrows from US sources also by linking the UN and other supranational agencies to a demonized "new world order" and the coming of the Antichrist (Herman 2001).

Irina Medvedeva and Tatiana Shishova, child psychologists and to this day the most influential debaters of the Parents' Movement, thus trace the allegedly satanic origins of the International Planned Parenthood Foundation (IPPF) from Margaret Sanger's well-known interest in Rosicrucianism and her endorsement of eugenics in the 1930s (the then predominant scientific paradigm) to Nazi mysticism, Aleister Crowley, homosexual Knights' Templars, the cult of Baphomet, and ancient Egyptian sects. With the benign aid of "liberal" Russian NGOs and corrupt state administrators, IPPF and allies such as the World Health Organization (WHO) are allegedly conducting a demographic war against Russia by proliferating an immoral and promiscuous lifestyle that, ultimately, will aggravate the already alarming abortion rates and lead to mass infertility due to STDs (Medvedeva and Shishova 2001). The strongly polemical prose relies heavily on biased or falsified information, hyperboles, and what Irvine (2004) in the US context calls depravity stories (i.e., unconfirmed urban legends about the disastrous effects of sexual education). Truth is immaterial to this kind of rhetoric, since its purpose is not to provide facts inasmuch as to shock and accommodate an emotional climate (Irvine 2004, 58). Russian depravity stories are usually about events in the West, as a way to underline the foreign origins of evil—English children are, as an example, said to begin their sexual lives at the age of nine and suffer from impotence by the age of twelve (Medvedeva and Shishova 1996).

The Sociopolitical Environment: Power and the Civil Sector

A significant part in "anti-sex" conspiracy narratives is played by a purported fifth column of corrupt Russian state administrators, liberal politicians, and NGOs, who are assumed to do the dirty job of the supranational agencies by promoting family planning and programs for sexual education and HIV prevention at the local level. The presumed evil intentions notwithstanding, these claims are correct insofar that Western aid agencies indeed were important for the emergence of a civil sector after the demise of the Soviet Union. The Yeltsin administration neither encouraged nor impeded civic activism, and in the chaotic 1990s people in general were too preoccupied with plain survival to have much time and energy left for collective mobilizations. Hence the "first generation" of NGOs largely comprised specialized advocacy organizations with permanent staff and facilities funded by Western grants. Predominant aims were human rights, gender equality, and other aspects of democracy building, as well as attempts to compensate the deficiencies of the crumbling sector of social welfare. The high Russian rates of abortions and

HIV infection made reproductive health a prioritized issue, and such projects were frequently carried out by Russian NGOs in cooperation with sectors of the state administration. They frequently turned out to be very productive, but the professionalization of the NGOs simultaneously estranged them from ordinary grassroots (cf. Jacobsson and Saxonberg 2013). In effect, the presumed new civil sector was perceived by many in terms of the old nomenklatura: a remote and privileged elite benefiting from resources unavailable to others (Hemment 2004). To the (thus far) relatively limited and marginalized flora of extreme nationalists and anti-sex activists, they were, in addition, the agents of hostile Western forces attempting to undermine Russian culture and sovereignty.

A few years after the beginning of the millennium, the political opportunities for civic action changed radically. In contrast to the Yeltsin administration, the Putin regime actively encourages the development of a civil society, on the condition that it serves a common national cause instead of advocating the interests of particular social groups (Henderson 2011). A federal Civic Chamber was created in 2004 to counsel the Duma on social issues and to distribute government funds to the civil sector, and the number of nonstate domestic funders has increased. Western funding has in the same period become politically inopportune and difficult to receive, due to nationalist policies and the fact that the relative economic stability has prompted foreign development agencies to leave Russia on their own accord.

Since the mid-2000s, mainstream official rhetoric has to an increasing extent revolved around patriotism, traditional morals (aka Orthodoxy), and family values—tropes that were formerly employed mainly in the distinctly Orthodox and/or ultranationalist sectors of the political spectrum. In spite of improved birthrates in the 2000s, the imminent "death of the nation" has remained pivotal, and so is the claim that the most effective remedy is pronatalist policy and a return to "tradition" (Rivkin-Fish 2006). Hence no enterprise today fails to include a profound concern for family and children in the presentation of its aims, be it within the state sector, the business world, or the "third sector" of nonstate organizations. The latter category includes a number of well-funded profamily organizations engaged in charity, educational projects, pro-life agitation, and demographic research. In contrast to, for example, the US Christian Right, these elite organizations do not simultaneously try to organize local grassroots networks (Irvine 2004), but they are solidly connected within the Russian power elite and, in some cases, associated with transnational profamily networks such as US-based World Congress of Families (cf. Morn 2013; Levintova 2014; Federman 2014).

The Parents' Movement, in contrast, represents an entirely different kind of social activism. It defines itself as grassroots and exhibits a deep skepticism to elites of all kinds, be it Kremlin or professionalized NGOs of any geographical origin or political orientation. As such, it is symptomatic for a general upsurge in grassroots mobilizations from the mid-2000s onward. According to Vorozheikina (2008), a similar boom of popular movements occurred in the Glasnost period, but it was thwarted by the "transitional" turbulence of the 1990s since, in short, it is difficult to pursue specific goals in an environment of general social collapse. Only with the relative economic stability of the 2000s could people once again address particular problems and believe that their influence may affect the powers that be. A contributing factor to the increase in grassroots engagement is the increased corruption and political repression of the Putin period. The new movements largely comprise a new proto-middle class, which is as dissatisfied with authority abuse as it is conscious of its own economic vulnerability. Educated and professionally experienced, the people in this category are capable and willing to organize themselves and to make claims about what they perceive as socially relevant (Chebankova 2013). At a more practical level, the proliferation of the internet is an important factor since it significantly enhances options to create and maintain networks in a country as vast as Russia (Zuev 2011; Gladarev and Lonkila 2012).

Social research has primarily focused on new grassroots movements less devoted to the present regime, for instance, trade unions, housing rights movements, environmental groups, or protests against rigged elections (Vorozheikina 2008; Gladarev and Lonkila 2012; Aron 2010). Less attention has been given to nationalist or conservative religious groups (for an exception, see Zuev 2011), who distrust the state apparatus as much as everybody else but blame its evils on transnational structures and global policy processes, while they endorse authoritarianism as such. Putin is usually revered as a strong and wise Tsar whose firm hand is perennially misled by his own corrupt administration and by his own backup party, United Russia. In the words of Anatoly Artiukh, leader of a Saint Petersburg parental organization:

> [Our] resistance . . . is not opposition against power [Putin], but its aid in restoring order in our country. The [liberal] opposition does not want order. Rather, it wants a "new world order." Which is when they take children from

> decent families and give them to pederasts. Or when they teach children masturbation instead of embroidery in school, with the help of German or Swedish cartoons. (Artiukh 2013, my translation)

Although such nationalist grassroots activists are loyal to the president's broad vision of a patriotic civil society, they may simultaneously be an impediment. They are difficult to control, and their ideological zeal often exceeds the more pragmatic objectives of Kremlin. In particular, this concerns overtly xenophobic groups, many of which have been outlawed as "extremists" for challenging official aims of interethnic harmony (Zuev 2011). One of them was in fact headed by a man who is now a prominent leader in the Parents' Movement, which indicates a potential ideological overlap.[4] Parental organizations are less controversial as they abide by the law and are engaged in less sensitive issues. As staunch opponents to official aims in the field of social policy, they are nonetheless (as I will explain further) frequently an annoyance to the authorities, who in reality are not as neatly divided into the opposing categories of "good Tsar" and "corrupt officials," as parental rhetoric would have it.

The Formation of Parental Grassroots Groups

Igor is the leader of a parental organization in a small town near Saint Petersburg. Now in his mid-50s, he acquired thorough organizational experience as a Komsomol leader in his youth and later from a professional life in the city administration. When we met, he was working as an administrator at a small factory, a comparatively insignificant position that, as he explained, he took on since his boss approves of the parental cause and gives him optimal scope to engage in the Movement.

His career as a parental activist started in 2008 when he conducted a local survey about intra-religious relations for the city administration: "But the people we met, most of them Orthodox, just said that 'so what, we don't have any problems with that [other religions], tell them [the city authorities] to do something about these clinics instead; we've had enough of our kids coming home with condoms and instructions about how to use them.'" Igor helped the parents to organize a protest manifestation, after which he joined some of them in the search for partners in the Saint Petersburg region. "We managed to borrow a conference hall, so we sent an open invitation to everyone we knew and asked them to pass it further. Some fifty persons showed up, and it turned out that everybody had been thinking in the same way for a long time, but without being sure if they were right. Since no strong organization was pursuing this question, we decided to organize ourselves instead." One participant at this meeting was a representative from the Saint Petersburg Diocese of the Russian Orthodox Church (ROC), which provided a free location for a second meeting. About half of the participants returned, and they developed a long-term strategy and set up working groups for different purposes.

They communicated with like-minded groups in other parts of Russia. Igor went to Yekaterinburg to see a local Parents' Committee well known for supporting new groups, and in late 2009 he joined some Moscow organizations in the arrangement of a series of nationwide congresses. In 2010, the first large public manifestation took place in Saint Petersburg—a "standing" (*stoyanie*) that blends elements of a religious prayer meeting with a picket line. By then, activists nationwide referred to themselves as a "movement," and the original clique of concerned Saint Petersburg parents had proliferated into a handful of different groups. A year later, they authored the Saint Petersburg Resolution together with seventy other organizations around the country.

Judging by other respondents and by existing sources on the internet, Igor's story is not unusual among parental activists or, according to Vorozheikina (2008), the new grassroots mobilizations in general. Some catalyst spurs informal networks of people—neighbors, coparishioners, friends, and acquaintances—to organize public meetings or spontaneous protests, after which some of them decide to consolidate their efforts into a nonprofit organization. The driving forces are usually middle-class professionals—Igor was once a civil servant, while others I met were engineers, journalists, entrepreneurs, and so forth—with some sort of organizational experience, whether it is from work, from the near-compulsory Soviet youth organization Komsomol, or from free time engagements related to children's schooling or hobbies. Until about 2010, such conservative mobilizations were usually targeting medical centers providing sexual education, while legal initiatives in the field of family policy became more common later. Dimitry, a journalist and an acquaintance of Igor's in Saint Petersburg, thus set up his parental committee in response to a controversial drafting of a municipal family policy in 2010 (which, he told me, was quietly withdrawn after a certain amount of parental pressure).

Another respondent, Olga, is a consultant on religious charity for a large bank and the chairwoman of an internet-based coalition for organizations defending the interests of multiple-child families. A mother of three, she created a web forum in 2006 when, in her opinion, a number of much-advertised pronatalist state policies regarding housing and monetary assistance turned out to sidestep the needs of this particular category of families. Not only is it a disadvantage legally, she said, but civil servants frequently look down upon parents with many children, considering them to be irresponsible and incapable of planning their lives (her opinion is supported by, for example, Lovtsova and Iarskaia-Smirnova 2005). The forum grew into a nationwide coalition embracing more than one thousand activists, and Olga has since then been one of the more prominent public figures in the parental opposition.

Her network is, just like Igor's, frequently supported by ROC representatives with practicalities such as free premises for family vacations or meetings. Officially, all four "traditional" religions are invited to join the parental struggle, but in practice, Orthodoxy permeates written propaganda as well as public manifestations. The "prayer standing" mentioned by Igor is a common form of manifestation, and a number of conservative clerics, some of them occupying high positions in the Church hierarchy, participate at a regular basis at parental public events. Nonetheless, few parental organizations are formally associated with the ROC, nor are activists uncritically loyal to the Church. The ROC is more heterogeneous than its public image indicates (cf. Papkova 2011), and the Parents' Movement should rather be seen as one of its most conservative lobbying groups.

Mutual assistance among parental organizations is far more important for the formation of new groups than is support by external actors. Igor mentions a trip to Yekaterinburg, where some of the first Parents' Committees were set up in the mid-2000s to combat a local program for reproductive health (it took them half a year to close it down). Making effective use of information technology, for instance, by virtual consultancy forums or webinars, these groups have invested considerable efforts in supporting new Parents' Committees all over the country. They also initiated the first attempts at nationwide cooperation, which in 2011 resulted in the most sustainable (although far from the only) coalition at the time, the Association of Parents Committees and Societies (ARKS).[5] Another such consolidating force is a Moscow-based coalition of ultranationalist Orthodox groups called "The People's Council" (*Narodniy sobor*), the agenda of which embraces not only family issues but also a return to monarchy, prevention of "unrestrained immigration," and mobilization against "immoral art" and homosexuality.

Associating themselves with many of the most influential and productive public debaters, the People's Council has for long constituted the movement's ideological nexus. Together with, among others, Olga and Igor, they also arranged a series of congresses. These "Parental Forums" gathered from 1,300 participants in 2009 to 4,000 in 2011, but they were preceded by a large number of smaller events.[6]

"Do It Yourself": Autonomy and Moral Integrity

Dimitry summarized the difference between the former cohorts of established NGOs and his own as follows: "Regardless of whether they have Western or Russian money, they're similar—professional and specialized in particular sectors, but they exist only as long as they have funding and they don't reflect real public opinion." Therefore, he explained, they are not the kind of tenacious organizations that everyone refers to as civil society. In this context, he used the word "professional" in contrast to *narodnyi*, "of the people," implying elitist isolation and a "sense of the game" (in Bourdieu's sense) with reference to power. The professionals are, in his view, more familiar with funders, state administrators, and politicians than they are with ordinary people and with "real" public opinion. The new grassroots movements, in contrast, consist of ordinary people who merely try to solve everyday problems in a communitarian and bottom-up (*snizu*) fashion, without being dependent on external actors.

Vorozheikina (2008) suggests that the proliferated distrust in the state and in formalized structures in general makes Russia comparatively fertile soil for grassroots activism since people have always relied on informal forms of cooperation. In the same vein, Dimitry and most of my other respondents emphasized what they considered to be a traditional Russian inclination to cooperate spontaneously, without paying respect (or even regard) to the absent or dysfunctional official structures of society. "[The movement] is just a spontaneous reaction of ordinary people who've had enough of the state neglecting its duties," Olga explained. "They've undermined the school system for a long time, so people set up reading clubs to give the children some education in literature and history. People organize themselves to fend off real threats from the state. . . . Like when the city handed over what used to be a good children's theater to a director whose latest ten shows have been nothing but untraditional orgies; people went mad, it became a huge scandal."

Most organizations thus combine public opinion work with activities aimed to compensate for what is already lost or what was never there. All of my respondents regularly engage in public manifestations, proliferation of information, petition writing, conferences, and so forth, but Olga also invests considerable efforts in organizing vacation homes for multiple-child families. Igor arranges Orthodox summer camps for children, and the main objective of Dimitry's group is family-friendly leisure activities. All of them are also engaged in "grassroots charity" such as assisting families in dire need by pooling resources (toys, clothes, money, help with renovations, legal advice, etc.) or finding others who can help out—"for instance," Olga said, "by asking a shop owner if he can donate a fridge to a destitute family—and if you ask in the name of an organization, it often works."

Due to the strong desire for autonomy, most parental groups intentionally disqualify themselves from receiving funding. Few of them are formally registered with the authorities, which is a prerequisite for engaging in any kind of financial operation.[7] "We see no point in registering," Igor explained, "it just ends up in more state control. And we don't have any sponsors or common property—everybody is just pooling their own resources, time, telephones, and so on." He added that some groups prefer to register, since they need donors to expand their charity work. Nobody holds this against them; however, one's moral credibility fares better without registration or funding. "Everybody knows that the one who pays also orders the music," Dimitry said. "But people know that we're not bought by anyone, not by the West, not by Russian sponsors, not by the state. So they trust us and listen to us—even the local authorities respect us because they know that we don't say what someone else has whispered to us beforehand."

Accusations against "being bought" are indeed frequently voiced at parental internet forums against activists who have allegedly stretched the boundaries of what is deemed acceptable. Political forms of patronage are as resented as financial ones, and Western-funded NGOs are thus despised not only due to their sponsors, but also for frequently having cooperated with state agencies in different projects. In the same way, the skepticism of the aforementioned elite profamily NGOs stems from their Kremlin connections inasmuch as from their oligarch financers.

The antipathy extends to the very concept of "politics," which is completely rejected. Dimitry was, for example, very careful to underline that his work had nothing to do with politics, although he simultaneously elaborated extensively on his efforts to lobby the city authorities. Political activism may indeed be dangerous in Russia, but the principal reason why he and others distance themselves from the concept is because to them, politics is more than just influencing governance; it is the opaque intrigues of a remote and self-interested elite caste of corrupt bureaucrats, and to be "political" is to communicate with them on their terms, to become one of them. Politics is thus the antithesis of everything that being "civic" is associated with—communitarianism, autonomy, and transparency.

However, activism by definition implies exerting influence on political actors, and some sort of dialogue is thus required. One strategy is to associate oneself with supposedly loyal politicians, such as United Russia deputy Vitaly Milonov (architect of Saint Petersburg's local ban on homosexual propaganda in 2012) or certain representatives of the Communist party, who all appear exempt from the taboo against political connections. Opinions are divided about membership in political parties. After I met Olga, I learned that she and some well-known Yekaterinburg leaders are members of United Russia. I take it as a strategic means to make themselves heard. Their choice is sharply criticized by ideological purists, while many others apparently trust that they are more dedicated to the movement than to the party.

Another strategy is professionalism, but in a different sense than elitist isolation or political dexterity. In the same interview, Dimitry expressed his high regard of a fellow activist: "He doesn't confront power, he just says 'I'm professional, I'm a jurist . . . ,' he can really evaluate things . . . and provides [neutral] information, and finally the deputies listen." Here, "professionalism" instead implies disinterested expert knowledge, a prerequisite for receiving the attention of power without compromising one's moral integrity. The emphasis on education and knowledge is hardly surprising since most prominent activists belong to the educated strata, and a large share of all the movement's events consists of seminars, roundtables, conferences, and public hearings, while a regular staff of experts (mostly psychologists, jurists, and clerics) occupies a central position in the movement as public debaters.

Many organizations, including the ones to which my respondents belong, attempt to lobby the authorities (in particular at local levels) by participating in, or co-arranging, public hearings, workshops, or various citizen commissions and advisory groups. Their credibility in these contexts stems from grassroots integrity as well as disinterested expert authority. As I interpret it, however, a fair number of activists are not convinced that the latter automatically gives moral immunity, but they are wary that lobbying might result in the aforementioned, less benign aspects of professionalism. In particular, the most ultranationalist and conservative Orthodox organizations consistently avoid direct interaction with authorities and restrict their activities to proliferation of information and public manifestations.

As I will return to, diverging positions in this respect have become increasingly common within the Parents' Movement along with its expansion and increased recognition in the established political field from 2010 onward. Nonetheless, the commentary in numerous internet debates simultaneously reveals a strong ethos of unity and a widespread opinion that schism as such is worse than ideological deviations. Many conflicts appear to remain at the individual level, while local groups often navigate pragmatically between potential partners in both camps.

The Agenda: Global Conspiracy, Russian Tradition, and Juvenile Justice

Such negotiations have intensified as the Movement has grown and as the focus of its attention has shifted from "immorality" in general to more specific legal initiatives and policy implementations. In 1997, the "anti-sex crusaders" stifled the development of a draft law about sex education in schools (Kon 1999), but the early rhetoric was nonetheless less focused on jurisprudence than on cultural values. In Melucci's terms, the anti-sex campaign laid the foundations of a post-Soviet conservative collective identity. By positioning Russian "tradition" in a new globalized world order and defining its enemies, it enabled social actors to recognize each other, and to a large extent it did so by appealing to emotions (Melucci 1989, 35). The civic aspects of this identity were yet to be developed, since the nascent opposition had not yet identified itself as a social movement and, thereby, as a civic actor.

In the mid-2000s, a new issue was introduced to the conservative pro-family agenda: the UN Convention of the Rights of Children (CRC). Russia already ratified the CRC in 1990, but for fiscal reasons (from my understanding), no comprehensive attempt was made to implement it legally until the mid-2000s. Parental activists refer to the resulting legislative transformation as *yuvenal'naya yustitsiia*, Juvenile Justice, or just YuYu. Originally, the eponym was an umbrella term for a number of reform projects targeted primarily at the youth penitentiary system, but they also addressed the dilemmas of socially vulnerable families and children. From the late 1990s onward, state administrators, social scientists, NGOs, and Western aid agencies have been cooperating in local pilot projects throughout Russia concerning, for example, youth courts, probation and rehabilitation systems, education on child rights, local Children's Ombudsmen, crisis hotlines, and so forth (Komarnitskiy 2010:441ff; CIDA 2009). Federal lawmakers followed suit from the mid-2000s onward with a number of reforms, frequently modeled on these pilots, aimed at protecting the rights of children and, in particular, improve the social protection of vulnerable children and families.[8]

The conservative opposition has never paid much attention to youth criminality, the main focus of the first Juvenile Justice projects. From the onset, the target was instead two very general aspects of the idea of Child Rights that have been the subject of reservations worldwide since the drafting of the CRC in the late 1980s. Firstly, the Convention is criticized for ignoring local conceptions of childhood and parent-child relationships in favor of a Eurocentric ideal of children as autonomous subjects (Schabas 1996). Secondly, legal implementations of the CRC by definition turn the state into the ultimate guarantor of the wellbeing of children. According to many critics, the right of parents to socialize their offspring as they see fit is thereby sidestepped, as are the civil rights to family autonomy and integrity of private life (Hafen and Hafen 1996).

In the Russian debate, emphasis has gradually shifted from Russia's position toward purported Western cultural imperialism to the supposedly conflicting interests of the state and the family respectively. I will therefore begin by strictly discussing ideological objections to Child Rights, and in the next section I will introduce protests of a more pragmatic nature against an escalating number of laws and policies that have been introduced since the mid-2000s.

In their seminal publication in 2006, "The Trojan Horse of Juvenile Justice," Medvedeva and Shishova insert the CRC and its agents (UNICEF and Russian NGOs promoting child rights) into the standard narrative about a Western liberal conspiracy against Russian sovereignty and tradition:

> Juvenile Justice implies such a disruption of child-parent relations, of social ties and of the entire Russian way of life, that previous reforms are mere Christmas crackers in comparison. As is well known, an important part of the globalization process (the building of single world government with an occult and Satanist ideology) is the destruction of the family. [The] mass perversion of children by mass media and, even, by school "innovations" aimed

> at eliminating parental authority . . . is not arbitrary scattered episodes, but a consistent policy of the globalist reformers. But as they admit themselves, they are hampered by the imperfection of our legal framework, which they use all their efforts to "improve." (Medvedeva and Shishova 2006, my translation)

Neither this text nor the numerous ones to come are unanimously negative to the CRC as such. The issue is rather how the treaty should be interpreted and by whom. Appeals to the Convention are often used to justify reforms that the Movement approves, for instance, obligatory religious education in schools or bans on homosexual "propaganda." International agencies and the forthcoming Russian juvenile system are assumed to implement the CRC to the disadvantage of Russian tradition. The activists argue that if abortions, sex, and brutality in mass media are not defined as violence against children, then this clause without doubt will be applied to a "light smack on the bum." The argument is lavishly illustrated with disparate depravity stories about children in Western countries reporting their parents to the authorities for light corporal reprimands, or for being grounded and having privileges withdrawn. Encouraged to report such "psychological abuse" to what activists consider as the totalitarian network of crisis hotlines, Children's Ombudsmen, and social workers, children will, according to the opponents, be removed from their families in order to be exploited for their final purpose—adoption to homosexual (i.e., pedophilic) couples in the West (Riabichenko 2013).

Basic to these arguments is an Orthodox view of the family as a mirror of the Church as well as of society. In written discourse it surfaces merely as occasional references to "Orthodox tradition" or, at best, the Fifth Commandment, but some of my respondents were careful to outline the logic more in detail. They brought it up spontaneously, presumably to avert an image of themselves as ruthless child abusers. The family, the Church, and society are all organized hierarchically with leaders entrusted with the right to discipline, they argued. If children do not learn to respect authority and boundaries at home, they will become asocial and a threat to the community. Physical punishment is a last-choice measure that must be taken with outmost consideration, but nonetheless it is necessary as an ultimate insignia of authority.

Other arguments (frequent also at parental forums) concern more down-to-earth aspects of socialization. Children do not know what is in their own best interest and cannot foresee consequences, and parents need to set clear limits. Moreover, it is argued, few adults were harmed by occasional and well-deserved bashings (physical punishments) in their childhood. A

Moscow activist added that children become verbal only at a certain age, and until then, all forms of communication are physical, indications of approval as well as the contrary. To him, the idea of banning even light corporal reprimands was thus as absurd as prohibiting hugs. As he put it, Russians in general value authority and corporality more than Westerners. Perhaps he is right—for example, Shmidt (2012a) suggests that the core of the controversy about Juvenile Justice resides in a Russian tendency to view children as essentially dependent and malleable, in contrast to the autonomous ideal of the CRC.[9] Her point deserves further empirical investigation, but here I abstain from conclusions in this matter. Essentializations of purportedly homogenous national cultures are fundamental to all nationalist ideologies, but in my own opinion, one of Russia's most typical traits is its extreme heterogeneity.

The Parents' Movement is primarily defined by the opposition against Juvenile Justice and Child Rights, but a conservative stance with regard to sexuality and gender is nonetheless fundamental to its self-image. In the early "morality rhetoric," references to homosexuality and feminism were made frequently but very briefly, as contributing factors to the problems of sex education and decreased birthrates. Since the first attempts to arrange gay pride parades in the mid-2000s, however, feminists and, in particular, the "gay lobby" have gradually received an increasingly central role in the alleged conspiracy. As recipients of Western funding and knowhow, these alleged promoters of an anti-Russian "gender ideology" are supposed to employ juvenile laws and authorities in a scheme aimed at eliminating natural sex differences, including heterosexual desire. Women's emancipation is, in contrast, addressed very sparsely, which is somewhat intriguing since the role of women as homemakers and mothers is usually central to conservative profamily movements. (In this case, moreover, about half of the leaders are female.) A tentative suggestion is that such arguments are superfluous. Most ordinary Russians endorse fathers as the main breadwinners and mothers as being responsible for the home and children, and neither parental activists nor public opinion object to supplementary female wage work. Also, there have not been many legal initiatives to protest. However, in 2012, a draft law on gender equality caught the attention of one of the most productive parental debaters. Her criticism does not concern its actual content, however, but the fact that the bill employs the term "gender" which, in her view, makes it a vehicle of the notorious "gender ideology" (Riabichenko 2013).[10]

Further Controversies: The Threat of an Omnipotent State

By 2010, the previous almost uniformly polemical and emotional rhetoric of parental debaters was supplemented with a more legalistic and dispassionate strand when a series of media reports appeared about child removals on unjustified grounds. Most of them concerned Russia, but more attention was given to a handful of cases involving Russian immigrants abroad (Finland in particular), who allegedly had suffered injustice by the child protecting authorities in their new countries. As a result, social services and child removals became high-profile news stories for a couple of years.

In the intensive media discussion, the Parents' Movement created a public platform for itself and managed to establish a discursive link between unjustified removals, Juvenile Justice, and the West. Parental debaters now spoke out as experts in mainstream mass media, contextualizing the seeming tide of child removals in Russia in relation to recent legal changes. A few years earlier, they had pointed out that the Eurocentric bias of the CRC would result in new normative grounds of the Russian system and, thereby, enable state intervention in any family deviating from Western standards, be it moral or material (cf. Terekhov 2007). Now, a number of legal amendments had broadened the definitions of "violence" and "neglect" in parent-child relations, introduced new and vague target categories (such as "dangerous life situation"), and permitted the removal of children from their families without a preceding court case. According to the Parents' Movement, these changes encouraged arbitrary interpretations by civil servants and, thereby, corruption. In some of the notorious cases, fabricated allegations of physical violence were said to have been used to blackmail parents, while other removals of children were allegedly justified on such loose grounds as an empty fridge or an untidy home. Olga was one of the first to point this out, since some of the incidents occurred within her network of multiple-child families. To her, she explained to me, this was the ultimate proof of the madness of the juvenile bureaucracy, since any common-sense human should understand that it is impossible for one with many children to have a constantly clean home and a permanently stocked fridge.

Whether or not the purported rise in unjust removals was actually true remains unclear—statistically, deprivations of parental rights have decreased since 2007, but figures obviously say nothing about fairness (cf. Shmidt 2012a). Facts notwithstanding, the image of a near-totalitarian system of child protection chimed well with already existing popular conceptions of this much-feared state agency. Parental activists had already for a few years predicted this nightmare and now it was seemingly coming true. Looming in the near future was, moreover, a new draft law project initiated in early 2010, which they feared would result in a coordinated and streamlined welfare agency immune to other legal authorities.

"The law on social patronage" was the latest in a long series of attempts to reform the outdated Soviet subsidiary welfare system, which grants predefined social categories (pensioners, disabled people, single mothers, etc.) fixed privileges and/or sums of money. Means-tested benefits for unexpected needs are poorly developed, so the only form of emergency assistance to families in crisis is a purportedly temporary place at an orphanage for the children. Since few parents ask for this "favor" voluntarily, most removals are forced and justified by the imminent danger of the child's life and health, and few children return to their parents.[11] The idea of the reform was, ironically, to amend these flaws and reduce the orphanage population, but since the bill proposed only medico-psychological aid and not monetary assistance (which crisis families usually need most), even liberal child rights advocates criticized it (c.f. Tsvetkova 2013).

From 2010 onward, new Parental Committees mushroomed all over the country, and Juvenile Justice was adopted as a top priority by an assorted cluster of already existing nationalist organizations and movements. As I take it, it was easier for people in general to relate to tangible everyday realities than to abstract future scenarios. The increased focus on jurisprudence and a new cohort of regular debaters contributed to a partial change of rhetorical style, in which references to religion and tradition were replaced with appeals to civil rights granted by the Russian Constitution. Among the new recruitments were thus, for the first time, secular groups (Dimitry's is one of them) and nationalist organizations that are more pro-Soviet than Orthodox. The proneness on apocalyptic dystopias remained in the parental rhetoric, but mainly in discussions pertaining to the notorious cases of children being removed from Russian immigrants by Western social services.

These families, most of them living in Finland, were depicted by Russian media as victims of false allegations of physical violence, usually because the children had mentioned in school that a parent had given them "a smack on the bum" (unfortunately, professional secrecy prevents the Finnish version from ever being told). The Parents' Movement managed to attach to itself some of the wronged parents and their advocates, who readily confirmed in public that their suffering was symptomatic for "the Western" Juvenile Justice system and an expression of downright Russophobia (cf. Höjdestrand 2014). Parental and mainstream media made extensive use of the entire battery of depravity stories, hyperboles, and straight falsifications—for example, Finland is accused of stripping children of Russian decent of their language and culture by systematically incarcerating them in concentration camps in Lapland (cf. Bekman 2010; Novikova 2014).

Both styles of rhetoric served to outline the self-image of the Parents' Movement. In debates pertaining to Russia, it promoted itself as the authentic voice of "the people," understood as a civic-minded citizenry standing up against a corrupt and debased state administration. When the cases of child removal abroad were at stake, it constructed itself rather as the voice of "the Russian people," threatened by a voracious and diabolic Western enemy.[12]

Success: The Movement Becomes Politically Correct

By 2010, however, hyperboles and falsifications were no longer rhetoric devices limited to a marginalized cohort of ultranationalists. A general tendency in the "patriotic turn" of the Russian regime since the mid-2000s is that it gradually appropriates symbols and discourses that formerly were deployed mainly by actors and groups more radical than the political mainstream (Zuev 2011; Laurelle 2009). Now, the Russian governing regime met ultranationalists halfway by adopting a rhetoric nearly as anti-Western and paranoid as the Parents' Movement's litanies about global conspiracy and moral warfare (cf. Ortmann and Heathershaw 2012). To the opportunistic popular press, the conservative narrative about child removals and Juvenile Justice was thus (from my understanding) a convenient way to prove one's political correctness, and occasional attempts at investigative journalism were drowned in the maelstrom of nationalist hyperbole and depravity stories.[13] Thus a causal link was established also in popular imaginaries between domestic authority abuse and a foreign system gradually being penetrated into Russia by a Western world already lost.

Finally, the anti-YuYu campaign found resonance among politically established actors. In 2010, the Communist Party, the ROC, Federal Child Commissioner Pavel Astakhov, and Elena Mizulina, head of the Duma Committee for Family, Women, and Children, officially distanced themselves from what they vaguely referred to as "the Western" model of Juvenile Justice. In the following years, many others followed suit, as it seems, with quite different motivations since Russian power is not a monolith with unequivocal objectives, as external observers often would suggest. Rather, objectives and agendas differ greatly between regions, various levels of the state apparatus, or just individuals (cf. Henderson 2011). The apex of federal power prioritizes geopolitics and macroeconomic issues, while social policy is addressed by subordinate and regional administrative levels. An officially promoted value such as "the good of the family" can thus be interpreted as a call for improved systems of child protection as well as the contrary, or just as a non-obliging buzzword.

Some of those who rejected "the Western model" probably agreed entirely with the Parents' Movement, while others merely used the YuYu controversy to demonstrate their own patriotism and dedication to "the people." Yet others—in particular state officials engaged in social policy—apparently tried to pacify the opposition by playing down the foreign element of the reforms, so that the much-needed transformation of a scandalously outdated and inefficient social sector eventually could be realized in practice. To the latter cohort belongs Elena Mizulina, who is the main official in charge of the reforms and who only a few years earlier was an ardent advocate of Juvenile Justice. As most other state administrators and experts on social policy at the time, however, she interpreted the term as an improvement of the systems dealing with youth at risk. The Parents' Movement, in contrast, has always applied the term to any legal reform that might challenge the authority of parents toward the state or toward children. Mass media, in turn, conveyed it roughly as "anything that authorizes the state to remove children," which was also the subject of the official renunciations, given the omnipresent media representations of the West as chronically family-hostile.

To Mizulina, a dismissal of "the Western model" of Juvenile Justice did not contradict a promotion of abovementioned draft law on social patronage—in her view, the bill would prevent excess removals of children, not the contrary. Parental activists, in contrast, considered this to be the most dangerous attempt to introduce Juvenile Justice so far, and once launched in March 2012, it was met by protest manifestations all over the country. The largest ones in Moscow reportedly gathered over 4,000 participants, and in the summer, activists gathered 140,000 petition signatures and delivered them to the Duma.

Throughout 2012 the parental rhetoric became increasingly triumphant, and in early 2013, a victory of sorts was achieved. Putin made a guest appearance at a parental congress, solemnly pledging to respect public opinion in the consideration of this draft law and others that "do not take Russian family traditions fully into account."[14] The loathed bill on social patronage somehow disappeared on its way through the readings in the Duma, even though there was no doubt that it would soon be replaced by new juvenile encroachments (which was also the case). More important was the fact that Putin's personal attention had confirmed the Parents' Movement as a worthy representative of an authentic and patriotic civil society. A commentator from the Congress notes, "[Speakers] proposed the idea of a new format of politics and of the birth of an authentic nationally oriented civic society" (Krivorotova 2013). "We won!" reads a statement by the coalition ARKS. "Our victory was possible only because the parental Orthodox community united with other patriotic forces who share the same civil positions."[15]

Reflection: Where Do We Go Now?

The above quotations conclude two vital criteria for the parental ideal about civicness. Firstly, patriotism excludes all purported liberals from the civil sphere, whether they are professionals or grassroots activists. Secondly, authenticity demarcates morally upright grassroots from any corrupt political establishment, be it domestic or foreign. Since 2012, however, the success of the Parents' Movement has made the latter aspect increasingly problematic. The rapid influx of new groups and movements resulted in increased heterogeneity, partly with reference to religiosity, but even more as regards to opinions about how to approach power and the authorities. As the movement has become politically opportune, established prolife NGOs and state agencies have approached parental leaders with proposals for joint coalitions or participation in citizen's advisory boards, for instance, under the Federal Child Commissioner or in cooperation with the Civic Chamber. Some have accepted, which has caused an intense debate. Another contentious issue is Sergei Kurginyan, leader of the largest new contribution to the movement, the pro-Soviet organization Essence of Time, which has become a nationwide movement on its own through the project "USSR 2.0." Kurginyan has a past not only as a theater director, a TV personality, and an academic, but also as a political analyst and a Kremlin advisor. To some, he is therefore a respected expert, while others find him deeply suspect. Still many of his critics agree that Putin would hardly have paid attention to the parental congress without Kurginyan's connections, and the novel opportunities to exert influence at higher political levels beg for a reconsideration of the moral implications of involvement with power.

Before Putin's speech, it was thus evident that profound schisms were underway. The issue is not the aims as such, since "traditional morals" and the core issues of the agenda imply little more than a rejection of the West, of homosexuality, and of state removals of children. Rather, the intensified discussions concern, in Melucci's (1989) terms, means and fields of actions, in other words, the ways in which these morals should be defended and on which arenas the struggle is to take place. As before, the main bone of contention is cooperation with elite structures and, by implication, also how "professionalism" should be managed in a benign way, without the negative consequences of elitism and isolation.

In effect, parental forums are increasingly preoccupied by the ethical implications of active citizenship. An increasing number of voices argue that it is not enough merely to represent the people's will and remain pure from corruption. When one is at war—which is how activists perceive the situation—more professionalism is needed, understood as expert competence and as a capacity to communicate and cooperate with the state administration.

The intensified debate does not imply a change in opinions inasmuch as a radically heightened awareness of the inherent difficulties in being and acting civically. Hence civicness as such has become crucial to the movement's collective identity. Until approximately 2012, parental activists were not invited to the more influential (and potentially polluting) political arenas, so neither purists nor pragmatists had to face, in practice, the long-term consequences of their own standpoints. The main issues now are thus not new, only more pertinent and painful than before.

Firstly, opinions vary about whether or not the Parents' Movement actually has acquired the required "civic capital" (to paraphrase Bourdieu) to enter new and foreign elite territories—to some, the new patriotic civil society is already a fact, while others lament what they see as an absence of skills, dedication, and faith. Secondly, and more important, the question remains whether or not one actually desires to risk the entire movement's existence by becoming immersed into the power structures, in spite of the apparent advantages. In this sense, activists are painfully aware of the same dilemma as is reflected in social research on civic organizations in Russia. The regime indeed actively attempts to pacify non-state organizations by absorbing them into its own structures (Ljubownikow, Crotty, and Rogers 2013), but such cooperation may simultaneously be very productive (Chebankova 2013). So far, the negotiations continue, as summarized by an anonymous voice:

> Parents are not . . . professional "warriors" in this uneven battle. They are just . . . learning to think strategically and work out tactics, to get familiar with and assimilate the methods of their adversaries. . . . Without doubt the non-professionals make many mistakes, but they have something essential—incorruptibility, they are uncompromising in their struggle against evil, they have a personal interest to protect their families, children, traditions, faith, folk and fatherland. . . . But there are also minuses, when the lack of professionalism, education, faith and so forth gives the enemy the opportunity to sipper through these cracks and lead the parental resistance astray.[16]

In the case of the Parents' Movement, different positions may or may not result in deepened schisms and, in the end, plural movements, but this is a case for future research.

Tova Höjdestrand, Associate Professor, Department of Sociology, Division of Social Anthropology at Lund University, Sweden

Tova Höjdestrand's present research traverses the areas of nationalism, social movements, transnational governance, and gender and sexuality. Her current project investigates how issues related to the intimate social sphere and reproduction are deployed in Russian nationalist discourse, and the interplay between patriotic moral mobilizations and policy-making at the national and transnational level. A previous project, published in her book *Needed by Nobody: Homelessness and Humanness in Post-Socialist Russia* (Cornell University Press, 2009), focused on processes of social exclusion, state surveillance, informal economy and survival strategies, social stigmatization, and identity formation.

Notes

1. Accessed September 30, 2014. http://blog.profamilia.ru/wp-content/uploads/2011/10/. Also available at the site is a slightly revised version of the Resolution in English, which was distributed to the representatives of all the member states of the European Council.

2. "Draft Recommendation on the rights and legal status of children and parental responsibilities" of the Committee of Ministers of the Council of Europe (CJ-FA-GT3, 2010, 2 rev. 5).

3. Accessed September 30, 2014. *Russkaia narodnaia linia* ("the Russian people's line," ruskline.ru) is a general patriotic, Orthodox, and monarchist news platform that covers parental issues very well (the main editor is a veteran in the movement), while *Yuvenal'naia yustitsiia—my protiv* ("Juvenile Justice—we're against," www.juvenaljustice.ru) is a protest site with an adjacent *Vkontakte* group (vk.com/stopjuvenaljustice) dedicated to the main item on the movement's agenda, which I will discuss further.

4. The most well-known case is Oleg Kassin, founder and leader of *Narodniy Sobor* (The People's Council), a leading coalition within the movement, who was once vice president of the quasi-fascist and xenophobic extreme nationalist organization Russian National Union (*Russk oenatsional'noeedinstvo*, RNE).

5. *Assotsiatsiia roditel'skikh komitety i soobshchestv*, ARKS.

6. For a video clip from the Forum held in 2011, see (accessed September 30, 2014) http://rutube.ru/video/701cd2d60207a718ed75997d091c77fc/.

7. For the mere status as a civil organization, a statute adopted at a foundational meeting is sufficient. The reluctance of parental groups to register is confirmed by the Ministry of Justice's register of nonstate, noncommercial organizations, where very few of the ones involved in the Parents' Movement are listed. One may add that many services offered to parental groups by private persons, the ROC, and others—be it free facilities, permissive work hours, printed materials, etc.—could most probably equal regular funding if the tax authorities ever cared to investigate them.

8. Some examples are the following: A federal system of youth courts (not yet taken), a strengthening of the legal authority of the child protective services (2008), new legal terms defining target categories (2009), the introduction of federal Child Commissioners (2010), harshened punishments for "cruelty against children" (2010), and new forms of social assistance (2012, 2013).

9. Shmidt (2012a) argues that the Russian tendency to perceive children as essentially dependent is reflected in the new legislation, which, in spite of its ostensible adherence to the CRC, transfers the overprotecting function from parents to the state. In some sense, her conclusion thus supports the claims of the conservative parental organizations; but as pointed out by Sherstneva (2013), she simultaneously appears to ignore paragraphs that explicitly state the right of children to have their opinions taken into account.

10. The battle against "gender ideology" is fought with considerably more passion by similar parental organizations in Ukraine, Poland, and other European countries with large Catholic populations. Discourse and arguments are strikingly similar everywhere, and in many countries the campaigns also appear to have begun at about the same time, from 2011 onward. They appear to be part of a globally coordinated project that began in the 1990s by various reactionary religious agencies (e.g., the Holy See or Evangelical Right organizations such as the aforementioned WCF) to return the world to "traditional values" (cf. Butler 2006), but it has intensified significantly in the past five years (cf. Korolczuk 2014; Case 2012).

11. Estimations vary of the number of children in state or foster care who are social orphans, in other words, those who are deprived of their parental rights but their parents are alive. According to the (relatively liberal) Orthodox news site *Pravoslavie i mir*, on March 15, 2014, there are 75% of social orphans in Moscow (Mendeleeva and Galperina 2014).

12. For an account in English of some of the Finnish cases, and for examples of the predominant style of rhetoric, see Kovalenko (2012) or Novikova (2014).

13. For an exception, see an unsigned article from the news agency IA Regnum, which among other things compares the number of children in state care in the respective countries. In 2010, 2.6% of Russia's children were in state or foster care, as compared to 1.3% of all Finnish

children (IA Regnum 2012). To this, one may add that in Western European countries, the percentage of children who remain permanently in state or foster care is considerably lower than in Russia (Shmidt 2012b).

14. Accessed September 30, 2014. http://eng.kremlin.ru/news/4973.

15. Accessed September 30, 2014. http://ruskline.ru/news_rl/2013/02/14/triumfalnaya_pobeda_roditelskogo_soobwestva_nad_yuvenalnoj_yusticiej/.

16. Accessed September 30, 2014 (my translation). http://ruskline.ru/news_rl/2012/12/28/davajte_pogovorim_o_glavnom.

Works Cited

Appadurai, Arjun. 1996. *Modernity at Large: Cultural Dimensions of Globalization.* Minneapolis: University of Minnesota Press.

Aron, Leon. 2010. "Russia's New Protesters." American Enterprise Institute for Public Policy Research. AIE Outlook Series, June 8. Accessed September 30, 2014. http://www.aei.org/publication/russias-new-protesters/.

Artiukh, Anatoly. 2013. "Ne speshite khoronit' Narodniy Sobor" [Don't Hurry to Bury the People's Council]. Accessed September 30, 2014. http://ruskline.ru/news_rl/2013/02/12/ne_speshite_horonit_narodnyj_sobor/.

Attwood, Lynne. 1990. *The New Soviet Man and Woman: Sex-Role Socialization in the USSR*. Bloomington: Indiana University Press.

Bekman, Iokhan [Bäckman, Johan]. 2010. "Iuvenal'naia iustitsiia: put' k fashizmu" [Juvenile Justice: The Road to Fascism]. Accessed September 30, 2014. http://ruskline.ru/analitika/2010/06/23/yuvenalnaya_yusticiya_put_k_fashizmu/.

Butler, Jennifer S. 2006. *Born Again: The Christian Right Globalized.* London, Ann Arbor: Pluto Press.

Case, Mary Anne. 2012. "After Gender the Destruction of Man? The Vatican's Nightmare Vision of the 'Gender Agenda' for Law." *Pace Law Review* 3 (3):802–818.

Chebankova, Elena A. 2013. *Civil Society in Putin's Russia.* London: Routledge.

CIDA (Canadian International Development Agency). 2009. "Juvenile Justice in Russia: Models, Design, and the Road Ahead." Accessed September 30, 2014. http://www.iicrd.org/system/files/Juvenile%20Justice%20Models%20Part%20I.pdf.

Federman, Adam. 2014. "How US Evangelicals Fuelled the Rise of Russia's 'Pro-Family' Right." Accessed September 30, 2014. http://www.thenation.com/article/177823/how-us-evangelicals-fueled-rise-russias-pro-family-right.

Fine, Michelle. 1988. "Sexuality, Schooling, and Adolescent Females: The Missing Discourse of Desire." *Harvard Educational Review* 58 (1):29–53.

Gladarev, Boris, and Markku Lonkila. 2012. "The Role of Social Networking Sites in Civic Activism in Russia and Finland." *Europe-Asia Studies* 64 (8):1375–1394.

Hafen, Bruce C., and Jonathan O. Hafen.1996. "Abandoning Children to Their Autonomy: The United Nations Convention on the Rights of the Child." *Harvard International Law Journal* 37 (2):449–493.

Hann, Chris, and Elizabeth Dunn. 1996. *Civil Society: Challenging Western Models.* London: Routledge.

Hemment, Julie D. 2004. "The Riddle of the Third Sector: Civil Society, Western Aid and NGOs in Russia." *Anthropological Quarterly* 77 (2):215–241.

Henderson, Sara L. 2011. "Civil Society in Russia: State-Society Relations in the Post-Yeltsin Era." *Problems of Post-Communism* 58 (3):11–27.

Herman, Didi. 2001. "Globalism's 'Siren Song': The United Nations and International Law in Christian Right Thought and Prophecy." *Sociological Review* 49 (1):56–77.

Höjdestrand, Tova. 2014. "Fosterland, familj och föräldraföreningar: moralisk mobilisering och myndighetsmisstro i dagens Ryssland"[Fatherland, Family, and Parental Associations: Moral Mobilization and Distrust in Authority in Contemporary Russia]. *Nordisk Østforum* 28 (4):329–354.

IA Regnum. 2012. "'Nizkiiy porog vmeshatel'stva'finskiy i peterburgskie eksperty o situatsii s rossiiskom det'mi" [A Low Threshold for Infringement—Experts from Finland and St. Petersburg about the Situation with Russian Children]. Accessed September 30, 2014. http://www.regnum.ru/news/fd-nw/piter/1582101.html.

Irvine, Janice M. 2004. *Talk about Sex: The Battles over Sex Education in the United States*. Berkeley: University of California Press.

Jacobsson, Kerstin, and Steven Saxonberg. 2013. "Introduction: The Development of Social Movements in Central and Eastern Europe." In *Beyond NGO-ization: The Development of Social Movements in Central and Eastern Europe*, edited by Kerstin Jacobsson and Steven Saxonberg. Farnham: Ashgate.

Komarnitskiy, Anatoly. 2010. Osnovy Iuvenal'naia Iustitsiia: Uchebnik [The Bases of Juvenile Justice: A Textbook]. St. Petersburg: Obshchestvo Znanie.

Kon, Igor. 1999. "Sexuality and Politics in Russia, 1700–2000." In *Sexual Cultures in Europe: National Histories*, edited by F. H. Eder, L. Hall, and G. Hekma. Manchester: Manchester University Press. Accessed September 30, 2014. http://sexology.narod.ru/publ012.html.

Korolczuk, Elżbieta. 2014. "'The War on Gender' from a Transnational Perspective: Lessons for Feminist Strategising." In *Proceedings of III International Gender Workshop "Are We Moving Forward or Backwards? Strategizing to Overcome Gender Backlash in Central and Eastern Europe"* September 2014, Berlin, organized by Heinrich Böll Foundation.

Kovalenko, Natalia. 2012. "Finland's Strange Policy towards Russian Children." Accessed September 30, 2014. http://english.pravda.ru/society/family/28–01–2014/126694-finland_juvenile_fascism-0/.

Krivorotova, Zhanna. 2013. "S'ezd roditelej Rossii glazami ego uchastnika" [The Congress of Russia's Parents through the Eyes of a Participant]. Website of the City Parents' Committee of Tiumen, February 25, 2013. Accessed September 30, 2014. http://arhiv1.tgrcom.ru/index.php/component/content/article/1490-2013-02-25-00-47-10.

Laruelle, Marlène. 2009. "Rethinking Russian Nationalism: Historical Continuity, Political Diversity, and Doctrinal Fragmentation." In *Russian Nationalism and the National Reassertion of Russia*, edited by Marlène Laruelle. London: Routledge.

Levintova, Hannah. 2014. "How US Evangelicals Helped Create Russia's Anti-Gay Movement." Accessed September 30, 2014. http://www.motherjones.com/politics/2014/02/world-congress-families-russia-gay-right.

Ljubownikow, Sergej, Jo Crotty, and Peter W. Rogers. 2013. "The State and Civil Society in Post-Soviet Russia: The Development of a Russian Style Civil Society." *Progress in Development Studies* 13 (2):153–166.

Lovtsova, N. I., and E. R. Iarskaia-Smirnova. 2005. "Demograficheskaia problema: kto vinovat i chto delat'?" [The Demographic Problem: Who is Guilty and What Should Be Done?]. *Mir Rossii* 4:78–104.

Medvedeva, Irina, and Tatiana Shishova. 1996. "Mezhdunarodniy proekt 'Polovoe vospitanie rossiyskikh shkol'nikov' i natsional'naya bezopasnost" [The International Project "Sexual Education of Russian School Children" and National Security]. Accessed September 30, 2014. http://lib.eparhia-saratov.ru/books/12m/medvedeva_shishova/ugliness/3.html.

———. 2001. "Zapakh sery" [The Smell of Sulfur]. Accessed September 30, 2014. http://www.pravoslavie.ru/jurnal/1332.htm.

———. 2006. "Troyanskiy kon' yuvenal'niy yustitsii" [The Trojan Horse of Juvenile Justice]. Accessed September 30, 2014. http://www.pravoslavie.ru/jurnal/061026200349.htm.

Melucci, Alberto. 1989. *Nomads of the Present. Social Movements and Individual Needs in Contemporary Society.* London: Radius.

Mendeleeva, Daria, and Anna Gal'perina. 2014. "Direktor detdoma, gde rasdali v sem'i vsekh detei—o tom, pochemu v Rossii stol'ko sirot" [The Director of an Orphanage that Placed All the Children into Families—Why are There So Many Orphans in Russia?]. *Pravoslavie i mir*, March 15, 2014. Accessed September 30, 2014. http://www.pravmir.ru/direktor-detdoma-gde-usyinovili-vseh-detey-o-tom-pochemu-v-rossii-stolko-sirot/?fb_action_ids=805386419480819&fb_action_types=og.likes.

Morn, Becca. 2013. "Homophobia Inc. and America's Newest Export." Accessed September 30, 2014. http://americablog.com/2013/10/homophobia-inc-americas-newest-export-hate-part-1-3.html.

Novikova, Inna. 2014. "Finland: Juvenile Fascism for 800 Million Euros." Accessed September 30, 2014. http://english.pravda.ru/society/family/28-01-2014/126694-finland_juvenile_fascism-0/.

Ortmann, Stefanie, and John Heathershaw. 2012. "Conspiracy Theories in the Post-Soviet Space." *Russian Review* 71 (4):551–564.

Papkova, Irina. 2011. *The Orthodox Church and Russian Politics.* Oxford: Oxford University Press.

Riabichenko, Liudmila. 2013. "Sodom ozhestochenno kroit mir pod sebya" [Sodom Is Frantically Cutting the World for Itself]. Accessed September 30, 2014. http://ruskline.ru/news_rl/2013/06/22/sodom_ozhestochyonno_kroit_mir_pod_sebya.

Rivkin-Fish, Michele. 2006. "From 'Demographic Crisis' to 'Dying Nation:' The Politics of Language and Reproduction in Russia." In *Gender and National Identity in Twentieth Century Russian Culture*, edited by Helena Goscilo and Andrea Lanoux. DeKalb: Northern Illinois University Press.

Schabas, William A. 1996. "Reservations to the Convention of the Rights of the Child." *Human Rights Quarterly* 18 (2):472–491.

Sherstneva, Natalia. 2013. *Kampanya protiv yuvenal'noiy yustitsii: analiz mobiliziruiushchikh freymov* [The Campaign against Juvenile Justice: An Analysis of the Mobilizing Frames]. Master's Thesis, European University Saint Petersburg.

Shmidt, Viktoriia. 2012a. "Tshchetnaya neostorozhnost" [Vain Negligence]. Accessed September 30, 2014. http://solinsky.livejournal.com/47769.html.

Shmidt, Viktoriia. 2012b. "Kak zashchishchat' detey" [How to Defend Children]. Accessed September 30, 2014. http://polit.ru/article/2012/10/26/children/.

Terekhov, Dmitry. 2007. "Vstrechaite—yuvenal'naia yustitsiia!" [Meet Juvenile Justice!]. Accessed September 30, 2014. http://ruskline.ru/analitika/2007/07/03/vstrechajte_-_yuvenal_naya_yusticiya.

Tsvetkova, Roza. 2013. "Sirota sirote rozn" [Every Orphan is Unique]. *Nezavisimaya Gazeta* February 19, 2013. Accessed September 30, 2014. http://www.ng.ru/ng_politics/2013-02-19/9_sirota.html.

Vorozheikina, Tatiana. 2008. "Samozashchita kak pervyi shag k solidarnosti" [Self Defence as the First Step to Solidarity]. Accessed September 30, 2014. http://polit.ru/article/2008/08/18/vorogejkina/.

Zuev, Dennis. 2011. "The Russian Ultranationalist Movement on the Internet: Actors, Communities, and Organizations of Joint Actions." *Post-Soviet Affairs* 27 (2):121–157.

2

Conservative Parents' Mobilization in Ukraine

Olena Strelnyk

Introduction

Since 2005, the Ukrainian state has been sounding an alarm over the country's low birthrate. Therefore, parents are considered to be a resource recruited to solve the country's demographic problem (Kabinet ministriv Ukrainy 2006). In this self-induced panic concerning demography and statehood, childhood has become politicized as well. For instance, the Ukrainian far-right party *Svoboda* (Freedom) promotes the prohibition of foreigners adopting Ukrainian orphans because "children are the treasure of the national gene pool" (quoted by Kotlyar 2013). Similarly, on the eve of the expected signing of the association with the EU on November 29, 2013,[1] both opponents and supporters of Ukrainian-European integration endlessly debated "the protection of children's futures." These political and social processes created very favorable conditions for the conservative parental mobilization that is centered on keeping what they consider to be national traditions as a basis of social wellbeing.

Parenthood emerged as a central topic in public discussions in independent Ukraine in the early 1990s because it links individuals, families, and their respective responsibilities to the new context of national state building. It appears that with time the debate on parenthood in the country has been infused with the element of "moral panic" (Cohen 2002) by frequently stating that the family is in crisis because of the decline of family values. Parental neglect and child abuse, orphans, and unattended children became the most talked about topics in the Ukrainian media; they became frequent subjects of state and regional social work and family policy programs and, lately, academic research. The period of 1990–2000 was also marked by the emergence of parents' organizations and their activism in many post-Soviet states. Researchers argue that parenthood became the new sphere of social solidarity (Chernova 2013) and part of the emergent civic society (Shpakovskaja 2013); for example, conservative movements, including parental movements, actively participated in the protest actions in Ukraine (Tsentr Doslidzhennya Suspil'stva 2013, 7).

This trend is connected to a more general sociocultural and political shift concerning the families and children in post–Soviet Ukraine. Even though the communist period was hardly monolithic concerning family policy and parenthood, during most of the Soviet Union's existence, children were declared a state and a public value, and the government took a major interest in their upbringing, especially on the ideological front. Beginning in early childhood, individuals in the Soviet Union were indoctrinated to follow the rules of society by obligatory participation in youth organizations such as the Little Octobrists, Young Pioneers, and Komsomol. The lives of children in the Soviet Union were shaped by state institutions to a larger extent than in many other societies. The Soviet authorities intended to provide children not only with education, but also "moral upbringing" (*vospitanie*) and leisure activities (Knight 2009, 791–798). In this social and political context, parents became rather passive in relation to childcare and educational institutions, and most importantly, vis-à-vis the state. As Knight pointed out, "Just as education and leisure provision were considered significant, not for developing the child as an individual, but rather for shaping adults who would contribute to the collective of Soviet society, so too the role of parents was considered to be primarily of social importance." In fact, the state considered this role as participation in raising communists and maintaining social order (795).

Around the time of the collapse of the USSR, the relation between the state, society, and family fundamentally changed. One of the first signs of this change was the 1988 emergence of *Komitet soldatskikh materej* (The Committee of Soldiers' Mothers), whose activity brought attention to human rights violations in Soviet (and later in Russian) military forces (Zdravomyslova 1999, 2000; Danilova 2004). How was parents' activism developed in newly independent Ukraine? What characterized the political background, cultural environment, and resources of the Ukrainian conservative parents' activism? This chapter focuses on an analysis of one of the most well-known parental movement organizations in the country, *Roditel'skiy komitet Ukrainy* (The Parents' Committee of Ukraine, PCU) and its activities between 2011 and 2014.

The conservative parents' movement in Ukraine developed with the use of significant material, human, financial, and organizational resources, both domestically and internationally. I argue that the PCU emerged and managed to actively and effectively participate in the increased number of protest actions in 2012–2013 mostly because of favorable social and political conditions. Newly dominant socially conservative rhetoric aided the consolidation of cooperation between the state, different religious forces (including Orthodox and Greek Catholic Church), and conservative parent activists (the PCU in particular). Contradictions between the geopolitical orientations of Ukraine toward the European Union (EU) and the Eurasian Customs Union (which includes Russia, Belarus and Kazakhstan) mattered as well. Preparations for the expected signing of the association agreement with the EU on November 29, 2013, created the favorable political opportunities for the alliance between the PCU and the state, which points to the controversial and inconsequential character of Ukrainian gender equality politics.

Theoretical Background and Sources of Data

The parents' movement in Ukraine is a typical example of conservative movements that focus on the past and orient their activities toward the revival of what they consider national traditions (Sztompka 1996, 345). I apply the concept of demographic nationalism (Yuval-Davis 1997) to analyze the roots of parental mobilization, and I use resource mobilization theory to explain how this type of social movement managed to gather and mobilize resources from both inside and outside their movement, gaining considerable attention and a following in contemporary Ukraine (McCarthy and Zald 1977; Jenkins 1983).

According to resource mobilization theory, social movements succeed through the effective mobilization of various types of resources and the development of political opportunities. Social movements may mobilize both material and nonmaterial resources. Material resources may include money, organizations, manpower, technology, and means of communication (including mass media). Nonmaterial resources can include legitimacy, loyalty, networks, personal connections, public attention, authority, moral commitment, and solidarity (Fuchs 2006, 106).

The cornerstone of nonmaterial symbolic resources the conservative parental movement mobilized is the very sensitive topic of childhood and children. This topic was framed as a basis of the movement's cultural and political legitimization. The main argument the conservative parents' movement promulgates is that children are very vulnerable socially and they need protection from homosexuality, pedophilia, "gender ideology," sexual education in schools, and some state policies; for example, juvenile justice laws (*yuvenal'na yustytsiya*) (Otkrytoe zajavlenie 2011; see also Höjdestrand in this volume).

International law defines juvenile justice as a body of laws that regulate the relationship between a state and juvenile offenders. Specifically, it means creation of special juvenile courts that protect children from the harsh punishments meted out in the criminal justice system; it spares them from being stigmatized as criminals and being imprisoned with adult criminals (Sherstneva 2014, 202). However, in the rhetoric of conservative forces in Ukraine, similar to Russia (Höjdestrand in this volume; Sherstneva 2014), juvenile justice is considered the system promoted by the morally degraded West and a tool of total state control over families. In particular, conservative movements view juvenile justice laws as a promotion of a wide authority of state social agencies that leads to controlling the parents, depriving them of parental rights, and destroying the relationships between parents and their children (Chto takoe juvenal'naja justicija 2 n.d.).

This chapter presents a case study of the Ukrainian social movement organization, *Roditel'skiy komitet Ukrainy* (The Parents' Committee of Ukraine, PCU), and its activities from 2011 to 2014. Although there is no information available on the date of the founding of the PCU, it has been active since 2010, and as of today it has branches in twelve (out of twenty-four) regions in Ukraine. The first large-scale event organized by the PCU was the Parents' Forum, which took place in Kiev in 2011. Since then, PCU has organized a number of meetings, conferences, and public protests all over the country. The activists officially claimed on their internet site that the organization's main purpose is "the consolidation of the parents' community for common actions aimed at overcoming the moral crisis in parents', youth's, children's and teenagers' environments, and strengthening historically traditional spiritual values in the public conscience."[2] The PCU's declared goal is to raise parents' self-consciousness and public engagement in organizing educational work with children, organizing events directed toward popularization of conservative family values, and organizing psychological and legal advice to parents, teachers, etc. The PCU opposes gender equality policy, sex education in schools, juvenile justice laws, homosexuality, abortions, family planning, and biotechnologies; for example, assisted reproductive technologies, as well as mandatory vaccination. Its representatives strongly criticize what they see as a threat to national values from Western family and gender policy; thus, the PCU appeals for the elimination of international organizations that promote gender equality programs and (what the PCU calls) "population control." In particular, the PCU views the EU's gender policy as dangerous because it allegedly equals the legalization of homosexual marriages, the adoption of children by homosexuals, and "propagation" of homosexuality to children (Maslennikova 2014).

The PCU has a well-developed website that links to all popular social networks, such as Facebook, *VKontakte,* and *Odnoklassniki.* As of December 2016, the number of subscribers on the PCU's site in *Odnoklassniki* was 833 and *VKontakte* was 2129. The content found on these networks is the same as PCU's website, and neither the PCU website nor the network pages serve as a space for discussions. Between January 2014 and January 2015, there were only twenty comments on the PCU website in the form of questions and/or supportive statements. The PCU also produced about one hundred videos that are freely available from Rodkom-TV, which is a channel on YouTube.

At the same time, the PCU is very active in publishing. It published and/or supported publishing a great number of copies of the organization's newspaper and books such as *Gender Education: How Your Children Will Be Made Homosexuals* (*Gendernoe vospitanie* n.d.), *Gender with its Warts: Through Gender Dictation to the Dictation of Homosexuality* (*Gender bez prikras* 2010–2011), *Juvenile Justice: How to Protect Oneself* (Roditel'skii komitet Ukrainy 2013), and *Analysis of Concepts and Programs of Sex Education in the Educational System of Ukraine* (Vseukrainskaya obshchestvennaya organizatsiya 2013).[3] The organization also distributed flyers and CDs about the harms of a gender equality policy, and it produced a significant number of teaching aids for educators. Moreover, the PCU organized three large Parents' Forums in Kiev in 2011, 2012, and 2013. According to the PCU's own account, there were 500 participants in the first forum and more than 1,000 in the second and third. The activists declare on the organization's website that among participants were representatives of the Ministry of Education of Ukraine, Ministry of Justice, deputies, teachers, scientists, lawyers, psychologists, and journalists, but in fact "they all were just parents who share concerns about their children."[4]

Two important reasons led to selecting this social movement organization as the research subject. First, the PCU is the most influential and visible conservative organization in Ukraine that presents itself as the parents' representative. Second, according to the network analysis produced by Ukrainian pro-equality activists, the PCU occupies a central position among the conservative organizations in Ukraine (Aktyvistky hendernoho rukhu 2013, 10–13).

The resources I used to substantiate the observations presented in this chapter principally come from PCU's website and materials produced by the organization. I also relied on secondary materials such as newspaper accounts of the PCU's actions, interviews with activists published in the media, and data from Ukrainian public opinion surveys illustrating the cultural values and legitimacy that the PCU claims to represent to indicate the likelihood of social support for the conservative parents' movement. Before I analyze the PCU's activities and resources it uses, I outline some important aspects of the Ukrainian context.

The Sociopolitical Context of Parents' Conservative Mobilization

In social movement studies, the sociocultural context of a movement's development has been a central element explaining the reasons for the emergence and success of activism (Williams 2004, 95). In particular, scholars of social movements have been paying careful attention to "the political-cultural or symbolic opportunities that determine what kind of ideas become visible, resonate with public opinion and are held to be 'legitimate' by the audience" (Kriesi 2004, 72). In a similar vein, it is useful to examine the political and cultural background that led to the political and public support of the conservative parents' movement in Ukraine.

Since the mid-1960s, a "second demographic transition" emerged in a number of industrialized countries. This process implies that marriages take place at a later age and parenting is postponed, with divorce rates increasing along with the number of cohabitations, increasing rate of "out of wedlock" births, and voluntary childlessness, etc. (van de Kaa 2003, 9–10). The trends associated with the second demographic transition have applied to Ukraine for the past twenty years. The age of marriage and giving birth to the first (and often the only) child has gradually risen in Ukraine, and public opinion toward cohabitation had become more permissive even before the 1990s. The number of cohabiting couples has also been increasing, similar to the number of children born outside of marriage. Moreover, the first decade of Ukrainian independence was marked by rapidly declining birthrates (Instytut demohrafiyi 2008a, 125). From 1990 to 2001 the number of newborns decreased by almost 43 percent (Instytut demohrafiyi 2008a, 60). The demographic decline was as dramatic as in Russia, which went through a similar political and socioeconomic transformation after the collapse of the USSR (ibid). In 1989, Ukrainian families had an average of 1.59 children (1.52 in cities and 1.77 in rural areas). In 2001, this rate was 1.44 on average (1.34 in cities and 1.65 in rural areas) (Instytut demohrafiyi 2008b, 19). Since 2002 the birthrate has been gradually rising, which is considered by demographers as a "post-crisis compensation," and the realization of previously suspended child-bearing intentions, as well as a short-term effect of changes in family policy. However, despite recent changes the birthrate in Ukraine is still one of the lowest in Europe, even though it is still higher than in Hungary, Greece, Spain, and Slovakia (United Nations 2013).

In contemporary Ukraine these trends—especially falling birthrates—have been met with an intense neotraditionalistic rhetoric and an alarmist discourse on low birthrate as a threat to national survival (Zhurzhenko 2008, 128–137). Yuval-Davis's term, "demographic nationalism," aptly captures this intense connection between national and demographic discourses. In the contemporary state-supported and media-enhanced political debate, fertility is still considered the basis of biological and symbolic reproduction of the nation. The birthrate decline and what is described as "depopulation" are regarded as the most important problems that determine the future of a nation (Yuval-Davis 1997). Such rhetoric of demographic nationalism is the part of the conservative discourse that the PCU presents on its website:

> The demographic crisis can be compared with anemia, which is a sharp decrease in blood cells that carry oxygen to all the organs and systems of the body. These vital cells of the state body are healthy families. We can say without any exaggeration: "Health of a family determines the health of the nation." (Maslennikova 2014)

In the rhetoric of demographic nationalism, women are cast as members of specific national collectivities, not as individuals, and certainly not as workers (as they had been during the Soviet period). The outcome of this intense political discourse is that it pressures some or possibly all women of reproductive age to have more children or, in the case of ethnic/religious minorities or otherwise marginalized women, to have fewer children (Yuval-Davis 1997, 22). In this discourse, a special symbolic role belongs to mothers and motherhood because their images symbolize the spiritual consolidation of the society around what is cast as the "eternal" values of a given national culture: traditions and language, its continuity of generations, and the survival and the future of the nation (Zhurzhenko 2008, 132). The Ukrainian historian Oksana Kis' stresses that "practically every nation in the period of national consolidation or national revival appeals to woman's and maternal symbols, and the idea of patriotism is embodied in the form of Woman-Mother," (2003, 156).

In the Ukrainian historical and cultural context, the cult of motherhood is fixed on the image of *Berehynya,* which is literally translated as "the one who protects, takes care of." In fact, the image of *Berehynya* is based primarily on the cult of motherhood, but not on the idea of women as persons with full and equal rights. The high symbolic status of the mother is intended to compensate for the painful reality of women's lack of rights and, at the same time, to re-impose a patriarchal model of motherhood as a woman's only destination (Kis' 2003).

The image of *Berehynya,* which has become a nearly sacred stronghold of the Ukrainian national idea, is based on at least two postulates. Firstly, it emerges from the idea of cult of the child as the unconditional value in premodern Ukrainian society. Secondly, it stresses the role of a mother as the most important role of a woman in Ukrainian national traditions (Kis' 2003). Thus, often with substantial state support, conservative parties and movements have declared abortion as fundamentally alien to the Ukrainian people's centuries-old traditions, "which were based on the religious outlook, a profound respect for human life and respect for the woman as a mother and a carrier of life" (Rezolyutsiya sympoziumu 2010). At the same time, Ukrainian governments attempt to achieve a balance: while stating that they aim to "keep national traditions," they also work for the modernization of the country with the framework of European integration. As of June 2015, from the current Ukrainian government's point of view, the country has made considerable progress regarding gender equality, fulfilling the conditions stipulated in the EU-Ukraine Association Agenda (*Informatsiya Pro implementatsiyu* 2014, 15–16).

State-sponsored efforts toward enhancing gender equality in contemporary Ukraine are framed as one of the main elements of the democratization process. Among the "proofs" of its commitment to gender equality, the government references its recent ratifications of a number of international conventions on gender equality, such as the Convention on the Elimination of All Forms of Discrimination against Women (1981), European Convention on Human Rights (1997), European Social Charter (revised in 2006), and Millennium Development Goals (2000). Ukraine also ratified a number of antidiscriminatory declarations and acts of the International Labor Organization, and was first in the Commonwealth of Independent States (CIS) region to pass a law against domestic violence in 2001. As of 2016, Ukraine and Kyrgyzstan are the only states from the CIS where the law on providing equal rights and opportunities for women and men was passed.[5]

However, even in the much acclaimed case of gender equality, there is a number of contradictions that reduce the effectiveness of these laws and the government's claims to democratic transformation. These contradictions include the conservative and antigender equality bills that were proposed between 2011 and 2013, since some discriminatory laws were passed. One of these laws, for instance, limits women's rights to enroll in the universities that train personnel for law enforcement agencies, effectively prohibiting women from joining and advancing in law enforcement. Similarly, in other areas of public life and public policy, recent Ukrainian governments produced an eclectic mix of laws and policies that express contradictory tendencies, including bowing to conservative discourse and following the rhetoric of gender equality. For example, in regional programs that ostensibly promote equal rights and opportunities for women and men, there are passages that appear to promote traditional gender roles, such as the contest for searching for the "*Berehynya* of our city" (*Rozporyadzhennya mis'koho holovy* 2013).

Official data and the results of studies on gender equality in Ukraine demonstrate the lack of effectiveness of government policy on equal opportunities and the instability of institutional mechanisms for providing gender equality. The contradictions between the legal principles on gender equality and the actual social processes in Ukraine are striking. Gender disparities,

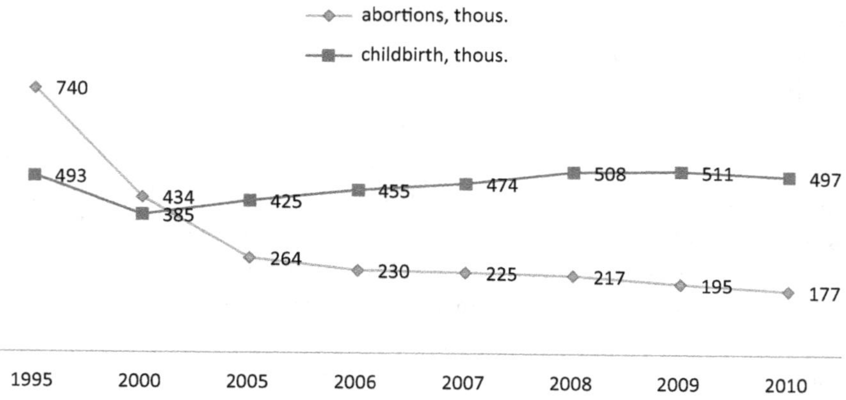

Fig. 2.1 Childbirth and abortions in Ukraine, 1995–2010 (Zhinky 2011, 44)

inequality, and open discrimination are rarely subject to public debate and thus are still far from being eliminated in many areas of public life. Attitudes toward gender ideals, and practices of gender relations are significantly asymmetric (Prohramma rozvytku 2007). For instance, the access of women to decision-making sphere is still limited. As of the beginning of 2016, only two women, Liliya Hrynevych and Ulyana Suprun, entered the Cabinet of Ministers of Ukraine in the roles of Minister of Education and Science, and Minister of Healthcare respectively. I argue that the inconsistencies in the Ukrainian governments' position and the deep contradictions between the laws promoting gender equality and social reality create openings in political opportunity structure that allow and encourage political pressures from the conservative parental movement in Ukraine.

Interestingly, Ukrainian demographic processes contradict the state-sponsored and conservative family discourses: while moral panic around abortion rises, the number of abortions drops. The rate declined almost by five times from 740 thousand per year in 1995 to 177 thousand in 2010 (see fig. 2.1).

"Moral panic" around demography, and especially abortion, as well as efforts toward strengthening the public image of women as first and foremost mothers, are accompanied by rather superficial efforts toward introducing more gender-equal regulations. These contradictions provide important symbolic resources and create political openings that conservative parental groups use.

Neotraditionalist Turn: Changes in Social Policy

Specific changes in social policy—some of which were only proposed, while others were implemented—demonstrate that the governments, as well as the Ukrainian Orthodox and United churches, far right parties, and parental activists pushing for those changes idealize a specific type of family. For example, the Family Code of Ukraine and the State National Program for Family Support for the Period until 2016 consider the family consisting of a married heterosexual couple with two (or more) children as a universal and ideal family model (Simeynyy kodeks Ukrayiny 2002; Kabinet ministriv Ukrayiny 2013). This model implies an outright stigmatization of what the government, right-wing forces, and conservative sociologists view as a "deviant" family, such as single parents and childless families, as well as specific practices such as abortion.

In reality, the state's family policy equals pronatalist policy, which focuses on demographic growth. In 2005, then President Victor Yushchenko established a new type of social benefit in the form of material assistance for family after the child's birth. This step was an important part of his pre-election, and then presidential program called "Ten Steps towards People" (Prohrama Presydenta 2005). President Yushchenko was one of the leaders of the "Orange Revolution" in 2004 supported by right-wing political party *Nasha Ukrayina* (Our Ukraine). Researchers analyzing Yushchenko's political image argue that it evolved from the "Revolutionary and Truth-Seeker" during the Orange Revolution to "Father of the Nation" after his inauguration. At mass events, Yushchenko appeared regularly accompanied by his family, emphasizing his fatherhood and having many children. Thus, the association between Yushchenko's family status and his patriarchal role in Ukrainian society was established (Dorohovskij 2006).

The trend toward introducing financial incentives for families continued until mid-2014. In 2013, the amount of the cash benefit grew to €3,000 (about 3,300 USD) after the birth of the first child, €6,000 after the second child, and €12,000 in the event of a third and subsequent children. These amounts are enormous considering that the average salary in Ukraine was €300 in 2013. In 2014, due to the economic crisis and the armed conflict in east of Ukraine, the amount of payment was reduced to approximately €2,000 (accounting for inflation at the time).[6] The state-mandated material assistance for a child's birth may have contributed to the increase in the birth rate, which, according to the data of the State Statistics Service, went from 9.0 newborns per 1,000 of the population in 2005 to 11.1 in 2013. However, Ukrainian demographers strongly criticized the cash benefit as an ineffective policy because its effect is projected to be temporary (Instytut demohrafiyi 2008b, 200; Dumanska 2013), while the media and experts noted the fertility increase among whom they call the "problem" population, particularly rural families (Den'gi na detjah 2011; Mel'nichuk 2014).

Neotraditionalist ideas also appeared in other proposed bills in Ukraine. There are four bills that merit attention because they focus on family policy, and at least in one case Ukrainian parental conservative activists were involved in its development. First, the bill on revision of the income tax rate was supposed to be calculated based on the number of children a taxpayer had (the bill also established exceptions for disabled persons). The maximum rate of taxation was to be 17 percent for childless citizens who had reached 30 years of age. This income tax bill was proposed in 2012 by Yaroslav Sukhyy (with support of President Yanukovich's party *Partiya rehioniv* [The Party of Regions] and Kateryna Lukyanova representing the right-wing political alliance *Nasha Ukrayina* [Our Ukraine] and *Narodna Samooborona* [People's Self-Defense]) (Proekt Zakonu 2012a). Ukrainian media, experts and public opinion reacted to the bill very critically, calling it a "tax on childlessness" (Vladina 2012) and it was never introduced.

Second, the bill on the revision of article 123 of the Family Code of Ukraine was proposed in 2011 by Kateryna Lukyanova as well. Her recommendation was that a term "married couple" could only refer to a male and a female couple who would be permitted to use assisted reproductive technologies including surrogacy, which is legal in Ukraine. The aim of this bill was to eliminate the possibility that a surrogate Ukrainian mother would allow a foreign homosexual couple to adopt a child (Proekt Zakonu 2011). The bill was voted on by *Verkhovna Rada* (Ukraine's Parliament) and passed, coming into force in 2012.

Third, there were bills to prohibit abortion except when the pregnancy threatened the mother's life. According to the current law, Ukrainian women can have an abortion if the pregnancy does not exceed twelve weeks. The first bill proposing limitations in access to abortion was proposed by Andriy Shkil, a nationalist member of the *Batkivshchyna* (Fatherland) party in 2012. The second bill was initiated by Ruslan Zelyk and Ruslan Martsinkiv, representatives of the far-right party *Svoboda* (Freedom) in 2013 (Proekt Zakonu 2013), but so far no restrictions have been passed or implemented.

Last, the PCU proposed a bill very similar to the one implemented in Russia (see Höjdestrand in this volume), to establish what they called "safe informational (media) space for children" labeling it "the prohibition of homosexuality propaganda." The bill suggested imposing criminal charges for those distributing information on homosexuality to minors, while avoiding defining what "homosexuality propaganda" means exactly (Proekt Zakonu 2012b).[7] Almost all Ukrainian churches, the Ukrainian Council of Churches, and many religious organizations expressed their support of the bill. After its registration in Verkhovna Rada, representatives of the organization Love against Homosexuality handed over 72,000 signatures in support of the criminalization of "homosexual propaganda" to the bill's authors. The PCU participated in the collection of these signatures (Bolee 70 tysjach 2011).

In the case of what is labeled as "homosexuality propaganda," the conservative campaign turned out to be successful. The bill against "homosexuality propaganda" was passed in the first reading (289 to 61 votes) in October 2012. In response, the group of deputies from the Parliamentary Assembly of the Council of Europe passed a declaration that called on the Ukrainian Parliament to withdraw this law because of its discriminatory nature. Leading international organizations, such as the Amnesty International, Human Rights Watch, and Equal Rights Trust made the same appeal and, as a result, further debate on the bill was deferred.

However, in July 2013, Vadim Kolesnichenko, the representative of a pro-Yanukovich and pro-Russian party, *Partiya rehioniv* (The Party of Regions), proposed the bill again. Revisiting this topic at a time when the details of Ukraine's association with the European Union were discussed in the *Rada* (Parliament) was highly significant because this bill was an attempt to wreck the association with the EU (Feder 2013). In 2013 and 2014, the deputies did not discuss the law, but they did not reject it either; although in May 2013, the Parliamentary Committee on freedom of speech proposed to reject the bill (Sheremet 2015). Only in January 2015 did the Verkhovna Rada stop consideration of the bill.

Casting homosexuality as a serious social problem that needs to be urgently confronted to protect children produced a welcome political opportunity to merge and consolidate different political forces. Olena Shevchenko, a director of the LGBT organization *Insayt* (Insight), sadly joked in an interview in 2013 to J. Feder, correspondent of *BuzzFeed* (USA), that legislators might disagree about being either on the side of the EU or Russia, but opposition to

LGBT rights was "the only thing that can consolidate our parliament" (Feder 2013). Political parties and conservative movements have used homosexuality as a tool for political mobilization. For instance, the social movement organization *Ukrainskij vybor* (The Ukrainian Choice), which was founded to protest the intentions of Ukraine's European integration, referred to the "threat of homosexuality" as the reason why Ukraine should avoid association with the EU. The Ukrainian Choice sponsored numerous large billboards all over the country in 2013 that stated, "The Association with the EU means same sex marriages."

The PCU and the conservative activist parents have been notable for their vocal protests against integration with the EU using the same argument. They have used the emergence of neotraditionalist discourses and policies as an opening in the political opportunity structure, while they aimed at strengthening this trend at the same time. In 2013 the co-chairman of the PCU, Aleksandr Skvortsov said, "We protest the signing of the EU association agreement because it will inevitably lead to the homosexualization of Ukraine" (Okolo 30 chelovek 2013). Talking with a reporter of *BuzzFeed* in his Kiev office in 2013, Skvortsov said that Ukraine's EU association agreement "establishes a dictatorship of homosexuality in relation to the whole society." Skvortsov claimed that the PCU was not officially encouraging the government and Rada to abandon all agreements with the EU, it just wanted to amend such an agreement to free Ukraine from the requirement of fulfilling EU rules that relate to "public morality" (quoted by Feder 2013).

The criticism of the international community due to the increasing number of discrimination cases, hate crimes, and violence against homosexuals usually targets Russia, but the public attitudes toward homosexuality in Ukraine provide an equally fertile soil for social mobilization of homophobic groups. The "homosexuality problem" is contributing to the consolidation of different political forces, not only conservative ones, especially when deliberating about children. Available research shows that the Ukrainian society in general shares homophobic views (see Martsenyuk 2012), and the level of homophobia rose from 2002 to 2011. In 2002, according to a survey conducted by Taylor Nelson Sofres Ukraine, by request of the LGBT organization *Nash Svit* (Our World), 49 percent of respondents negatively answered the following question: "Should homosexual people have the right to raise children?" In 2011, the same response to the identical question was

69 percent, based on the survey of 1,200 respondents with a representative sampling by sex, age, region, and type of settlement (Uroven' gomofobii v Ukraine 2011).

The conservative movement uses what they label the "homosexuality problem" as a tool to gain further influence. This movement declared that it is of the utmost importance to "protect" children from homosexuality, since, as they claim, homosexuality is connected with, or equals, pedophilia. For instance, on the conservative network website "Stop gender" (https://stopgender.wordpress.com/), the following interactive question is posed: "Is it necessary to prohibit homosexuality propaganda that reaches the underaged?" The website proudly stated that 93 percent of its visitors had answered "yes" to this internet "survey."[8]

During 2013 conservative organizations in Ukraine focused on preparing for the signing of Ukraine's EU association agreement. The PCU indicated that "homosexualization" was the main obstacle to the EU association, and it stated that it was a threat to national values. As part of the PCU's protest repertoire, it organized two roundtables in 2013 in Verkhovna Rada. The topic of the first such gathering was "Does European choice of Ukraine necessitate the acceptance of same-sex relations?" and the second one was titled "The necessity of preserving family values in Ukraine." In October 2013, the PCU organized mass protests in what they saw as defense of traditional family values, particularly against the EU Association Agreement. In November 2013, the PCU was one of the main actors to organize protests in defense of traditional family values with the following slogan: "Traditional family—JA, Homosexualisation—NEIN" near the German Embassy. Not surprisingly, during the 2013–2014 protests the PCU supported the anti-*Maidan* and anti-EU actions.

However, the PCU's ardent anti-EU rhetoric can reduce public support for its conservative agenda in the future, because sociological research indicates more positive attitudes toward the EU association after the *Maidan* revolt between November 2013 and February 2014. In the twenty years since such research is available, the number of EU supporters has not exceeded the number of supporters who are in favor of closer collaboration with the previous Soviet states; for example, in 2013, 45 percent of respondents supported the idea of entry into the Eurasian Customs Union of Russia, Belarus, and Kazakhstan, and 42 percent were in favor of joining the EU (Vorona 2013, 7–8). The situation changed after the *Maidan* protest. During the February to March 2014 period, 51 percent of Ukrainians expressed their support of the

EU association, and 33 percent were ready to vote for entry into the Customs Union (Tsentr sotsialnykh 2014).

Material Resources of the Ukrainian Conservative Parents' Activism

Mobilization around "the prohibition of homosexuality propaganda" shows that the PCU, together with other conservative groups, aims to influence not only public opinion, but political decisions as well. The question is how to explain the emergence of a movement in a country where the general scarcity of resources available to grassroots social initiatives has been further deepened by the contemporary political and economic crisis. To this end, I will employ one of the most well-established theories of social movement literature, which focuses on rational actors and operates under the assumption that availability of resources enhances the likelihood of collective action. In this section I apply a typology of resources that the PCU uses employing five main categories: social-organizational, human, material, moral, and cultural resources (Edwards and McCarthy 2004).

I will begin with discussing social-organizational resources, defined as infrastructure, social networks, and organizations (Edwards and McCarthy 2004, 127). The PCU is an integral part of the network of organizations representing conservative agenda, which includes religious and proreligious groups and political parties such as *Pravoslavnyj roditel'skij komitet* (Orthodox Parents' Committee), *Hristianskoe dvizhenie za zhizn'* (Christian Movement for a Life), *Ljubov' protiv gomoseksualizma* (Love against Homosexuality), Stop Gender, *Molodost' neravnodushna* (Youth is not Indifferent), the pro-Russian and anti-EU social movement organization *Ukrainskij vybor* (The Ukrainian Choice), and the far-right party *Svoboda* (Freedom). Ukrainian gender equality activists who conducted a network analysis of conservative movement organizations defined two types of relationships between them. One type of relationship consisted of networks of solidarity or "formal partnerships," while the other type is characterized by cognitive networks, which implies awareness of identical or similar activities of different social agents.

According to the report presented by the gender equality activists, the PCU occupies a central position in the network of conservative groups through its significant amount of input and output connections, making it a strong link in the web of formal partnerships. Also in the cognitive network, although Ukrainian Choice has the largest centrality index, the PCU occupies a strong central position as well because its members work closely with both Ukrainian Choice and Freedom. Such close cooperation among these three groups may seem controversial because of their differing political orientations (Aktyvistky hendernoho rukhu 2013, 12–13), but these networks together may qualify as a "social movement industry" as defined by McCarthy and Zald (1977, 1219).

The PCU cooperates with conservative, family-oriented organizations and networks not only in the country, but also abroad. It is a part of The World Congress of Families (WCF), which "is an international network of pro-family organizations, scholars, leaders and people of goodwill from more than sixty countries, that seek to restore the natural family as the fundamental social unit and the 'seedbed' of civil society (as found in the UN Universal Declaration of Human Rights, 1948)."[9] Founded in 1997 by Allan Carlson as part of the project of The Howard Center for Family, Religion, and Society in Rockford, Illinois, in recent years the WCF has become very active in the region, and according to news reports it is supported by Russian state-sponsored organizations such as the Sanctity of Motherhood. Due to close cooperation between the WCF and the PCU, the recent International Parents' Forum, which took place in June 2014, was held in Yalta, Crimea. According to information on the WCF Internet site, it featured the representatives of "pro-family organizations and civil society from Ukraine, Russia, Belarus and Moldova" with the PCU as one of the main local organizers.[10]

Second, the PCU utilizes important human resources, which include activists' labor, experience, skills, and expertise. Successful social movements develop a wide expert base that reaches beyond the national arena to the international arena. Due to its extensive international networks, the PCU often invited experts from France, Serbia, Russia, Finland, and the United States as speakers for its press conferences and forums. The majority of events that the PCU and related conservative groups organized were conducted with support from academics and scholarly representatives who use their academic position to legitimize their own proreligious ideas. For instance, Antonina Yevtodyuk, the head of the Ukrainian public association *Khrystyyanskyy rukh Za zhyttya* (Christian Movement for Life) is an associate professor at Lviv National Technical University. Similarly, one of the leaders of the PCU is an associate professor at a Ukrainian university. Thus, the PCU has well-established human resources both domestically and internationally.

Third, complementing the social-organizational and human resources, material resources including monetary resources, property, office space, equipment, and supplies are of importance. The PCU is officially registered as a charitable organization that sustains itself from donations and voluntary contributions, but it is difficult to discern to what extent people support the organization financially. Judging from the scope of its activities, the PCU has well-established material resources both domestically and internationally, but the sources of the organization's revenues are unclear. According to Ukrainian LGBT activist Yuriy Frank, the PCU's sponsors are American conservatives and Protestant fundamentalists (Traicija kak bezuslovnoe blago 2013, 8). Since there are no official records of the PCU finances, this information is impossible to verify, but this argument is particularly curious in the context of the rhetoric of Ukrainian conservative organizations, because they are the ones who blame the LGBT movement for "destroying traditional values using the money of the West" (Frank 2013, 21).

The fourth type of resources are nonmaterial resources, which may include conferred legitimacy, solidarity, and celebrity's support as expressed in the media and by public awards. The PCU has substantial resources in this regard. The most recent Parents' Forum in 2013 was organized in cooperation with the Ministry of Education, the Patriarch of the Orthodox Church of Moscow Patriarchate, Yuriy Miroshnychenko, who was President Yanukovych's representative in the Parliament, and some of the Ukrainian deputies and members of Parliament's Committees for family and education. As a result of what the PCU calls a moral crusade, it seems that the PCU succeeded in getting substantive support from various political forces in Ukraine and possibly also from abroad. This shows that the PCU differs from grassroots organizations in Russia, analyzed by Tova Höjdestrand in this volume, who seek autonomy from state representatives and politics. At the same time, such strong connections to the Yanukovych regime negatively affect the PCU given the current political situation in Ukraine.

The Ukrainian Cultural Environment as a Resource for The Conservative Parents' Mobilization

Material resources, however, are not the only ones that activists can use. By moving inductively through the cultural resources that social movements use in particular settings, the "boundaries of the legitimate" and the cultural resonance of symbolic repertoires emerge as important. The cultural environment is the array of values that are widely and deeply held as well as solidly institutionalized, and a movement has to work with the socially acceptable norms and values in order to affect change (Williams 2004, 98–99). Williams emphasizes two analytic requirements for a systematic analysis of the cultural environment: "boundedness" and "resonance." Boundedness refers to a range of symbolic elements from which a movement can draw or which may become a source of constraint on possible movement actions and ideas. Boundedness helps set analytic boundaries on what is culturally relevant at a particular time and place. "Resonance" in turn means that "some cultural elements will be more important and held more dearly. Even within the boundaries of the legitimate, cultural effectiveness will vary. The variation will occur across groups within the general population, across issue areas or arenas of social life, and over time, depending on events. In social movement terms, some cultural resources—such as frames, or symbols, or ideologies—will resonate and others will not" (ibid, 101).

In the case of the PCU, I concentrate on traditional values or those values that are framed as such (for example, religiousness) and the level of trust in the state as the main issues that could resonate with the conservative movements' ideas. A cultural environment is a dynamic rather than a static concept, and Ukraine went through considerable social and political changes, including the modifications in political discourses and public attitudes in its most recent past. While what the movement calls "traditional values" and the rate of religiousness are rather stable, peoples' attitudes toward European integration and the level of trust in the state institutions changed considerably in 2014 and 2015, and these social changes will probably create the new environment for conservative mobilization.

As already indicated, the key slogan of Ukrainian conservative rhetoric has been "back to tradition." The concept of "traditional values" has been used as an ideological marker that is not critically perceived, for example, the numerous contradictions between the "Perfect Mother" cult (*Berehynya*) as a national Ukrainian tradition and the reality of mothering practices in pre-modern Ukrainian society are not addressed. The notion of "traditional values" in the PCU's rhetoric assumes the idealization of the family in pre-modern Ukraine, and the fetishizing of Christian values, traditional (patriarchal) gender roles, as well as the high morality and spirituality of Ukrainians. At the same time, the solidification of independent Ukrainian national identity is not an explicit part of the PCU's activities because they have a strong affiliation to Russian and Orthodox political groups and culture. For instance, the PCU mainly uses the Russian language on its websites and publications, it actively involves experts from Russia for participation in its actions, and texts by Russian conservative organizations and activists are placed on the PCU website.[11] The PCU is active mainly in the Russian-speaking central, eastern, and southern regions of Ukraine and enlists the Orthodox Church's (which is under the leadership of the Moscow Patriarchate) support as well.

In sociological discourse, the term "traditional values" means the orientation toward family, health, work, and material well-being, which are considered as opposite to individualistic and emancipatory values of freedom, personal independence, and self-realization. Applying this interpretation, sociological research confirms the resurgence of traditional values in Ukraine (Ruchka and Naumova 2013, 292–293). In 2013, 57 percent of Ukrainians expressed their support for "people who firmly uphold stable, life-affirming customs, traditions and rules" (ibid, 294).

Modernization produces social changes and development that enhance the importance of individual freedom and self-realization. Modernization and its accompanying value changes are characterized by a shift from traditional to secular-rational values, and the modification of the values of survival to self-expression (Inglehart and Welzel 2005). However, modernization and the values of self-expression do not simply appear as a consequence of time passing. Ukrainians' value orientations did not change significantly from 1991 to 2009. The persistently most highly ranked "basic values" are family, health, work, and material well-being (Savelyev 2013). In the context of neotraditionalist discourse, conservative parents' movements are successful because they use political means to create a false alternative between tradition and modernization, and play on the fears of modernization (Tradicija kak bezuslovnoe blago 2013).

The influence of religion, which could be seen as an important cultural background of parents' conservatism and part of boundedness for our analysis here, remains quite controversial in post-Soviet Ukraine. Religion in Ukraine has previously undergone a process of laicization similar to other European countries, with Ukrainians becoming more secular and individual-centered. Still, in 2008, Ukraine ranked seventh in terms of people's religious identification among 23 countries (Parashchevin 2009, 13). Over 70 percent of Ukrainians gave a positive answer to the following question: "Are you affiliated with a particular religion or belief?" In comparison, only 47.1 percent of Russians gave an identical answer. The vast majority of Ukrainians (91%) describe themselves as Christian believers. Of this group, 39 percent belong to the three major Orthodox Churches (Moscow Patriarchate, Kiev Patriarchate, and Ukrainian Autocephalous Orthodox Church), 44 percent indicated that they had no affiliation with a particular church, and 8 percent were affiliated with Greek Catholics (ibid, 21).

The impact of religious affiliation is highly significant in some regions, such as western Ukraine, where many of the self-proclaimed religious people (31%) belong to the Greek Catholic Church (ibid, 22). Unlike the eastern part of Ukraine, the western part is characterized by historically higher levels of religiosity in terms of both people's religious affiliations and practices (Parashchevin 2009). Sociological surveys show Greek Orthodox Catholics as more unwavering in their faith in God, with a higher likelihood of believing in all components of Christian doctrine, a greater trust in the church, and more willingness to rely on religious leaders' intervention in political life in comparison to Orthodox believers. It should be noted that the western part of Ukraine has also a significantly lower crime rate (Informatsiyno-analitychnyi tsentr 2013b), lower number of abortions (Informatsiyno-analitychnyi tsentr 2013a), lower incidence of HIV/AIDS (*VIL-infektsiya v Ukrayini* 2014, 6), and is characterized by a higher birth rate (Panchenko and Krikunenko 2015), which may be interpreted as reflecting the continuing influence of religion and traditions.

In addition to religion, the other significant cultural resource and option of "resonance" for the Ukrainian parental movement's conservatism regards the low level of trust in the state. The activities of the PCU are directed toward protecting children from the state and its institutes; for example, from juvenile justice, sex education in school, and mandatory vaccination. This explains wide resonance to the PCU's activities. In 2013, 67 percent of Ukrainians said they distrusted the president, 77 percent said that they did not trust the Ukrainian Parliament, 72 percent distrusted the state government, and 60 percent did not trust the local government (Tarasenko and Sakada 2013, 73). Eighty percent of Ukrainians distrust the courts and the law enforcement agencies. From 2006 to 2013, only the level of trust in non-governmental organizations and charity funds increased slightly (Stepanenko 2013, 124). Distrust in the state and its various institutions provides an important background to the activities of the Ukrainian parents' conservative movement. According to the conservative interpretation, juvenile justice is a state's intervention aimed at gaining full control over families. In this view, the juvenile justice agencies can inspect any family under the guise of childcare and label any behaviors as socially dangerous to impose state's control over family.

The two social institutions that Ukrainians trust most are the media and a church. In 2015, sociological surveys indicated that 58.8 percent of Ukrainian people trusted religious authorities (Ukrayintsi naybil'she doviryayut' 2016). With a country undergoing profound social changes over the past twenty years, the church is trusted more than other institutions because it offers not only material resources such as networking options, but also cultural coherence, of importance also to conservative parents' mobilization.

Conclusion: The New Configuration of Political Space of the Parents' Conservative Activism in Ukraine

Parenthood in contemporary Ukraine is turning into a form of social citizenship. Since the emergence of the independent Ukrainian state in 1991, the state-level and broad political demand for parenthood as a civic, demographic, national, and patriotic duty has become a reality. Parents—in practice mostly mothers—are recruited to solve what authorities see as demographic problems, for the transmission of national cultural values and traditions and for the tasks of nation-state building. Along with parenthood, childhood has also become politicized. The notion of "children's vulnerability" emerged as the most fertile soil for a moral panic, it became a focus of public and political consolidation, and served as an argument even in geopolitical discussions concerning the entry of Ukraine into the European Union.

The conservative parents' activism in Ukraine has well-established material, cultural, human, financial, and organizational resources both domestically and internationally. These resources have served the movement to impede social changes concerning the European integration of Ukraine. On the one hand, the conservative parents' initiatives are a form of parental (active) citizenship. On the other hand, these activities have led to "moral panics" concerning the "threat to children" from the European Union and the "morally degraded" West instead of serious public discussions about childcare as an important public value.

The activities of conservative forces in Ukraine, including parents' activism from 2010 to 2013, were supported by (1) the governments' attempt to balance "keeping national traditions" and the modernization of the country with the eventual aim of integrating with the EU, (2) contradictions between geopolitical orientations toward the EU and the Eurasian Customs Union, and (3) the controversial and inconsequential character of Ukrainian gender equality policy.

After the *Maidan* Revolution (November 2013–February 2014), the configuration of political opportunities for conservative mobilization in Ukraine changed. Despite public concern about the possible legitimation of extremist forces in the new Ukrainian parliament after the revolution, neither the far-right party *Svoboda*, which had been elected to Parliament during the previous session, nor *Pravy sektor* (The Right Sector) managed to enter Rada in 2014 by party lists. These parties' representatives have only six directly elected district (*okruh*) members out of 423 deputies in the Rada. In the official discourse this development means a loss of political legitimacy for the far-right forces as a stronghold of Ukrainian conservatism.[12] Throughout 2014 and until early 2015, neither Ukrainian nor pro-Russian conservatives undertook any notable political action and they did not sponsor any bills on family and parenthood. In January 2015, the bill on "prohibition of homosexuality propaganda" was finally removed from the political agenda.[13] With the background of armed conflict in Eastern Ukraine, the discourse on European integration strengthened in the Central and Western regions of Ukraine, which reduced the political opportunities of the anti-EU and pro-Russian PCU. The *Maidan* revolution and the armed conflict in the eastern part of Ukraine have led to a new round of civic society activities including parental initiatives, such as *Materi Maydanu* (Mothers of Maidan) and the movement of Soldiers' Mothers. Hopefully, future research will show the new areas, directions, and trends of such initiatives as well as provide an answer to the question whether new actors will engage with conservative forces, such as the PCU, and what their potential will be for social change in contemporary Ukraine.

Olena Strelnyk, Postdoctoral Research Fellow, Department of Sociology at Taras Shevchenko National University of Kyiv, Ukraine

Olena Strelnyk received her PhD in Sociology in 2004 at Kharkiv National University, Ukraine. The title of her PhD Thesis is "Gender Inequality and Woman's Social Status in Contemporary Ukrainian Society." Her current research focuses on mothering practices and mothers' activism in contemporary Ukraine. She is the author of more than fifty articles on gender issues, family, parenthood, and social policy in Ukraine. In 2015, she was designated an Andrew Carnegie Fellow (visiting scholar at Institute for Research on Women and Gender, University of Michigan, United States; 2016).

Notes

I am grateful to Elżbieta Korolczuk for comments on an early version of this paper. I am also grateful to Ina Dimitrova and Tova Höjdestrand for their elaborate and useful comments. I am thankful especially to Katalin Fábián for the very meticulous text editing.

1. Ukrainian president Victor Yanukovych planned to sign the association with the EU but did not do it. He said that Ukraine did not refuse to sign an association agreement but offered the format of trilateral negotiations with Ukraine, EU, and Russia. This caused the protests in Ukraine known as "*EuroMaidan*" (or *Maidan*).

2. Accessed June 29, 2015. http://rodkom.org/цели-и-задачи-мы-объединились-чтобы.

3. It is hard to identify the real publishers of these brochures because they include no information about the date of publication and other requirements for any print production. For instance, "Gender with its warts: Through gender dictation to the dictation of homosexuality" was published by "All-Ukrainian Parents' Movement." All of these brochures are available at the PCU website. At least two of them ("Juvenile Justice. How to Protect Oneself" and "Analysis of Concepts and Programs of Sex Education in the Educational System of Ukraine") were published directly by the PCU.

4. Accessed June 29, 2015. http://rodkom.org/цели-и-задачи-мы-объединились-чтобы.

5. The Ukrainian law passed in 2005. It is remarkable that the title of the law does not include the term "gender equality" but "providing the equal rights and opportunities for women and men." I suppose that these changes were also induced from below and Ukrainian women's non-government organizations were at the helm of pressuring the government to accomplish these legal changes.

6. The first installment of this payment (10,320 UAH) is paid immediately after the birth of the child and the rest is paid in equal parts of 860 UAH a month for 36 months.

7. This bill was proposed in 2012 by Yevhen Tsarkov (Communist Party), Kateryna Lukyanova and Liliya Hryhorovych (right-wing political alliance *Nasha Ukrayina* and *Narodna Samooborona*), Pavlo Unhuryan (*Batkivshchyna),* Yuliya Kovalevska, and Taras Chornovil (a pro-Yanukovich party *Partiya rehioniv*).

8. This website is not officially connected to the PCU, but there are links to it in brochures promoted on the website of PCU. Accessed June 29, 2015. https://stopgender.wordpress.com/

9. Detailed information on the WCF is available on network's internet site: http://worldcongress.ru/english/static-en/152-world-congress-of-families.html

10. http://worldcongress.ru/english/142-international-parents-forum-takes-place-in-yalta.html.

11. See, for instance, (accessed July 1, 2015) http://rodkom.org/2014/6067.html#more-6067.

12. During the *Maidan* protests, the overall style of the average citizens' thinking and political sympathies took a sharp turn to the right-wing ideas (Mayerchik 2014). As of 2015, a right-wing discourse is the dominant one in state and media discourses in western and central Ukraine. Thus, in June 2015 the Ukrainian Ministry of Education passed the "Conception of National and Patriotic Education of Children and Youth," the content of which could be regarded as militaristic and nationalistic (Serhiyenko 2015). The new political, security, and

cultural context, as well as the new configuration of political space, will probably create the new background for conservative mobilization in Ukraine.

13. Today, political and everyday attitudes toward homosexuality are often hostile. Despite current Ukrainian President Petro Poroshenko's voiced support for LGBT rights, as shown in public statement that he does not see any reason to prohibit organization of the Gay Pride in 2015 because to demonstrate is a constitutional right of every citizen of Ukraine, Gay Pride in Kyiv was attacked by far-right nationalist groups (see Interfax Religion, June 5, 2015, accessed July 31, 2015, http://www.interfax-religion.com/?act=news&div=12071).

Works Cited

Aktyvistky hendernoho rukhu [Activists of the Movement for Gender Equality]. 2013. "Vzayemodiya konservatyvnykh i prorelihiynykh orhanizatsiy ta politychnykh partiy v mezhakh anhtyhendernoho rukhuv Ukrayini" [Interaction between Conservative and Pro-Religious Organizations, and Political Parties in the Context of Anti-Gender Movement in Ukraine]. *Genderniy zhurnal "Ya"* 3 (34):10–13.

"Bolee 70 tysjach ukraincev potrebovali ot Verhovnoj Rady zapretit' propagandu gomoseksualizma" [More than 70 Thousand Ukrainians Demanded Verkhovna Rada to Ban the Promotion of Homosexuality]. 2011. Accessed July 2, 2015. http://love-contra.org/index.php/news/issue/845/.

Chernova, Zhanna. 2013. "Roditel'stvo v sovremennoj Rossii: politika gosudarstva i grazhdanskie iniciativy" [Parenthood in Contemporary Russia: State Policy and Civic Initiatives]. (*Monitoring obshhestvennogo mnenija The Monitoring of Public Opinion*) 7 (113):51–61

"Chto takoe juvenal'naja justicija" [What is Juvenile Justice?]. Accessed July 1, 2015. http://rodkom.org//аналитика/ювенальная-юстиция.

Cohen, Stanley. 2002. *Folk Devils and Moral Panics*. New York: Routledge.

Danilova, Natalja. 2004. "Pravo materi soldata: instinkt zaboty ili grazhdanskij dolg?" [The Right of Soldier's Mother: The Instinct of Care or Civic Duty?]. In *Semejnye uzy: modeli dlja sborki*, edited by S. Oushakine, 188–210. Moskva: NLO.

Dembitskyi, Serhiy. 2013. "Sotciolohichna diahnostika hromadskoyi aktivnosti v Ukrayini" [Sociological Diagnostics of the Current State of Civil Activity in Ukraine]. In *Ukrainske suspilstvo 1992–2013. Stan ta dinamika zmin*, edited by V. Vorona and M. Shulga, 113-119. Kyiv: Instytut sotsiolohiyi NAN Ukrayiny.

"Den'gi na detjah: 10 tys. ukrainok rozhajut radi nazhivy kazhdyj god" [Money on Children: 10,000 Ukrainian Women Give Birth for Profit Each Year]. 2011. *Muzhskoj zhurnal M-Port*, August 11. Accessed January 18, 2015. http://mport.ua/psycho/1552695-Dengi-na-detyah-10-tis-ykrainok-rojaut-radi-najivi-kajdii-god.

Dorohovskij, Konstantin. 2006. "Viktor Yushchenko: zhazhda vlasti—nichto, imidzh—vsjo?" [Victor Yushchenko: Thirst for Power Is Nothing, Image Is Everything?]. Accessed January 12, 2015. http://h.ua/story/15212/.

Dumans'ka, V. P. 2013. "Monetarnyy pronatalizm: otsinka efektyvnosty" [Monetarist Pronatalism: The Evaluation of Efficiency]. *Demohrafiya ta sotsial'na ekonomika* 1 (19):28–36.

Edwards, Bob, and John D. McCarthy. 2004. "Resources and Social Movement Mobilization." In *The Blackwell Companion to Social Movements*, edited by David A. Snow, Sarah A. Soule, and Hanspeter Kriesi, 116–152. Malden, MA: Blackwell.

Feder, J. Lester. 2013. "Gomofobija. Pole bitvy—Ukraina" [Homophobia. The Battlefield Is Ukraine]. *Glavkom* 13, November 2013. Accessed July 2, 2015. http://glavcom.ua/articles/15337.html.

Frank, Jurij. 2013. "Kto finansiruet gomofobiju v razvivayushchikhsya stranakh" [Who Finances Homophobia in Developing Countries]. *Genderniy zhurnal "Ya"* 3 (34):20–23.

Fuchs, Christian. 2006. "The Self-Organization of Social Movements." *Systemic Practice and Action Research* 19 (1):101–137.

"Gender bez prikras. Cherez gendernuju politiku k diktature gomoseksualizma." [Gender with Its Warts: Through Gender Dictatorship to the Dictatorship of Homosexuality]. 2010–2011. Accessed July 2, 2015. http://issuu.com/stopgender/docs/broshura-gender-bez-prikras1?e=2877601/2632961.

"Gendernoe vospitanie. Kak iz vashih detej budut delat' gomoseksualistov" [Gender Education: How Your Children Will Be Made Homosexuals]. Accessed July 2, 2015. https://stopgender.files.wordpress.com/2012/01/genderne-vihovannja.pdf.

Informatsiya "Pro implementatsiyu poryadku dennoho asotsiatsiyi Ukrayina—ES u 2014 rotsi" [Information "On Implementation of the EU-Ukraine Association Agenda in 2014"]. 2014. Kyiv: Kabinet Ministriv Ukrayiny.

Informatsiyno-analitychnyy tsentr "Info-Light." [The Information and Analytical Centre "Info-Light"]. 2013a. "Dynamika ta heohrafiya abortiv v Ukrayini u 2005–2012 rokakh" [Dynamics and Geography of Abortion in Ukraine in 2005–2012]. Accessed July 2, 2015. http://infolight.org.ua/content/dinamika-ta-geografiya-abortiv-v-ukrayini-2005–2012-roki.

———. 2013b. "Pokaznyky zlochynnosti v rozrizi oblastey Ukrayiny za 2011–2012 roky" [Crime Rates in the Regions of Ukraine in 2011–2012 Years]. Accessed July 2, 2015. http://infolight.org.ua/maps/pokazniki-zlochinnosti-v-rozrizi-oblastey-ukrayini-za-2011–2012-roki.

Inglehart, Ronald, and Christian Welzel. 2005. *Modernization, Cultural Change, and Democracy. The Human Development Sequence.* New York: Cambridge University Press.

Instytut demohrafiyi ta sotsial'nykh doslidzhen imeni M. V. Ptukhy NAN Ukrainy, Derzhavnyi komitet statystyky Ukrainy [Ptoukha Institute for Demography and Social Studies of the National Academy of Sciences of Ukraine, The State Statistics Committee]. 2008a. *Naselennya Ukrayiny. Narodzhuvanist' v konteksti suspil'notransformatsiyykh peretvoren'* [The Population of Ukraine. Fertility in the Context of Social Transformation Changes]. Kyiv: Adef-Ukraina.

Instytut demohrafiyi ta sotsial'nykh doslidzhen' imeni M. V. Ptukhy NAN Ukrainy, Ukrayinskyy tsentr sotsial'nykh reform [Ptoukha Institute for Demography and Social Studies of the National Academy of Sciences of Ukraine, the Ukrainian Centre for Social Reforms]. 2008b. *Shliub, simia ta ditorodni oriientatsii v Ukraini* [Marriage, Family and Reproductive Orientations in Ukraine]. Kyiv: Adef-Ukrayina.

Jenkins, Craig J. 1983. "Resource Mobilization Theory and the Study of Social Movements." *Annual Review of Sociology* 9:527–553.

Kabinet ministriv Ukrainy. 2006. "Stratehiia demohrafichnoho rozvytku v period do 2015 roku" [The Strategy of Demographic Development to the Year 2015]. Accessed July 2, 2015. http://zakon1.rada.gov.ua/laws/show/879–2006-п.

Kabinet ministriv Ukrainy. 2013. "Derzhavna tsilova prohrama pidtrymky simi do 2016 roku" [The State Program of Family Support to the Year 2016]. Accessed July 2, 2015. http://zakon2.rada.gov.ua/laws/show/341–2013-п.

Khmel'nyts'ka oblasna rada [Khmel'nyts'ky Regional Council]. 2011. *Khmel'nyts'ka oblasnaprohrama zabezpechennya rivnykh prav ta mozhlyvosteyzhinok i cholovikiv na period do 2015 roku* [Khmel'nyts'ky Regional Program on Providing the Equal Rights and Opportunities for Women and Men in the Year 2015].

Kis', Oksana. 2003. "Materinstvo i detstvo v ukrainskoi traditsii: dekonstruktsija mifa" [Motherhood and Childhood in Ukraine: The Deconstruction of a Myth]. In *Sotcial'naya istoriya. Zhenskaya i gendernaya istoriya*, edited by Natalia Pushkar'ova, 156–172. Moscow: Rossiyskaya Politicheskaya Entsiklopediya.

Knight, Rebecca. 2009. "Representations of Soviet Childhood in Post-Soviet Texts by Liudmila Ulitskaia and Nina Gabrielian." *Modern Language Review* 104 (3):790–808.

Kotlyar, Anna. 2013. "Mama VS Mother." *Zerkalo nedeli. Ukraina*, January 18. Accessed July 2, 2015. http://gazeta.zn.ua/socium/mama-vs-mother.html.

Kriesi, Hanspeter. 2004. "Political Context and Opportunity." In *The Blackwell Companion to Social Movements,* edited by David A. Snow, Sarah A. Soule, and Hanspeter Kriesi, 67–90. Malden, MA: Blackwell.

Martsenyuk, Tamara. 2012. "The State of the LGBT Community and Homophobia in Ukraine." *Problems of Post Communism* 59 (2)(March-April):51–62.

Maslennikova, Galina. 2014. "Natsional'naja demograficheskaja bezopasnost' i semejnoe obrazovanie" [National Demographic Security and Family Education]. Accessed July 2, 2015. http://rodkom.org/2014/6007.html#more-6007.

Mayerchik, Maria. 2014. "On Occasion of March 8th. Recasting of Meanings." *Krytyka*, March 8. Accessed 31 July, 2015. http://krytyka.com/en/community/blogs/occasion-march-8th-recasting-meanings#sthash.71dNI6KO.dpuf.

McCarthy, J. D., and M. N. Zald. 1977. "Resource Mobilization and Social Movements." *American Journal of Sociology* 82 (6):1212–1241.

Melnichuk, Julija. 2014. "Deti—kak sredstvo dlja poluchenija deneg" [Children as a Means of Receiving Money]. *Zhitomirskaja oblastnaja obshhestvenno-politicheskaja gazeta Ekho,* January 15. Accessed July 2, 2015. http://exo.net.ua/exo/5201–2014–01–15–09–10–58.

"Okolo 30 chelovek protestovali u posol'stva Germanii protiv propagandy gomoseksualizma" [About 30 People Protested Near the German Embassy against Homosexuality Propaganda]. 2013. *Interfax.Ukraine*, November 5. Accessed July 2, 2015. http://interfax.com.ua/news/general/173425.html.

"Otkrytoe zajavlenie ukrainskih obshhestvennyh objedinenij ob antisemejnyh dejstvijah organov i struktur OON" [The Open Statement of Ukrainian Public Associations about Anti-Family Activities of the UN Agencies]. 2011. Accessed July 2, 2015. http://sovest.dnepro.org/2011/4193.html.

Panchenko, Aleksandr, and Irina Krikunenko. 2015. "Demohrafiya z minusom: tilky v chotyrokh oblastyakh ta Kyyevi naselennya pryrostaye za rakhunok narodzhuvanosti" [Demography with Minus: Population Grows Only in Four Regions and in Kiev]. *Segodnia. Ua*, January 29. Accessed July 2, 2015. http://www.segodnya.ua/ukraine/demografiya-s-minusom-na-dvuh-ukrainok-prihoditsya-tri-rebenka-a-nado-hotya-by-pyat-587931.html.

Parashchevin, Maksym. 2009. *Relihiya ta relihiynist' v Ukrayini* [Religion and Religiousness in Ukraine]. Kyiv, Instytut polityky, Instytut sotsiolohiyi NAN Ukrayiny.

Proekt Zakonu. 2011. "Pro vnesennya zmin do statti 123 Simeynoho kodeksu Ukrayiny (shchodo vyznachennya bat'kiv dytyny, narodzhenoyi v rezultati zastosuvannya dopomizhnykh reproduktyvnykh tekhnolohiy)" [The Bill on Amendments to Article 123 of the Family Code of Ukraine (Concerning the Identification of the Parents of a Child Born as a Result of Assisted Reproductive Technologies)]. Accessed July 2, 2015. http://w1.c1.rada.gov.ua/pls/zweb2/webproc4_2?id=&pf3516=8212&skl=7.

———. 2012a. "Pro vnesennya zmin do statti 167 Podatkovoho kodeksu Ukrayiny shchodo perehlyadu stavky podatku na dokhody fizychnykh osib" [The Bill on Amendments to Article 167 of the Tax Code of Ukraine on the Revision of the Tax Rate on Personal Income]. Accessed July 2, 2015. http://w1.c1.rada.gov.ua/pls/zweb2/webproc4_2?id=&pf3516=10112&skl=7.

———. 2012b. "Pro vnesennya zmin do deyakykh zakonodavchykh aktiv (shchodo zakhystu prav ditey na bezpechnyy informatsiynyy prostir)" [The Bill on Amendments to Certain Legislative Acts (To Protect the Children's Rights on Safe Information Space)]. Accessed July 2, 2015. http://w1.c1.rada.gov.ua/pls/zweb2/webproc4_1?pf3511=45128.

———. 2013. "Pro vnesennya zmin do deyakykh zakonodavchykh aktiv Ukrayiny (shchodo zaborony shtuchnoho pereryvannya vahitnosti abortiv)" [The Bill on Amendments to Certain Legislative Acts of Ukraine (Regarding the Prohibition of Abortion)]. Accessed July 2, 2015. http://w1.c1.rada.gov.ua/pls/zweb2/webproc4_1?pf3511=46457.

Prohrama Prezydenta Ukrayiny Viktora Yushchenka. 2005. "10 krokiv nazustrich lyudyam, 2005–2009" [The Program by President of Ukraine Victor Yushchenko, "Ten Steps Towards People"]. Accessed July 2, 2015. http://www.president.gov.ua/docs/10krokiv.pdf.

Prohramma rozvytku OON, Instytut sotsiolohiyi NAN Ukrayiny [INDP in Ukraine, Institute of Sociology of the NAS of Ukraine]. 2007. *Henderni stereotypy ta stavlennya hromadskosti do hendernykh problem v ukrayinskomu suspil'stvi* [Gender Stereotypes and Public Attitudes to Gender Issues in Ukrainian Society]. Kyiv.

Rezolyutsiya sympoziumu "Moral'no-etychni aspekty shtuchnoho pereryvannya vahitnosti" [The Resolution of the Symposium "Moral and Ethical Aspects of Abortions"]. 2010. Kyiv. Accessed July 2, 2015. http://wolua.org/ru/news/symposium-2010.html.

Roditel'skii komitet Ukrainy. 2013. Juvenal'naja justicija: kak zashhishhat'sja? [Juvenile Justice. How to Protect Oneself?]. Kiev.

Rozporyadzhennya mis'koho holovy Chervonohradskoyi miskoyi rady L'vivs'koyi oblasti Pro provedennya miskoho konkursu "Berehyni nashoho mista" [Mayor's Order of the Chervonograd City Council About City Competition "Berehinya of Our City"]. 2013. March, 26. Accessed December 26, 2016.

Ruchka, A., and M. Naumova. 2013. "Tsinnosti i typy tsinnisnoyi samoidentifikatsii v suchasnomu sotsiumi" [Values and Types of the Value Identification in the Present-Day Society]. In *Ukrains'ke suspil'stvo 1992–2013. Stan ta dinamika zmin,* edited by V. Vorona and M. Shulga, 285–297. Kyiv: Instytut sotsiolohiyi NAN Ukrayiny.

Savelyev, Yu.B. 2013. "Tsinnisnyy vymir suspil'noho rozvytku: superechnosti zmin tsinnostey v protsesi modernizatsiyi" [Value Dimension of Social Development: Contradictions of Values Changes in the Process of Modernization]. In *Problemy rozvytku sotsiolohichnoi teorii: kontseptualizatsiya tsinnisnykh zmin u suchasnomu suspilstvi*, edited by V. Sudakov and O. Kutsenko, 34–39. Kyiv: Taras Shevchenko National University of Kyiv.

Serhiyenko, Stanislav. 2015. "Choho chekaty vid vprovadzhennya natsionalno-patriotychnoho vykhovannya" [What to Expect from the Implementation of National-Patriotic Education]. *Spilne. Commons. Journal of Social Criticism*, July 2. Accessed July 31, 2015. http://commons.com.ua/автор/sergiyenko-stanislav/.

Sheremet, Svyatoslav. 2015. "V parlamente reshyly nevozvrashchat'sya k zapretu 'propahandy homoseksualyzma'" [The Parliament Decided Not to Return to "Homosexuality Propaganda" Prohibition]. *Correspondent*, January 21. Accessed July 2, 2015. http://blogs.korrespondent.net/blog/politics/3469255/.

Sherstneva, Natalia. 2014. "Why are Children's Rights So Dangerous? Interpreting Juvenile Justice in the Light of Conservative Mobilization in Contemporary Russia." In *Women's History in Russia: (re)Establishing the Field*, edited by M. Muravyeva and N. Novikova, 193–215. Newcastle upon Tyne: Cambridge Scholars Publishing.

Shpakovskaja, Larisa. 2013. "Diskursivnye praktiki roditel'stva: politicheskie vyzovy i aktual'nye problemy" [The Discursive Practices of Parenthood: The Political Challenges and Urgent Problems]. *The Bulletin of Tomsk University* 1 (21):236–248.

"Simeynyy kodeks Ukrayiny" [A Family Code of Ukraine]. 2002. Accessed July 2, 2015. http://zakon1.rada.gov.ua/laws/show/2947-14.

Stepanenko, Volodymyr. 2013. "Hromadski orhanizatsii u paternalistskomu suspilstvi" [Non-governmental Organizations in a Paternalistic Society]. In *Ukrainske suspilstvo 1992–2013. Stan ta dinamika zmin. Sotsiolohichnyy monitorynh [Ukrainian Society 1992–2013. Current State and Dynamics of Changes. Sociological Monitoring]*, edited by V. Vorona and M. Shulga, 120–127. Kyiv: Instytut sotsiolohiyi NAN Ukrainy [Institute of Sociology of the NAS of Ukraine].

Sztompka, Peter. 1996. *Sotsiologija sotsial'nikh izmenenij* [The Sociology of Social Changes]. Moskva: Aspect.

Tarasenko, V., and M. Sakada. 2013. "Pro stan hromadyanskosti ukrayinskoho suspilstva" [On the Current State of Civicism of Ukrainian Society]. In *Ukrainske suspilstvo 1992–2013. Stan ta dinamika zmin*, edited by V. Vorona and M. Shulga, 67–77. Kyiv: Instytut sotsiolohiyi NAN Ukrainy.

"Tradicija kak bezuslovnoe blago v konservativnoj ritorike (po materialam publichnoj diskussii)" [A Tradition as an Absolute Value in Conservative Rhetoric (Based on Public Debate)]. 2013. *Genderniy zhurnal "Ya"* 3 (34):4–9.

Tsentr doslidzhennya suspil'stva [The Centre for the Research on Society]. 2013. *Protesty, peremohy i represiyi v Ukrayini: rezultaty monitorynhu 2012 roku* [Protests, Victories, and Repressions in Ukraine: Results of the Monitoring of the Year 2012]. Edited by V. Ishchenko. Kyiv.

Tsentr sotsial'nykh ta marketynhovykh doslidzhen SOCIS [The Centre for Social and Marketing Studies SOCIS]. "Dani zahalnoukrayinskoho sotsiolohichnoho doslidzhennya na pochatok bereznya" [The Data of All-Ukrainian Sociological

Survey at March]. 2014. Accessed July 1, 2015. http://www.socis.kiev.ua/ua/press/tsentr-sotsialnykh-ta-marketynhovykh-doslidzhen-sotsys-proponuje-do-vashoji-uvahy-dani-zahalnou.html.

Ukrayintsi naybil'she doviryaut' tserkvi ta volonteram [Ukrainians Trusted a Church and Volunteers above All]. 2016. In *Ukrayins'ka pravda. Zhyttya*, January 15, 2016. Accessed January 2, 2017. http://life.pravda.com.ua/society/2016/01/15/206550/.

United Nations. 2013. "World Population Prospects." The 2012 Revision. New York. Accessed July 2, 2015. http://esa.un.org/wpp/documentation/pdf/WPP2012_%20KEY%20FINDINGS.pdf.

"Uroven' gomofobii v Ukraine" [The Level of Homophobia in Ukraine]. 2011. Accessed July 2, 2015. http://gay.org.ua/publications/poll2011.pdf.

van de Kaa, Dirk J. 2003. "The Idea of a Second Demographic Transition in Industrialized Countries." Accessed July 2, 2015. http://www.ipss.go.jp/webj-ad/webjournal.files/population/2003_4/kaa.pdf.

VIL-infektsiya v Ukrayini. Informatsiynyy byuleten. [HIV-Infection in Ukraine. Information Bulletin]. 2014. 42.

Vladina, Viktorija. 2012. "Chto podnimet v Ukraine nalog na besdetnost'" [What the Tax on Childlessness Will Raise in Ukraine]. *Tsenzor. Net*, March 2. Accessed June 23, 2015. http://censor.net.ua/resonance/198962/chto_podnimet_v_ukraine_nalog_na_bezdetnost.

Vorona, V. 2013. "Sotsial'ni zahrozy i sotsial'nyi potentsial realizatsii interesiv narodu Ukrainy" [Social Threats and Social Potential for Realizing Interests of Ukrainian People]. In *Ukrainske suspil'stvo 1992–2013. Stan ta dinamika zmin*, edited by V. Vorona and M. Shulga, 3–15. Kyiv: Instytut sotsiolohiyi NAN Ukrainy.

Vseukrainskaya obshchestvennaya organizatsiya "Roditel'skii komitet Ukrainy" 2013. "Analiz koncepcii i programm seksual'nogo prosveshchenija v sisteme obrazovanija Ukrainy" [Analysis of Concepts and Programs of Sex Education in the Educational System of Ukraine]. Accessed July 2, 2015. http://rodkom.org/wp-content/uploads/2011/04/Анализ-концепции.pdf.

Williams, Rhys H. 2004. "The Cultural Contexts of Collective Action: Constraints, Opportunities, and the Symbolic Life of Social Movements." In *The Blackwell Companion to Social Movements*, edited by David A. Snow, Sarah A. Soule, and Hanspeter Kriesi, 91–115. Malden, MA: Blackwell.

Yuval-Davis, Nira. 1997. *Gender and Nation*. Thousand Oaks, CA: SAGE.

Zdravomyslova, Elena. 1999. "Peaceful Initiatives: The Soldiers' Mothers Movement in Russia." In *Towards a Women's Agenda for a Culture of Peace*, edited by I. Breines, D. Gierycs, and B. Reardon, 165–180. Paris: UNESCO Publishing.

Zdravomyslova, Elena. 2000. "Civic Initiatives: Soldiers' Mothers Movement in Russia." In *Politics of Civil Society: A Global Perspective on Democratisation*, edited by H. Patomaki, 29–42. Helsinki: NIDG Working Paper 2.

Zhinky v Ukrayini, statystychnyi zbirnyk. [Women in Ukraine, Statistical Almanac]. 2011. Kyiv: Derzhavna sluzhba statystyky.

Zhurzhenko, Tatiyana. 2008. *Gendernyye rynki Ukrainy* [Gender Markets of Ukraine]. Vil'nyus: EHU.

3

Constructing Parenthood and Nation in Bulgaria through New Reproductive Technologies

Ina Dimitrova

Introduction

The aim of the text is to illuminate and explore one core set of frames, constructed and mobilized around the issues of infertility and assisted reproductive technologies (ARTs) in Bulgaria. It argues that these frames are organized predominantly around the notion of "deservedness" of parenthood, a notion, which adequately captures some crucial features of the self-descriptions and public representations, employed by the respective activist organizations. The successful embedding of the infertile within the "deservedness" framework, which provides a culturally resonant "schemata of interpretation" (Snow et al. 1986, 464), aptly redefines the private, individual suffering and turns it into a public and national problem. Relying on a hybrid cultural texture, combining the still typical Bulgarian high valorization of parenthood (and especially motherhood), the demographic gloom haunting the country, and the ever popular postsocialist transitional neoliberal rhetoric, focusing on the need to praise and protect the productive from the "burdensome" citizens, the patient organizations engage actively in an interpretative work, constructing the infertile couples as a valuable resource, as yet not a fully recognized "reserve" of authentic and responsible parenthood. This legitimizes their demand for increased public support and state funding.

In the first part of the paper I shall briefly describe the conceptual background of the study and its empirical base. In the second part, I outline the local context of ARTs activism, and then in the third part, I analyze the specific ways of constructing the abovementioned core set of frames, which are especially visible when applied in the different contexts of facing "outsiders," who must be persuaded, kept aside, or denounced.

Empirical and Conceptual Background

Data collection for the analysis includes the relevant online discussions in two internet forums—BG Mamma and the *Zachatie* (Conception) Association forum—fifteen semistructured interviews and a review of media publications, and the results of several already conducted qualitative studies of individuals and communities struggling with infertility in Bulgaria.[1] BG Mamma is the leading Bulgarian online venue for discussions, sharing information and experiences, and providing emotional support among future and present parents (predominantly women) with thousands of users and numerous themes, subthemes, and threads. The portal is not dedicated exclusively to infertility, but many of the themes are associated with it. The second forum is part of the online activities of the Association *Zachatie*—an activist organization, which, together with another non-governmental organization (NGO) *Iskam Bebe* (I Want a Baby), are the main patient organizations in the country, supporting people struggling with infertility. They provide information on reproductive health and current treatment opportunities, educate the public and raise awareness, and also fight for introducing state regulations and public funding. In April 2014 the Zachatie forum had 31,845 users and about 14,000 themes in its different subforums.

The semistructured interviews were conducted in April 2014. About half of the respondents are some of the most active users of the Zachatie forum (mostly local or global moderators), who are at the same time intensively engaged in the activities of the Association. The second group of respondents was recruited from a subforum (on the BG Mamma portal) of patients of one of the most renown private clinics in Bulgaria—*Nadezhda* (Hope). My point in designing the interviewing process in such a way was to register the differences (if there are any) between patients engaged in activist work and patients who are not. Actually, the ways of responding for the informants of these two groups were different, and it is worth mentioning here the specific reactions of the individuals working for the Association. As a whole, they demonstrated a very high level of internal solidarity, apparent suspicion, and mistrust toward "outsiders." Directly or indirectly they expressed their concern that any research attempt threatens their public image and the image of getting pregnant through assisted reproductive technologies by voluntary or involuntary misinterpretation, due to the lack of personal experience, information, and sensitivity, presumed to characterize everyone who does not "walk in their shoes." They rejected being "used as animals" for research and testing, stated that research should be focused only on scientific, technical, and legal facts and details and not on "attitudes and emotions," and interpreted the inquiry as an attempt to state or suggest something (incorrect or abusive), to send a message, or to influence the public attitudes—not as an effort to familiarize the society or the scholarly community with their beliefs, convictions, general views, and position. The activists considered the researchers addressing such issues as intruders, qualifying their efforts to collect empirical data as attempts to use them and their forum as "guinea pigs." The second group of respondents demonstrated no such cautiousness and also no great interest in participating (six women responded out of the twenty-five invited).[2]

The theoretical background of the analysis of the data collected for this study is the broad and bourgeoning field of research on patient groups and health movements, with a special focus on movement framing in its interplay with the specific cultural environment, captured by the notion of "cultural resonance" (Williams and Kubal 1999). Such resonance is crucial since it "increase[s] the appeal of a frame by making it appear natural and familiar" (Gamson 1992, 135) and "captures the interrelations between movement frames and the cultural environment and helps answer questions about the construction and potency of movement framing" (Kubal 1998, 542).

Social movement scholars demonstrate a steady interest in framing processes as an especially revealing dimension of the movements' mobilization, dynamics, construction of identities, formulation of grievances, etc. Drawing on the pioneer analyses of Goffman (1974) and the interactionist tradition, this perspective views "movement actors . . . as signifying agents actively engaged in the production and maintenance of meaning for constituents, antagonists, and bystanders or observers" (Benford and Snow 2000, 614). Illuminating and understanding the interpretive work of social movements has been deemed crucial for capturing their performance and interrelations with other actors, such as the state and media for example. This is interpreted as a "cultural turn" in the social movements research toward "bringing meaning back in" and has focused on the ways in which movements have used symbols, language, discourse, identity, and other dimensions of culture to recruit, retain, mobilize, and motivate members (Williams 2004, 93). In this framework the notion of cultural resonance is introduced as a means to illuminate the processes of "projection of movement power in the public sphere . . . Movement discourse, ideologies, and actions must be culturally resonant—coherent within some shared cultural repertoire—if they hope to strike bystander publics as legitimate, or neutralize oppositional positions" (Williams 1995, 105). In other words, a movement's public claims must have a "cultural power" (Williams 2004, 93).

In what follows I demonstrate how ART's activism in Bulgaria benefits from the specific local configuration of socially and culturally available opportunities (Benford and Snow 2000), which influence the dynamics of the movement and play an important role in determining its success and effectiveness. Among the cultural resources from which the ART activists can draw on, there are some elements, which effectively resonate with the majority of the audience. As I mentioned above they could be grouped as follows: the traditionally praised, "valuable above all," parenthood and, especially, motherhood, the belief in and uncritical acceptance of technological innovation and its broad application (Simeonov and Krachunova 1993, 18; Boyadzhieva et al. 1994; Dimitrova 2012), the current fears about the "endangered Bulgarian nation," and the postsocialist, neoliberal affirmation of the citizens' responsibilities and productiveness. Consequently, when the activists' self-descriptions are embedded in these thematic lines, they successfully attain cultural resonance, which could be summarized under the heading of "deservedness" of parenthood. It is worth emphasizing that there exists no "anti-ART" movement—conservatively, religiously, or anti-technologically motivated—on the Bulgarian public scene. There are some unpopular conservative groups (such as the Society and Value Association) affirming family values, and they are strongly against surrogate motherhood but not against assisted reproduction as a whole. In such a sense, the "outsiders" whom the ART activists try to persuade, keep aside, or denounce are not particular social actors, but rather a blended imaginary construct, composed of claims conceived as threatening and harmful. They shall be addressed in the third part of the text.

Local Context

Even among the EU countries, which all face unprecedented demographic challenges due to aging populations, the demographic picture in Bulgaria is rather bleak. The demographic gloom deepens due to the high mortality rate and a fertility rate below the replacement level, and it continuously generates disturbing forecasts for the future population "quality" and quantity of Bulgarian nation.

This murky picture of the national future is, however, not something novel. In fact, for most of twentieth century, the demographic considerations have been firmly on the political agenda and a matter of public concern. The fear of population decline and finding the relevant governmental response became social and cultural focal points as early as the late 1930s and the first half of the 1940s. In this period the depopulation anxiety become linked to the debates on modernization, on "degeneration" and social hygiene measures, on the need to stimulate the "revival" of family and to affirm motherhood as woman's national duty, and on the relevant social policy counteracting these calamities.[3] In fact, here are the roots of the socialist and postsocialist pronatalist demographic policy: the latter are "a continuation rather than a novel departure in modern Bulgarian history. As such, they attest the long history of the state's attempts to respond to domestic needs and serve the national cause" (Baloutzova 2011, 251). Before 1945, the pronatalist politics was mainly part of the social and welfare policies, while later—during the socialist period—it became narrowly linked to the official party ideology. The state introduced not only encouraging policies, but also some restricting and punitive measures, for example, restrictions in the abortion regulations and bachelors' taxation. Against this historical background it would be revealing to explore population policy and fears of demographic decline not only within social welfare framework (as before 1945) or as part of a certain ideology (as during socialist period), but also as a context of the advancing biotechnological opportunities.

The demographic concern, provoking numerous alarming predictions and pronatalist appeals, was in the focus of the public interest in Bulgaria also during the post-1989 period, proving to be a convenient demagoguery technique employed for a wide spectrum of issues. It gives rise to a nationalistic discourse, which enjoys special attention in the media, molds public attitudes, and could be discerned in the political platforms of the left and nationalistic parties but also in governmental decrees on regional and national levels. This discourse is given voice by prominent intellectuals, political experts, scholars, and renowned artists. The employed vocabulary bristles with expressions such as "demographic apocalypse," "Bulgarian national disaster," "collapse of the state," "ethno-demographic erosion," "third national catastrophe," etc. (Kotseva 2011, 342). In this context, not only the decline in birth rates, but also the prospect of outnumbering of ethnic Bulgarians by the ethnic minorities (Roma and ethnic Turks) is conceived as a threat.

On a European level, besides the more traditional alleviating measures such as the introduction of pronatalist legislation, different incentives, and work and family reconciliation policies, the use of assisted reproduction technologies has been recently seriously considered as having the potential to increase birth rates, thereby helping to offset against the trend of population aging (Grant et al. 2006; Hoorens et al. 2007). Despite some counterarguments that such claims are grossly overestimated (te Velde et al. 2008), this perspective is keenly embraced in Bulgaria by the key social actors in the field of the ARTs and by some political forces. Although no actual effective state pronatalist policy is being introduced in the country and no conditions for reconciliation of work and family are being set up, this rhetoric appears to be an effective means for gaining public support and attracting resources for ARTs.

The enactment of the relevant policy regarding ARTs is rooted exclusively in the framing of these technologies as a measure against the demographic crisis of the Bulgarian ethnos, opposed to the fecund minorities and especially the Roma minority. The "depopulation" fear effectively molds the public attitudes today and the usual way of representing infertility and respectively—the regulation of the use of assisted reproduction technologies—is as a national problem (Kotseva and Todorova 2005; Panayotova and Todorova 2007). In this context, the "health care providers and their patients are consonant on the point that infertile couples are an important demographic resource" (Panayotova and Todorova 2009, 63), which must be reflected in government decisions and measures to expand the access to ARTs.

ARTs have been available in Bulgaria since the end of the 1980s, when the first IVF baby was born in 1988. The use of these technologies has been regulated since 2005, when a program was initiated reimbursing the cost for IVF medications (Panayotova and Todorova 2009, 65). The crucial step in making ARTs more accessible is the establishment of the Fund for Assisted

Reproduction in the beginning of 2009, which reimburses up to three IFV attempts. This is considered the first major achievement of the patient organizations, since the pressure they managed to exert on the decision makers was considerable. The Fund has contracts with almost thirty hospitals and clinics, offering ART, and the majority of them are private. There are also other private clinics, which have no contract with the Fund and the patients must cover all the expenditures themselves. Since the beginning of 2014, the NGO Iskam Bebe has launched a campaign, aiming at convincing the policy makers to cover partially another three attempts. Another success for the activist organizations was the elimination of the age limit for performing ART procedures, which until 2011 was 43 years old and now is broadly defined as "menopause" (the public Fund still reimburses the costs only for patients of age up to 43 years). Besides the Fund many municipalities in the country are allocating additional funding for couples from the respective regions.

The establishment of the Fund was justified by focusing on its national importance—"at least" 4,000 children were "promised" in the first year of its functioning. Some syndical organizations also supported the establishment of the Fund, stating that the Bulgarian government should pay attention to the recent EUROSTAT data, demonstrating that the state has taken the lead in the rankings of countries with the greatest decline in birth rates—a development "more dreadful" than its last place position in the rankings for per capita income. In this declaration the existence of the Fund was again bound with the "national interests" (Dnes.bg 2008). In the National Assembly transcripts of the Healthcare committee discussion, key phrases were "the children that the state needs" and "the infants of Bulgaria" (National Assembly 2008). The overcoming of the demographic crisis was again in the focus, when the legislative initiative for settling the issue of surrogate motherhood—another opportunity for assisted reproduction—was launched in 2011 by a member of the parliamentary group of the nationalist political party Attack.

This central rhetorical figure of a vanishing nation haunts several official documents. As early as 1998 in the *National Program for Infertility Treatment*, it was clearly stated that the demographic situation is a "national disaster," but the "national program for IVF treatment shall increase the number of births in Bulgaria in the near future" (Kotseva and Todorova 2005, 223). The rise of fertility rates "through improved access of women to in vitro procedures" is one of the key objectives of the Ministry of Health for 2011 (Ministry of Health 2011).

In the *Report for the Realization of the National strategy for Demographic Development of Republic of Bulgaria 2006–2020*, it is stated that "it is widely accepted" that infertility specialists could render assistance to 70 percent of the families with reproductive problems, whose estimated number is 270,000, and "their efforts would contribute to multiplying the Bulgarian nation with 189,000 desired children. . . . If we assume that the couples would like to have not only one but two children, the number grows to 378,000. It is important to note that in these cases the children are very much desired, their parents take greater care of them and provide very good conditions for raising and nurturing." The same claim is featured in the *Plan for Fulfillment of the National Strategy for Demographic Development of Republic of Bulgaria for 2011* as well as in the mentioned above IMRO project for demographic measures "Bulgaria–2050."[4]

ART activism in Bulgaria benefits from the political opportunistic structure, as well as from the current cultural environment. In what follows I demonstrate how the parenthood discourse, employed by the ART movement, appears to possess palpable symbolic power due to its cultural resonance.

Images of "Quality Procreation" in Bulgaria

Exemplary Parents

The promises of assisted reproduction have not only quantitative but also a manifest "qualitative" dimension. One central frame, constructed and employed by the patient organizations, is the characteristic profile of the (future) parents of children, conceived after assisted reproduction procedures. In one of the first self-presentations of the nonprofit organization Iskam Bebe, it is stressed that the infertility statistics are not sheer numbers; they refer to "brave and strong-minded people with exceptional sensitivity, well-paid occupations, unambiguous strivings and one great dream—the dream of their lives. . . . Their dignity could be measured only by ascending a heavenly stairway—only upwards with confidence in the good and with prayers" (Ariston S Foundation 2008). In a petition to the media, Zachatie directly underlines the class distinctions, which have become more and more visible and painful during the postsocialist transition:

> We are young, intelligent and educated people, awaiting their chance to bring up their children. We are not like those, queuing up for social welfare, and multiplying the army of the illiterate and unemployed. . . . Lack of information

> and accountability, violation of law and rules—this is the "reward" for our efforts as conscientious citizens by those people, whose salaries we pay from our own pocket!

In this statement another master frame is mobilized—the postsocialist, neoliberal image of the decent, productive, and responsible members of the society needing protection from the irresponsible and burdensome ones, who are a drain on public resources. The heightened sensitivity especially toward the "irresponsible parents" could clearly be seen in a special and very popular theme on the Zachatie website: "How long shall we tolerate the irresponsible parents?" It comprises 45 pages of a sometimes very heated debate, which was initiated in 2010 and is still active and open for new posts; in April 2014 it had 63,414 views. The motivation to establish the thread is to discuss different measures, which would provide better parental care and investment on a national level and would prevent people from using children solely as a source of child benefits, which encourages irresponsible and "unlimited" procreation (this is a popular image of the Roma minority, for example, which is eagerly circulated by the media). Repeated in the discussions, cases of child abuse and neglect even provoke some of the participants to mention the efficacy of the practice of compulsory sterilization of (Roma) minorities. The other target of indignation are the irresponsible parents, inhabiting the rural regions, "where the poverty and ignorance produce monsters."[5]

The focus on responsibility as a central characteristic of parenthood is common among the respondents, and often they interpret it in an extreme form: their descriptions usually involve characterizations as "complete devotion" and "wholehearted dedication." Consequently, the interviewed generally support the claim that motherhood is the primary role of women and the most important source of meaning in their lives.

When the respondents were asked to describe the couples struggling with infertility through ART, two different images emerge, both stressing to a certain extent their "deservedness." The first one repeats the self-presentation of the patient organizations and is usually focused on their better education, higher intelligence, and income. One respondent describes the infertile as follows: "Most of them are good looking, orthodox Christians, older than 30; they are educated, with good jobs and good income. . . . They come from the bigger cities and many of them live together as cohabitants without being married" (respondent 2). They are also "young, able-bodied, paying their taxes" (respondent 3).

Another respondent directly invokes the fact of using modern biotechnologies as an indicator of intelligence and sophistication: "The whole procedure is not suitable for plain people. They definitely are quite intelligent and purposeful" (respondent 4). The same respondent adds that "the responsibility of the people who have chosen this way, and their desire to overcome the difficulties at any price and their tenacity," must be recognized and rewarded by the rest of society. The other informants also affirm that the couples usually are "highly educated and with good jobs" (respondent 6). Using ARTs is clearly imagined as a sign of a person's economic position in the society: "At least one of the couple must have good job. In Bulgaria, there is no chance to take advantage of ARTs without a good income" (respondent 5). Although the Fund reimburses up to three attempts, the respondent here underlies the fact that, firstly, only a limited number of women/couples would be listed for receiving annual funding and, secondly, that there are different preliminary and concomitant medical tests and examinations, which the patients must cover themselves.

The other typical way of negotiating "who we are" is through stressing the lack of difference between the "outsiders" and "our group" and especially the open possibility of "outsiders" to join them: "The things mentioned (in the question) are not relevant as characteristics (education, career, age, etc.)—tomorrow it could be you" (respondent 3). This point is further connected with construing infertility as a "scourge," which shall engulf more and more couples, making the issue of deservedness (of parenthood through public support) so self-understanding that it becomes pointless since it is a matter of national concern as this respondent implies.[6] This is very clearly captured in the following statement: "Infertility is not a result from the lifestyle or someone's choice. It can affect everyone, every family and turn their life upside down. No one is protected from this tragedy and society owes to itself the maturity to recognize the problem and support its solution" (Respondent 7). And the same point from a more confrontational stance, "Every sixth couple in the world has a reproductive problem, so if someone does not know yet (what it feels like), sooner or later they shall understand, the world is small." (Respondent 3). This general attitude that only those who experience the same suffering could "judge" or participate in the decision-making process concerning the social conditions, affecting the infertile, is typical not only for the Bulgarian context.[7]

Thus, besides the special qualities of the infertile couples making them deserving parents, the other set of core frames is focused on the exceptionally demanding nature of ARTs, which are so devastating that only the strong could persevere. And even this makes them deserving: the society "must know that even the fact that they have chosen this way is enough to offer them support because it is not a bed of roses, not at all" (Respondent 2).

A central dimension of the ARTs discourse is the crucial difference, negotiated and sustained by the community of ARTs activists, between "ART parents" and "parents without reproductive problems." It is nicely captured by one of the respondents, who claims that the special qualities of the first influence the way they become parents and perform their parenthood:

> It is not easy or right to generalize, but as a user (and a moderator) of a forum with huge number of participants, I could say that the vast majority of the people with reproductive problems are intelligent, educated people. . . . In every case there are exceptions, but surely most of them have good social standing and are about or above the average IQ level. *Consequently* (italic mine, I.D.), they are much more conscious of their parenthood, more aware of this responsibility, and more ready for it. This does not mean that the people without reproductive problems do not possess these qualities, but it is impossible to deny that as a whole people have children because "the time has come" or "this is what all do" and so on, without being really aware whether they are ready for parenthood. On the other side, when you fight for years to become a parent, you have much more time to prepare yourself, to reflect, to "attune" yourself. This is different. (Respondent 1)

And she adds: "If I had no problems getting pregnant I would have acted in more perfunctory manner (as a parent)." According to another respondent, the parental attitude of those without reproductive problems is different because they "think of their parenthood as something given and for them it is simultaneously a joy and also an obligation, a burden" (Respondent 7).

Better Children

The construction of the ART parents as the decent, responsible, educated, and higher earning power segment of society is coupled with and reinforced by the other central dimension of deservedness—the "quality" of the future children. As I have already stressed above, the children conceived through ARTs are usually described as follows: they are "very much desired, their parents take greater care for them and provide very good conditions for rising and nurturing" (Ministry of Labor and Social Policy 2007). The same claim is found in the *Plan for Fulfillment of the National Strategy for Demographic Development of the Republic of Bulgaria for 2011*. These children also "have higher grades in school, go to elite colleges and universities and are more successful in their future lives" (Kotseva and Todorova 2005, 223).

This reproductive "stratification" (Colen 1995) is eagerly undertaken by the patients and activists, who, in their online discussions, often engage in comparisons between the normally conceived children and those conceived after assisted reproduction procedures, calling the latter "conceived with greater love" and "waited more eagerly."[8] The imagery of decent, suffering, and devoted families, who are finally blessed with "much desired children, who get more care" than the "ordinary," spontaneously conceived ones, reveals a crucial aspect of the framing of assisted reproduction in Bulgaria. Thus, namely the opportunity for a "procreation of higher quality," warranted by the fact that the future parents are well off and are ready to provide a loving family environment and greater parental investment.

This issue of the quality of parenting and its consequences for the children conceived by assisted reproduction is addressed also in the educational articles on the Zachatie website. In the article "Families of 'Test Tube Babies'" the author presented some results from studies, focusing on the question of whether the method of conception has some stable impact on the parent-child relationship and the child development. The sources of information are selected in such a way that ART parenthood is depicted in most favorable terms, demonstrating its superior quality.

When the respondents were asked whether they believe in the suggestions that couples who have conceived with ARTs invest more than the couples with spontaneously conceived children, they are almost unanimous in their affirmative attitude and usually reply "Yes, absolutely." The reasons, which are usually mentioned, are the long and painful striving toward parenthood, the "fight, which is hard, long, and tormenting," and the view of parenthood as a "reward" (Respondent 7).

It is interesting to note here that within the ART context in Bulgaria children are perceived as a "reward"—as part of a relation of exchange or as compensation—but not as a "gift." Thus, they are not necessarily accepted "just as they are." This is clearly demonstrated through the common conviction among the respondents that they will not continue a long waited pregnancy by ARTs if the fetus has been diagnosed prenatally with some genetic condition, such as Down syndrome. One of the women even stated, "The aim of every woman with reproductive problems is not to see herself pregnant, but to give birth to a healthy baby" (Respondent 3). In the same vein, they all express very positive attitudes toward the possibility of preimplantation diagnosis. This confirms again the conclusions, made in other studies of ARTs in Bulgaria, that the attitudes toward them are "embedded in the broader, generally positive cultural discourse of science and technology. . . . Bulgarians expressed very high levels of trust in science and scientists" (Panayotova and Todorova 2009, 63).

Going back to the ART children's qualities, it must be stressed that many of the respondents believe that they are really "special," as they are often called. One of the respondents even exclaims: "Yes, they are different! They are loved more!!!" and adds, "These couples will create children, who will become worthy citizens and shall not be mere human rabble" (Respondent 8). Another one states, "They are special children, who combine the best of the genes of their parents" (Respondent 11). The respondents are obviously convinced that the fact that these children are long waited and "really desired" provides them something extra, which is missing in the spontaneously conceived ones. One respondent underlines that the difference is not in the "result" (the child), but in the process of conception: "five minutes of groaning versus the hard work of a whole team of medical professionals" (Respondent 3).

Asking questions about the children conceived by assisted reproduction is tricky, because in most cases the respondents immediately become distrustful and suspicious of unfavorable assumptions motivating such inquiries. One respondent says, "Nothing should be stressed (with regard to them). They are like the other children; they are not aliens or genetically modified. They are not different . . . in any aspect" (Respondent 7). And another one exhorts, "It is high time to put an end to such discussions, because even posing the question (Do you think that the children, conceived by assisted reproduction, are in some way—positive or negative—different?) presupposes the possibility of such difference" (Respondent 10).

The unwillingness to discuss ART children is an effect of another very powerful frame residing at the heart of the ART discourse in Bulgaria: the striving to present reproductive technologies in completely positive terms and to safeguard them from mentioning critiques, doubts, and moral dilemmas. The activist community successfully constructs a discursive opposition: they are the progressive, well informed, and enlightened citizens who have set themselves free from the ignorance and prejudice, which still haunt the backward public, stuck in the past. This attitude toward the rest of society is common for all respondents—with no exceptions they depict Bulgarian society as far from being ready to accept the technological innovation, unwilling to support people with health problems like infertility, and attempting to deprive them of their rights to healthcare and happiness. According to them this society is also hostile to their children, but in fact, in Bulgaria there is no strong and visible discourse arguing that children, conceived through ARTs, are in some way "damaged." In contrast to some other contexts, for example Poland, there are no prominent conservative and religious communities who openly criticize "IVF parenthood" in the country (Korolczuk 2014).[9]

Simultaneously, the activist organizations, as mentioned above, invoke rather conservative frames for their activities, appealing exactly to the traditional and patriarchal societal values. It is interesting to look more closely at one media presentation of the Iskam Bebe foundation. Here the conservative frames are clearly visible. Among the facts explaining why infertility is so widely distributed are mentioned the societal pressures on women to postpone pregnancy, the availability of birth control pills, the diminishing value of the conventional nuclear family, the separation between procreation and sexual relations, and women's "emancipation" efforts. These views are expressed fully in the following exhortation from a public presentation of the Association's activities: "Let's look at ourselves—how do we express our feminine essence? It may seem funny, but on the Bali Island, for example, there is no problem with infertility—they venerate the plumpness of women and the latter do not put themselves on a diet and do not wear trousers." It is followed by the warning that "something has gone wrong with nature," which is accompanied by several photos of a pregnant man and of women soldiers, weight lifters, and boxers (Iskam Bebe Foundation 2007).

In such a way, the patient organizations engage in a curious hybrid strategy, which could be called "reactionary techno-progressivism." It is evident not only in the demographic and nationalist arguments employed, but also in the fact that their campaign for public financial and symbolic support does not involve the issue of access to ARTs by same-sex couples, for example. With regard to the attitudes of the patient organization toward this issue, one of the respondents (a member of Zachatie) says, "For some (of the activists) the fight for maximally broad access to ARTs is unacceptable, since it is unpractical—there are more painful issues. . . . The moral dimension of the problem for me is unquestionable, but Bulgarians are conservative and most often they say 'no'" (Respondent 7).

Besides the dilemmas of access, other main concerns regarding ARTs and their long-term consequences are also neglected or deliberately not brought to the light of public discussion. Perhaps the most painful issue for the activists and for the patients as whole is the possible increased risk for adverse health outcomes in the children born after assisted reproduction. There are studies supporting these fears.[10] The general conclusions of European Society of Human Reproduction and Embryology, for example, are that the absolute risk after ART is small, the risks of inherited and de novo chromosomal aberrations are higher after intracytoplasmic sperm injection (ICSI), and some of the increase is thought to be related to parental characteristics and not to the procedures, but more information and monitoring is needed. Nevertheless, as the analysis of data from the National Birth Defects Prevention Study—a population-based, multicenter, case-control study of birth defects—concludes, "Some birth defects occur more often among infants conceived with ART. Although the mechanism is not clear, couples considering ART should be informed of all potential risks and benefits" (Reefhuis et al. 2009; Zhu et al. 2006).

This crucial focus on informing and counseling the patients and providing the current available information, despite the lack of conclusiveness, generates serious concern in the Bulgarian setting around ARTs. The possible risks of assisted reproduction are deliberately omitted in the positive and pronatalist framing of the issue and are rejected by the activists and infertile people, if in some form they appear in the public space. They are denied, for example, by renowned medical specialists in the field who claim that "there is no higher disease incidence, no disabilities or malformations. And even if there are, they do not occur more often in comparison with the naturally conceived children. This is proved with 100% certainty" (Blitz 2010).

Relevant and up-to-date information is not available on the websites of the leading patient organizations and is not present in the informed consent form, which must be signed by the couples prior to the procedures. On the internet site of the nonprofit organization Iskam Bebe, the answer of the question "should we expect some complications after ICSI?" is, "Today this procedure is practiced all over the world and the scientists are unanimous—there is no higher disease occurrence, no higher mortality rates and no higher incidence of birth defects among children, conceived in this way." A media account of the same organization clearly states, "IVF babies are not more ill, born with more malformations or different in any way—they are simply waited more eagerly" (Iskam Bebe Foundation 2007). The private clinics also reject the possibility of even slightly higher risks: "Such a possibility does not exist. The defective embryos, even those which are spontaneously conceived, usually do not develop" (Olimed 2014).

The aforementioned divide between the "ignorant and backward" public opinion and the "progressive community" of patients appears again in the opinion of a psychologist, affiliated at a private ART hospital, working also for one of the leading patient organizations. In an e-mail to the author on October 22, 2012, she stresses, "If the statement that the ART infants are 'more defective' goes public, this would only deepen the negative attitudes. . . . Those, having reproductive problems, will continue using ARTs just because they do not have another choice and the impression that this involves risks is not beneficial neither to them nor to society." Such attitude clearly compromises the right to informed consent of potential patients.

It is important to note that patients themselves actively contribute to the elimination of all possible doubts in the health of the future children conceived by assisted reproduction and the elevated risks associated with infertility or infertility treatment. Obviously, they are convinced that such information could have a negative impact on the public attitudes and could possibly diminish the symbolic public support and lead to a withdrawing of resources. As I already mentioned, the patients prefer not to discuss such issues and there are few online discussions on the topic. They are nevertheless quite indicative. One good example for the resistance to depict ARTs in any way different than in positive terms is seen from the reactions of the patients, provoked by a publication of a pediatrician on her personal blog. In a special article she mentions the information about the slightly elevated risks. This sparks a wave of scorn and rage against her—numerous comments are published in the blog and a special thread is established in the Zachatie forum. There the article is characterized as "scandalous," "offensive," "ridiculous," "misleading" and "unprofessional," directed "personally toward all our children, conceived and born after ART," who are in fact "created with more love (perseverant, proven and conscious) than many from the hastily conceived children" (Zachatie 2010). The author is accused of a lack of competence and being completely ignorant; there are even suggestions in the discussion to bring a lawsuit against her. The situation is similar in the other online discussions; the profound mistrust is retained, for example, even when the renowned *British Medical Journal* (BG Mamma 2008b) is mentioned as a source. This local phenomenon "illuminate[s] the crucial sociological point that movement frames do not require 'validity' for successful claimsmaking, but rather must display a degree of cultural resonance, or cultural viability, with intended audiences to ensure strong public claims" (Kokler 2004, 833).

Conclusion

The article presented and analyzed some core framing strategies adopted by the patient organizations of people with reproductive problems in Bulgaria. Its main conclusion is that this health movement invokes culturally resonant frames, which greatly enhance its efforts to gain public support—being symbolic as well as financial. The infertile persons in Bulgaria purposefully and willingly portray themselves as a valuable resource in a critical situation—critical in terms of demographic collapse, but also in terms of societal and family values. In such a sense, infertility is not only a universal threat, which shall affect a growing part of the population, but especially a "scourge" for the educated, decent, productive, and responsible members of a society. Unlike other health movements in Bulgaria—for example, the organizations for people with rare genetic diseases or for parents of children with disabilities—the local framing of the problem is not limited by the "social value" of infertile persons: "other health social movements might bring fewer cultural resources to their activities in terms of the social value of the victims portrayed in accounts of their cause, impacting upon their ability to convince audiences that their disease is a serious public problem" (Kokler 2004, 837). This allows them to bring together diverse representational elements, to embed them in culturally resonant matrices, and to construct their specific reactionary techno-progressivist discourse of deservedness.

Ina Dimitrova, Associate Professor at the Department of Philosophy and History, Plovdiv University, Bulgaria and honorary lecturer at the Department of Philosophy, Sofia University, Bulgaria

Ina Dimitrova's research interests include ethical, social, and legal implications of the new biotechnologies, patient activism, and ethics of parenthood and procreation. Her book *Prenatal Diagnosis and Biopolitics in Bulgaria* (2012) analyzes the expert discourse on the practice of selective abortion and the local processes of responsibilization of parenthood. Her previous research projects were focused on the ways of governing poverty in Bulgaria from a historical perspective and the concept of reflexivity as a phenomenon of the social world and knowledge.

Notes

1. See, for example, Assenova (2007), Kotseva (2011), Panayotova and Todorova (2007, 2009).

2. Similar reactions face also other attempts at recruiting respondents or conducting surveys in Bulgaria. See, for example, Assenova (2007).

3. For a detailed account see Baloutzova (2011).

4. The discourse of the "reproductive reserve" in Poland is very similar. See, for example, Hryciuk and Korolczuk (2015).

5. This discourse of the irresponsible procreation of the undeserving poor and "dependent" individuals could be fruitfully further analyzed using the notion of "controlling images," which operate aiming to justify the domination over certain groups in society (Collins 2000).

6. This is one of the key ongoing social and bioethical controversies around ARTs worldwide: should we define infertility as a disease similar to diabetes, for example (since it is not "treated" or "cured" but its side effects are managed), and provide public funding? Or, do we have no reason to go beyond the idea that reproductive rights are purely negative rights and entitle the infertile with subsidiary positive rights, which impose a kind of obligation on society to help them reproduce? Another way to pose the question is whether we have a right to procreate and how it could be grounded. See, for example, Robertson (1994) and Purdy (1996).

7. See, for example, Korolczuk (2015) for the Polish context.

8. The online discussion is very revealing on the meaning of the phrase "precious baby," used for the children that are conceived after ARTs (BG Mamma 2008b).

9. The Polish context is, for example, radically different in this respect, where a conservative public campaign exists, led primarily by the Catholic Church, stressing the "monstrosity" of the IVF children. See, for example, Korolczuk (2014) and Radkowska-Walkowicz (2012).

10. One of the most cited is published in 2002 in *The New England Journal of Medicine* (Hansen et al. 2002). It found a 9% rate of major birth defects in infants born after IVF and an 8.6% rate of major birth defects in infants born after ICSI. The control group of naturally conceived infants had a 4.2% rate of major birth defects. Similar results report several studies, conducted during the last years: "compared with spontaneously conceived babies, the ART singletons had 2.1 times the risk of septal heart defects, they also had 2.4 times the risk of cleft lip and palate, 4.5 times the risk of esophageal defects, 3.7 times the risk of anal and rectal defects, and 2.1 times the risk of hypospadias" (Macintosh 2010, 278). Other possible complications are the following: cardiovascular risk factors in IVF children (Ceelen et al. 2009), ART twins are more likely than spontaneously conceived twins to be admitted to a neonatal intensive care unit and hospitalized in the first three years of life (Hansen et al. 2009), umbilical cord anomalies (Delbaere et al. 2007), increased risk of stillbirth (Wisborg et al. 2010), and cerebral palsy (Zhu et al. 2010). Similar results could be found also in Mitsiakos et al. (2009), Bonduelle et al. (2005), and Davies et al. (2012). Recent studies continue to stress the risks (Hansen et al. 2013; Kelley-Quong et al. 2013; Farhi et al. 2013).

Works Cited

Ariston S. Foundation. 2008. "Iskam Bebe Foundation." Accessed April 15, 2014. http://foundation.ariston-s.com/index.php?page=partners&partnerID=1.

Assenova, Assya. 2007. "Moralni problemi pri oplozhdane in vitro" [Moral Issues in In Vitro Fertilization]. PhD Diss., Sofia University.

Baloutzova, Svetla. 2011. *Demography and Nation. Social Legislation and Population Policy in Bulgaria, 1918–1944*. Budapest-New York: CEU Press.

Benford, Robert, and David A. Snow. 2000. "Framing Processes and Social Movements: An Overview and Assessment." *Annual Review of Sociology* 26:611–639.

BG Mamma. 2008a. "What Do You Think about Embryonal Reduction?" Accessed April 12, 2012. http://www.bg-mamma.com/index.php?topic=307245.15.

———. 2008b. "Why In Vitro Babies Are Delivered via C-section?" Accessed April 12, 2014. http://www.bg-mamma.com/index.php?topic=339552.20.

Blitz. 2010. "Assoc. Prof. Iliya Vatev: I Have Created More Than 1000 Babies In Vitro." Accessed April 20, 2014. http://www.blitz.bg/article/18451.

Bonduelle, M., U.-B. Wennerholm, A. Loft, B. C. Tarlatzis, C. Peters, S. Henriet, C. Mau, et al. 2005. "A Multi-centre Cohort Study of the Physical Health of 5-year-old Children Conceived after Intracytoplasmic Sperm Injection, In Vitro Fertilization and Natural Conception." *Human Reproduction* 20 (2):413–419.

Boyadjeva, Pepka, Ivan Tchalakov, and Krastina Petkova. 1994. Naukata—Zhivot Izvan Laboratoriyata [*Science—Life outside Laboratory*]. Sofia: Academic Publishers.

Ceelen, M., M. M. van Weissenbruch, J. Prein, J. J. Smit, J. P. Vermeiden, M. Spreeuwenberg, F. E. van Leeuwen, and H. A. Delemarre-van de Waal. 2009. "Growth During Infancy and Early Childhood in Relation to Blood Pressure and Body Fat Measures at Age 8–18 Years of IVF Children and Spontaneously Conceived Controls Born to Subfertile Parents." *Human Reproduction* 24 (11):2788–2795.

Colen, Shellee. 1995. "Like a Mother to Them: Stratified Reproduction and the West Indian Childcare Workers and Employers in New York." In *Conceiving the New World Order: The Global Politics of Reproduction*, edited by Faye D. Ginsburg and Rayna Rapp, 78–102. Berkeley: University of California Press.

Collins, Patricia H. 2000. *Black Feminist Thought: Knowledge, Consciousness, and the Politics of Empowerment*. New York: Routledge.

Davies, Michael, V. Moore, K. Willson, Ph. Van Essen, K. Priest, H. Scott, E. Haan, and A. Chan. 2012. "Reproductive Technologies and the Risk of Birth Defects." *The New England Journal of Medicine* 366:1803–1813.

Delbaere, I., S. Goetgeluk, C. Derom, D. Bacquer, P. De Sutter, and M. Temmerman. 2007. "Umbilical Cord Anomalies Are More Frequent in Twins after Assisted Reproduction." *Human Reproduction* 22 (10):2763–2767.

Dimitrova, Ina. 2012. Prenatalna Diagnostika i Biopolitika v Bulgaria [*Prenatal Diagnostics and Biopolitics in Bulgaria*]. Sofia: East-West Publishers.

Dnes.bg. 2008. "Syndical Organizations Supporting the In Vitro Program." Accessed April 12, 2014. http://www.dnes.bg/obshtestvo/2008/12/17/sindikalni-organizacii-v-podkrepa-na-programata-quot-in-vitro-quot.62776,2.

Farhi, A., B. Reichman, V. Boyko, S. Mashiach, A. Hourvitz, E. J. Margalioth, D. Levran, I. Calderon, R. Orvieto, A. Ellenbogen, J. Meyerovitch, R. Ron-El, and L. Lerner-Geva. 2013. "Congenital Malformations in Infants Conceived Following Assisted Reproductive Technology in Comparison with Spontaneously Conceived Infants." *Journal of Maternal, Fetal, and Neonatal Medicine* 26 (12):1171–1179.

Gamson, William A. 1992. *Talking Politics*. New York: Cambridge University Press.

Goffman, Erving. 1974. *Frame Analysis: An Essay on the Organization of Experience*. New York: Harper Colophon.

Grant, Jonathan, Stijn Hoorens, Federico Gallo, and Jonathan Cave. 2006. "Should ART Be Part of a Population Policy Mix? A Preliminary Assessment of the Demographic and Economic Impact of Assisted Reproductive Technologies." Santa Monica, CA: RAND Corporation.

Hansen, Michèle, Jennifer Kurinczuk, Carol Bower, and Sandra Webb. 2002. "The Risk of Major Birth Defects after Intracytoplasmic Sperm Injection and In Vitro Fertilization." *New England Journal of Medicine* 346 (10):725–730.

Hansen, Michèle, Lyn Colvin, Beverly Petterson, Jennifer Kurinczuk, Nicolas de Klerk, and Carol Bower. 2009. "Twins Born Following Assisted Reproductive Technology: Perinatal Outcome and Admission to Hospital." *Human Reproduction* 24 (9):2321–2331.

Hansen, Michèle, Jennifer Kurinczuk, Elizabeth Milne, Nicolas de Klerk, and Carol Bower. 2013. "Assisted Reproductive Technology and Birth Defects: A Systematic Review and Meta-analysis." *Human Reproduction Update* 19 (4):330–353.

Hoorens, Stijn, Federico Gallo, Jonathan Cave, and Jonathan Grant. 2007. "Can Assisted Reproductive Technologies Help to Offset Population Ageing? An Assessment of the Demographic and Economic Impact of ART in Denmark and UK." *Human Reproduction* 22:2471–2475.

Hryciuk, Renata, and Elżbieta Korolczuk. 2015. "Konteksty upolitycznienia macierzyństwa i ojcostwa we współczesnej Polsce" [Politicizing Motherhood and Fatherhood in Contemporary Poland]. In *Niebezpieczne związki. Macierzyństwo, ojcostwo i polityka [Dangerous Liaisons. Motherhood, Fatherhood and Politics]*, edited by Renata E. Hryciuk and Elżbieta Korolczuk, 11–44. Warsaw: Warsaw University Press.

Iskam Bebe Foundation. 2007. "Fulfill Your Dream! And . . . Pay It Forward." Accessed April 15, 2014. http://img.dfbulgaria.org/conference/Presentation_Iskam_bebe_BDF.pdf.

Kelley-Quon, Lorraine I., Chi-Hong Tseng, Carla Janzen, and Stephen B. Shew. 2013. "Congenital Malformations Associated with Assisted Reproductive Technology: A California Statewide Analysis." *Journal of Pediatric Surgery* 48 (6):1218–1224.

Kokler, Emily. 2004. "Framing as a Cultural Resource in Health Social Movements: Funding Activism and the Breast Cancer Movement in the US 1990–1993." *Sociology of Health and Illness* 26 (6):820–844.

Korolczuk, Elżbieta. 2014. "Terms of Engagement. Redefining Identity and Infertility On-line." *Culture Unbound: Journal of Current Cultural Research* 6 (22):431–449.

———. 2015. "Those Who Are Full Can Never Understand the Hungry: Challenging the Meaning of Infertility in Poland." In *The Identity Dilemma. Social Movements and Identity Dilemma*, edited by Aidan McGarry and James Jasper, 170–191. Philadelphia: Temple University Press.

Kotseva, T. 2011. "Demografskiyat problem vav fokusa na publichnite diskursi v nachaloto na XXI vek" [The Demographic Problem in the Focus of Public Discourses in the Beginning of 21st Century]. *Sociological Problems* 3–4:340–364.

Kotseva, Tatyana, and Irina Todorova. 2005. "Socialno konstruirane na bezplodieto v balgarskoto obshtestvo" [Social Construction of Infertility in Bulgarian Society]. *Sociological Problems* 3–4:215–243.

Kubal, Timothy J. 1998. "The Presentation of the Political Self: Culture, Mobilization, and the Construction of Collective Action Frames." *Sociological Quarterly* 39:539–554.

Macintosh, Kerry. 2010. "Brave New Eugenics: Regulating Assisted Reproductive Technologies in the Name of Better Babies." *University of Illinois Journal of Law, Technology and Policy* 2:257–310.

Ministry of Health. 2011. "Report on the Fulfillment of Objectives for 2010, Appendix 2."

Ministry of Labor and Social Policy. 2007. "Report for the Realization of the National Strategy for Demographic Development of Republic of Bulgaria 2006–2020." Report period 2006–2007.

Mitsiakos, George, Evaggelia Giougi, Christos Tsakalidis, Maria Kourti, Hlias Chatziionnidis, and Paraskevi Karagianni. 2009. "A Case of Adams-Oliver Syndrome Following in Vitro Fertilization." *Human Reproduction* 24 (6):1529–1530.

National Assembly of the Republic of Bulgaria. 2008. "National Assembly Archive." Accessed April 12, 2014. http://www.parliament.bg/bg/archive/2/3/164/steno/ID/1132/.

Olimed. 2014. "Frequently Asked Questions." Accessed April 13, 2014. http://www.invitro-olimed.eu/index.php?page=faq.

Panayotova, Julia, and Irina Todorova. 2007. "Asistirani reproduktivni tehnologii v Bulgaria. Konstruirane na ravnopostavenostta ot poziciyata na lekari i specialisti" [Assisted Reproductive Technologies in Bulgaria. Constructing Equity from the Point of View of Medical Professionals]. In *Etikata v Bulgarskoto Zdraveopazvane* [Ethics in Bulgarian Healthcare], edited by Emilia Marinova and Sashka Popova, 510–519. Sofia: Simel.

———. 2009. "Cultural Meanings in Assisted Reproductive Technologies: Women's Voices from Bulgaria." In *Assisting Reproduction, Testing Genes. Global Encounters with New Biotechnologies*, edited by Daphna Birenbaum-Carmeli and Marcia Inhorn, 61–85. New York: Berghahn Books.

Purdy, Laura. 1996. *Reproducing Persons*. Ithaca, NY: Cornell University Press.

Radkowska-Walkowicz, Magdalena. 2012. "The Creation of 'Monsters': The Discourse of Opposition to In Vitro Fertilization in Poland." *Reproductive Health Matters* 20 (40):30–37.

Reefhuis, J., M. A. Honein, L. A. Schieve, A. Correa, C. A. Hobbs, and S. A. Rasmussen. 2009. "Assisted Reproductive Technology and Major Structural Birth Defects in the United States." *Human Reproduction* 24 (2):360–366.

Robertson, John. 1994. *Children of Choice*. Princeton: Princeton University Press.

Simeonov, Emil, and Maria Krachunova. 1993. "Genetichno konsultirane v pediatrichnata praktika" [Genetic Counseling in Pediatric Practice]. *Pediatrics* 1:16–20.

Snow, David A., Rochford E. Burke, Steven Worden, and Robert D. Benford. 1986. "Frame Alignment Processes, Micromobilization and Movement Participation." *American Sociological Review* 51:464–481.

te Velde, Egbert, Marinus Eijkemans, Beets J. Gijs, and Dik F. Habbema. 2008. "Can Assisted Reproductive Technologies Help to Offset Population Ageing?" *Human Reproduction* 23 (9):2173–2175.

Williams, Rhys H. 1995. "Constructing the Public Good: Social Movements and Cultural Resources." *Social Problems* 42:124–144.

———. 2004. "The Cultural Contexts of Collective Action: Constraints, Opportunities, and the Symbolic Life of Social Movements." In *The Blackwell Companion to Social Movements*, edited by David A. Snow, Sarah Soule, and Hanspeter Kriesi, 91–115. Malden: Blackwell Publishing.

Williams, Rhys H., and Timothy Kubal. 1999. "Movement Frames and the Cultural Environment: Resonance, Failure, and the Boundaries of the Legitimate." *Research in Social Movements, Conflicts and Change* 21:225–248.

Wisborg, Kirsten, Hans J. Ingerslev, and Tine B. Henriksen. 2010. "IVF and Stillbirth: A Prospective Follow-up Study." *Human Reproduction* 25 (5):1312–1316.

Zachatie. 2010. "Risks, Related with In Vitro Conception." Accessed March 10, 2014. http://www.zachatie.org/forum/index.php?topic=42317.msg709434#msg709434.

Zhu, Jin Liang, Dorte Hvidtjørn, Olga Basso, Carsten Obel, Poul Thorsen, Peter Uldall, and Jørn Olsen. 2010. "Parental Infertility and Cerebral Palsy in Children." *Human Reproduction* 25 (12):3142–3145.

4

In the Name of the Family and Nation: Framing Fathers' Activism in Contemporary Poland

Elżbieta Korolczuk and Renata E. Hryciuk

Introduction

Fatherhood and fathering have only recently become a topic of public debate in Poland, though the first fathers' groups were formed in the late 1980s and early 1990s. Postdivorce conflict over child custody was introduced to the broader public in 1995 when the popular and widely discussed film, *Tato* (*Daddy*, directed by Michał Ślesicki), was released. This film features the story of a man who saves his daughter from his psychotic ex-wife with the help of *Stowarzyszenie Obrony Praw Ojca* (Association for the Defense of Fathers' Rights), a Warsaw-based organization. The film focuses on the custody issue, but the authors make it clear that this is just part of the contemporary "war of the sexes."

The film can be interpreted as a Polish pop-cultural manifestation of backlash (Faludi 1991), in presenting the story of a highly successful cameraman, whose stay-at-home depressed wife files for divorce and gets sole custody of their only child. The protagonist decides to kidnap the young daughter to protect her from a psychologically unstable mother. Despite his apparent lack of parenting experience, he is portrayed as a sympathetic and caring father, whereas the mother is depicted as a villainess and a danger to her child, instigated by a vicious man-hating feminist friend. *Daddy* can also be seen as a reflection of the gendered dimension of post-1989 social and economic change (Funk and Mueller 1993; Gal and Kligman 2000), as the protagonist tries to live up to the new ideal of an engaged caring father while simultaneously trying to be a successful entrepreneur in the film industry. The film highlights an important yet little researched aspect of the post-1989 transformation of gender order, namely the alteration of discourses and practices of fathering, which the social activism of fathers both reflects and influences.

Contemporary studies on fathers' groups concentrate on industrialized Western countries, with a specific focus on Australia, Canada, and the United States (Collier and Sheldon 2006; Crowley 2008; Flood 2012). Little is known of fathers' activism in other cultural and social settings, although an online worldwide directory of fathers' activism lists organizations and groups that exist in India, Japan, and Turkey, as well as in postsocialist and post-Soviet contexts, for example, Poland, Hungary, Czech Republic, and Ukraine. There is also a scarcity of comparative studies. This analysis hopes to fill this gap, albeit only partially, by examining the local specificity of the Polish fathers' movement in a comparative perspective.

Fathers' activists use specific frames and rights claims that are embedded in locally relevant discourses regarding fatherhood/motherhood and gender, as well as the most resonant social problems and needs. This chapter examines fathers' activism in contemporary Poland, focusing on the ways in which activists frame the problem, their claims and expected outcomes, and on the specificity of fathers' activism in a postsocialist context in comparison to other cultural and political environments. We apply analytical tools of social movement theory, specifically the notion of framing, which we define as a process of interpretation and meaning production in a given political, cultural, and social context. We distinguish three main frames that the Polish activists employed: (1) "misogynist" frame, which highlights fathers' rights as men's rights, (2) "state violence" frame, which focuses on the state violating fathers' rights as citizens, and (3) "equality" frame, which stresses fathers' engagement as part of a gender equality agenda. We show that each of these types of self-representation and arguments combine, to a different degree, transnational and local discourses on fathering, masculinity, and the family, reflecting the hybrid nature of contemporary discourses and ideals of fathering.

This chapter begins with outlining theoretical inspirations and methodology. We then present how fathers' activism has been conceptualized in international scholarship and how the emergence of organizations and networks of fathers have been explained in different social and cultural contexts, including the Polish context. In the following sections we present the results of our study, discussing the types of fathers' organizations that exist in Poland and the main frames they employ in a comparative perspective. Concluding remarks focus on the similarities and specificities of the Polish case in comparison to other national contexts where fathers' activism exists.[1]

Theoretical Inspirations and Methodology

Most studies on fathers' groups and organizations use the interpretive approach of the sociology of family and/or gender studies, although there is a growing body of scholarship that employs social movement theory to study this phenomenon (e.g., Blais and Dupuis-Déri 2012; Wojnicka and Zierkiewicz 2014). We apply social movement theory to examine how Polish activists interpret the problem to which they mobilize and how they formulate their claims and goals. We analyze the constructivist and interpretive dimensions of collective action and apply the concept of framing, which we define as an interpretive process involving the activists' construction of meaning within specific cultural, political, and social context (Zald 1996). Following other scholars we focus on the frames, used in a contextual or indexical sense, as a dividing line that keeps some elements in view and others out of view (Benford and Snow 2000; Williams and Benford 2000). Thus, we examine how the choice of frames is related to (1) the movement's processes (if they serve the aims of coalition building capacity) and (2) media resonance and its outcomes (if they increase the visibility and effectiveness of the claims, e.g., in terms of influencing policy-making processes).

We used a variety of sources to obtain data on the Polish fathers' groups. Because much of the parents' activism takes place on the internet we began by reviewing online resources such as the web pages of fathers' groups, their public discussion forums, Facebook pages, and relevant blogs. We also reviewed mainstream media digital repositories by analyzing articles on Polish fathers' activism since 2004 that were published in daily publications, such as *Gazeta Wyborcza* and *Rzeczpospolita*, and weekly publications, such as *Polityka*, *Wprost*, *Newsweek*, and *UważamRze*, which together represent a wide array of ideological orientations. The third important source of information was public debates and open forums. Some of these debates were organized by the media (e.g., *Daddy. Non-Fiction* debate organized in Warsaw by *Gazeta Wyborcza* in 2012), while others emerged through the initiative of state institutions, such as *Forum dla Rodziny* [Family Forum], organized by the prime minister's office in 2013. We also attended expert seminars for participant observation; for example, in 2013 we went to an open meeting of fathers' groups and representatives of the state organized under the auspices of the Plenipotentiary for Equal Status. Similar debates were held by non-governmental organizations (NGOs), such as the Institute for Public Affairs in 2013 and 2014. We examined the visibility of fathers' movements during such events measured by the presence of the activists and their participation in discussions, and we analyzed how they publicly framed their claims. Attending various debates and meetings also helped us identify and contact the most active fathers' groups and individuals, many of whom we later interviewed.

In the second stage of information gathering, we collected detailed information on the claims of the father's groups and their personal and institutional motivations—through individual, open-ended interviews with ten representatives (leaders and/or members of the management board) of fathers' groups in the capital (Warsaw) and other larger cities in Poland (Katowice, Olsztyn, and Lublin). Most of our interviewees were men, which obviously reflects the gender composition of the fathers' movement; but because some women were engaged in daily activities of some organizations, we also interviewed executive female members of two organizations, one supporting member who helps fathers in her capacity as a trained psychologist, and the representative of *Forum Matek* (Mothers' Forum). The latter is the only women's organization that supports fathers' activists. In fact, one of its leaders is the mother of a man who initiated one of the fathers' groups. We also conducted two additional interviews with women working in state institutions who collaborated extensively with fathers' activists (one person worked in the ministry and one was a judge involved in custody cases).[2] The interviews lasted between 30 minutes and 3.5 hours; all except two were recorded and transcribed. Additionally, in November 2014 we observed participants of one fathers' group meeting that regularly takes place in Warsaw. We anonymized the quotes from the interviews and did our best to delete information that could identify informants, such as the name of the organization they represent.

As feminist scholars, we do not share many of the views expressed by our informants and their interpretations of the sources of the problems divorced fathers encounter. Thus, we faced a number of epistemological, moral, and political challenges when studying groups with whose values and orientations we do not sympathize (see, e.g., Esseveld and Eyerman 1992). We addressed some of these challenges by focusing on gaining a full understanding of the views and interpretations as expressed by fathers' groups and by engaging in a meaningful conversation with the fathers; for example, in January 2015 we presented the preliminary outcomes of our research at the Institute of Ethnology and Cultural Anthropology in Warsaw, to which the activists were invited (two of them took part in the meeting and the following discussion). We also attempted at allowing our informants to speak for themselves, which is why we included some extensive quotes, while interpreting the arguments in relation to the local and transnational social, political, and cultural context.

Explaining the Emergence of Fathers' Activism: A Comparative Perspective

Fathers' activism is usually interpreted as part of men's movements along with other currents: men's liberation, antifeminist or profeminist, and various spiritual and more traditional strands, including Christianity (Flood 2012, 419). It is a heterogeneous phenomenon, present in different political and social contexts and traversed by various ideologies. Internationally the fathers' movement consists mostly of groups that focus specifically on the rights of fathers who are noncustodial parents, though some have a broader agenda, including changes in practices and ideals of fatherhood, for example, they promote a new model of the engaged father.

Researchers studying this phenomenon in industrialized countries point to four main reasons why fathers' movements have emerged in different contexts over roughly the same period of time (Bertoia and Drakich 1993; Crowley 2006; Flood 2012). These include (1) changes in demographic trends and family composition, (2) cuts in welfare spending and reducing help for families and single-parent households, (3) changes in ideals and practices of parenthood, and (4) the rise of conservative and religious movements that highlight the need to defend "traditional family values" and strengthen the authority of fathers. All of these trends were also present in Poland, although there are some significant temporal, sociocultural, and political specificities of the Polish context. In the following section we will discuss the similarities and differences regarding the emergence and proliferation of fathers' activism in Poland in a comparative perspective.

First, there is a demographic trend in Western industrialized countries that "fewer men enter fatherhood and more leave it" (Hobson and Morgan 2002, 2). It reflects a broader shift in family patterns that include declining birth rates, growing divorce rates, and a ratio of cohabiting couples, as well as single-parent families. A similar trend can be observed in contemporary Poland where the post-1989 economic, political, and social transformation greatly affected the family structure and gender relationships. The changes included declining fertility rates (from 2.32 in 1985 to 1.26 in 2006), decreasing number of marriages, and increasing rates of divorces, separations, and extramarital births. The ratio of single parents, mostly women, grew from 14 percent in 1988 to 19 percent in 2002. Meanwhile, the rate of unemployment rose rapidly (in the case of females from 15.7% in 1994 to 20.3% in 2003), which significantly undermined the economic stability of Polish families (Hryciuk and Korolczuk 2010; Szelewa 2015).

Second, since the 1980s there has been a tendency in most Western welfare states to significantly reduce, or even withdraw, support for "solo mothers" (Hobson and Morgan 2002, 2). In addition to neoliberalism's call to reduce the scope of welfare, another rationale for this change is that the state should not substitute for fathers who are not willing to take financial responsibility for their offspring, and the withdrawal of welfare provisions would result in enhancing fathers' engagement and cuts in the state's spending. Blais and Dupis-Deri (2012) show that the emergence of fathers' groups in some countries was linked directly with more stringent administrative measures regarding child support, as was the case in the early 1990s in the UK, where at the time 70 percent of absent parents, mostly fathers, made no support payments.[3] When the government established the Child Support Agency to induce such payments, a broad coalition was formed to oppose the initiative (2012, 32). A similar dynamic was found in Canada, where fathers' groups began to emerge in response to the local legislatures' efforts to enact reforms of the divorce law and introduce the mandatory collection of child support.

In Poland, drastic cuts to welfare expenditures, such as the state-owned childcare system, were implemented in the early 1990s along with the introduction of neoliberal models of economy, negatively affecting many families' economic conditions (Szelewa 2015). The growth in the number of divorced parents with children, combined with rising unemployment and the state administration's lack of interest in this issue, resulted in an increasing problem with paying child maintenance. In Poland, as in other countries such as Latvia, Lithuania, Luxemburg, and Portugal, child support was guaranteed by a special state-controlled fund, the Alimony Fund,[4] established in 1974 to provide for the children when the parent who was obliged by the court to pay was not able or not willing to do so. The Alimony Fund "loaned" money to the children and was supposed to collect it from the nonresident parent, nearly always the father; this system worked reasonably well until the early 1990s (Desperak 2008; Hryciuk and Korolczuk 2013). In the decade between 1980 and 1989, the average number of children entitled to monthly payments from the Alimony Fund increased by 34 percent, but the average rate of monies collected by the state was a relatively stable 58 percent of the sum "loaned" to the children. However, for the next decade the number of persons entitled to fund support increased by 348 percent, and the state was able to retrieve only 18 percent of the money spent (Kłos and Szymańczak 2003, 8). Due to increased costs generated by the Alimony Fund, it was liquidated in 2004 to meet the budgetary deficit requirements of joining the European Union (EU). After mass protests of single mothers during 2002–2007, AF was reinstated in 2007, although today it is mean-tested; thus if a mother of one earns a minimal wage she is ineligible to receive payments from the fund (Hryciuk 2017; Hryciuk and Korolczuk 2013). This increases pressure on fathers to pay child maintenance, especially in cases when the mother works and does not receive any state support. Consequently, many of the contemporary Polish fathers' groups focus on this issue, and some of the activists oppose paying child support claiming that the current system turns them into "ATMs"—they are expected to pay but have no rights to contact their children.

Third, in international literature the emergence and proliferation of fathers' activism is often linked to contemporary changes in ideals and practices of parenthood (Crowley 2008). Motherhood and fatherhood as a norm, and its related practices, have become an arena in which changes and negotiations concerning the shape of the gender contract are played out.[5] They have become a disputed terrain where different views and needs coexist and clash (Hryciuk and Korolczuk 2015; Kubicki 2009). Tensions are considerable, and shifts concerning values and norms related to parenthood do not necessarily coincide with how fathers and mothers behave. In most developed countries today, fathers are expected to be involved in everyday family life and to provide care, but men's actual participation in raising and caring for children has not changed much, with the exception of the educated middle class and some particular countries, such as Sweden—where gender equality has become a well-established norm (Clarke and Popay 1998; Rodin and Åberg 2013).

According to this explanatory model, fathers' activism reflects the tensions resulting from the growth in divorce and separation, norms of "new fatherhood," changes in the legal regulation of postdivorce family life, and shifting discourses in law and broader society regarding parenting and equality (Flood 2012, 237). This is also the case in Poland, where fatherhood has become an important topic in the public sphere and sociological inquiry (Fuszara 2008; Krajewska 2008; Kubicki 2009; Sikorska 2009; Suwada and Platin 2014; Wojnicka and Ciaputa 2011). The tone of the public debate oscillates between hopeful accounts of the new trend toward engaged and caring fatherhood, often termed "daddyism" (*tacierzyństwo*) (Budrowska 2008; Bierca 2013; Sikorska 2012), and the gloomy vision of the crisis of fatherhood that supposedly results from "getting rid of traditional roles without establishing new ones" (Gębka 2006, 118; see also Dzwonkowska-Godula 2011). The latter grim tone reflects a broader trend within conservative segments in Polish society. The Catholic Church has repeatedly issued warnings against the demise of the "normal" and "traditional" family and highlighted the dire social consequences of this process. Both the Church and conservative elites ascribe partial responsibility for this trend to the "contemporary man," who is all too often not a responsible father and husband but rather "an absentee, tyrant, or deserter" (Korab 2006, 2). However, the source of the problem is usually found in postmodern sexual ethics (or rather lack of thereof), which stems from feminism, sexual revolution, and emancipation of sexual minorities (Graff and Korolczuk 2017).

The public debate on fatherhood in Poland signals the discrepancy between the new model of an engaged father, who shares caring responsibilities with the mother as promoted in the public sphere, and the social reality where men do not engage in fathering. Contemporary sociological studies on unpaid domestic work and care in Poland show that changes in opinions on fathering do not necessarily translate into changes in behaviors (CBOS 2013).[6] Whereas images of gender-equal parenting appear more often in the media (the press, TV series, or soap operas) (Arcimowicz 2009; Łaciak 2008), men do not necessarily engage in actual care to a much greater extent than their fathers (Fuszara 2008).

At the same time, the new generation of Polish men appears to be more open to new ideals of fathering. In 2013, just two years after introducing new regulations enabling men to take two weeks of paid "daddy leave" after the birth of a child, over 130,000 Polish fathers (approximately 50% of those who were entitled) went on such leave. The very high response rate shows that changes in social policy can induce men to take paternal leave, and some fathers' groups aim at strengthening this trend. These activists promote engaged fatherhood, although, as we will discuss in more detail, it does not necessarily mean that they promote full gender equality in all aspects of family life.

Finally, in explaining the emergence and proliferation of fathers' movements internationally, some scholars point to the rise of conservative and religious currents, among them antifeminist men's activism (Eldén 2002; Blais and Dupuis-Deri 2012). They argue that some groups, especially the fathers' rights strand, represent "organized backlash to feminism" (Flood 2012, 235). Indeed, a considerable segment of the fathers' movement can be seen as a countermovement to feminism. This is also the case in Poland, where post-1989 changes included the revival of nationalism and increased political power of the Catholic Church with its focus on "traditional family values" and a strong critique of feminism, gender equality, and sexual and reproductive rights. Thus, some fathers' groups in Poland claim that men are in crisis because of the growing influence of feminists and the ongoing "feminization" of society. Introducing gender equality policies and norms, in their opinion, translates to discrimination against fathers, which is reflected in family law and divorce procedures (Wojnicka 2013). For example, fathers' organization *Dzielny Tata* (Brave Dad) joined the opposition to ratification of the Council of Europe Convention on preventing and combating violence against women and domestic violence in 2015, and its activists occasionally engage in direct actions against local feminist movements, such as distributing billboards with antifeminist slogans in Warsaw in 2014.[7]

Comparison of the conditions that led to the emergence of fathers' activism in different contexts shows that fathers' activism can be interpreted as a transnational phenomenon that is typical for late modernity with its characteristic culture of individualism, growing divorce rates, and single-parent families (Flood 2012). At the same time, despite some striking similarities in the social trends activists respond to and goals they claim to pursue, there are some differences between specific countries and groups. The differences include how the activists frame fathers' rights, what their views are on gender equality and feminism, and the level of their involvement in political advocacy and other contentious actions (cf. Saxonberg, Åberg and Rodin, Strelnyk, and Karzabi in this volume).

The Three Strands of Fathers' Groups in Poland

The first Polish fathers' organization was established in 1988, but today there are over twenty NGOs concerned solely or mainly with the issue of fatherhood (Wojnicka 2013). In this section we give an account of fathers organizing in Poland and discuss the similarities and differences between the main strands of activism in terms of organizational characteristics, the choice of strategies, levels of cooperation with the state, and the goals the activists pursue.

It is difficult to account for the exact number of active contemporary Polish fathers' organizations and groups, and it is even harder to estimate their accurate membership because some organizations are active mostly online and members of others may not meet on a regular basis. Complicating the exact count, a growing number of individuals and loose networks have become active online, and some of these activities turn into NGOs, while the existing ones often cease to undertake activities after a time (Badzian 2010). Organizations we interviewed varied in terms of number of official members or people engaged in daily activities. Some of the groups, such as Brave Dad, claim to have a large membership even though they appear to consist of just a few men who gather around a charismatic leader, and others such as *Centrum Praw Ojca i Dziecka* (Center for Fathers' and Children's Rights) have larger memberships. This latter NGO has a group of six executive members providing services to help men in legal proceedings, about 180 regular members who pay fees, and a formal organization that men can call on when they need legal support. There are also other organizations that claim to have very large memberships. For example, the leader of one organization claimed they have over 1,600 members and another declared there were over 20,000 men who contacted them face-to-face, via telephone, or email every year. However, it is difficult to verify these claims of membership and appeal. As one of our interviewees concluded, there are few leaders, many of whom are fathers fighting for custody for their children; there are supporters, often lawyers or psychologists; and there are fathers who contact these organizations, but they just want help rather than to engage in social activism. Most of our interviewees agreed, however, that the number of fathers seeking help and support is growing, mostly due to growing rates of divorce and what activists claimed as the "emancipation of Polish women who are rewarded for getting a divorce because they get the kids and the money (in the form of child support)" (Interview with male leader, Warsaw, October 23, 2013).

Examining the strategies, goals, and frames that the fathers' groups used, we distinguished three strands of fathers' activism in Poland: groups of (1) "angry fathers"; (2) "fathers' advocates," and (3) "engaged fathers." All three strands overlap in terms of actual engagement of individual activists and forming coalitions, although internal conflicts also divide the fathers' movement (Śledzianowski 1999; Krajewska 2008; Wojnicka 2013).

As in other countries, all groups stress the social importance of fatherhood and fathering, and they claim their goal is to improve the situation of fathers, families, and children. Despite the important role of Catholicism in Poland, and in contrast to some other countries such as the United Sates, activists hardly ever stress religious elements, with the notable exception of *Fundacja Cyryla i Metodego* (Cyril and Methodius Foundation) located in Lublin, which will be discussed later.

The differences between the organizations and networks we studied concern the choice of strategies, levels of cooperation with the state, their goals, and the frames they employ. These strategic differences also reflect the family situation of men who joined them, which attests to the utmost importance of "private" experiences and the emotional component in fathers' activism (Wojnicka and Zierkiewicz 2014). Bertoia and Drakich (1993) observe that in the United States, most men appear to join fathers' groups mainly for personal reasons and personal gain, focusing on their private troubles. In Poland this depiction applies to the men active in the first two strands, but not the third. In the first two types of fathers' groups, the activists are most frequently recently divorced fathers who are still involved in court proceedings, whereas the third group of "engaged fathers" consists mostly of men who are married and do not have traumatic experiences with custody battles.

The first strand of activism comprises numerous informal groups and formal organizations of "angry fathers" (Bertoia and Drakich 1993), that Wojnicka and Zierkiewicz termed "hard-core antifeminists" (2014). The best example of this type of organization in Poland is Brave Dad, based in Warsaw. Members organize both online and offline, attracting considerable public attention to the concerns of postdivorce fathers. Brave Dad is known for its use of highly contentious strategies, such as sit-ins in front of Parliament and

Fig. 4.1 Group of activists during the "Fathers Demand Equality!" demonstration organized by fathers' rights organization Brave Dad on the occasion of the meeting arranged by the Government Plenipotentiary for Equal Treatment, Agnieszka Kozłowska-Rajewicz, on December 12, 2013, which was held to discuss discrimination of fathers in custody cases. The demonstration took place in front of the prime minister's office in Warsaw, where the meeting was organized. Photo by Elżbieta Korolczuk.

the courts, organizing marches and demonstrations, and employing controversial symbols and slogans, often strongly antifeminist ones. Due to their radical tactics they have become one of the most visible fathers' groups in Polish media, although such a choice of strategies makes it difficult to establish cooperation with more moderate groups and state institutions.

The second strand, which we termed "fathers' advocates," shares many of the convictions of the first group, but its activism focuses mostly on service provision, engaging in political lobbying, and it only rarely participates in direct protests. Organizations such as *Śląskie Stowarzyszenie Obrony Praw Ojca* (Silesian Association for the Defense of Fathers) and *Centrum Praw Ojca i Dziecka* (Center for Fathers' and Children's Rights) provide legal and emotional assistance to fathers.[8] In contrast to lawyers, which some of the fathers cannot afford, the activists offer personal case management, supporting the members in legal battles and helping them navigate the complexity of family laws. Some executive members engage in political advocacy, establishing adhoc

Fig. 4.2 "Stop discrimination of fathers!" and "Alternate care." Photo taken during the "White T-shirts March" organized to protest against the discrimination of fathers in custody cases. The march was organized by fathers' rights organization Brave Dad and held on May 21, 2015, in the center of Warsaw. Photo by Elżbieta Korolczuk.

coalitions with other groups in response to political openings. Some fathers' groups such as Warsaw-based Center for Fathers' and Children's Rights claim that they help not only men but also women in custody or child support cases.

The third group comprises organizations that promote "engaged fathering," such as Warsaw-based *Fundacja Akcja* (Action Foundation), *Fundacja Cyryla i Metodego* (Cyril and Methodius Foundation) located in Lublin, or *Fundacja Ojcostwo Mistrzostwo* (Fathers as Champions Foundation), which is active in Warsaw and in other smaller Polish cities. Most of these NGOs were established in the 2000s. They focus on popularizing engaged fatherhood, education, and consciousness raising campaigns addressed to fathers, and they sometimes also offer mediation and individual therapy for family members in time of crisis. The activists concentrate on increasing and deepening the quality of fathering, and problems stemming from postdivorce parenting such as custody and child support are not the main focus of their agenda. Some of these groups deliberately avoid debating these highly controversial and deeply politicized issues. One of the leaders we interviewed declared that he stopped cooperating with the group of postdivorce fathers because he did not want to deal with "fathers claiming that the child support, which amounts to 80 euro per month, is excessive" (Interview with male leader, Warsaw, February 12, 2014). In contrast to the first and second groups, the activists promoting "engaged fathering" do not build on their own divorce and postmarital conflict experiences, but rather stress (e.g., on the NGOs' website) that they are happily married, as if to distance themselves from organizations representing divorced men. This group of fathers' NGOs focuses on influencing public debate on fathering, and at times they also engage in political advocacy along with the other two strands of fathers' groups.

The "engaged fathers" strand is the most successful in establishing cooperation with state institutions as well as other NGOs. For example, *Action Foundation* was the most active member of *Forum na Rzecz Odpowiedzialnego Ojcostwa,* (Forum for Responsible Fatherhood), established in 2008, which worked with the state institutions to change the laws regarding custody. The forum's activities attest to the effectiveness of fathers' groups that are able to make use of the political openings, such as the one created in 2007 after the general elections. These openings included the appointment of the new Government Plenipotentiary for Equal Treatment, Elżbieta Radziszewska, who endorsed the conservative fathers' groups' agenda. With her support, the representatives of five organizations that made up the forum organized meetings with top state officials and advocated for changes in the Family and Guardianship Code in 2009 concerning the enforcement of courts' decisions to allow fathers to have contact with their children, and to present the court with an educational plan for children during the divorce. These changes were passed in the Parliament, although today most members of fathers' organizations do not see them as a success because in practice it proved to be very difficult to enforce both parents' compliance with the provisions of the new laws. Introduction of an educational plan for children, which both parents were supposed to agree on, turned out to be counterproductive. Since many parents were not able to agree on such a plan, many judges decided to give custody to one parent only, usually the mother, automatically restricting custody rights of the other parent; also, the percentage of cases where custody was given to both mother and father dropped under this period (from 41% in 2009 to 33% in 2012) (*MS: Zmiany prawa*, 2013). Consequently, further amendments in the Family and Guardianship Code were introduced in 2015, stating that children have the right to have contact with both parents; thus decisions to restrict custody rights should be made only in special cases.

Framing Fathers' Activism in Contemporary Poland

There are some recurrent frames that fathers' activists use that were identified across different countries (Bertoia and Drakich 1993; Crowley 2006; Wojnicka 2013; Saxonberg in the present volume). The fathers' activists often claim they are victims of discrimination and injustice in family courts and other state institutions. They want to reestablish paternal authority and have unhindered access to their children after divorce, blaming mothers and/or state institutions for the growing divorce rates and difficulties that fathers encounter after divorce.

The choice of frames stems partly from emotional and contextual factors, such as the fact that men usually join fathers' groups after experiencing a painful divorce and the loss of contact with their children, but it also depends on local cultural and political trends. For example, in the United States contemporary fathers' activism operates in the context of the growing concern about "the epidemic of fatherlessness" and dire social consequences of growing up in single-parent families, especially in African-American communities (Crowley 2006; Dowd 2000). In response to this trend, organizations such as the National Fatherhood Initiative promulgate the view that engaging men (especially men of color) in fathering is the key to solving many social and economic problems including poverty, emotional, and behavioral problems as well as maternal and child health (National Fatherhood Initiative). Similar views also appear in Germany where lack of father figures has been interpreted as one of the reasons for the emergence of authoritarian tendencies (Ostner 2002). References to the social consequences of fatherlessness are also made in the texts and statements of some of the Polish fathers' organizations, especially the ones that collaborate with American organizations (sometimes in the form of translated texts), but this theme is by no means the most prevalent one.

In Poland we identified three main frames employed by different strands of the fathers' movement. It should be stressed, however, that these frames do not necessarily correspond with the three different organizational strands presented above. Rather, the representatives of a specific group may use different frames depending on the context and audience, even though some leaders and groups tend to prefer one or another specific frame. We argue that this flexibility of choice regarding which frames they use reflects the hybrid nature of contemporary discourses and ideologies of fatherhood in Poland. In this case, hybridity refers to flexibly fusing different and contradictory discourses on fatherhood such as the patriarchal vision of an all-powerful father and the new ideal of a sensitive and caring man.

Misogynist Frame

The first frame highlights fathers' rights as men. At its core lies the assumption popular among fathers' rights activists in Poland and elsewhere (such as the United States and Canada) that fathers are discriminated against by the alleged "maternal preference in awarding custody, maternal control of the children, and maternal financial privilege" (Bertoia and Drakich 1993, 597–598). The activists demand a more gender-equal approach, but in their utterances equality is usually limited to court decisions on custody, whereas issues such as fathers' leave or the need for fathers' greater engagement in everyday care are not discussed.[9] This frame represents women, "feminized" family courts and feminism in general as the main adversaries of fathers. In texts published on the Polish fathers' internet sites, and even in the interviews we conducted with leaders of these groups, some activists refer to women as cunning and ruthless gold-diggers, who use the children as "hostages" to "rip off" ex-husbands, treating them as ATMs.[10] As one of our male interviewees explained, "it is because women always look for men to provide for them. Women are like monkeys, they would not let go of one branch before they find another" (Interview with male leader, Warsaw, November 23, 2013). These fathers attribute their individual problems to feminism, political correctness, and moral laxity that, in their view, the state supports and strengthens in its social policies related to custody and divorce. This helps the activists legitimize their claims to gain full custody rights, placing the reasons for crises in marriage outside of fathers themselves and beyond their control (Kubicki 2009).

Characteristic of this misogynistic type of framing is militant language on both the textual and visual levels. Court cases are compared to "battles" and the fathers have to "fight" in "the war over children" and against the mothers who "sabotage" fathers. Women are depicted as possibly dangerous to their children: on the webpage of Brave Dad, there is a page dedicated solely to cases of women who murdered their children.[11]

Typical of this frame is its highly emotional tone. Fathers who appear on videos are often agitated and angry when they talk about their love for children

Fig. 4.3 "We fight for the right to raise our children." Photo taken during the "White T-shirts March" organized to protest against the discrimination of fathers in custody cases. The march was organized by fathers' rights organization Brave Dad and held on May 21, 2015, in the center of Warsaw. Photo by Elżbieta Korolczuk.

and the emotional pain of separation (see also Wojnicka and Zierkiewicz 2014). They make clear that they are the victims. One of the activists, in a short film posted on the NGOs page, describes taking away his son as the "murder" committed against the father, and on the internet site of Brave Dad there is a drawing depicting a man who hanged himself on a tree, with a woman and a child on a swing on the other side of the tree who seem to be having a good time.[12]

This frame combines different and often contradictory elements of "caring" and "patriarchal" masculinity. For example, men are presented as highly emotional, attached to their children, and generally good caring parents. During demonstrations and public meetings they often carry the pictures of their children and stress how much they value the family.

At the same time, the frame also heavily stresses "traditional" patriarchal masculinity with its critique of women's emancipation, focus on solidarity among men, and the need for men to regain control and take back "their right place"

Fig. 4.4 "Family, family, family . . ." Photo taken during "White T-shirts March" organized to protest against the discrimination of fathers in custody cases. The march was organized by fathers' rights organization Brave Dad and held on May 21, 2015, in the center of Warsaw. Photo by Elżbieta Korolczuk.

in society. To further enhance the strong male community image, the video of the official Brave Dad anthem depicts a group of stern-looking men, a rapper getting a tattoo, and a military unit doing exercises on the polygon (Biały feat Magda 2011). Radical, highly emotional and sensational, such messages attract some deeply disenchanted fathers, but it also discourages others and increasingly impedes cooperation with state institutions and other NGOs and movements, such as women's organizations—although Brave Dad, for example, has cooperated with some women's groups that oppose feminism and gender equality.

Focusing on the frame of "fathers' rights as men" is common among fathers' rights activists all over the world, but in contemporary Poland this frame is highly politicized and infused with nationalist and xenophobic discourse and imagery. The activists eagerly employ national symbols, including the Polish national anthem, make references to Polish military history and patriotic literature; for example, they use images of medieval knights in full armor with the logo of Brave Dad on the banners, which they display at marches and on their website. This historicizing, hero-invoking stance is also reflected in making alliances with right-wing conservative groups and participating in the events organized by these environments, such as the nationalist marches organized to celebrate Polish Independence Day.

The leaders of Brave Dad claimed in the interview that the group's occasional alliance with right-wing organizations reflects their desperation to find support rather than their actual political views. However, the use of homophobic, xenophobic, or anti-Semitic language during interviews and in texts published online suggests otherwise. For example, some activists claim that their rights as heterosexual men are being restricted whereas homosexual men will soon get the right to adopt children, which supposedly shows how unjust and corrupt the current political and judicial system is. Other ethnic/religious/sexual minority groups are targeted as well. For example, in a recent report on the activism of fathers' rights in Poland in a conservative TV channel, Republika, one of the activists accused Anna Grodzka, by then an MP and the only transsexual Polish politician, of attempting to "put him into jail for fighting for his children" (*Zadanie specjalne* 2013). The following passage, published on the front page of the Brave Dad internet page, also demonstrates that antifeminism is often interwoven with xenophobic and even anti-Semitic discourses on the textual level:

> [Mothers] do everything to rip fathers off. It goes like this: the wife asks her husband to take a loan and buy a flat, and when he does so, she moves out and takes the child as a hostage and demands a ransom. This is done in order

> to make the father pay the loan and child support. If the father refuses, the mother . . . this Jewish slut, moves out to find another sucker. . . . The law that has been introduced by the Jewish-Communists (*żydo-komunę*) makes you kidnap your own child if you want to stay in touch with him. (www.dzielny-tato.pl, accessed on September 10, 2014)

A misogynist frame is not only a part of the transnational antifeminist discourse, it is also a manifestation of a conservative trend in contemporary Polish society within which antifeminism is intimately linked to (gendered) nationalism and xenophobia (Graff 2008; cf. Yuval-Davis and Werbner 1999). The latest stage of this trend in Poland is the "war on gender," which involves targeting feminists, LGBT organizations, sex educators, state administrators, and ultimately all groups and individuals promoting ideals of gender equality, advocating for sex education in schools, and defending the rights of sexual minorities—all of whom conservative groups and representatives of the Catholic Church see as their enemies (Grzebalska 2015, Graff and Korolczuk 2017, Korolczuk 2014). Some fathers' networks openly support "the war against gender." For example, one of our interviewees claimed that

> the ideology of feminism has conquered both the USA and Europe, and they are now infused by gender ideology which creates even more of a fuss in the sphere of the family. When something becomes fashionable, this does not necessarily mean that it is good. (Interview with male leader, Warsaw, December 4, 2013)

Within this framework the fight for fathers' rights as men exceeds the interest of individual fathers, and it becomes an element of a broader struggle against liberal and feminist influences in the contemporary world. In early 2015, the Brave Dad Party appeared as a new political party. Its leaders claim that they will not only oppose discrimination against fathers in courts, but also deal with other social and economic problems, such as reprivatization, which they refer to as "economic swindles" and "selling-off of national assets." This shows that even though fathers' activists often denounce politics, in practice the boundary between civil society, understood as grassroots organizing, and political society of party politics is porous.

State Violence Frame

The second frame, "state violence," highlights fathers' rights as citizens and focuses on the relationship with the state rather than ex-spouses or women in general. This framing problematizes what activists perceive as the partiality of judges toward mothers and it stresses the inefficiency of the

Polish legal system, as well as "the state's arbitrary intervention in the private sphere."[13] As one of our interviewees stated,

> once you enter the court, everything becomes a problem. One needs to know how to behave, which documents to present, when and how to approach the judge. If you enter the court, even with your knowledge and education, you would know how difficult it is to talk to those in power. (Interview with male leader, Lublin, December 12, 2013)

Whereas the first misogynist frame stresses that women are guilty of a masculinity crisis and discrimination toward fathers, the second strand highlights the state-sponsored violation of fathers' rights. The dominant emotion that this frame displays is powerlessness vis-à-vis state institutions, which are usually but not necessarily represented by women. The imbalance of power between individual and the state makes it crucial to support other men who are in the same situation, and to share information about how court proceedings work. Even though the activists are not lawyers, they can offer insider knowledge that strengthens individual fathers' sense of agency and confidence.

Stressing that men are victims of state violence and injustice is part of the framing that the fathers' groups have applied in many countries, including Australia, the United States, and Spain (Flood 2012; Municio-Larsson and Pujol Algans 2002). In the Polish context, the belief that the state is an oppressor is further strengthened by recent history and the interpretation that the judiciary system—the 1964 Family and Guardianship Code, as well as Family Consultative and Diagnostic Centers (RODK) established in 1983, are all remnants of the state socialist period.[14] Thus, the frame of "state violence" reflects the argument that the state controls the private sphere and "destroys the family" in order to take control of citizens. According to this narrative, fathers are fighting a losing battle as citizens because they suffer from the imbalance of power and knowledge between them and the judicial system. Many activists who use this frame also argue that the feminization of the judiciary, which is interpreted as one of the main factors behind what they see as blatant discrimination against fathers, was inherited from communist times. Even if, according to some activists, male judges are just as hostile to fathers as female judges are, others still claim that "they are usually the sons of the female judges who were themselves divorced and raised their sons in hatred and contempt toward their fathers" (Interview with male leader, Warsaw, November 23, 2013).

The frame of "state violence" reflects the hegemonic narrative in Poland that the communist period is at the root of many contemporary social and institutional evils in the country. Following the internal logic of this argument, it is necessary to dismiss and/or denigrate all possible achievements of the communist era, among them welfare-state institutions and emancipation of women through labor market participation. All remnants of the communist state institutions have to be liquidated in the process of democratization of the country—this concerns both the very idea of state intervention within the private sphere and specific state institutions, such as the RODKs, that are supposed to offer diagnostic and counseling services in the case of postmarital conflicts over custody.

In the narratives of some of the leading activists, the fight for the elimination of RODK that they started becomes not only a necessity, but it is an equivalent to a patriotic mission that needs to be accomplished.

> These centers (RODK) were established (in the 1980s) to destroy the democratic opposition. They were supposed to take away the activists' children and isolate these kids in state-run juvenile correction facilities. This was supposed to weaken the democratic opposition working to dismantle the communist system. A lot changed after 1989 . . . but not the law. (Fabisiak 2015)

In the framework of state violence, fathers fighting for custody rights are fighting not only on behalf of themselves and their children, but on behalf of all citizens oppressed by the Polish state corrupted by its past. The fathers' activities are interpreted as an effort to get rid of the sick "remnants" of the communist system, and their activism becomes legitimized as an integral part of the process of normalization and democratization in the country.

Gender Equality Frame

The third frame concerns fathers' activism and engagement as part of a gender equality agenda. Comparable to other contexts, Polish fathers' groups define "gender equality" in terms of equal chances for custody and equal treatment in court cases. As in the case of Czech or Ukrainian activists (Saxonberg and Karzabi in the present volume), many fathers stress their equal competences when it comes to taking care of their children, but they usually subscribe to the patriarchal vision of gender roles as complementary rather than equivalent. An example of such attitude was one of our interviewees who expressed the opinion that the fathers' groups' fight for joint custody will "help women because they will be relieved of half of the work," but gave the following account of his family life prior to divorce:

> My wife complained about me, she kept saying that I don't help her with the baby. And yes, I used to organize parties for my friends. He was just a little kid by then, he was a year old. It is hard to say what I could do as a father, what could I do? I couldn't breastfeed him, I couldn't take care of him, because fathers are supposed to get involved in children's lives at a later stage. (Interview with male leader, Warsaw, November 23, 2013)

This shows that the expression "half of the work" may not reflect the actual amount of caring that fathers do, especially in the case of younger children. In fact, most fathers' activists seem to be of the opinion that during the first couple of years it is the mother who should be the primary or even sole care provider to the child. When asked if they would like to have full custody of their children, most interviewees stated that they want to have contact with them, but they did not seek full custody and do not envision themselves as the main care providers. The activists' responses reflect a view that is rather common in Poland, namely that "the mother is more important in the first period of a child's life, and [men] do not really see a space for the father during this period" (Suwada and Platin 2014, 516).

This narrow interpretation of gender equality is not unique to Poland, even though in other sociocultural contexts, such as Canada, some fathers' groups tend to employ a broader interpretation of this term. These activists focus on "co-parenting and continuing parent-child relationships, [which] are couched in the deeply held principles of "equality" and "right"" (Bertoia and Drakich 1993, 592). Such framing may resonate well in the Anglo-Saxon context, but in the case of the Polish fathers' movement, the promotion of "gender equality" is often explicitly linked to the "traditional" family and Catholic values, in support of both engaged fatherhood and the limited interpretation of equality in parenting. Within this framework some elements of the patriarchal model of fathering (which references fathers' responsibility, control, and reliability as values) are combined with a new ideal of "engaged fathering" (which involves spending time with a child and providing child care). It appears, however, that it is the patriarchal norm that guides practice.

An illustrative example of the ambiguous character of equality framework can be found on the internet site of the Cyril and Methodius Foundation. This organization states that its mission is stimulating interfaith dialogue and counteracting discrimination in relation to gender, faith, nationality, and beliefs. The main target audience of the foundation is fathers who are offered education and training to help them become responsible, engaged parents able to balance professional and familial obligations. Among educational materials targeted for fathers one can find many articles and tutorials explaining issues such as "masculinity and fatherhood," "how to protect your family," or "providing the children with what they need." One of the articles—which, according to the information provided, was originally published on the Christian site Mateusz.pl—includes the paragraph in which anonymous authors explain that

> when God created a woman from man's rib to help him . . . he was aimed at perfection and complementary vision of mankind, which is reflected in gender differences. . . . One aspect of gender differences concerns the emotional sphere. Men are usually undemanding or even blind to emotions. In a marriage he wants to build a small financially stable state on a solid background, of which he would be a sole ruler. (Tatonet.pl)

This passage is by no means unique. It shows how the idea of gender equality is being reinterpreted according to fathers' organizations' own aims.

Highlighting gender equality in the different-but-equal sense appears as a strategic choice that is used in specific contexts to achieve the organizations' goals. Referencing gender equality helps to counteract negative opinions that fathers' activists fight for their own interests rather than on behalf of children and society in general. It also enables some of the fathers' organizations to establish cooperation with other NGOs, including women's groups. Such framing also facilitates collaboration with the state as it fits the (limited) way in which the notion of gender equality has been implemented in Poland in the context of gender mainstreaming and pronatalist social policy (Hryciuk and Korolczuk 2015).

Conclusions

We identified three main frames that the Polish fathers' groups' activists employed: (1) "misogynist" frame, (2) "state violence" frame, and (3) "gender equality" frame. Each of these frames combines, to a different degree, transnational and local discourses on fathering, the family, and gender. Different fathers' groups employ them interchangeably, depending on the context, which reflects the hybrid nature of contemporary ideals of fatherhood and practices of fathering, where hybridity connotes flexibly mixing conservative, nationalist, and postmodern elements.

This amalgamation of apparently contradictory aspects points to the contentious character of contemporary discourses and practices of fatherhood and gender. It shows that what we witness today is not an inevitable transition from an imagined traditional patriarchal model to a gender-equal one, but rather the emergence of a hybrid model that combines select elements of the various, otherwise rather incompatible, norms and ideals. For example, some components of the gender equality agenda, such as fathers taking an active part in their children's upbringing, have become an integral part of the contemporary Polish ideal of fathering, whereas others, such as fathers' financial responsibility for children after divorce, have not. Thus, the meaning of the notion of "engaged fatherhood" or "daddyism" remains negotiable and varies depending on the context in which this issue is discussed.

The analysis of the Polish fathers' activism shows that this case bears a significant resemblance to fathers' movements in other countries, in their common focus on custody, antifeminist rhetoric, and conditionality of fathers' financial responsibility for children after divorce. This is hardly surprising given that analyses show many connections and commonalities between groups operating in different national contexts and internationally (Flood 2012). Some scholars even propose to use the term "fathers' rights movement" to refer to these groups as they function either within national boundaries or across them (Collier and Sheldon 2006, 2).

There are also some significant differences between the frames that fathers' activists use, which reflects specificity of the local context and also considerable diversity within a single national context. Polish activists only marginally discuss issues central in other countries, such as the social ills resulting from fatherlessness, which is a theme prominent in the United States and Germany, or promotion of active fatherhood as a way to increase the fertility rate, which is a frame present in contemporary Russia and Ukraine (Åberg and Rodin; Karzabi in this volume). There are also no fathers' groups in Poland framing their claims in terms of social and economic discrimination of specific groups of men, for example, disabled fathers as in the case of Ukraine (Karzabi in this volume). Finally, in contrast to most fathers' organizations in Sweden and some in other countries such as the United States and Canada, Polish activists only note the need for gender equality for both men and women in the context of court proceedings after divorce: they merge elements of gender-equal parenting practices with the patriarchal vision of masculinity claiming that men should be in full control over women and children.

The types of frames that social movements use reflect themes that have wide social resonance or concepts that are held in reverence in the national culture. This explains why fathers' groups use the threat of the "fatherless nation" to gain social resonance in the United States but not in Poland, where fatherlessness is not perceived as a social problem and where the local national gendered imagery sanctions absent fathers and self-sacrificing mothers. Local specificity of the Polish fathers' movement is also reflected in how the activists of the militant fraction of the movement effectively combine nationalist and anticommunist rhetoric with an antifeminist stance. They employ nationalist and xenophobic discourses, interpreting their fight as part of what they perceive as the larger social conflict concerning national identity and post-1989 transformation. The activists tend to attribute what they see as discrimination against fathers to the legacy of the previous state-socialist political system, with its model of the state as a superior power intervening in the private matters of the family, marginalizing citizens' own interests and promoting gender equality and feminism. In arguing that discrimination of fathers in Poland results from social policies introduced under communism, they link their fight with a larger cultural trend toward de-communization and democratic consolidation of the country. Similarly, opposing feminism and gender equality discourses and practices allows them to become part of a broader campaign against liberal forces that allegedly endanger the Polish nation and ultimately Christian civilization.

Renata E. Hryciuk, Assistant Professor, Institute of Ethnology and Cultural Anthropology, University of Warsaw, Poland

Renata Hryciuk is an anthropologist, Latin Americanist. Her recent research projects focus on social movements (parents' activism in Poland) and the impact of heritage tourism on local foodways and gender roles in Oaxaca (Southern Mexico). She was awarded research grants from the Mexican government (1999–2000, 2005–2006, 2011, 2016–2017), Norwegian government (2006), Swedish Institute (2011–2012), and Swedish Research Council (2012–2014). She is the co-editor (with Agnieszka Kościańska) of a two-volume reader in gender and anthropology, *Gender: An Anthropological Perspective* (in Polish), and (with Elżbieta Korolczuk) she co-edited two volumes: *Farewell to the Polish Mother? Discourses, Practices, and Representations of Motherhood in Contemporary Poland* (in Polish) and *Dangerous Liaisons: Motherhood, Fatherhood and Politics* (in Polish), and (with Joanna Mroczkowska) *Food: Anthropological Perspective. (Post)socialism* (in Polish).

Elżbieta Korolczuk, researcher, School of Culture and Education, Södertörn University, Sweden

Elżbieta Korolczuk, PhD is a sociologist working at Södertörn University in Sweden. She also teaches at the Gender Studies Centre at Warsaw University in Poland. Her research interests include social movements, civil society and gender (especially motherhood/fatherhood, assisted reproductive technologies and feminism). Recently, she conducted research on parental activism and social and legal implications of assisted reproduction in Poland, and on gender and political cultures of knowledge. She co-edited (with Renata E. Hryciuk) two volumes (in Polish): *Farewell to the Polish Mother: Discourses, Practices and Representations of Motherhood in Contemporary Poland* (2012), which explores ideologies and practices of motherhood in Poland, and *Dangerous Liaisons: Motherhood, Fatherhood and Politics* (2015), which focuses on the intersection between motherhood, fatherhood, and politics in Poland and Russia. Most recent publications include an edited volume (with Kerstin Jacobsson) *Civil Society Revisited: Lessons from Poland* published by Berghahn Books in April 2017.

Notes

1. We are grateful to Katalin Fábián, Kerstin Jacobsson, Katarzyna Wojnicka, and colleagues who took part in the seminar held at the University of Gothenburg in June 2015 and at the seminar at the Institute of Ethnology and Cultural Anthropology University of Warsaw in January 2015, for offering helpful comments on earlier versions of this chapter. Our research was supported by the Swedish Research Council-funded project, "Institutional Constraints and Creative Solutions: Civil Society in Poland in Comparative Perspective" (grant 421–2010–1706).

2. All respondents are anonymized and interviews are assigned the name of the city and date. We anonymized not only the activists, but also professionals because they spoke off the record. We are very grateful to our interviewees for agreeing to talk to us and to have us at their meetings. All quotes are translated by the authors.

3. Most researchers use the term "child support" or "child maintenance" to stress that these are payments made to the children and not to the ex-spouse (as is alimony). Although Polish law allows for paying alimony to the ex-spouse in some cases (e.g., disability) it is a very rare practice. Child support payments are commonly referred to as alimony, as reflected in the name Alimony Fund (*Fundusz Alimentacyjny*). Thus, we use the term "alimony" and "child support payment" interchangeably when referring to money paid to the resident parent by a nonresident one to cover child-raising expenses.

4. Welfare systems differ in how they may guarantee child support payments. In some cases, the state guarantees such payments, as in Austria, Estonia, Germany, Hungary, Italy, and Sweden. In others, local authorities are the grantors, as in the Czech Republic, Denmark, and Finland. In a third group of cases, a special administrative agency is responsible as in The Netherlands and the UK. In other countries where such institutions exist, child maintenance can also be guaranteed by private agencies or insurance companies (Beaumont and Mason 2014).

5. Following Anna Titkow (2014, 250), we define the "gender contract" as a set of rules and principles that organize the relationship between men and women on institutional, cultural, and individual levels.

6. CBOS' report "On women's role in the family" (2013) shows that even though gender equal arrangements are preferred by most respondents, women are still disproportionally more engaged in everyday tasks such as cleaning, ironing, washing dishes, and taking care of children.

7. The billboards feature a depiction of a small angel-like child and the slogan reads "Feminists! Use your brains before intercourse! Stop fucking around!" The phrase "stop fucking around" is a wordplay which connotes both having sex and saying something nonsensical, the message being that the right to abortion would not be needed if only feminists refrain from having unprotected sex.

8. As already indicated, there are some overlaps between organizations and strands. Both of these groups cooperate with *Brave Dad*, but they remain separate in their organizational structures with their own repertoire of goals, strategies, and activities.

9. When asked about these issues during interviews most activists answered that they did not see any connection between promoting fathers' leave and engagement and getting custody after divorce.

10. The gender of the activists did not determine if they accepted such a view or not, as the case of a group called *Forum Matek* (Mothers' Forum) shows. This small but vocal group of well-educated, middle-class retired women provides the fathers' groups with legal expertise and administrative work (e.g., helping individual fathers in preparing for cases in courts), and it supports them during public meetings and protests, promoting misogynist and antifeminist views. The leaders of Mother's Forum are also active in political lobbying, writing letters to state authorities, and taking part in meetings with authorities.

11. Last accessed January 12, 2015. dzielnytata.pl/mord.htm. The implied message is that although domestic violence is most often attributed to men, mothers are dangerous to their children, too. The first photo on the page depicts a well-known Polish feminist activist saying that "violence is gendered and it is of a male gender," while the rest of the page contains clips from newspapers depicting mothers accused of murdering their children.

12. Last accessed on May 22, 2015. www.dzielnytata.pl. The drawing features the articles in civil and penal laws ("Art. 26 KC, 58 KRiO i 107 KRiO") that the activists perceive as discriminatory against fathers. For example, Article 26 of the Civil Law states that the child should live with the parent who has custody or with whom the child currently resides.

13. The quote is a translation of a Brave Dad activist's statement made during a TV program on fathers' rights activism on TV Republika (*Zadanie specjalne* 2013).

14. Family Consultative and Diagnostic Centers (RODK) were established by the ordinance of the Ministry of Justice. Such centers engage psychologists, counselors, and educationists to provide guidance, care and diagnostics to family courts in cases including minors (Gronowska 1990).

Works Cited

Arcimowicz, Krzysztof. 2009. "Wizerunek ojca w polskich mediach" [Fathers' Images in Polish Media]. In *Nowi mężczyźni. Zmieniające się modele męskości we współczesnej Polsce* [*New Men. Changing Models of Masculinity in Contemporary Poland*], edited by Małgorzata Fuszara, 187–221. Trio: Warszawa.

Badzian, Dorota. 2010. "Ojcowie w polskich sądach rodzinnych jako ofiary męskiej dominacji" [Fathers in Polish Family Courts as Victims of Male Domination], unpublished B.A. thesis, Institute of Ethnology and Cultural Anthropology, University of Warsaw.

Beaumont, Karolina, and Paul Mason. 2014. *Child Maintenance Systems in EU Member States in Gender Perspective.* Accessed June 12, 2015. http://www.europarl.europa.eu/RegData/etudes/note/join/2014/474407/IPOL-FEMM_NT%282014%29474407_EN.pdf.

Benford, Robert D., and David A. Snow. 2000. "Framing Processes and Social Movements: An Overview and Assessment." *Annual Review of Sociology* 26:611–639.

Bertoia, Carl, and Janice Drakich. 1993. "The Fathers' Rights Movement." *Journal of Family Issues* 14 (4):592–615.

Biały feat Magda. 2011. "Walczę do końca" [I Will Fight till the End]. November 10. Accessed January 21, 2015. https://www.youtube.com/watch?v=3369MuOZTCs.

Bierca, Marta. 2013. "'Tacierzyństwo' w sieci—analiza nowego trendu i jego socjologiczne aplikacje" ['Daddyism' Online—Analysis of New Trend and Its Sociological Implications]. *InterAlia. A Journal of Queer Studies* 8:78–90.

Blais, Melissa, and Francis Dupuis-Déri. 2012. "Masculinism and the Antifeminist Countermovement." *Social Movement Studies* 11 (1):21–39.

Budrowska, Bogusława. 2008. "Tacierzyństwo, czyli nowy wzór ojcostwa" ['Daddyism' as the New Model of Fatherhood]. *Kultura i Społeczeństwo* 52 (3):123–151.

CBOS. 2013. "On Women's Role in the Family." Accessed January 12, 2015. http://www.cbos.pl/SPISKOM.POL/2013/K_030_13.PDF.

Clarke, Sue, and Jannie Popay. 1998. "'I'm Just a Bloke Who's Had Kids': Men and Women on Fatherhood." In *Men, Gender Divisions and Welfare*, edited by Jannie Popay, Jeff Hearn, and Jeannette Edwards. London: Routledge.

Collier, Richard, and Sally Sheldon, eds. 2006. *Fathers' Rights Activism and Law Reform in Comparative Perspective.* Oxford and Portland: Hart Publishing.

Crowley, Jocelyn Elise. 2006. "Organizational Responses to the Fatherhood Crisis: The Case of Fathers' Rights Groups in the United States." *Marriage and Family Review* 39 (1–2):99–120.

———. 2008. *Defiant Dads: Fathers' Rights Activists in America.* Ithaca: Cornell University Press.

Desperak, Iza, ed. 2008. *Homofobia, Mizoginia i Ciemnogród? Burzliwe Losy Kontrowersyjnych Ustaw* [*Homophobia, Misogyny, and Backwardness. Controversial Regulations in Poland*]. Łódź: Omega Praxis.

Dowd, Nancy. 2000. *Redefining Fatherhood*. New York: New York University Press.

Dzwonkowska-Godula, Krystyna. 2011. "Publiczny dyskurs o współczesnym ojcostwie w Polsce" [Public Discourse on Contemporary Fatherhood in Poland]. In *Karuzela z mężczyznami* [Merry-go-round with Men], edited by Katarzyna Wojnicka and Ewelina Ciaputa, 113–138. Oficyna Wydawnicza Impuls: Kraków

Eldén, Sara. 2002. "Gender Politics in Conservative Men's Movements: Beyond Complexity, Ambiguity and Pragmatism." *NORA—Nordic Journal of Feminist and Gender Research* 10 (1):38–48.

Esseveld, Johanna, and Ron Eyerman. 1992. "Which Side Are You On? Reflections on Methodological Issues in the Study of 'Distasteful' Social Movements." In *Studying Collective Action*, vol. 30, edited by Mario Diani and Ron Eyerman. London: SAGE.

Fabisiak, Michał. 2015. "Dzielny Tata." Last modified July 20. http://dzielnytata.pl/RODK.htm.

Faludi, Susan. 1991. *Backlash: The Undeclared War Against American Women*. New York: Three Rivers' Press.

Flood, Michel. 2012. "Separated Fathers and the Fathers' Rights Movement." *Journal of Family Studies* 18 (2–3):235–245.

Funk, Nanette, and Magda Mueller, eds. 1993. *Gender Politics and Post-Communism: Reflections from Eastern Europe and the Former Soviet Union*. New York: Routledge.

Fuszara, Małgorzata, ed. 2008. *Nowi mężczyźni? Zmieniające się modele męskości we współczesnej Polsce* [*New Men? Changing Masculinity Models in Contemporary Poland*]. Warszawa: Trio.

Gal, Susan, and Kligman Gal, eds. 2000. *Reproducing Gender. Politics, Publics and Everyday Life after Socialism*. Princeton, NJ: Princeton University Press.

Gębka, Mikołaj. 2006. "Trzy pytania o kryzys ojcostwa" [Three Questions Concerning the Crisis of Fatherhood]. *Roczniki Socjologii Rodziny* XVII:117–137.

Graff, Agnieszka. 2008. "The Return of Real Men and Real Women: Gender and EU Accession in Three Polish Weeklies." In *Global Empowerment of Women*, edited by C. Elliot, 191–212. London and New York: Routledge.

Graff, Agnieszka, and Elżbieta Korolczuk. 2017 (forthcoming). "Worse than Communism and Nazism Put Together': War on Gender in Poland." In *Anti-Gender Campaigns in Europe Mobilizing against Equality*, edited by Roman Kuhar and David Paternotte. London: Rowman & Littlefield International.

Gronowska, Bożena. 1990. "The Role of Personality Diagnosis in Decisions of Judges in Juvenile Cases." In *Erziehung und Strafe: Jugendstrafrecht in der Bundesrepublik Deutschland und Polen—Grundfragen und Zustandsbeschreibung Taschenbuch*, edited by Wolff von Jörg and Andrzej Marek, 176–184. Berlin: Forum Verlag.

Grzebalska, Weronika. 2015. "Poland." In *Gender as Symbolic Glue: The Position and Role of Conservative and Far Right Parties in the Anti-Gender-Mobilization*, edited by Eszter Kováts and Maari Põim, 83–103. Budapest: FEPS.

Hobson, Barbara, and David Morgan. 2002. *Making Men into Fathers: Men, Masculinities and the Social Politics of Fatherhood*. Cambridge: Cambridge University Press.

Hryciuk, Renata E., and Elżbieta Korolczuk. 2010. "Poland." In *Encyclopedia of Mothering*, edited by Andrea O'Reilly, 990–992. Thousand Oaks, CA: SAGE.

———. 2013. "At the Intersection of Gender and Class: Social Mobilization Around Mothers' Rights in Poland." In *Beyond NGO-ization. The Development of Social*

Movements in Central and Eastern Europe, edited by Kerstin Jacobsson and Steven Saxonberg, 49–70. Farnham: Ashgate.

———. 2015. "Konteksty upolitycznienia macierzyństwa i ojcostwa we współczesnej Polsce" [Politicizing Mothering and Fathering in Contemporary Poland]. In *Niebezpieczne związki. Macierzyństwo, ojcostwo i polityka* [*Dangerous Liaisons. Motherhood, Fatherhood and Politics*], edited by Renata E. Hryciuk and Elżbieta Korolczuk, 11–44. Warszawa: Warsaw University Press.

Hryciuk, Renata E., 2017. "On the Disappearing Mother. Political Motherhood, Citizenship, and Neoliberalism in Poland." In *Civil Society Revisited. Lessons from Poland*, edited by Kerstin Jacobsson and Elżbieta Korolczuk. New York, Oxford: Berghahn.

Kłos, Bożena, and Jolanta Szymańczak. 2003. *Fundusz Alimentacyjny* [*Alimony Fund*]. Biuro Studiów i Ekspertyz, Kancelaria Sejmu [Bureau for Research and Professional Assessment, Chancellery of the Sejm]. Warszawa.

Korab, Kazimierz. 2006. "Kryzys i odradzanie się ojcostwa. Przykład inicjatywy Tato. net" [Crisis and Rebirth of Fatherhood. The Example of Tato.Net Initiative], presentation during the National Day of Life, special session held at Polish Parliament. March 23. Accessed January 20, 2015. http://old.tato.net/engine.php?attr=c3RyPTQ3NSZnbTozJm1pZDozJmxhbmdpZDox.

Korolczuk, Elżbieta. 2014. "'The War on Gender' from a Transnational Perspective—Lessons for Feminist Strategizing." In *Proceedings of III International Gender Workshop "Are We Moving Forward or Backwards? Strategizing to Overcome Gender Backlash in Central and Eastern Europe."* Berlin.

Krajewska, Anna. 2008. "Konteksty ojcostwa" [Contextualizing Faterhood]. In *Nowi mężczyźni. Zmieniające się modele męskości we współczesnej Polsce* [*New Men. Changing Models of Masculinity in Contemporary Poland*], edited by Małgorzata Fuszara. Warszawa: TRIO.

Kubicki, Paweł. 2009. "Przemiany ojcostwa we współczesnej Polsce" [Transformation of Fatherhood in Contemporary Poland]. In *Być rodzicem we współczesnej Polsce. Nowe wzory w konfrontacji ze współczesnością* [*To Be a Parent in Contemporary Poland. New Ideals in Confrontation with Contemporary World*], edited by Małgorzata Sikorska, 77–105. Warszawa: Warsaw University Press.

Łaciak, Beata. 2008. "Medialny obraz mężczyzn w relacjach małżeńskich i rodzinnych" [Media Representation of Men in Family and Marriage]. In *Nowi mężczyźni. Zmieniające się modele męskości we współczesnej Polsce* [*New Men. Changing Models of Masculinity in Contemporary Poland*], edited by Małgorzata Fuszara, 151–187. Warszawa: TRIO.

"MS: Zmiany prawa ws. opieki nad dziećmi po rozwodzie na razie niewskazane" [Ministry of Justice: Changes in Custody Laws are Inadvisable]. 2013. *Onet*, December 20. Accessed July 20, 2015. http://wiadomosci.onet.pl/kraj/ms-zmiany-prawa-ws-opieki-nad-dziecmi-po-rozwodzie-na-razie-niewskazane/p2gr2.

Municio-Larsson, Ingegerd, and Carmen Pujol Algans. 2002. "Making Sense of Fatherhood: The Non-Payment of Child support in Spain." In *Making Men into Fathers*, edited by Barbara Hobson, 191–212. Cambridge: Cambridge University Press.

"National Fatherhood Initiative." Accessed February 12, 2015. http://www.fatherhood.org/father-absence-statistics.

Ostner, Ilona. 2002. "A New Role for Fathers? The German Case." In *Making Men into Fathers—Men, Masculinities and the Social Politics of Fatherhood*, edited by Barbara Hobson, 150–167. Cambridge: Cambridge University Press.

Rodin, Johnny, and Pelle Åberg. 2013. "Fatherhood across Space and Time: Russia in Perspective." *Baltic Worlds* 6 (3–4):21–28.

Sikorska, Małgorzata. 2009. *Nowa matka, nowy ojciec, nowe dziecko. O nowym układzie sił w polskich rodzinach* [*New Mother, New Father, New Child. On New Power Relations in Polish Families*]. Warsaw: Wydawnictwa Akademickie i Profesjonalne [Academic and Professional Publishers].

———. 2012. "Życie rodzinne we współczesnej Polsce" [Family Life in Contemporary Poland]. In *Współczesne społeczeństwo polskie* [*Contemporary Polish Society*], edited by Anna Giza and Małgorzata Sikorska. Warsaw: PWN.

Śledzianowski, Jan. 1999. *Zranione ojcostwo* [*Wounded Fatherhood*]. Kuria Diecezjalna: Kielce.

Suwada, Katarzyna, and Lars Platin. 2014. "On Fatherhood, Masculinities, and Family Policies in Poland and Sweden: A Comparative Study." *Polish Sociological Review* 4 (188):509–524.

Szelewa, Dorota. 2015."Polityka rodzinna w Polsce po 1989 roku: od familializmu prywatnego do publicznego?" [Family Policy in Poland after 1989: From Private to Public Maternalism?]. In *Niebezpieczne związki. Macierzyństwo, ojcostwo i polityka* [*Dangerous Liaisons. Motherhood, Fatherhood and Politics*], edited by Renata E. Hryciuk and Elżbieta Korolczuk, 105–132. Warsaw: Warsaw University Press.

"Tatonet.pl." Last modified January 17, 2015. http://www.tato.net/tatonet_en/warto-przeczytac/wazne-tematy/581-meskosc-ojcostwo.

Titkow, Anna. 2014. "Kontrakt płci" [Gender Contract]. In *Encyklopedia gender* [*Encyclopedia of Gender Studies*], edited by Monika Rudaś-Grodzka et al., 250–252. Warsaw: Czarna Owca Publishers.

Williams, Rhys H., and Robert D. Benford. 2000. "Two Faces of Collective Action Frames: A Theoretical Consideration." *Current Perspectives in Social Theory* 20:127–151.

Wojnicka, Katarzyna. 2013. "Męskie ruchy społeczne we współczesnej Polsce: Wybrane ustalenia i wnioski" [Men Social Movements in Contemporary Poland: Selected Findings and Conclusions]. *Acta Universitatis Lodziensis Folia Sociologica* 47.

Wojnicka, Katarzyna, and Ewelina Ciaputa. 2011. *Karuzela z mężczyznami* [*Merry-go-round with Men*]. Kraków: Oficyna Wydawnicza Impuls.

Wojnicka, Katarzyna, and Edyta Zierkiewicz. 2014. "Emocje w ruchach społecznych na przykładzie ruchu obrony praw ojców i Amazonek w Polsce" [Emotions in Social Movements: The Example of Fathers' Movements and Amazones in Poland]. *Studia Socjologiczne* 4 (215):209–234.

Yuval-Davis, Nira, and Pnina Werbner, eds. 1999. *Women, Citizenship and Difference*. London and New York: Zed Books.

"Zadanie specjalne" (Special Task), Episode 17. 2013. Accessed January 12, 2015. http://telewizjarepublika.pl/Zadanie-specjalne-odc-17–201314,video,601.html#.VMZp2ixybIV.

Zald, M. N. 1996. "Culture, Ideology and Strategic Framing." In *Comparative Perspectives on Social Movements*, edited by Dough McAdam, J. D. McCarthy, and M. N. Zald. Cambridge: Cambridge University Press.

5

Civil Society and Fatherhood in Russia: The Case of Daddy-Schools in Saint Petersburg

Pelle Åberg and Johnny Rodin

Introduction

In the Russian context, the state and development of civil society, as well as the space that exists for civic activism in general, have been much debated during the last few decades. It has been claimed that Russian legislation introduced during the last decade has severely limited this space and the possibilities for forming and maintaining civil society organizations that are independent from the state and able to fulfill an advocacy and watchdog function vis-à-vis the state and government.

At the same time, there appears to be space enough for civic activism, as long as such efforts are not strongly politicized in any oppositional way but rather complement those of the state. What are often said to be results of political and legislative developments in Russia are a strengthened state and large parts of civil society being increasingly, not least financially, dependent on the state. Thus, the borderland between civil society and the state may have been partly redefined. Civil society organizations often operate in this and other borderlands, such as the one between civil society and the private sphere of the family. These borderlands are also discussed in this chapter.

The empirical focus of this chapter is "daddy-schools," in Russian *papa shkoly*, which have been established in and around Saint Petersburg during the last eight years. These daddy-schools constitute cases of social activism and, more specifically, male parental activism in contemporary Russia. The focus and activities of the daddy-schools are also connected to demographic matters and issues of the decreasing population of the Russian Federation, which are high on the political agenda in Russia. At least, that is one way of framing issues concerning family life, parenting and, in these specific cases, fatherhood.

The activities and organization of these daddy-schools are connected both to the borderland between civil society and the private sphere, since fatherhood is clearly connected to the family, and to the borderland between civil society and the state. The relations between the daddy-schools and the state are even more interesting due to how relations between civil society and the Russian state in general have developed in recent years.

Thus, questions to be addressed in this chapter are the following: How do actors in the daddy-schools manage their relations with the state? How do actors in the daddy-schools navigate in the borderland between civil society and the state as they try to promote their issues in a repressive political environment? How do the Russian daddy-schools frame their questions and operations to gain legitimacy and influence within their specific cultural, political, and social context?

The chapter is linked to two theoretical themes: civil society and social activism, on the one hand, and research on fatherhood as a social institution and on currently prevalent discourses on fatherhood in the Russian context on the other hand. The chapter thus complements previous research in several ways. It adds to existing research on Russian civil society and civic initiatives in the Russian context. It also addresses the nexus between the public and the private as well as the gender dimension of civil society activities. Finally, it contributes to the currently underresearched issues of fatherhood in Russia.

The study is based on documentation from the organizations and on interviews performed primarily with the initiators of the daddy-schools in Russia and with current moderators (i.e., those leading and managing the daddy-groups). Before analyzing this material, we will elaborate on the conceptual lens used to further our understanding of the Russian daddy-schools as well as the context in which the daddy-school activities exist.

Civil Society in Borderlands

Civil society, social activism, civic engagement, active citizenship, social movements, and other related concepts are complex and there is no consensus concerning how they should be defined or how they relate to each other. The purpose of this chapter is not to bring clarity to this debate, but it is necessary to link to these discussions to some extent in order to present the theoretical perspective applied to the Russian daddy-schools, the development of which we argue should be understood as a civic initiative, in other words, an initiative that came into being through the civic engagement of individual citizens in a bottom-up fashion.

Civil society is often argued to entail voluntary organizations and informal networks and the actions undertaken by individuals within these organizations and networks (see for instance Alexander 2006; Jeppsson Grassman and Svedberg 2007; Kymlicka and Norman 1995). It is also negatively defined by many scholars who distinguish civil society from the state and the market. An issue rarely addressed is the relation between civil society and the intimate sphere of the family and household (Ginsborg 2013). However, for this particular text that dimension is important given the overall topic of this chapter and the book as such. Hence, we elaborate below on the two borderlands of primary interest for this chapter: civil society and the family, and civil society and the state.

Civil Society and the Family

Many researchers treat civil society as separate, not only from the state and the market, but also from the family sphere, arguing that civil society relations are built on a different rationality than the other spheres (cf. Alexander 2006; von Essen and Sundgren 2012; Jeppsson Grassman and Svedberg 2007; Nautz, Ginsborg, and Nijhuis 2013). In this text, we will use this view as a point of departure. Thus theoretically, society can be divided into four different spheres: the state, the market or business sphere, civil society, and the family or private sphere. Each sphere is based on different logics or rationalities. For instance, the market sphere is based on a calculative rationality in which relationships are exchangeable. The civil society sphere, on the contrary, is based on an ideal-based rationality where actors and relationships are not easily exchanged since they are based on shared identities and ideologies (Sjöstrand 2000).

This kind of differentiation, not least concerning the division between a public sphere and a private sphere, has implications for a discussion that has been central to feminist writing for about two hundred years, in other words, the dichotomy between the private and the public as part of a critique of liberal thinking and the patriarchal elements in that strand of thought. Several feminist thinkers argue that the dichotomy between the public and the private only serves patriarchal interests since, in liberal theory, men are the ones related to the public sphere whereas women have their "natural" position in the private sphere, which also leads to a devaluation of women's work. This causes some to argue that the private sphere of domestic life is a central part of the public sphere and civil society (cf. Okin 1991; Pateman 1983). However, as discussed by Ginsborg (2013), merging these two spheres is theoretically problematic since, as noted above, the spheres are built on different rationalities, and the type of relations between actors are different. In the private sphere of the family, relations are intimate to an extent that is not shared by civil society. And, we cannot choose our birth family, meaning that these relations are not voluntary, which is an important trait of civil society relations.

For this particular text, the borderland between civil society and the family is important since fatherhood, as will be discussed further below, contains both a public and a private dimension. Parenthood in general, as well as fatherhood, clearly relate to the private sphere of the family but also influences and is influenced by various processes in the public sphere.

Civil Society and the State

Civil society and the state are generally seen as separate, hence the term "non-governmental organizations," which is frequently used to refer to one form of civil society organizations. However, there is no consensus concerning what the relationship between the state and civil society is or should be. Some researchers see civil society and the state as separate but mutually complementary. Many agree that a civil society cannot develop in isolation from the state and the market since the spheres influence one another (Diamond 1999; Evans Jr. 2002; Keane 1988). Much research also claims that the state is important for the development of civil society by providing necessary conditions and creating space for independent and voluntary organizational activity (cf. Edwards 2004; Putnam 2002; Skocpol 1999).

Some take a more conflict-oriented approach, emphasizing the function civil society can have in challenging the state when this is necessary. This more confrontational view of the relations between civil society and the state has its roots partly in the fact that civil society came into prominence in the context of the oppositional movements in Eastern Europe where the relationship was very much construed as civil society *against* the state (Howard 2003). Thus, even though there is a widespread consensus in the research community about the distinction between civil society and the state as two separate societal spheres, there is disagreement concerning how they are related to each other and whether this relationship is dominated by conflict or cooperation and compromise.

One approach to the issue of how the different societal spheres relate to each other is to emphasize the interrelation, rather than the separation, of the spheres. In fact, the spheres are constantly interacting and also tend to overlap one another. Thus, the boundaries are blurred (Åberg 2008; Nautz, Ginsborg, and Nijhuis 2013), which is why we focus on different borderlands between civil society and other societal spheres.

Civil Society in Russia

There is an immense amount of studies discussing civil society in Russia, historical legacies, the weakness of civil society in many parts of the former Soviet Union, the impact of foreign funding on civil society development, and so on (see for instance Howard 2003; Ljubownikow, Crotty, and Rodgers 2013; Mendelson and Glenn 2002; Uhlin 2006; Weigle 2002).

There is no consensus concerning what, if any, "real" civil society existed during Soviet times and no consensus concerning what the future may hold or what the status actually is today. However, what is frequently claimed is that there was an upsurge of civil society organizations and collective action during the late 1980s, followed by a sharp decline in activity in the 1990s and then a new upsurge in the last decades (Ljubownikow, Crotty, and Rodgers 2013; Weigle 2000; Weigle 2002). However, one problem sometimes raised concerning studies of Russian civil society is that they have frequently been based on a Western notion of what a civil society structure is (Fröhlich 2012; Hann 2004).

For instance, concerning contemporary Russia, there is research indicating that a Russian-style civil society is emerging, where civil society organizations "maintain strong and dependent relationships with the state" (Ljubownikow, Crotty, and Rodgers 2013, 154). This has sometimes been perceived as troublesome for civil society development in Russia, suggesting the development of civil society organizations that are primarily, or even exclusively, a "longer arm" of the state, although some research argues that this only holds true for parts of contemporary Russian civil society (Chebankova 2009; Fröhlich 2012; cf. Evans Jr. 2006, 152).

The close relations between civil society organizations and the Russian state can be connected to political, legislative, and financial issues. In 2008, for instance, tax privileges for non-governmental organizations (NGOs) were reduced, which made government contracts much more important, and subsequently the space for service delivery on the part of civil society organizations has also been codified in legislation (Chebankova 2012, 395). Simultaneously, other legislative changes have made it much more difficult for Russian organizations to obtain foreign funding (Crotty 2009; Fröhlich 2012, 376f).

A number of political and legislative developments in Russia during the last decade strengthened the state, leading to a current situation in which the state greatly influences civil society development (Ljubownikow, Crotty, and Rodgers 2013). Legislative changes during the Putin administration have, for instance, been tools used to accomplish greater state control over civil society organizations. A case in point is the "NGO Law" introduced in 2006 through which increased demands were placed on civil society organizations to register and report their activities and finances (Chebankova 2009; Crotty 2009; Fröhlich 2012, 374f).

Recent research argues that the space for contentious action in contemporary Russia, restricted as it may be given quite recent legislative changes, may lie with, or be "hidden" within, noncontentious, nonpolitical, service-oriented activities. By providing, for instance, welfare services, and thereby fulfilling needs not addressed by the state, civil society organizations can gain legitimacy in the eyes of the state. This legitimacy may subsequently open up doors for the same organizations to also influence policies and legislation in their area of expertise (Fröhlich 2012; cf. Jacobsson and Saxonberg 2012; Jakobson and Sanovich 2010). Thus, providing services and at least appearing as a nonpolitical organization can be understood as a "framing" exercise (cf. Benford and Snow 2000) and points to the importance of exploring the borderland between civil society and the state. Civil society organizations need to frame their goals in ways that resonate with culturally, politically, and otherwise accepted norms (cf. Fröhlich 2012, 376). In the case of Russian daddy-schools, this may mean focusing on their social contributions in terms of working to reduce domestic violence and promoting active fathers as a way to increase the fertility rate and the welfare of Russian families rather than on ambitions for political or legislative change.

Fatherhood In and Outside Russia

Apart from civil society, fatherhood is of central concern here since our empirical cases are Russian daddy-schools. However, fatherhood is also of more general concern due to the demographic situation in Russia, which has led the Russian state to be active in the field of family policies, etc.[1] At the same time, fathers and fatherhood are largely neglected. While issues concerning family, children and parenthood are high on the political agenda in Russia, fatherhood remains both underresearched and underemphasized in the political and public debate (Rodin and Åberg 2013).

There is, however, a significant body of research on fatherhood outside of the Russian context. In recent decades, researchers have generally studied fatherhood from the perspective of social constructivism. From this perspective, fatherhood is a politicized social construction, located in the intersection between the public and the private spheres. Discourses on fatherhood are expressions of struggles between different normative pressures from political, religious, and social authorities and institutions as well as from more personal and private relations (Hobson and Morgan 2002). Thus, there is no fixed truth about what fatherhood is, rather its meaning changes over time. What is considered to be "good" or "appropriate" fatherhood and how individuals live up to those ideals are bound by history and sociopolitical context, or more concretely by the ideologies and practices associated with being a father (Doherty, Kouneski, and Erickson 1998; LaRossa 1998; Marsiglio et al. 2000).

Previous research has generally argued that in many countries, fatherhood has changed over time. The predominant role for the father in many contexts has been to act as the breadwinner, in other words to be the provider and decision-maker in the family, but not to be especially involved in childrearing or other tasks in the household. This also implies that the father's/man's primary role is in the public, not the private, sphere (Lamb 2000; Kimmel 2008). Today, an alternative model exists where the father is more active in all aspects of family life, taking on also a nurturing and caring role vis-à-vis the children. This is sometimes called the "new" or "responsible" fatherhood and is based on a more equal relationship between man and woman in the family, where the father takes on a greater role in the private sphere (Eränta and Moisander 2011; Williams 2008).

Fathers' engagement is not only deemed to be a good in itself but is also discussed as a contributing factor in reducing domestic violence, improving the health of mothers, fathers, and children, and promoting improved gender equality, among other things (e.g., Kimmel 2008; Rossi 1984). Thus, active fatherhood, although intimately connected to the private sphere, is connected to various public and societal benefits as well.

There is a vivid discussion concerning the interplay between the private and the public sphere in theoretical debates about civil society. Similarly, fatherhood is connected to both the private and the public spheres. It is clearly a private matter, relating to issues of the family, but fatherhood is also influenced by what happens in the public sphere and it has implications for the public sphere.

In the Russian context, the development of fatherhood ideals has been somewhat different than in the Western context (see Rodin and Åberg 2013). It has been argued that the role of the father in Russia, and in Eastern Europe in general, before Soviet times was weaker than the situation in Western Europe and the United States. A traditional family model in Russia frequently included multigenerational households where the older generation dominated the younger. Even though it was still a patriarchal family model, it was not necessarily the father who was the head of the family but frequently a male from an older generation (Hajnal 1965; Laslett 1983).

The Soviet system and the gender contract that was part of that system subsequently led to certain developments concerning views on family, parenthood, and fatherhood. Even if Soviet social policies went through different phases, as elaborated by Chernova (2007), one of the most prominent features was the lack of a clear role for the Soviet father. The model can be described as "only mothers have children. Fathers are ignored by societal institutions and by society at large" (Chernova 2007, 139, authors' translation). The father's place was in the public sphere as a worker and a defender of the motherland. In the private sphere of the family he did not really have a purpose since the state had taken over the role as the main provider, making it very difficult for the man to uphold the role of a breadwinner (Rodin and Åberg 2013). Moreover, fathers today are clearly excluded from the state and public discourses that appear to be part of a cultural legacy that stretches back through Soviet times and beyond (Aivazova 1998; Rotkirch 2000).

Fathers and fatherhood are neither present in state guideline documents on demographic policy, nor are they given much space in the constitution of the Russian Federation (Rodin and Åberg 2013). When norms concerning fatherhood and the role of fathers *are* parts of public discourses, the model discussed primarily resembles that of a traditional breadwinner, which was discussed above, in other words a "new" or more active fatherhood does not appear to be commonplace in Russian discourses. However, the ability to fulfill a role as breadwinner is, of course, also dependent on a number of social and economic conditions and we should also remember that the behavior of fathers has to be viewed as separate from how the *ideal* of fatherhood is understood.

Organizing to Promote Active Fatherhood in Russia

The empirical focus in this chapter concerns the daddy-schools that have been established in and around Saint Petersburg during the last eight years. In the following sections we will present the daddy-schools, what they are all about, how they have developed, and how they can be understood.

The material consists of interviews with nine organizers and moderators of daddy-schools. Moderators lead the activities in the daddy-schools. A focus group interview has also been conducted with organizers and moderators. All interviews have been recorded and subsequently transcribed before being coded and analyzed.

Apart from this, we have performed participant observations of the daddy-school activities, taking part in the meetings of three different daddy-groups in Saint Petersburg and Novgorod. Finally, documents from the organizations/networks have been analyzed.

The Birth and Development of a Civic Initiative

First, to get an idea of the civic initiative discussed here, it should be noted that the daddy-schools in Saint Petersburg, in terms of their numbers, are a quite marginal phenomenon. However, that says very little about the potential impact of their activities.

No official records exist, but on average, since the first daddy-school started in 2008, a few hundred fathers-to-be have participated in their activities each year. In 2014, there were ten daddy-schools in operation in and around Saint Petersburg. The number has varied somewhat over time depending on the number of fathers who are interested and where there are individuals interested in becoming moderators.

Of course, there is also the issue of what groups these activities reach. Even though several moderators claim that there is variation among the participants in terms of socioeconomic background and status, the level of education, etc., it still appears that the vast majority of the participants are quite well-educated and have a fairly good economic status. Alexander Malyshev has shown, albeit based on a rather small sample, that almost 80 percent of the participants in the daddy-schools have a university degree. Moreover, almost 60 percent of the participants can afford expensive goods (excluding apartments) (Malyshev 2013, 41), which means that they could be considered to be middle class. Based on interviews with daddy-school-participants, Olga Bezrukova has shown that the daddy-school-participants are generally more likely to hold norms of gender equality and "new fatherhood" than the population in general, although their actual behavior does not always follow suit (Bezrukova 2012, 269). It is hardly surprising that the daddy-school participants hold such norms since much research has found that progressive ideas most frequently first take root among the middleclass (Bezrukova 2012; LaRossa 1998).

The story of the daddy-school-initiative begins in 2007 when the individuals who became founders and developers of the daddy-schools met each other, as well as representatives from Swedish organizations, at a conference dealing with domestic violence. The would-be enthusiasts for the daddy-schools attended the conference as a result of their employment at social welfare offices and similar institutions in Saint Petersburg. At this conference it was mentioned in passing that something called "daddy-groups" existed in Sweden for the purpose of encouraging men to discuss issues of fatherhood and family life with other men. This sparked an interest among some of the Russian attendees. Eventually, this led to further contact with Swedish organizations and ensuing cooperation, and in November of 2008, the first Russian daddy-school was organized in Saint Petersburg by some of the attendees from the above-mentioned conference. Thus, the development of the Russian daddy-schools is also a case of transnational cooperation between civil society organizations and can be connected to the voluminous literature on such issues, as well as to the impact of foreign contacts and funding on Russian civil society. However, the Russian daddy-schools survive without foreign funding, and the exploration of the transnational contacts is a theme in its own right, to be developed in future studies. Thus, we refrain from further analyses of these contacts in this particular text.

The daddy-schools provide a program of seminars where men meet to discuss topics related to parenting from a male perspective. The specific topics they address can vary depending on the interests of the participants but frequently include different aspects of childbirth, early stages in a child's development, and responsible fatherhood, which is natural given the daddy-schools' aim of promoting more active fathers. The groups function in a bottom-up fashion, providing the participants with substantial influence over the program's contents. A moderator leads the group meetings.

The moderators are volunteers who do not receive any financial or other form of compensation for their engagement in the daddy-schools, and the activities are neither parts of the state machinery nor parts of the for-profit business sphere. Hence, it is safe to claim that the work of the moderators and the activities of the daddy-schools are parts of civil society. In the introduction we interpreted our cases as examples of male parental activism. The moderators could, from such a perspective, be viewed as the first line of activists. The participants cannot so easily be understood as activists, although their participation could be an expression of a wish to change gender roles and of them holding or being curious about alternative norms concerning what being a man and a father means.

Organizationally, no formal registration of the daddy-schools took place until 2010, when an organization called Northern Way (formed by some of the enthusiasts behind the daddy-schools) was registered. Today, ten individual daddy-schools exist in and around Saint Petersburg, but they are still neither registered organizations nor formal parts of Northern Way. Thus, the local organization and the activities of the daddy-schools are more accurately described as a network than as organizations. However, the daddy-schools share a value-base and a specific format, based on a nonhierarchical, grassroots ethos. Several respondents claim to share a group identity with the other people involved, based on a shared interest and belief in the methods used and in the importance of promoting more active and involved fathers. One of the key actors of the daddy-schools expresses the postulate that unites them all as follows:

> We do not work to satisfy the curiosity of men but we have two goals: to preserve the family and the child's right to be raised in a complete family and the prevention of domestic violence. (Interview, November 22, 2012, authors' translation)

During the last two years, those who initiated the daddy-school activities and who are now involved in Northern Way have also begun to expand the activities to start daddy-schools outside of Saint Petersburg. Currently a daddy-school also exists in Novgorod, and more schools are about to be started in Petrozavodsk and Archangelsk.

What is the Purpose of Daddy-Schools?

One may wonder what is new about these ideas in the Russian context. First, we have already noted that fathers are not really present in the larger discourses of parenthood and family. Second, when the role of fathers *is* discussed, it tends to be viewed as that of a traditional breadwinner, whereas the more active fatherhood ideal is not commonplace. The active, involved, and nurturing father who is involved in all aspects of family life is, however, precisely what the daddy-schools aim to promote, which is evident in the following quotation from one of the founders of the daddy-schools:

> To me everything is very clear. It is all about the man's active actions in childrearing. Not formal actions but everyday, practical, ordinary tasks that the wife usually performs—he also has to do the same every day. That is, not just say hello, pat on the head, ask about how the day has been and play. . . . It is important to teach men to talk to other men about their children—that is not commonplace. Men should be actively involved . . . the involved father is he who takes the child to the doctor, takes the child for a walk—not just on weekends but as she [the mother] does. The involved father performs the same tasks as his wife does. (Interview, November 22, 2012, authors' translation)

According to several respondents, this is what all activists who are involved in the daddy-schools unite around. Hence, they are aiming to introduce issues that are currently neglected by other segments of society—a part often played by social movements and civil society organizations that also has the potential for influencing policy. Some of the respondents express similar attitudes where a connection is also made between a more active type of fatherhood and gender equality.

> We are trained to be allowed to drive a car; we learn in order to manage a profession. But, to become a parent, no learning is required. People seem to believe that will come by itself. To our regret, it does not come by itself. You should work on all of this. We should raise the status of the parents and the status of the father, and in this you should definitely speak of equality. (Interview, April 25, 2012, authors' translation)

This quote demonstrates the ambition of the daddy-schools to change norms concerning the father's role in the family, in other words, to change norms concerning the private sphere through the activities of this civil society initiative.

Finally, it should be noted that our respondents argue that the methods and techniques used are crucial for furthering the ambition of the daddy-schools, in other words, teaching men how to be more involved fathers. These methods are also argued to be something new or different in the Russian context. The active involvement of fathers, not only in the family and the care of the children, but also their active involvement as participants in the daddy-schools, is emphasized (cf. Berggren et al 2010). A number of moderators argue that it is very unorthodox in Russia to base learning activities on the participants' active involvement in the group and on their questions, concerns and wishes. In such a participant-oriented learning environment, the teacher, expert, or in these cases the moderator, is not a lecturer but someone who facilitates the discussion between the participants. Several moderators have also claimed to have witnessed unfamiliarity with such a model of interaction each time a new daddy-group gathers for the first time.

Thus, the originality (in a Russian context) of the daddy-schools not only concerns the contents of the activities or the view of fatherhood promoted, but also the methods employed and the nonhierarchical relations between moderators and participants.

> It is not just about making men more consciously aware of their role as fathers but to involve the men so they actively participate in this [the activities of the daddy-schools; in their own learning]. Without the involvement of the men themselves, it will all turn into an organization arranging lectures for the general public. We have sufficiently competent experts who can, well, make people aware of the scientific point of view. But I would make the involvement of the men the priority, with everything else coming after. Because that is the greatest difficulty—getting the men to become involved. (Interview, November 22, 2012, authors' translation)

With this vision as a background to the development of the daddy-schools we must also note that the perspective of this civic initiative has produced results, not only in terms of getting fathers-to-be to participate. Changes have also occurred in regional as well as federal legislation in line with, and as a result of, the activities of the daddy-schools. However, this will be covered in the coming sections where we will discuss the activities, strategies, and outcomes of the daddy-schools in relation to the different borderlands in which civil society organizations operate.

Organizing Activities and Influencing Participants

The aim expressed by daddy-school-representatives is to change the attitudes of fathers toward the family and their role in child-rearing. This aim is also a consequence of an ambition to contribute to a number of public benefits that have been discussed previously such as reducing domestic violence, contributing to the welfare of children, and potentially increasing the number of children born (Berggren et al. 2010). Thus, the ambition of the daddy-schools has both public and private dimensions that position them in the borderland between the public and the private, which is also one of the borderlands that concern civil society, albeit possibly the least explored one.

The issue of recruiting fathers-to-be to become participants is an issue of central concern and has been so since the very start of the daddy-school activities. Recruitment of participants is frequently discussed among the moderators, even more than issues of methods and practice. The moderators have found different strategies for attracting would-be participants. Most of them clearly state that the most common way for fathers-to-be to come into contact with the daddy-school is through their wives or partners. Hence, good relations with maternal care units, where mothers-to-be take part in educational activities but where questions of the fathers' role are downplayed, have been important for the recruitment of participants throughout the years (cf. Malyshev 2013). One of the moderators describes the importance of being present at maternal care units as follows:

> In these groups [at the maternal care unit] we explained about our activities, that we are here to help you [the mothers], that when we speak to men we emphasize that the man should help you from the birth of the child and be included before the birth, he should understand you better. . . . Most of the time it was women [that called the daddy-school] and said: "sign my husband up" . . . Sometimes the man himself phoned and wondered, "Have I come to right place? It is supposed to be some form of daddy-school, something for fathers-to-be my wife told me." (Interview, April 26, 2012, authors' translation)

Several of the daddy-schools said recruitment at maternity care units was the single most important source of participants, which also connects to the issue of relations between the daddy-schools and the state or parts of the public administration, which will be further explored in the next section.

So, what can be said about the outcome of the daddy-school activities in terms of impact on those fathers who participate? There is no hard evidence, and measuring the effects of this kind of activity for an individual is inherently difficult. From the point of view of the moderators though, they stress how participation has opened up new arenas for the fathers. There are several instances where the men who met in the daddy-groups have maintained contact, both with the daddy-schools but even more frequently with each other. Several moderators have also witnessed a normalization of discussing child behavior and child-rearing issues between men. In that sense, those involved with the daddy-schools argue that a change in attitudes and perhaps norms concerning fatherhood indeed has taken place as a result of the daddy-school activities.

One of the moderators also stressed how men who would most likely never meet in "ordinary life" have come together, which validates conclusions stemming from previous research on civil society (Diamond 1994; de Tocqueville 1997). Thus, new social ties can be forged through participation in the daddy-schools, something that researchers have deemed important for the creation of social capital (see, e.g., Putnam 2000). However, we should also remember the question posed earlier concerning who participates in the daddy-schools. As already stated, a majority seems to come from groups that are quite well-educated and who are in a decent financial situation. But, that is the majority, not everyone. Thus, the potential for being a meeting place, as expressed by more than one of the moderators, is an important part of the activities.

Regarding the organization of the daddy-schools, the formalization of their activities through the foundation of Northern Way in 2010 has not, according to different moderators as well as respondents from Northern Way, led to increased institutionalization or centralization. The daddy-schools are not headed or governed by Northern Way, but the legal status of having a registered organization was needed in order to open a bank account, apply for funding, and take up a more official status. Respondents, both from Northern Way and different daddy-schools, portray Northern Way as being, or at least trying to be, a resource hub for the various groups of fathers meeting together with a moderator. The head of Northern Way, who has also been one of the real enthusiasts behind the development of the daddy-schools from the very beginning, states that

> most groups that have been founded with our support continue to maintain contact. . . . We support each other and keep a unified direction because we, when new groups are founded, tell everyone who uses our support that the only way for a group to get into our community and call themselves a daddy-school is to stick to the main principles: it has to be a men's group, it should involve men on the basis of the main goals of our operation, that is, the good of the child, the prevention of domestic violence, and equal possibilities for participating in child-rearing. It is only through these principles that we unite them. Legally, these relations are not registered. (Interview, November 22, 2012, authors' translation)

The founders of the daddy-school activities emphasize that Northern Way is primarily a support structure for when there is a new daddy-school initiative about to start activities and in the initial stages of development. A conscious choice of avoiding the creation of hierarchical institutional structures is frequently stressed. As in the case of parental committees in Russia analyzed by Tova Höjdestrand (in this volume), the lack of hierarchy is an important organizational principle. Some, however, also consider what the future will hold.

> Northern Way is not a governing organ at this time and it will most likely not become one either. And no one needs that. If they [potential moderators] find it interesting they will do it in their city districts. Someone does it, someone else takes a break from it, new [initiatives] arise. . . . On the other hand, we think that perhaps we should create something, like a method center, a supporting resource structure to be placed at Northern Way. (Interview, November 21, 2012, authors' translation)

Thus, whether the informal network structure of the daddy-schools will remain or if some degree of institutionalization will take place is unclear at this point. This may also be influenced by other societal developments and, not least, the relations to the state, which is what we will now turn our attention to.

Daddy-Schools, the Public Sphere, and the Russian State

Since the very start of their activities in 2008, the daddy-schools have received quite a lot of attention. This can be exemplified by the interest from the media that was evident from the beginning.

> There was a lot of attention from the mass media. When the daddy-groups started we had such an occasion. There is a newspaper called *My City District* [freely translated] and I know a female journalist there. And I talked to her once and mentioned that there was a daddy-group. She said, "Wow, how exciting," and wrote an article. Before it was printed it was published on their website. And literally within one hour, three television networks called me . . . there were a number of reports on the daddy-schools on different TV channels. (Interview, November 21, 2012, authors' translation)

This interest from the mass media has remained relatively high, and there is a belief that in general this has also sparked a more general interest in fatherhood, exemplified by new shows on the radio and on TV, such as the TV-show *School for Young Fathers* (freely translated) and the radio show

Young Dads. The daddy-schools in Saint Petersburg have also been noticed in national media and newspapers and even abroad, because the initiative was described in a series of stories in the largest Swedish newspaper, *Dagens Nyheter*, as well as in another Swedish newspaper, *Aftonbladet* (Erlandson 2009; Letmark 2012a; Letmark 2012b).

Representatives of the daddy-schools and Northern Way believe that the Russian media's interest is due to the fact that these activities were indeed something new and original in the Russian context. The idea of a discussion group exclusively for fathers and based on participant activity rather than distribution of expert knowledge was, in this context, something unheard of and therefore attracted attention.

Thus, the daddy-schools have gained much attention from the media but also from the regional authorities. Neither the daddy-schools nor Northern Way as an organization has taken on an oppositional, political role, which may be interpreted as one of the reasons why the relations with the regional and city authorities are described by respondents as good. According to those who are active in Northern Way and the daddy-schools, this is precisely due to the schools not taking on an oppositional role but rather framing their activities as being for the benefit of the city of Saint Petersburg, as well as inviting and including politicians and representatives from the public administration to their events. The activists have attempted and, it seems, succeeded in framing their activities and ambitions as being in line with state interests. This confirms conclusions drawn by other researchers who have identified this kind of relation as providing space for civil society organizations in contemporary Russia (cf. Fröhlich 2012).

Several of those involved in the daddy-schools have regular employment inside the state structures, normally in the field of social welfare. One moderator argues that this in itself is important since it is easier to change things and get access to those in charge when you are on the "inside." The networks that moderators have built through their employment are referred to as important for disseminating information but are probably also important for providing legitimacy to the activities they undertake.

Of course, given these connections between those active in the daddy-schools and the state, it is possible to question the independence and grassroots character of the daddy-schools. But, according to the material that we have analyzed, the daddy-schools appear to be relatively independent. They fill a social function in a policy field that is also high on the political agenda, which has made state representatives favorable to the actors and activities in the daddy-schools since these schools deal with a perspective that the state has largely neglected.

Usually, the daddy-schools have also been organized in the offices of various institutions and centers in the field of social welfare. How this structuring or placement of the activities came about is described as an organic process.

> Those who became and become interested [in running a daddy-school] are usually those people who work in the field of social welfare, and they work in different places that are connected to social issues. Therefore, it is, in a natural way, convenient for them to gather a daddy-group and understand that this form can be used in their activities . . . and they do it in their places of work. That came to be in a natural way. It is understandable that if I work here it is more convenient for me to do it [the daddy-school] here. (Interview, November 21, 2012, authors' translation)

The good relations to the authorities are also demonstrated by how Northern Way and actors involved with the daddy-schools have repeatedly been invited to participate in meetings with state administration, including the city governor. Respondents claim that they have managed to have a real impact on political and legislative developments, exemplified by how one of their initiatives—that it should be possible for fathers to be present, free-of-charge, during the delivery of their child—is now a reality, even on the federal level.

Furthermore, since July 2012, the family policy of Saint Petersburg states that every city district should have a daddy-school (*The concept of family policy in Saint Petersburg* 2011, 33). Even the concept of daddy-schools (*papa shkoly*) has been inscribed in this formal document, a concept that was introduced by the civic initiative we study in this chapter. Several of our respondents stressed this with great pride as evidence for how their activities have influenced policy processes.

That the state appears to be positive toward the activities of the daddy-schools can be further exemplified by how an article about daddy-schools was published in *Rossiyskaja Gazeta*, which is a government daily newspaper in which, among other things, official decrees and promulgations of new laws are published (Vasilishina 2012). Hence, this newspaper has a strong official status.

The development and outcomes of the daddy-schools' activities support findings in previous research indicating that one way for civil society organizations to gain influence in Russia today is to first gain legitimacy by providing nonpolitical services, and then use that legitimacy to also have an impact on policies and legislation (cf. Fröhlich 2012; Jakobson and Sanovich 2010).

The formal status of having daddy-schools inscribed in the family policy is, thus, a source of pride and also a potential future means of obtaining funding since it means that public resources will be made available for such activities. The state also seems to be embracing the activities more in practice. Close to seventy state-run maternity care units in Saint Petersburg have developed activities aimed at fathers-to-be since 2012. However, several respondents also see potential dangers in the wake of a more formal status and more concrete interest from the state. The funding made available can lead to the establishment of new groups, which may diverge from the methods and ideas that have so far kept the daddy-schools together.

> Here we see a certain risk in that they will be called daddy-schools or daddy-groups but in reality will not be as they should. Perhaps they will have a symbolic meeting, *call* it a daddy-group but [content-wise and method-wise doing something different] . . . and then the denigration of the idea begins. (Interview, November 21, 2012, authors' translation)

> We are worried that a large number of groups will arise that will formally be called daddy-schools. . . . When money becomes available, many may have a more formal attitude and no one will force them to maintain any unity. That is why we talk of difficulties. But we fought for this so that there could be as many groups as possible of our kind that are interested in working with men and getting men involved. (Interview, November 22, 2012, authors' translation)

Thus, what is expressed is a fear that the idea of establishing daddy-schools will be co-opted by other forces and be turned into something that violates the original ambition and practice of the currently existing daddy-schools.

Conclusions: Active Fathers in the Borderlands between Civil Society, the State, and the Family

What have we learned from this exploration into the development of the Russian daddy-schools? First, organizationally, the daddy-schools are quite loosely structured, mostly resembling a network, with the organization Northern Way as a resource in structuring, developing, and initiating activities. Such a network is also believed by previous research to be strengthened by, among other things, a strong common narrative, in other words, a storyline that the actors involved share a belief in, and also by methods and strategies that are shared between the participants in the network (cf. Cohen 2007). Our analysis shows that the daddy-schools are well-developed in these aspects, and they coalesce around common values such as lack of hierarchy, exchange of experiences and ideas, equality (including gender equality), and active fatherhood.

Then, as discussed in previous research on civil society and the relations between the public and the private spheres, it is important for the man to take on a greater role in the private sphere and in child-rearing if the woman is to expand her involvement in the public sphere. Initiatives like the daddy-schools studied here may benefit a development in that direction through their ambition to promote a new, active fatherhood. The ambition of the daddy-schools to influence norms concerning fatherhood also illustrates the borderlands between the private and the public and between the private sphere and civil society.

To what extent the daddy-schools have actually changed the attitudes of the participants is difficult to ascertain since it would require a study of the participants before and after having participated in the daddy-schools. In addition, there is also the possibility that the daddy-schools are, at least partly, "preaching to the choir." As shown above, the majority of participants are what can be described as progressive middle-class, a stratum of society which in many contexts already holds more progressive norms than the general public. It is even more difficult to estimate whether the activities have led to any changes in behavior. Accomplishing behavioral changes also depends on many other factors, including structural ones and financial possibilities.

What we can say, however, is that this initiative has created a meeting place for fathers, which is rare in Russian society. A new arena for discussing masculinity and male parenting has been created where fathers-to-be can discuss issues that are otherwise not on the agenda and where they can meet people they would otherwise not meet. Thus, the number of social ties, which is believed to further the development of social capital, can increase. Another way of framing this is that the activities of the daddy-schools create an arena where issues related to the private sphere are discussed and worked on in a civil society setting.

The daddy-schools have also brought media attention to the issue of fatherhood and have left an imprint on regional legislation. Hence, at a more implicit and general level it seems reasonable to assume that the daddy-schools have played a role for normative change. Influencing changes concerning norms and practices related to the private sphere of the family shows how civil society affects the private sphere.

What we also see is that there is clearly a space for civic initiatives and civic engagement in contemporary Russia. However, we should remember that the organization and the activities studied here have not taken a political, or at least not an outspoken oppositional, role but have nurtured good relations with the state machinery. These good relations are rooted in the nonpolitical stance taken by the daddy-schools and by those active within them but also in their ability to present, or frame, the activities as an important service having positive results for state-set goals (such as increasing the fertility rate and reducing domestic violence), although using a different strategy and focusing on a different target group. Even if the daddy-schools framed themselves as nonpolitical or service-oriented, that does not mean that they *are* nonpolitical. Indeed, the activities of the daddy-schools have influenced policies, for instance, by increasing the possibilities for fathers to be present during the birth of their child(ren) and further exemplified by how the notion of daddy-schools has been incorporated in the family policy of Saint Petersburg.

In relation to the Russian state, the daddy-schools are attempting to promote a different normative position concerning the kind of fatherhood that is desirable or, at the very least, to get issues of fatherhood on the agenda. The promotion of active fatherhood in Russia via these civic initiatives may, however, not be a counter-discourse, but rather complementary to the state's, where civil society organizations and citizen initiatives take up issues that are not addressed by the state.

Thus, our study supports the findings in previous research that a way for civil society organizations to have a political impact in a nonconducive context is to frame their issues in a way that legitimizes them as service providers in the eyes of the state. Only then, by proving themselves useful and nonthreatening by providing services, can civil society actors get the opportunity to also use their voice and fill an advocacy role. All of this also clearly positions the daddy-schools in the borderland between civil society and the state. Given previous research discussing the limited space available for social activism and civil society in contemporary Russia, it appears that this is a space in the borderland between civil society and the state where civic initiatives are tolerated or even encouraged, that is, *if* civil society actors manage to frame their ambitions and strategies in a way that resonates with the cultural and political values of the surrounding society.

The analysis of the Russian daddy-schools has demonstrated that such activism can also have an impact on a policy level. However, cooperation with the state and especially the financial support now available from state institutions in Saint Petersburg is also believed to imply a risk that the ideas, methods, and practices will be co-opted or transformed in a negative way, thus demonstrating the potential dangers of working in the borderland between civil society and the state.

Pelle Åberg, Associate Professor in Political Science, Department of Social Sciences, Ersta Sköndal Bräcke University College and researcher at the Center for Baltic and East European Studies (CBEES) and the School of Social Sciences, Södertörn University, Stockholm, Sweden

Pelle Åberg's research primarily deals with various aspects of civil society, including transnational relations as well as research on Sweden, Estonia, and Russia. His previous publications include studies of transnational cooperation between civil society organizations (*Translating Popular Education: Civil Society Cooperation between Sweden and Estonia*, Stockholm University, 2008; "Change in Motion or Processing Change" in *Nordic Civil Society at a Cross-Roads*, Nomos, 2011); in-depth studies of Swedish civil society, especially in the field of popular education ("Myths and Traditions as Constraints or Resources? Path Dependency and Decoupling Strategies among Civil Society Organizations," *Journal of Civil Society*, 2015; "Managing Expectations, Demands and Myths: Swedish Study Associations Caught Between Civil Society, the State and the Market," *Voluntas*, 2013), and fatherhood in Russia ("Fatherhood Across Space and Time: Russia in Perspective," *Baltic Worlds*, 2013).

Johnny Rodin, PhD in Political Science, researcher at the Center for Baltic and East European Studies (CBEES) and the School of Social Sciences, Södertörn University, Stockholm, Sweden

Johnny Rodin's research has primarily focused on various aspects of public policy with a particular emphasis on elite studies in Russia. His publications analyze regional politics, population- and family policies as well as fatherhood in the Russian context. He is the author of the monograph *Rethinking Russian Federalism: Federal Policies and Intergovernmental Relations from Yeltsin to Putin* (2008). He contributed articles such as "Understanding the Fertility Crisis in Eastern Europe During Transition—An Ideational Approach" in *Ambio*, 2011 and "Fatherhood Across Space and Time: Russia in Perspective" in *Baltic Worlds*, 2013.

Note

1. Russia has experienced significant demographic problems with a population decline of around 0.5% annually for the last twenty years (in total, a decline of about 8 million individuals since 1991).

Works Cited

Åberg, Pelle. 2008. *Translating Popular Education: Civil Society Cooperation between Sweden and Estonia*. Stockholm: Stockholm University, Department of Political Science.

Aivazova, Svetlana. 1998. *Russkie zhenshchiny v labirinte ravnopraviia: Ocherki politicheskoi teorii I istorii* [*Russian Women in the Labyrinth of Equality: Essays on Political Theory and History*]. Moscow: RIK.

Alexander, Jeffrey C. 2006. *The Civil Sphere*. Oxford: Oxford University Press.

Benford, Robert D., and David A. Snow. 2000. "Framing Processes and Social Movements: An Overview and Assessment." *Annual Review of Sociology* 26:611–639.

Berggren, Mats, Nikolay Eremin, Stanislav Kazansky, Vladimir Martsenyuk, Vladimir Motygin, and Andrey Turovets. 2010. *Father School: Step by Step*. Moscow: Best-print.

Bezrukova, Olga. 2012. Praktiki otvestvennogo otsovstva: "papa-shkola" i sotsialnyi kapital [The Practices of Responsible Fatherhood: Daddy-Schools and Social Capital]. Vestnik Saint Petersburg University. Seriia 12, Vypusk 3.

Chebankova, Elena. 2009. "The Evolution of Russia's Civil Society under Vladimir Putin: A Cause for Concern or Grounds for Optimism?" *Perspectives on European Politics and Society* 10 (3):394–415.

———. 2012. "State-Sponsored Civic Associations in Russia: Systemic Integration or the 'War of Position'?" *East European Politics* 28 (4):390–408.

Chernova, Zhanna. 2007. "Model' sovetskogo otsovstva: diskursivnye predpisanija" [Model of Soviet Fatherhood: Discursive Prescriptions]. In *Rossiiskii Gendernyi Poriadok* [*Russian Gender Order*], edited by Yelena Zdravomysleva and Anna Temkina, 138–168. Saint Petersburg: European University of Saint Petersburg.

Cohen, Jean L. 2007. "Civil Society and Globalization: Rethinking the Categories." In *State and Civil Society in Northern Europe: The Swedish Model Reconsidered*, edited by Lars Trägårdh, 37–66. New York: Berghahn Books.

The Concept of Family Policy in Saint Petersburg 2012–2022. 2011.

Crotty, Jo. 2009. "Making a Difference? NGOs and Civil Society Development in Russia." *Europe-Asia Studies* 61 (1):85–108.

Diamond, Larry. 1994. "Toward Democratic Consolidation." *Journal of Democracy* 5 (3):4–17.

———. 1999. *Developing Democracy. Toward Consolidation*. Baltimore: The Johns Hopkins University Press.

Doherty, William, Edward Kouneski, and Martha Erickson. 1998. "Responsible Fathering: An Overview and Conceptual Framework." *Journal of Marriage and Family* 60 (2):277–292.

Edwards, Michael. 2004. *Civil Society*. Oxford: Blackwell Publishing.

Eränta, Kirsi, and Johanna Moisander. 2011. "Psychological Regimes of Truth and Father Identity: Challenges for Work/Life Integration." *Organization Studies* 32 (4):509–526.

Erlandson, Åsa. 2009. "Ryska pappagrupper—En sensation" [Russian Daddy-Groups—A Sensation]. *Aftonbladet*, January 28.

Essen, Johan von, and Gunnar Sundgren. 2012. "Vilse i civilsamhället" [Lost in Civil Society]. In *En mosaik av mening: Om studieförbund och civilsamhälle* [*A Mosaic of Meaning: On Study Associations and Civil Society*], edited by Johan von Essen and Gunnar Sundgren, 21–68. Gothenburg: Daidalos.

Evans Jr., Alfred B. 2002. "Recent Assessments of Social Organizations in Russia." *Demokratizatsiya* 10 (3):322–342.

———. 2006. "Vladimir Putin's Design for Civil Society." In *Russian Civil Society: A Critical Assessment*, edited by Alfred B. Evans Jr., Laura A. Henry, and Lisa McIntosh Sundstrom, 147–158. Armonk: M.E. Sharpe.

Fröhlich, Christian. 2012. "Civil Society and the State Intertwined: The Case of Disability NGOs in Russia." *East European Politics* 28 (4):371–389.

Ginsborg, Paul. 2013. "Uncharted Territories: Individuals, Families, Civil Society and the Democratic State." In *The Golden Chain: Family, Civil Society, and the State*, edited by Jürgen Nautz, Paul Ginsborg, and Ton Nijhuis, 17–39. New York: Berghahn Books.

Hajnal, John. 1965. "European Marriage Patterns in Perspective." In *Population in History: Essays in Historical Demography*, edited by David Glass and David Eversley, 101–143. London: Edward Arnold.

Hann, Chris. 2004. "In the Church of Civil Society." In *Exploring Civil Society: Political and Cultural Contexts*, edited by Marlies Glasius, David Lewis, and Hakan Seckinelgin, 44–50. London: Routledge.

Hobson, Barbara, and David Morgan. 2002. "Introduction: Making Men into Fathers." In *Making Men into Fathers. Men, Masculinities and the Social Politics of Fatherhood*, edited by Barbara Hobson, 1–24. Cambridge: Cambridge University Press.

Howard, Marc Morjé. 2003. *The Weakness of Civil Society in Post-Communist Europe*. Cambridge: Cambridge University Press.

Jacobsson, Kerstin, and Steven Saxonberg. 2012. "Introduction: A New Look at Social Movements and Civil Society in Post-Communist Poland and Russia." *East European Politics* 28 (4):329–331.

Jakobson, Lev, and Sergey Sanovich. 2010. "The Changing Models of the Russian Third Sector: Import Substitution Phase." *Journal of Civil Society* 6 (3):279–300.

Jeppsson Grassman, Eva, and Lars Svedberg. 2007. "Civic Participation in a Scandinavian Welfare State: Patterns in Contemporary Sweden." In *State and*

Civil Society in Northern Europe: The Swedish Model Reconsidered, edited by Lars Trägårdh, 126–164. New York: Berghahn Books.

Keane, John. 1988. *Democracy and Civil Society: On the Predicaments of European Socialism, the Prospects for Democracy, and the Problem of Controlling Social and Political Power*. London: Verso.

Kimmel, Michael S. 2008. *The Gendered Society*, 3rd edition. Oxford: Oxford University Press.

Kymlicka, Will, and Wayne Norman. 1995. "Return of the Citizen: A Survey of Recent Work on Citizenship Theory." In *Theorizing Citizenship*, edited by Ronald Beiner, 283–322. Albany: State University of New York Press.

Lamb, Michael. 2000. "The History of Research on Father Involvement." *Marriage & Family Review* 29 (2–3):23–42.

LaRossa, Ralph. 1998. "Fatherhood and Social Change." *Family Relations* 37 (4):451–457.

Laslett, Peter. 1983. "Family and Household as Work Group and Kin Group." In *Family Forms in Historic Europe*, edited by Richard Wall, 513–564. Cambridge: Cambridge University Press.

Letmark, Peter. 2012a. "Svenska papparollen—nu på export" [The Role of the Swedish Dad—Now on Export]. *Dagens Nyheter*, June 26.

———. 2012b. "Pappagrupp kan bryta destruktiva monster" [Daddy-Group Can Break Destructive Patterns]. *Dagens Nyheter*, June 27.

Ljubownikow, Sergej, Jo Crotty, and Peter W. Rodgers. 2013. "The State and Civil Society in Post-Soviet Russia: The Development of a Russian-Style Civil Society." *Progress in Development Studies* 13 (2):153–166.

Malyshev, Alexander. 2013. *Impact of Gender-Sensitive Social Services on the Transformation of Parental Values and Practices in Today's Russia*. Saint Petersburg: Tuskorara.

Marsiglio, William, Paul Amato, Randal Day, and Michael Lamb. 2000. "Scholarship on Fatherhood in the 1990s and Beyond." *Journal of Marriage and Family* 62 (4):1173–1191.

Mendelson, Sarah E., and John K. Glenn, eds. 2002. *The Power and Limits of NGOs: A Critical Look at Building Democracy in Eastern Europe and Eurasia*. New York: Columbia University Press.

Nautz, Jürgen, Paul Ginsborg, and Ton Nijhuis. 2013. "Introduction." In *The Golden Chain: Family, Civil Society, and the State*, edited by Jürgen Nautz, Paul Ginsborg, and Ton Nijhuis, 3–16. New York: Berghahn Books.

Okin, Susan M. 1991. "Gender, the Public and the Private." In *Political Theory Today*, edited by David Held, 67–90. Oxford: Polity Press.

Pateman, Carole. 1983. "Feminist Critiques of the Public/Private Dichotomy." In *Public and Private in Social Life*, edited by Stanley I. Benn and Gerald F. Gaus, 281–303. London: Croom Helm.

Putnam, Robert D. 2000. *Bowling Alone: The Collapse and Revival of American Community*. New York: Simon & Schuster.

———. ed. 2002. *Democracies in Flux: The Evolution of Social Capital in Contemporary Society*. Oxford: Oxford University Press.

Rodin, Johnny, and Pelle Åberg. 2013. "Fatherhood across Time and Space. Russian Fatherhood in Perspective." *Baltic Worlds* 6 (3–4):21–28.

Rossi, Alice. 1984. "Gender and Parenthood." *American Sociological Review* 49 (1):1–19.
Rotkirch, Anna. 2000. "The Man Question: Loves and Lives in Late 20th Century Russia." Helsinki: University of Helsinki, Department of Social Policy Research Report 1/2000.
Sjöstrand, Sven-Erik. 2000. "The Organization of Nonprofit Activities." *Voluntas* 11 (3):199–216.
Skocpol, Theda. 1999. "How Americans Became Civic." In *Civic Engagement in American Democracy*, edited by Theda Skocpol and Morris P. Fiorina, 27–80. Washington, DC: Brookings Institution Press.
Tocqueville, Alexis de. 1997. *Om demokratin i Amerika, bok 2* [Democracy in America, vol. 2]. Stockholm: Atlantis.
Uhlin, Anders. 2006. *Post-Soviet Civil Society: Democratization in Russia and the Baltic States*. London: Routledge.
Vasilishina, Yulia. 2012. "Ottsovskiy instinkt" [Paternal Instinct]. *Rossiyskaja Gazeta*, October 18.
Weigle, Marcia A. 2000. *Russia's Liberal Project. State-Society Relations in the Transition from Communism*. University Park, PA: Pennsylvania State University.
———. 2002. "On the Road to the Civic Forum: State and Civil Society from Yeltsin to Putin." *Demokratizatsiya* 10 (2):117–146.
Williams, Stephen. 2008. "What is Fatherhood? Searching for the Reflective Father." *Sociology* 42 (3):487–502.

6

Fathers' Activism in Ukraine: Contradictory Positions on Gender Equality

Iman Karzabi

Introduction

This chapter analyzes the social activism of fathers, a new form of parental activism in Ukraine. Thus far, parental activism in Ukraine has been analyzed, but scholars have tended to study mothers' mobilizations (Hrycak 2006, 2007; Phillips 2008). In a country where family issues continue to be perceived as predominantly mothers' concerns, with minimal childcare involvement of fathers, the emergence of several fathers' organizations promoting greater participation of fathers in family life appears as an important development concerning gender equality. Thus, the main purpose of this chapter is to discuss the potential links between the promotion of fathers' participation in childcare and the advancement of gender equality in the context of fathers' activism in contemporary Ukraine.

International research on fathers' movements demonstrates that these movements are mostly composed of organizations that defend fathers' rights, which focus on the custody and the rights of divorced fathers, and often express strong antiwomen and antigender equality statements (Korolczuk and Hryciuk; Saxonberg in this volume; Crowley 2006; Dragiewicz 2008; Flood 2010, 2012; Kaye and Tolmie 1998; Rhoades 2006). In Ukraine, fathers' non-governmental organizations (NGOs) focus their activity on promoting the participation of fathers in parenting. Thus, their goals appear as similar to those of feminist movements, which stress the importance of fathers' participation in family life and domestic duties as a condition for the advancement of gender equality in both the private sphere and broader society. Consequently, even though in Ukraine fathers' organizations rarely make statements about gender equality in general terms, these groups are seen as new actors in the promotion of gender equality along with main stakeholders, for example, the representatives of the Ukrainian government and experts engaged in introducing gender equality policies and practices in the country. The reality, however, is more complex.

In this chapter, the term "gender equality" is understood as being related to the division of power (Okin 1989; Scott, Conway, and Bourque 1989). Inequalities between men and women are based on the uneven power distribution related to decision making, access to financial resources, etc., coming from differentiated gender roles and the fact that women provide almost all parenting-related tasks. This has an impact on women's careers, participation in politics, etc., consequently putting women at a disadvantage and in a subaltern position compared to men. Thus, I analyze the position of fathers' activists on gender equality beyond the sharing of parenting responsibilities they directly promote. I focus in particular on their opinion on the equality of roles attributed to mothers and fathers in the private sphere, understood in terms of sharing all duties and power equally as well as between men and women in general. The main objective of this chapter is to analyze whether or not these new actors undermine the patriarchal gender order that persists in current Ukrainian society.

The study is based on interviews conducted with leaders and members of the four main fathers' groups in Ukraine, as well as an analysis of textual materials, internet sites, and policy documents of these organizations. The empirical data demonstrates a paradox in which fathers' organizations defend the principle of equality of rights between fathers and mothers and promote fathers' involvement in family life, yet they fail to undermine the gendered division of labor and attribution of the primary caregiving role to mothers. The activists use the concept of gender equality in a very narrow and limited way, which does not necessarily translate into promoting more gender-equal society. In particular, some organizations express patriarchal views on the division of gender roles and assert the superiority of what they perceive as fathers' roles in the family and in society.

This chapter begins by presenting the origins of fathers' NGOs in Ukraine and their typology. Next, it concentrates on the activities of these organizations that are related to gender equality, analyzing how they consider this principle in their official documents and public actions. This is followed by a more detailed look at the activists' positions on the distribution of gender roles and on the country's existing gender inequalities, based on interviews conducted with representatives of fathers' organizations. The last part of the chapter examines their ability to influence the decision making in the areas of family and gender equality policies as well as the trends toward their cooptation by public authorities. In the conclusions I reflect on the paradoxical effects of the fathers' activism for the sake of gender equality.

Methods of Data Collection

This chapter is based on empirical data collected during my several visits to Ukraine from 2008–2013, lasting a total of ten months. The analysis concentrates on the period prior to the pro-European demonstrations that took place in November 2013 in Kiev and the armed conflict that subsequently began in eastern Ukraine between pro-Russian separatists and the Ukrainian army.

I conducted interviews with representatives of the four main fathers' organizations both in the capital and in other regions during my last visit to Ukraine in August–October 2013. These organizations are the following: Ukrainian Union of Brave Fathers (*Soyuz Muzhnikh Tatusiv*), located in the city of Donetsk in eastern Ukraine; Union of Single-Parent Families of Ukraine (*Ob'ednannia Batkiv-Odinakiv Ukrainy*), in the capital Kiev; International Center of Fatherhood (*Mezhdunarodnyj Centr Otsovstva*) in Kiev; and Ukrainian Network of Schools for Fathers (daddy-schools or *Tato-shkoly* in Ukrainian), with headquarters in the city of Vinnitsa in central Ukraine; it coordinates a network of Schools for Fathers all over the country. I call these groups the "main" fathers' organizations because they were the most visible in the media, they are mentioned in official documents, and were also named by several informants in Ukraine when asked about men's NGOs they knew of.[1] I conducted nine in-depth, open-ended, and face-to-face or telephone interviews with presidents, directors, campaign coordinators, and regular active members of these four organizations. I complemented these interviews by participant observation during some events organized by the NGOs under study, analyzing these organizations' documents and websites and reviewing information available from the media. I also interviewed a number of other stakeholders involved in gender equality policies in Ukraine (governmental bodies, international organizations, women's NGOs, etc.).[2]

The "Crisis of Masculinity" and the Birth of the Ukrainian Fathers' Movement

The Ukrainian fathers' movement emerged in the mid-1990s when the situation of men and the problems men face in the country began to be frequently discussed in political circles and in the media.[3] The figures from the Ukrainian State Statistical Service (2014) indicating men's low life expectancy (63 years in the early 2000s and 66 years in 2013) and poor health prove the deterioration of men's social status. Already in the mid-1990s, alarmist discourses about declining birth rates provoked reforms of family policies and a resurgence of state involvement in the promotion of responsible fatherhood (Zhurzhenko 2004, 2012). Due to the lack of economic means, the government proclaimed that parents must assume full responsibility for the material provision, education, health, and preparation for the adult lives of their children. In this context, fathers' participation in these activities was seen as key to encouraging families to have more children and to meet all children's needs. International influences, for example, stemming from the participation of a Ukrainian state delegation in the 1995 World Conference on Women in Beijing also had an impact on the local level. Due to the geopolitical trends and the desire of the Ukrainian government to join the European Union, particularly after the 2004 Orange Revolution, Ukraine began promoting equality of women and men in all social spheres, including the family, at least in political discourses and official documents (Tolstokorova 2012; Hankivsky and Salnykova 2010; Strelnyk in this volume). In fact, Ukraine is a pioneer country in the post-Soviet region when it comes to the official machinery of gender equality; already in 2005 the country adopted the Law on Ensuring Equal Rights and Opportunities of Women and Men, which aims to advance gender equality in all domains and clarifies the responsibilities of each government branch in this area.[4]

Thus, in the context of local demographic problems and the process of Westernization and Europeanization of the country, the Ukrainian government began paying more attention to the question of fatherhood, which translated into legal changes. Firstly, the first Family Code of independent

Ukraine, adopted in 2002, recognizes the equal role of both parents in providing care and education for their children. The three-year maternity leave was extended to fathers and is now called "parental leave," even though the father can take the leave only after the mother uses her first four months. This leave can last until the baby is three years old. Additionally, instead of family benefits being paid to the mother, today the Family Code indicates that payments should be directed to the parent who is actually raising the child. The Code additionally eliminated women's privileges in custody or alimony regulations, introduced during the Soviet period.[5]

Despite political fluctuations in the country, the promotion of gender equality is rarely presented in political discourse as a way of liberating women from their double burden of family and professional responsibilities. The motivation of the Ukrainian government to foster gender equality in the private sphere stems mostly from the belief that these measures will turn around Ukraine's worsening demographic indicators, ameliorate men's health and social problems, and improve children's well-being (Zhurzhenko 2012). Such legal changes are also a way to prove that Ukraine is a truly European country and is ready to adopt European Union rules in this area, as stated in the EU-Ukraine Association Agenda. This does not mean, however, that changes in law are followed by changes in practices. Despite these legal advances, the participation of fathers in family life remains limited compared to that of mothers. According to a study conducted in 2013 by the League of Social Workers of Ukraine, only 1 percent of Ukrainian fathers entirely or partially take the three-year parental leave, compared to 93 percent of Ukrainian mothers, who remain the primary caregivers (League of Social Workers of Ukraine 2013).

Ukrainian fathers' organizations often quote the data on difficult demographic situation and poor men's health, presenting the return of men to family life as a solution to men's social problems in Ukraine, as well as a key to solving the demographic problems, especially the decline in birth rates. Contemporary Ukrainian fathers' NGOs present their aim of strengthening men's involvement in parenting as a radical change from the model of masculinity promoted during the Soviet period, which they argue remains influential. The activists claim that during the Soviet period, men in the family were marginalized because one of the main aims of the state was to undermine the rule of the father-patriarch in the private sphere as a potential obstacle to family members embracing Soviet ideology. Existing scholarship confirms such a view, showing that nurturing, childcare, and emotional attachment to a baby never formed a legitimate part of Soviet hegemonic masculinity (Bureychak 2012; Kukhterin 2000). Legislation and welfare policies were directed exclusively at mothers and children, without any mention of paternal involvement in raising children. The gender division of care work was maintained with remarkable constancy despite the many changes in social and family policies during the decades of Soviet rule (Ashwin 2000; Kay 2006, 2007; Zdravomyslova and Temkina 2002).

Ideals and practices of parenthood shaped by the Soviet past have been maintained in the contemporary period. Consequently, the current predominant image of male parents in Ukraine is that of minimally engaged fathers, participating much less in nurturing and parenting than mothers, who devote 4.5 times more spare time to home duties than men (League of Social Workers of Ukraine 2013). Men are seen first and foremost as breadwinners and they defer to their female partners to take care of children's physical, emotional, and cognitive needs (Koshulap 2012). According to fathers' NGOs, the marginal position of fathers in family life is a social problem and it has negative consequences on men's status in society and men's health as well as the well-being of families. Fathers' activists share the conviction that Ukrainian masculinity is in crisis and the predominant model of man-breadwinner should be transformed to that of the involved father. However, contrary to men's organizations in other countries, such as the United States (Crowley 2006, 2008), they attribute the marginal position of fathers in family life to the legacy of the Soviet regime rather than to the influence of feminist social movements. All organizations under study share this understanding of the origin of the current crisis of masculinity, even though their repertoires of action and specific goals vary.

Typology of Ukrainian Fathers' NGOs

Fathers' organizations in Ukraine are heterogeneous regarding their origins and activities. Although they are not as numerous as in some other countries, including the United States or Australia, they are almost as diverse as the organizations described by scholars in these Western countries. This may stem from the fact that some Ukrainian fathers' organizations were established with the help of foreign organizations and maintain strong connections with them, although there are also some groups that have been set up in a bottom-up fashion, after their founders experienced personal difficulties, and without any international help.

In Ukraine, one finds nearly the same subsets of fathers' organizations that Anna Gavanas (2002) distinguished in the United States. These include

- "Pro-marriage groups" that see the family as foundational to society and focus on the centrality of the fathers' involvement in family life for its stability. In Ukraine, this type of fathers' organization is represented by the International Center of Fatherhood.[6] It was set up by a seminary-trained pastor within the Evangelical Church in partnership with a USA-based pro-marriage group, the American National Center for Fathering (Gavanas 2002).[7] The Ukrainian and American Centers, in close cooperation, promote the view that fathers have a central role to play in the transmission of "traditional" family values to children and they are chosen for this mission by God.

- "Fragile families' organizations" defending the rights of fathers in difficult economic and social situations. In the American context such groups focus mostly on fathers from ethnic minorities, while in Ukraine these types of fathers' groups focus on economic and social inequalities affecting disabled and single fathers. The Ukrainian Union of Brave Fathers and the Union of Single-Parent Families of Ukraine can be categorized into this group. In contrast to the latter, which addresses the issues of all single-parent families, the Union of Brave Fathers, set up by a disabled father, defends the rights of disabled single fathers, considered by the NGO as the most "vulnerable" and "unprotected" group of parents.[8]

- "Pro-feminist" men's organizations stress the need for more gender equality and employ arguments which resemble those used in feminist social analysis. In the United States these organizations are mostly constituted of men from university circles, in Ukraine this type of fathers' group is represented by an organization working at a more operational level putting in place training for fathers called "schools for fathers"(daddy-schools or *tato-shkoly* in Ukrainian), the Ukrainian Network of Schools for Fathers.[9] This organization, set up in partnership with Swedish men's groups and using methodology and materials developed in Sweden, describes Ukrainian society as patriarchal and unfavorable for both men and women because it imposes narrow sets of social roles, based on persistent gender stereotypes (Martsenyuk, Motygin, and Shestiuk 2009). The Ukrainian Network encourages fathers to adjust to the evolution of the gender contract in which women seek to share professional and political responsibilities with men, while men share family responsibilities with women. Thus, the main activity of this NGO is to provide fathers with all the necessary practical knowledge related to childcare by means of a special course called "school for fathers." Their functioning is very similar to those of the daddy-schools in Russia described by Åberg and Rodin in this volume, and the organizations in both countries cooperate and develop their trainings with the assistance of the same partner organizations in Sweden.[10]

Anna Gavanas (2002) also defined a fourth type of fathers group in the United States, namely the "fathers' rightists," focusing on the custody and the rights of divorced fathers, and often expressing strong antiwomen statements. The fathers' rightists claim that fathers are deprived of their rights and are subject to systematic discrimination as fathers and as men in a system biased toward women and dominated by feminists, in particular through the legal system favoring mothers (Flood 2012: 235). These are often the most active and visible fathers' groups in many Western countries (Crowley 2006; Flood 2010, 2012; Kaye and Tolmie 1998; Rhoades 2006). Other chapters in this volume demonstrate that such groups also exist in the region, for example, in Poland and the Czech Republic (Korolczuk and Hryciuk; Saxonberg). In Ukraine, however, there are no such organizations, and main fathers' groups focus their activity on the promotion of fathers' rights, understood as access to social benefits or symbolic recognition of the father's role. This mismatch is likely due to the Ukrainian local context where the essentialist role of mothers as primary caregivers is also widely accepted among fathers' activists. As will be shown later, fathers are mostly viewed as complementary caregivers, which may explain the fact that after divorce, having full or joint custody is rarely sought by men in Ukraine today.

Fathers' organizations in Ukraine also vary in terms of the repertoires of their actions. Previous research on social activism in the Ukrainian context has shown that even though there are some grassroots initiatives in the country, in most cases activism is channeled into formalized, bureaucratic, professionalized organizations that spend most of their time on grant management and are distant from citizens' concerns (Hrycak 2006, 2007; Pishchikova 2011). This does not seem to be the case for fathers' NGOs, which combine different forms of activism. They provide direct assistance to fathers including the distribution of humanitarian aid, organizing training to teach men how to be caring fathers and to lead political lobbying activities, and occasionally also mass mobilizations to promote involved fatherhood. This chapter concentrates in particular on fathers' organizations' actions oriented toward gender equality, in their lobbying activities toward the government.

Fathers' Activism and the Promotion of Gender Equality

In this section I analyze how fathers' activists define gender equality in their official documents and their actions targeting the authorities and the general public. All the studied organizations stress the importance of gender equality in their lobbying activities toward the government. However, they often refer to the "equality between men and women," highlighting the need for equal treatment and recognition of fathers, rather than to the term "gender," which is difficult to translate into Ukrainian and Russian.[11] I classify equality oriented fathers' groups' activities into three types. These include efforts concerning (1) legal reforms to entitle fathers with the same rights as mothers pertaining to paternity leave and single-parent subsidies; (2) the symbolic recognition of the importance of fatherhood in the same way as for motherhood, in particular through the creation of a specific national Father's Day; and (3) equal access of fathers to knowledge related to childcare.

1) Legal Reforms to Counteract Discrimination toward Fathers

The Ukrainian Union of Brave Fathers focuses on the rights of disabled single fathers; however, it lobbies for all fathers' rights to supplementary paternity leave. Today, Ukrainian fathers can benefit from almost three years of paid parental leave, which places Ukraine among countries with most favorable regulations in this respect, even though in practice men rarely take parental leave. However, the activists point to the fact that today only the mother is entitled to maternity leave of four months related to the pregnancy and the birth. A father may take parental leave only after the mother's first four months end. Consequently, the union activists demanded the creation of a supplementary two-week paternity leave that the father can use immediately following the birth of a baby. As the director of the organization explained to me in an interview,

> We find it unjust that babies spend their first months of life mostly with their mothers. The law does not provide any legal opportunity for fathers to stop working and care for his family during this crucial period, as it happens in other countries. It is important to create a link between a baby and his father as soon as possible. If not, the baby will be too attached to his mother and the father can quickly feel that he has become an outsider. (Interview, September 11, 2013, author's translation)

However, despite the persistent lobbying for such a legal solution, no legal changes have been introduced. The response of the members of Ukrainian Parliament to the demands of the Ukrainian Union of Brave Fathers indicated that the issue attracted their attention but such measures are financially unaffordable.

Another organization, the Union of Single-Parent Families of Ukraine, was more successful in lobbying for legal change. It succeeded in obtaining the abrogation of gender-based discriminatory regulations regarding widowed or divorced fathers, which prevented them from receiving government assistance equivalent to that received by single mothers. As the leader of the NGO explained to me, even though the majority of single-parent families in Ukraine are constituted by a mother with her children, there are also many single fathers in the country. Some of them raise several children alone. Thus, single fathers mobilized to change the situation where

> all Ukrainian laws regarding lone-parent families referred only to the social rights of single mothers, without any mention of single fathers. It is completely unjust that they had been excluded from the right to receive a financial subsidy from the government, from favorable conditions provided by labor legislation to this kind of social group, from priority in receiving social housing, etc., from all of the benefits that are allocated to single mothers. (Interview, September 4, 2013, author's translation)

To obtain gender equality in the area of social rights of single fathers and mothers, in 2010 the Union of Single-Parent Families of Ukraine initiated a lobbying campaign. The activists wrote letters to several members of Parliament, local administrators, ministers, and the president. The director of the NGO also publicized these problems in newspapers and on television.[12] Finally, in July 2013, the law n° 239-VII "on the guarantee of the quality of rights of single mothers and single fathers" was adopted in Ukraine.[13] It eliminated gender-based discrimination regarding access to social provisions for single parents, giving fathers access to state help comparable to the support single mothers get.

This case shows that Ukrainian fathers' organizations are able to successfully petition the authorities, and they have made some considerable gains. At the same time, not all groups have been effective in changing the law. Successfully eliminating discrimination toward fathers accessing already existing social provisions for single parents can be explained by the changes in political context, especially the Ukrainian government's aspiration to join the EU. This process strengthened the government's commitment to abrogate all gender-based discrimination in national legislation, as stated in the EU-Ukraine Association Agenda that became effective in 2009.[14] However, it turned out to be much more difficult for the Ukrainian Union of Brave Fathers to introduce two-week paternity leave for fathers, analogous to the one that mothers get. This may be related to the relatively high costs of universal leave for fathers as stated by Ukrainian authorities, combined with a range of socioeconomic obstacles to active fatherhood as discussed by Åberg and Rodin in this volume (e.g., low family income and housing problems), as well as the deeply rooted belief that mothers should be primary caregivers.

2) Symbolic Recognition of Fatherhood

In 2006, the International Center of Fatherhood began a lobbying campaign to create an official Father's Day in Ukraine. The aim was to create a new public holiday promoting the importance of fathers in raising and educating children and to show that fatherhood is as important as motherhood. The organization found it unjust that only Mother's Day was widely celebrated in the country. Thus, the center aimed to create a Father's Day in Ukraine that would have the same rank as International Women's Rights Day, celebrated on March 8th and which has been a public holiday in the country since the Soviet period; it is generally synonymous with Mothers' Day in Ukraine.[15]

To attract the government's attention to the issue, the International Center of Fatherhood began by consulting with Ukrainian citizens to add legitimacy to the proposal. More precisely, the center organized public meetings in several Ukrainian cities to explain the importance of the project and collected ten thousand signatures from citizens supporting this initiative. Members of the organization subsequently met several ministers and members of Parliament to lobby for the creation of Father's Day. The campaign was successful: since 2009, Father's Day (*Den' Bat'ka*) has been celebrated every third Sunday of September in Ukraine. The International Center of Fatherhood has become a privileged governmental partner in the organization of the celebrations. In Fall 2013, following persistent lobbying from the center, the Ministry of Social Affairs proposed to the president of Ukraine to promote the Father's Day to the status of an official national holiday (of the same rank as March 8th). However, the decision on the Ministry's proposition is still pending because of the political instability in the country since November 2013.

This issue turned out to be the source of conflict between different fathers' groups. The previously discussed fathers' NGO, the Ukrainian Union of Brave Fathers, has also attempted to advocate for the creation of a Fathers' Day (*Den' Tata*) but opposed the event that was put in place by the government and the International Center of Fatherhood. Firstly, the Union activists criticized the fact that Fathers' Day is called "*Den' Bat'ka*" in Ukrainian, a term that means not only "father's day" but also "parent's day." The Union proposes renaming the holiday *Den' Tata* to emphasize that this day is devoted specifically to fathers. Secondly, the current Father's Day is celebrated on the third Sunday in September, whereas the Union advocates that this day should be celebrated on May 19th, the day of the official registration of the Ukrainian Union of Brave Fathers, as it was the first fathers' organization in the country and the first to lobby for the creation of a Father's Day. Apparently, their struggle concerns both symbolic recognition of the fathers' role and their own importance as the pioneers of fathers' activism in Ukraine. Despite a lack of success, the union continues its campaign, mostly by sending letters to different ministries and administration, and the activists celebrate their own alternative *Den' Tata* annually. This conflict reflects power struggles between different fathers' groups, particularly regarding the cooperation with public authorities, and indicates that despite similar agendas, the activists find it difficult to cooperate (see also Korolczuk and Hryciuk in this volume).

3) Equal Access to Knowledge Related to Childcare

The Ukrainian Network of Schools for Fathers claims that in order to encourage fathers to take a more active part in family life, it is first necessary to provide them with all necessary knowledge related to parenting. According to the activists, fathers feel excluded from the transmission of knowledge about childcare. They point to the fact that most handbooks, internet sites, or existing training for future parents are addressed to women. To fill this gap, the organization developed a special course exclusively for fathers called daddy-schools or *tato-shkoly* in Ukrainian. Today, daddy-schools function in half of the Ukrainian regions, training hundreds of fathers every year.

The courses, targeting fathers-to-be, are based on the program that has been operating for several years in Sweden. It includes such topics as knowledge regarding pregnancy, the health of the mother and the baby, practical childcare, and advice on the procedures for requesting government benefits for families with children, as well as gender equality principles and prevention of domestic violence. Both official documents and the internet site of the organization stress that the aim is to combat stereotypes concerning fatherhood and motherhood based on patriarchal social norms and to emphasize the need for more equality between men and women in private and public spheres (Martsenyuk, Motygin, and Shestiuk 2009). In this respect, the Ukrainian Network of Schools for Fathers is the only fathers' organization in the country that officially defines gender equality not only in terms of fathers' rights and status, but also as interaction between men and women based on the same rights, duties, and equal distribution of power. However, as I will show later in this chapter, there is a significant discrepancy between ideology and practice, between the theoretical basis of the organization and its everyday activity.

Activist Fathers' Positions on Gender Equality: from Indifference to Appraisal of Patriarchy

In the following section I analyze in more detail the activists' views on, and their understanding of, gender equality. Such an analysis is important, since fathers' organizations have been recognized as new actors in public debate on gender equality. In interviews conducted with various stakeholders involved in gender equality policies in Ukraine (including administrators in charge of governmental policies, researchers, representatives of international agencies, etc.), the respondents unanimously stated that they view the activities of fathers' organizations as an important step in advancing gender equality in the country. Actions aimed at more equal division of childcare responsibilities between mothers and fathers are generally viewed by all my informants as a key element of introducing equality between men and women in all spheres of public and private life. Although women's groups remain hesitant about the emergence of fathers' groups, fearing marginalization, they are not opposed to them because in the Ukrainian contexts such groups do not openly express antifeminist positions, as is the case of fathers' rightists in other countries. Given this growing public recognition of fathers' groups and their partnership with government institutions, the purpose of this research was also to understand the activists' position on gender equality beyond the scope of the reforms for which they lobby, as presented in previous parts.

Detailed analysis of the opinions of fathers' activists expressed during interviews challenges the view that promoting fathers' rights and their more active participation in family life translates into the promotion of equality between men and women more generally, a view that is often taken for granted by the stakeholders I interviewed. My analysis shows that Ukrainian fathers' organizations principally focus on the child-father relationship, and their stance on the subject of the division of childcare work is usually limited to general statements about the positive influence of the involvement of fathers in children's care and education. Activists rarely talk about gender equality in the family in terms of equal distribution of all household tasks between men and women, for example, cleaning, cooking, etc. Moreover, they seem oblivious to the persistent gender inequalities in Ukraine that primarily and significantly affect women and stem from the fact that women carry out most unpaid care work: for example, the gender wage gap in contemporary Ukraine is more than 30 percent (Libanova 2012; Hankivsky and Salnykova 2012). In the context of men's low involvement in family life and insufficient public child-care infrastructure, women with small children, especially those with few qualifications and lacking a work record, have little chance of getting a job, and young, married women—prospective mothers—are particularly strongly discriminated against in the labor market (Libanova 2012; Zhurzhenko 2012).

Fathers' activists often stress equal capacities of both parents when it comes to taking care of the children, but most subscribe to "traditional" visions of gender roles as complementary rather than equivalent. Thus, fathers' groups promote the participation of fathers in child raising but do not necessarily embrace the idea of gender equality understood as sharing all responsibilities concerned with parenting and home duties on an equal basis. In fact, they do not challenge the role of mothers as primary caregivers. Additionally, the new ideal of involved fathering, which implies spending time with children, as promoted by Ukrainian fathers' groups, is often combined with some elements of the traditional patriarchal model of family, based, for instance, on fathers' control and superior role in educating children.

The interviews conducted with leaders and members of the four organizations under study identified three main characteristics of the position on gender equality that most fathers' activists take: some of them ignore the inequalities suffered by women; some promote patriarchal views on gender roles while others display a mere formal engagement in promoting gender equality.[16]

Although all activists participating in the study highlighted the discrimination that fathers suffer in Ukrainian society, they tended to disregard the gender-based inequalities faced by women. When the leaders of the fathers' organizations were asked about gender inequality in Ukraine and the importance of greater paternal participation in care, they never mentioned the double burden of professional and home duties women face and its impact on women's careers, participation in politics, and their personal fulfillment. The Union of Single-Parent Families of Ukraine represents a typical case in this regard. According to the organization's leader, fathers and mothers in single-parent families face the same difficulties and have to combine multiple working occupations to guarantee sufficient financial resources for their families. Although the organization mostly directs its help to single fathers, it also occasionally assists single mothers. During the interview, the leader of the organization completely dismissed the discrimination that mothers confront in contemporary Ukrainian society as women, such as the fact that occupational gender segregation leaves Ukrainian women in jobs that are less stable and provide lower income; therefore, if they become head of a single-parent family, they consequently face greater financial hardships than men.[17] The organization disregards this disparity and focuses on the (very real) difficulties faced by single fathers, neglecting, however, a variety of ways in which single mothers are additionally disadvantaged.

The patriarchal views articulated by fathers' organizations range from stereotypical and essentialist views on the roles fathers and mothers play in child raising, to affirming the superiority of the father, as in the case of some Czech activists (see Saxonberg in this volume). While the activists representing Union of Brave Fathers expressed stereotypical views about the role of the mother, which the activists see as devoted mostly to the private sphere and dependent on her male partner, the International Center of Fatherhood places a patriarchal view of gender roles at the core of their ideology and ideal model of the family. Generally, the majority of the fathers' NGOs refer to a singular model of the family: a heterosexual nuclear family, which is based on the notion of gender differences and the complementarity of men's and women's roles. In this vein, several activists expressed the opinion that homosexual couples cannot be considered "a family."

During his interview with me, the leader of the Union of Brave Fathers emphasized that he always tries to spread an "honorable" image of women because women are "a weak part of humanity" and men should behave like a "knight" to "protect" them (Interview, September 11, 2013, author's translation). Such behavior should include the participation of men in family tasks, in addition to supporting the family financially, but men participate rather as women's helpers than as equals or the persons in charge of care activities.

The president of the International Center of Fatherhood, which works closely with the Ukrainian government, expressed more radical statements, claiming that men and women have different innate "natures" and "behaviors" as parents. He drew on biblical metaphors to discuss gender relations, arguing that men are fundamentally different from women and fathers and mothers have different God-given roles in the family. He affirmed in an interview that

> men and women accomplish unique and complementary roles in children's education. The role of the mother is to provide emotional protection and kindness to children. The father provides material security and helps children build their self-assertion. The father teaches the son to be a gentleman and to share his love; the mother teaches the daughter to be a real lady and to receive love. The parents can never replace each other in these roles and this complementarity is essential for the balanced development of children. (Interview, August 26, 2013, author's translation)

Thus, this group links "the decline of fatherhood" to changing gender roles. A close reading of the training materials created by his organization showed that the organization strongly defends the superiority of men within the family, stating that "the husband is superior to the wife and God is superior to the man. Man is responsible for his family in front of God" (Marchenko 2013, 39–42, see also Korolczuk and Hryciuk in this volume). The president of the center explained this statement to me in an interview claiming that the privileged role and mission of the father has been given to him in biblical commandments in which God is first of all a father. Thus, men have been chosen by God as fathers living on Earth for the transmission of biblical commandments to their sons, who will become fathers and in turn transfer these values to their male offspring. Without the participation of fathers, moral and spiritual values cannot be transferred from one generation to another. The role of the mother is clearly secondary according to this perspective. While fathers provide what they see as appropriate discipline to children, encourage independence, and teach self-discipline, motherhood is characterized by the binary opposite: it is cautious, "soft," and offers comforting child-rearing practices. Hence, according to the organization, although children need both parents, the father in particular is irreplaceable (Interview, August 26, 2013, author's translation).

The superiority of men is also reflected in the public sphere, as the NGO stresses the social responsibility of fathers for the well-being of the whole society. As stated in the training materials, "If fathers do not spend time with their children and do not transfer God's message from one generation to another, this leads the society to destruction and death" (Marchenko 2013, 42). Such a position echoes the fear of a "fatherless nation" spread by neoconservative groups and organizations in the United States, which should come as no surprise, given the close cooperation between the center and its American donors who initiated the establishment of the organization. Given the current wave of nationalism and growing importance of religion in public life, we can expect this message to gain in popularity in the country (cf. Strelnyk in this volume).

Finally, even the activists who appear as committed to promoting gender equality do not necessarily promote it in everyday practice. The Network of Schools for Fathers is the only fathers' NGO in the country that has a clear vision of the patriarchal traditions of Ukrainian society and is formally committed to combating gender-specific stereotypes throughout all the trainings of daddy-schools. Such a strong commitment to combating gender inequality probably reflects the close connections with the Scandinavian sponsors; however, the organization finds it difficult to adjust these ideas to the Ukrainian context. Such a conclusion results from a close examination of the activities of the organization, proving that its formal commitment to promoting gender equality is not always matched by its actions.

The gender-sensitive approach applied by the Network was developed in the framework of the cooperation of the organization with the Swedish profeminist groups, such as Men for Gender Equality, which assisted the NGO in developing its training materials. Officially, the concept of gender as well as the socially constructed gender inequalities and stereotypes form key elements of the trainings. All teachers are expected to use these materials in the schools. As stated in the methodology book of the Ukrainian Schools for Fathers, "the gender equality part of the course is essential and is the only one that is compulsory in the training, while the choice of other themes can be made according to the interests of the participants" (Martsenyuk, Motygin and Shestiuk 2009, 48).

However, in my interviews conducted with some schools' trainers, they revealed that the topic of gender equality was omitted by most of them because they considered this issue to be too controversial. The trainers felt that the Schools for Fathers course was too short and it was impossible to discuss such a complex issue within only a few hours. Moreover, they did not feel that they themselves had received enough training to address all controversies that this part of the course can raise. As stated by one of the trainers,

> fathers come with stereotypes that have been forged since their childhood and it is hard to convince them within only a few hours that care and nurturing are not women's natural qualities and that fathers can replace them. They mainly

> want to learn very practical things about childcare to be able to spend some time with their kids and to help their wives, but they have difficulties imagining that they can become the main childcare providers and that the mother can be the main provider of financial resources for the family. (Interview, September 25, 2013, author's translation)

The question is also to what extent have these schools actually changed the attitudes of the participants? Åberg and Rodin (in this volume) stress that answering such a question would require a study of the participants before and after participating in trainings. The interviews I conducted with some of the daddy-school trainees in Kiev suggest that participation in courses does not result in changing the views on gender order that many participants shared before they entered training. After following the training course, and although they stressed the will to become engaged parents, most fathers I talked to saw their role only as complementary to those of mothers, as occasional childcare providers. They claimed that they could not imagine themselves being the main caregiver to their child because "they have to guarantee necessary financial resources for their family," and "men have other social missions to accomplish and cannot spend all their time with their family" (interview, September 25, 2013, author's translation). This shows that despite its formal commitment to gender equality, these schools generally provide fathers mostly with practical knowledge regarding childcare. It also confirms other scholars' assessments that feminism and gender equality as international concepts are rearranged by social actors according to local cultural and social contexts (e.g., Hrycak 2006).

Establishing Partnerships with the State: Political Openings for Fathers' Organizations

All the organizations under study not only seek to promote the reforms that are to benefit Ukrainian fathers, but also try to influence public policies more generally, for example, by becoming governmental partners. This gives them the possibility of influencing the decision-making process on family and gender equality issues, despite their controversial positions on the issue. In general, the activists approve both state support and state intervention in the sphere of the family. This sets them apart from some fathers' movements in other contexts, especially from fathers' rightists, who often oppose the state, seeing it as too intrusive and powerful in relation to the family.

Researchers have shown that these groups usually insist the state should stop intervening in the private sphere of the family, for example, by providing divorced women with alimony and child custody (Flood 2012; Municio-Larsson and Pujol Algans 2002). As shown by Korolczuk and Hryciuk in this volume, Polish fathers' rights groups also proclaim that the state aims to control the private sphere and to destroy the family in order to introduce a new political system, which is a trend supposedly reflecting the communist legacy. In contrast, Ukrainian fathers' organizations do not oppose the state. Rather, they see the recent interest of the Ukrainian government in men's issues as a political opening and an attempt at establishing a close collaboration with the authorities (see also Åberg and Rodin in this volume). My analysis shows the growing influence of fathers' groups as to formulation and implementation of public policies pertaining to family and gender equality. These two policy fields are interconnected in the country and are often administered by the same public authorities.[18] As shown above, fathers' organizations have succeeded in cooperating with the government in promoting fathers' social rights and position. The cooperation between state and civil society has become more frequent in recent years along with the growing influence of conservative groups in Ukraine as shown by Strelnyk (in this volume).

In this section, I discuss how the structure of political opportunities has become more open for fathers' organizations in recent years. In contrast to the Soviet period when the subject of the men's vulnerability was a taboo, today the Ukrainian authorities tend to view fathers' issues as a problem that should be addressed by the state rather than merely as a private concern. As is often the case in the region, in Ukraine the issue of fatherhood has entered the public debate in the context of two important trends, which include the demographic crisis as well as the gender equality discourse and regulations brought by the process of Westernization, and Europeanization, of the country. This explains why Ukrainian authorities acknowledge the activities of fathers' NGOs and rely on their expertise and services.

Some organizations, for example, the Union of Single-Parent Families of Ukraine and the Union of Brave Fathers, developed close links with several elected members of national Parliament and local authorities, whereas the most conservative fathers' organization in the country, the International Center of Fatherhood, became influential on the national level.[19] The International Center of Fatherhood became a governmental partner in defining family policy in 2012 when the Ministry of Social Affairs decided to include the activists in the group of experts working on the "Governmental program of social help to families for the period from 2013 to 2016," which was a roadmap for future family policies. The program was adopted on May 15, 2013, and due to the lobbying of the center, it includes many references to the importance of the promotion of responsible fatherhood.[20] The International Center of Fatherhood also became an official member of the Public Council, established by the local authorities of the city of Kiev as a consultative structure on the questions on family and gender equality policies.[21]

Lobbying of fathers' groups also had an impact on the Ukrainian government's latest "Program on the realization of gender equality for the period 2013–2016" adopted in September 2013.[22] This program states that there should be training activities for parents promoting equal division of parental responsibilities, organized in partnership with civil society organizations. It is likely that fathers' groups will be privileged governmental partners in the implementation of these measures, strengthening their existing cooperation.

The Ukrainian Network of Schools for Fathers, formally engaged in promoting gender equality, is also already engaged in cooperation with local Ukrainian authorities. Members of the Network are partners in implementing regional family and gender equality policies that promote more responsible fathering through the trainings organized at daddy-schools. Their cooperation with public authorities, however, remains limited mostly to service-providing, and their ability to promote the principle of gender equality in a broader sense is narrow. As discussed by Åberg and Rodin in this volume, the service provision can be a way of legitimating the expertise of the organization in the eyes of public authorities and can then be used as a means to fill an advocacy role. However, the Ukrainian Network of Schools for Fathers does not seem to be looking to take such a role.

These trends show that there have been significant openings in the political opportunity structure, thus enabling fathers' groups to exert influence on the public discourse and regulations.[23] However, this mostly concerns groups expressing conservative and patriarchal views on families and gender roles. The fathers' groups that are formally involved in the promotion of the gender equality tend to focus on service provision, rather than becoming involved in advocacy. Consequently, even though there are no fathers' rightists groups in Ukraine, the influence of existing conservative organizations may impede the promotion of gender equality in Ukraine, as it was the case in other countries with active fathers' rightist's groups.

Conclusions

In comparison to fathers' groups studied in other countries, the fathers' organizations in Ukraine appear in some respects similar and in some different. In contrast to fathers' rights movements in the United States, Canada, Czech Republic, or Poland that focus mostly on custody issues, fathers groups in Ukraine do not address this issue. Rather, they fight for specific welfare provisions and promote more general social change in regard to fathers' attitudes and the participation of fathers in childcare. Comparably to organizations that operate in other cultural and social contexts, they use political lobbying, organize campaigns for the symbolic recognition of the importance of fatherhood, and fight for the access of fathers to the knowledge related to parenting. The activists promote equal treatment of fathers in all legal provisions, aiming at changing the remaining discriminatory laws and regulations. Their activities have resulted in some important reforms that promote fathers' participation in family life. As a result of their activities, Ukrainian fathers' organizations have also gained considerable political, public, and media resonance in recent years. The activities of these organizations are viewed as an important contribution to the advancement of gender equality within the family and in society more generally, despite this not being the organizations' primary goal.

However, examination of the ideologies and activities of these organizations in more detail reveals a paradox. Although equality between men and women is an important element of their rhetoric, a closer look shows that they employ a narrow notion of equality, mostly based on the equality of rights that does not necessarily echo the feminist definition of this term. The fact that these organizations promote involved fatherhood does not equate to promotion of gender equality in the family and in broader society, which is understood in terms of sharing both care and power equally. Some accounts reported here unveil a masculinist construction of equality that obfuscates the gendered inequalities and experiences of mothers and fathers. Moreover, some organizations express patriarchal views on the division of gender roles and assert the superiority of what they perceive as fathers' roles in the family and in society, making their position even closer to fathers' rightists' declarations in other countries. Given the partnership of conservative organizations with the government, it is obvious that their contribution to policy-making can be an impediment to gender equality promotion in the country. Also, the existing profeminist fathers' groups formally engaged in combating the patriarchal gender order in current Ukrainian society do not engage in advocacy, leaving the space for the growing influence of conservative groups.

Fathers' groups have adopted the language of gender equality but not the feminist spirit of equality. Most Ukrainian fathers' groups do not undermine the unequal distribution of power between men and women, despite the novel image of "caring" masculinity they appear to promote. Their opinions and actions reflect how, in contemporary Ukrainian society, "progressive" ideas and trends overlap and intersect with the patriarchal discourses. Arguably, the latter will be exacerbated in the nearest future, due to the current increase in nationalism and rise of conservative religious groups in the country.

Iman Karzabi, PhD, Center for International Studies and Research, Institute of Political Science of Paris (Sciences Po), France

Iman Karzabi's research interests focus on gender equality policies, violence against women, and NGO and social movements in postcommunist countries, particularly in Ukraine and Belarus. In her PhD thesis, she explores how transnational gender dynamics and domestic priorities, such as demographic issues, impact gender equality, family policies, and gender contract between women and men. Recently, she co-organized an international conference in Paris, on Gender and Nationalism in Post-Soviet Countries.

Notes

1. These four organizations do not represent an exhaustive cartography of all fathers' organizations and groups currently active in Ukraine. There are other organizations, for example, Men Against Gender-Based Violence. However, it is difficult to know if this latter organization still functions because no information is available on the internet on their current activities and no contact information is provided.

2. I am grateful to the *Institut Emilie du Châtelet* and the *Association Française des Femmes Diplômées des Universités* (AFFDU) for providing the financial assistance that allowed me to organize several stays in Ukraine to collect empirical data. I am also grateful to Loretta G.

Platts, a health researcher with an interest in the region, who attentively read several drafts of this article and provided valuable comments.

3. I use the term "movement," here understood as a "collective action by people with common purposes" (Tarrow 1998), because though these groups operate independently, they pursue some shared goals.

4. The text of the law is available in English (last accessed July 16, 2015): http://www.legislationline.org/download/action/download/id/3426/file/Ukraine_law_on_ensuring_equal_rights_and_opportunities_of_women_and_men_2005_e.pdf.

5. The Family Code of Ukraine is available in English at (last accessed July 26, 2015) http://www.familylaw.com.ua/docs/FAMILY_CODE_OF_UKRAINE.doc.

6. The website of the organization in English (last accessed July 1, 2015) is http://icfatherhood.org/.

7. The website of the organization (last accessed July 1, 2015) is https://www.fathers.com/.

8. The Ukrainian Union of Brave Fathers does not have a website; however the details about its history and main activities can be found on the following page in Ukrainian (last accessed July 16, 2015): http://gurt.org.ua/news/recent/15403/#lastcomment. The website of the Union of Single-Parent Families of Ukraine in Ukrainian (last accessed July 16, 2015) is www.mytato.com.ua.

9. The Facebook page of the Network in Ukrainian (last accessed July 16, 2015): https://www.facebook.com/papanet.ua.

10. Both organizations are members of the Men Engage Alliance, an international network of men's organizations involved in the promotion of gender equality, which is coordinated in Europe by the Swedish NGO Men for Gender Equality (accessed on July 16, 2015) (http://menengage.org/). The organizations of both countries are also involved in the project "Men Can Do It," concerning social work with men in post-Soviet countries and Northern Europe (accessed on July 16, 2015) (http://www.mencandoit.org/#!about/cij1). Moreover, the leaders of the organizations in Ukraine and in Russia participated in the publishing of a common methodological manual on the establishment of schools for fathers (accessed on July 16, 2015) (http://menengage.org/resources/father-school-step-step/).

11. Also, this term is controversial in Ukraine since it is often associated exclusively with LGBT rights, which some fathers' organizations openly oppose (cf. Strelnyk in this volume).

12. All the actions conducted by the organization, including the letters sent to the government and copies of newspaper articles and a video with the interviews of the director of the organization can be viewed on the organization's Facebook page (in Ukrainian): https://www.facebook.com/pages/Объединение-Родителей-одиночек-Украины/189284017817792 and on the website of the organization (last accessed July 1, 2015): www.mytato.com.ua.

13. Available (in Ukrainian) (last accessed on July 28, 2014) on http://zakon4.rada.gov.ua/laws/show/239–18.

14. The text of the Association Agenda signed by the EU-Ukraine Cooperation Council in November 2009 is available in English (last accessed July 16, 2015) at http://www.eeas.europa.eu/ukraine/docs/2010_eu_ukraine_association_agenda_en.pdf.

15. The official Mothers' Day was introduced in Ukraine in 2000 and is celebrated on the second Sunday in May. However, March 8th, Women's Rights Day, remains synonymous with Mothers' Day in Ukraine and is a national public holiday.

16. During the interviews, I chose not to introduce the word "gender" as it is not used by fathers' organizations for the reasons explained above. Instead, I used "equality" of men and women.

17. Interview conducted on September 4, 2013.

18. On the national level, the Ministry of Social Affairs is responsible for both family and gender equality policies.

19. For example, the Union of Brave Fathers celebrates its alternative Father's Day in the city of Donetsk with the support of local authorities. The Union of Single-Parent Families of Ukraine could get the financial assistance of some MPs for the development of its activities toward single fathers.

20. The Program is available in Ukrainian (last accessed July 28, 2014) at http://zakon2.rada.gov.ua/laws/show/341-2013.

21. More detailed information on the Public Council can be found on the following link (last accessed July 28, 2014) in Ukrainian: http://sms.gov.ua/.

22. The Program is available in Ukrainian (last accessed July 16, 2015) on http://zakon4.rada.gov.ua/laws/show/717-2013-%D0%BF.

23. Evidently, there are also significant closings related to the current crisis in Eastern Ukraine that significantly change the priorities of the state and issues that appear in the public debate.

Works Cited

Ashwin, Sarah. 2000. *Gender, State and Society in Soviet and Post-Soviet Russia.* London, New York: Routledge.

Bureychak, Tetyana. 2012. "Masculinity in Soviet and Post-Soviet Ukraine: Models and Their Implications." In *Gender, Politics and Society in Ukraine*, edited by Olena Hankivsky and Anastasia Salnykova, 325–361. Toronto: University of Toronto Press.

Crowley, Jocelyn E. 2006. "Organizational Responses to the Fatherhood Crisis: The Case of Fathers' Rights Groups in the United States." *Marriage and Family Review* 39:99–120.

———. 2008. *Defiant Dads: Fathers' Rights Activists in America.* Ithaca, New York: Cornell University Press.

Dragiewicz, Molly. 2008. "Patriarchy Reasserted Fathers' Rights and Anti-VAWA Activism." *Feminist Criminology* 3:121–144.

Flood, Michael. 2010. "Fathers' Rights and the Defense of Paternal Authority in Australia." *Violence Against Women* 16:328–347.

———. 2012. "Separated Fathers and the 'Fathers' Rights' Movement." *Journal of Family Studies* 18:235–245.

Gavanas, Anne. 2002. "The Fatherhood Responsibility Movement: The Centrality of Marriage, Work and Male Sexuality in Reconstructions of Masculinity and Fatherhood." In *Making Men into Fathers: Men, Masculinities, and the Social Politics of Fatherhood*, edited by Barbara Hobson, 213–244. Cambridge: Cambridge University Press.

Hankivsky, Olena, and Anastasia Salnykova. 2010. "Gender Mainstreaming in Post-Soviet Ukraine: Application and Applicability." *Journal of Communist Studies and Transition Politics* 26 (3):383–408.

———. 2012. *Gender, Politics and Society in Ukraine.* Toronto: University of Toronto Press.

Hrycak, Alexandra. 2006. "Foundation Feminism and the Articulation of Hybrid Feminisms in Post-Socialist Ukraine." *East European Politics and Societies* 20:69–100.

———. 2007. "Gender and the Orange Democratic Revolution in Ukraine." *Journal of Communist Studies and Transition Politics* 23:152–179.
Kay, Rebecca. 2006. *Men in Contemporary Russia: The Fallen Heroes of Post-Soviet Change?* Aldershot, Burlington: Ashgate.
———. 2007. "Caring for Men in Contemporary Russia: Gendered Constructions of Need and Hybrid Forms of Social Security." *Focaal: European Journal of Anthropology* 50:51–65.
Kaye, Miranda, and Julia Tolmie. 1998. "Fathers' Rights Groups in Australia and Their Engagement with Issues of Family Law." *Australian Journal of Family Law* 12:19–67.
Koshulap, Iryna. 2012. "Cash and/or Care: Current Discourses and Practices of Fatherhood in Ukraine." In *Gender, Politics and Society in Ukraine*, edited by Olena Hankivky and Anastasia Salnykova, 362–384. Toronto: University of Toronto Press.
Kukhterin, Sergei. 2000. "Fathers and Patriarchs in Communist and Post-Communist Russia." In *Gender, State and Society in Soviet and Post-Soviet Russia*, edited by Sarah Ashwin, 71–89. London, New York: Routledge.
League of Social Workers of Ukraine. 2013. *Doslidzhennia potreb batkiv pid chas povernennia ikh do profesiinoi diialnosti pislia vidpustky dlia-dohliadu za dytynoiu* [Study of Parents' Needs during Their Return to Work after Parental Leave]. Kyiv. Accessed August 1, 2015. http://znovudoroboty.org.ua/ua/biblioteka/dokumenty-proektu/137-doslidzhennia-potreb-batkiv-pid-chas-povernennia-ikh-do-profesiinoi-diialnosti-pislia-vidpustky-dlia-dohliadu-za-dytynoiu.
Libanova, Ella. 2012. *Analytical Research on Women's Participation in the Labour Force in Ukraine*. Kyiv: The United Nations Population Fund. Accessed August 1, 2015. http://www.unfpa.org.ua/files/articles/4/28/Analytical%20research%20on%20women's%20participation%20in%20the%20labour%20force%20in%20Ukraine%20(EN).pdf.
Marchenko, Alexander. 2013. *Sila otsovstva: Obratit serdsa otsov k Detiam* [*The Force of Fatherhood: Turn Fathers' Hearts to Children*]. Kyiv: Mezhdunarodnyj Centr Otsovstva [International Fathering Center].
Martsenyuk, Volodomyr, Volodomyr Motygin, and Olena Shestiuk. 2009. *Tato-Shkola: Yak Stvoriti ta Zabespechiti Stale Funkcionuvannya. Metodichnyj Posibnyk* [*School for Fathers: How to Set Up and Guarantee a Stable Development. Methodological Handbook*]. Vinnytsia: FOP Daniliyuk. Accessed August 1, 2015. www.unicef.org/ukraine/ukr/7.1_Tato_School_Book.pdf.
Municio-Larsson, Ingegerd, and Carmen Pujol Algans. 2002. "Making Sense of Fatherhood: The Non-Payment of Child Support in Spain." In *Making Men into Fathers: Men, Masculinities and the Social Politics of Fatherhood*, edited by Barbara Hobson, 191–212. Cambridge: Cambridge University Press.
Okin, Susan. 1989. *Justice, Gender, and the Family*. New York: Basic Books.
Phillips, Sarah D. 2008. *Women's Social Activism in the New Ukraine: Development and the Politics of Differentiation*. Bloomington: Indiana University Press.
Pishchikova, Kateryna. 2011. *Promoting Democracy in Postcommunist Ukraine: The Contradictory Outcomes of US Aid to Women's NGOs*. Boulder, CO: First Forum Press.
Rhoades, Helen. 2006. "Yearning for Law: Fathers' Groups and Family Law Reform in Australia." In *Fathers' Rights Activism and Legal Reform in Comparative Context*, edited by Richard Collier and Sally Sheldon, 125–146. Oxford: Hart Publishing.

Scott, Joan W., Jill Conway, and Susan C. Bourque. 1989. *Learning about Women: Gender, Politics and Power.* Ann Arbor: University of Michigan Press.

State Statistics Service of Ukraine. 2014. *Average Life Expectancy at Birth in Ukraine.* Kiev: Institute for Demography and Social Studies named after M. V. Ptukha of the NAS of Ukraine. Accessed August 1, 2015. http://database.ukrcensus.gov.ua/MULT/Dialog/view.asp?ma=7&ti=Average+life+expectancy+at+birth+in+Ukraine+%28years%29&path=../Quicktables/KEY_IND/1/&lang=2&multilang=en.

Tarrow, Sidney. 1998. *Power in Movement: Social Movements and Contentious Politics*, 2nd ed. Cambridge: Cambridge University Press.

Tolstokorova, Alissa. 2012. "A Mosaic Model of Gender Democracy in Ukraine." In *Gender, Politics and Society in Ukraine*, edited by Olena Hankivsky and Anastasia Salnykova, 29–53. Toronto: University of Toronto Press.

Zdravomyslova, Elena, and Anna Temkina. 2002. "Krizis Maskulinnosti v Pozdnesovetskom Diskurse" [The Crisis of Masculinity in Late Soviet Discourse]. In *O Muzhe(N)stvennosti: Sbornik Statei* [*About Masculinity: Anthology of Articles*], edited by Sergei Ushakin, 432–451. Moscow: Novoe Literaturnoe Obozrenie.

Zhurzhenko, Tatiana. 2004. "Strong Women, Weak State: Family Politics and Nation Building in Post-Soviet Ukraine." In *Post-Soviet Women Encountering Transition: Nation Building, Economic Survival, and Civic Activism*, edited by Kathleen Kuehnast and Carol Nechemias, 23–43. Washington, DC: Woodrow Wilson Press.

———. 2012. "Gender, Nation and Reproduction: Demographic Discourses and Politics in Ukraine after the Orange Revolution." In *Gender, Politics and Society in Ukraine*, edited by Olena Hankivsky and Anastasia Salnykova, 131–151. Toronto: University of Toronto Press.

7

Down and Out in a "Femo-Fascist" State: The Czech Fathers' Discussion Forum

Steven Saxonberg

Introduction

Much has been written about postcommunist women's organizing, but postcommunist men's organizing has hardly been studied. The focus of this article is on fathers' groups, since they are the most visible men's groups in the Czech Republic. In Western countries (including Australia), many men's and fathers' movements have developed. However, at least some of these men's organizations usually have a profeminist orientation, and in a few countries some part of the men's movement was an offshoot of the feminist movement. Yet, with the exception of the League of Open Men (LOM) organization, Czech fathers' associations have been openly hostile to feminism. Rather than focusing on broad social and political issues such as the gendered division of labor in society, how to raise children, how the role of fathers should change in the family, etc., Czech fathers' organizations focus almost exclusively on the emotionally charged issue of shared child custody and the perceived bias of the courts, which almost always award custody to the mothers rather than awarding joint custody.

So far, theories of the sociology of emotions have not been applied to postcommunist men's movements; yet, the case of the Czech men's movement makes for an interesting study to explore the roles of emotions because—in contrast to the women's movement in this country—the men's movement has tended to be very aggressive and confrontational, while the women's movement has been more professionalized and low-keyed, relying more on factual arguments than on desperate pleas. As theorists of social movements have noted, the manner in which activists frame their arguments plays a central role in their ability to gain support from a wider public. If they frame their arguments in a way that is culturally resonant, they are more likely to gain support. But as theorists of the sociology of emotions point out, injustice frames are potentially powerful because of the emotions that they invoke. Thus, in analyzing the main father's online discussion forum, a forum that is independent of any particular men's organization, this chapter will analyze what kinds of injustice frames the participants use and see to what extent insights from the sociology of emotions can explain these choices.

This chapter proceeds by first discussing its methodology and data. Second, it will briefly give an overview of the fathers' organizations in the Czech Republic, and then it moves on to discuss fathers' activism in relation to the Czech local context and analyzes the fathers' discussion forum. In analyzing the discussion forum, the analysis will concentrate on the main injustice frames and arguments that participants use: (1) feminism has turned the legal system against fathers; (2) women are the cause of the breakups of families, yet men are the ones who suffer because the welfare/judicial system supports the mothers; and (3) fathers are just as good or even better parents than mothers in raising children, but they are not allowed to do so. In analyzing these arguments and injustice frames, special emphasis is placed on the role of emotions.

Method

This chapter focuses on an analysis of the main Czech discussion forum for fathers. To give background information that allows one to relate the forum discussions to the men's movement in general, this chapter also relies on interviews conducted with the leaders and main activists in all the father groups in the country that agreed to be interviewed, as well as on an analysis of their websites (Saxonberg and Janoušková 2013). Further background information comes from articles from all the Czech nationally distributed newspapers between 2009 and 2013.

This chapter focuses on the fathers' discussion forum and examines the injustice frames that the fathers use. Gruszczyńska (2006, 101) notes that the anonymity of the internet creates "safe spaces" for participants. As Korolczuk (2014) notes, this anonymity sometimes allows activists to display views that differ from the official views of organizations. Similarly, forum participants enjoy anonymity, which allows them to display their views more bluntly than organization leaders, who have some incentives to tone down their language in order to gain wider support from society.

Another reason why internet forums are important for understanding the Czech father's movement is that because the fathers' organizations are small and lacking in resources, online activism becomes a cheap mechanism for them to inform potential supporters both of their ideas and of upcoming protest events, which these potential supporters might be willing to join. As scholars of online activism have noted, the internet provides an important form of "alternative media" (e.g., Stein 2009) for those organizations that have trouble getting access to the public media (when it does not sympathize with them) and it also provides a cheap form of communication for organizations that lack resources to use other forms of communication (Brossi, Landa, and de Zarate 2012). Stein (2009, 752–753) observes that besides allowing social movements to provide communication, the internet also assists action and mobilization (by informing the population of upcoming events). Furthermore, the internet promises interaction and dialog, it makes lateral linkages, and promotes fundraising and resource generation, but also important for this study, it "serves as an outlet for creative expression." It also allows for specific internet-based forms of protest actions (Earl 2010; Theocharis 2012). In the case of the Czech fathers' movement, internet-based forms of protest actions have mainly taken the form of encouraging e-mail letter writing campaigns, by providing sympathizers with pre-written e-mails that they can copy and send to authorities.

I have chosen one discussion forum for fathers, which allows for activists at all levels to participate—including those who do not belong to any particular organization (http://tatove.info/diskuse.html). The forum is connected to the homepage of the informational site tatove.info, which translates to daddy.info. This site is devoted to giving information to fathers about a variety of topics. In contrast to the father organizations, this website does not emphasize the custody issue, but rather sees it as one of many issues concerning fathers. The webpage does not make clear who the editor(s) is/are and presents itself in neutral terms in the sense of not having a political agenda or supporting any particular view. It is the only independent fathers' forum available, but one fathers' organization, *Spravedlnost dětem*, has its own discussion forum, which is directly connected to this particular fathers' rights group. Since http://tatove.info/diskuse.html is a neutral site, it is open to all possible views. There is no reason to assume that all participants are members of any fathers' groups, although some might be. A couple of times one men's group (Střídavka) did in fact use its name in participating in the forum as a way of mobilizing support for its petition on joint custody.[1] Thus, the forum http://tatove.info/diskuse.html provides a wider range of views than a forum connected to a particular organization.

I analyzed the discussion forum from April 11, 2010, until September 17, 2012. In total there were 169 threads with people participating 310 times, 148 usernames were used, and the total text comprised 22,832 words. Of course, 148 usernames do not mean that 148 people participated, as some people could use multiple usernames and sometimes several people could use the same one.

A possible bias of relying on a discussion forum for ascertaining the views of supporters of fathers' organizations is that those belonging to the middle class are more likely to have access to the internet than the working class, the marginalized, and poor. However, this middle-class bias likely reflects the characteristics of father's rights activists in the Czech Republic and in other contexts (Crowley 2012; Flood 1996). As in the case of the leaders of fathers' organizations, the participants in the discussion forum seem to mostly be professionals or entrepreneurs. For example, the head of fathers' organization K213 is officially titled "Ing. Jiří Fiala," which means he has a master's degree in engineering (which in the Czech Republic includes economics). Meanwhile, the head of Stridavka.cz is an investment banker.[2] The current head of *Unie otců*, Valentin Papazian, is a social worker with a master's degree, who in 2014 was a candidate for a small, new conservative party for the EU elections, while the organization's former head has a master's degree.[3]

Evidence for the middle-class bias of the participants in the discussion forums comes from the usernames that they give themselves. One participant used the Czech word "doktor," while another used the English translation "doctor." Just the fact that this man chose the English spelling also indicates that he is well educated. Another example is that one man chose the username JUDr., which means the person has a doctor's degree in law. Some are also obviously very knowledgeable about the IT world, as they do things like start their own discussion forums (e.g., Náměty, August 16, 2010

[12:58]), which also indicates that they are well educated. One of them also admits to owning his own enterprise (Petr, September 6, 2010 [19:55]). Of course, it is possible that some participants have different backgrounds, but there were not any indications given in either their choice of usernames or in what they wrote about themselves that would give reason to believe that any of the participants have working-class backgrounds or belong to marginalized social groups. The evidence of their class backgrounds backs up previous studies of the men's rights movements in the United States that indicate that the vast majority of activists have middle-class/professional backgrounds (Crowley 2009).

Since father activists seem to mostly consist of well-educated professionals and entrepreneurs, they have the knowledge of how to use the internet, which they can use to inform the public of their views and to mobilize people for protest events. Their views and emotional-confrontational style isolate them from the kinds of revenue sources that most Czech women's groups rely on (such as governmental grants and support from international organizations), thus, the reliance on the internet compensates to some extent for their limited access to resources.

The analysis was based on the critical discourse analysis method in the sense that I analyzed the contents in order to understand the power structures in the gender relations that stand behind the participants' views (van Leeuwen 1993; Fairclough 1995). Using critical discourse analysis, one does not simply "deconstruct" the discourse as in postmodern types of discourse analysis, but rather one tries to find and point out the connection with the discourse and power structures. In the post-modern version, by contrast, one applies discourse analysis in order to show that certain terms are not being used objectively and, therefore, one focuses on the possible interpretations of the terms. Thus, one concentrates on the text more than on the relationship between texts and society. Because this chapter uses critical discourse analysis, rather than deconstructing the main terms in the discourse, I highlight the link between the types of male dominance in Czech society (where most women work but have trouble competing with men as women leave the labor market for long periods raising children) and the type of discourse that develops—in other words, the fathers' activists do not question these normalized social arrangements that give men a great advantage in the public sphere, and they instead concentrate on the main issue that may visibly disadvantage them: child custody.

In applying critical discourse analysis, I followed the grounded theory approach in analyzing what main injustice frames were used. As Goulding (2005) points out, even when applying grounded theory, one starts with some theoretical knowledge and knowledge of previous studies. Thus, already in my previous research on the Czech men's movement, I identified some basic elements of the injustice frames, such as the notion that fathers are good carers, but they are not allowed to have custody over their children due to the feminized character of the courts (Saxonberg and Janoušková 2013). Consequently, I used these as my starting point in the current analysis of the posts. The coding was based on "directed content analysis," which draws on "prior research, [where] researchers begin by identifying key concepts or variables as initial coding categories" (Hsieh and Shannon 2005). Thus, from the theories of the sociology of emotions, for example, I wanted to see whether those participating indicated at all what kinds of jobs and status they had and what kinds of emotions they used, since theoretically a loss of status leads to feelings of anger. Consequently, in coding the posts I searched for any indications of their profession and names as well as any indications of how their living conditions and status might have changed due to divorce. Finally, I examined which kinds of emotions are expressed in specific posts.

Czech Father Organizations

At the time of this study, in 2012–2013, there were six father's organizations active in the Czech Republic, plus a seventh organization that is not officially registered but runs its own internet site and organizes various types of protest events. One of them refused to be interviewed or have any contact with me, so I have left them out of this analysis.

The only men's organization to have become professionalized that engages in lobbying activities, joining governmental committees, and applying for grants to run projects and write reports is LOM (League of Open Men). It has three full-time employees, over 800 fans on Facebook, multisource financing, and provides a broad spectrum of services to public. In contrast to the other fathers' organizations it gets financing that comes from public sources such as the Ministry of Labor and Social Affairs and the Ministry of the Interior as well as the European Social Fund. Similar to organizations that promote "engaged fathering," discussed by Korolczuk and Hryciuk (in this volume), LOM advocates such issues as active fatherhood, the harmonization of work and family, the presence of the father during childbirth, etc. However, they do not explicitly encourage fathers to share in the parental leave time or argue for changes in parental leave policies to encourage fathers to go on parental leave. Nevertheless, they are the one fathers' organization that works against traditional gender roles and, for example, they run campaigns supporting fathers' care for children (*Táta dneska frčí*). Their focus on changing legislation contrasts with the American father's rights activists in Crowley's (2006) study, where only 17 percent of the activists whom she interviewed were interested in changing policies and most joined organizations for getting emotional support. Their focus also shows some similarities with the fathers' groups oriented toward gender equality in Poland and activists engaged in "daddy schools" in Russia (Korolczuk and Hryciuk; Åberg and Rodin in the present volume).

The five remaining organizations are K213, *Unie otců* (the Union of Fathers), *Aliance pro rodiče a děti* (The Alliance for Parents and Children), *Český svaz mužů* (the Czech Union of Men) and *Spravedlnost dětem* (Justice for Children). In addition, there is also the group *Stridavka.cz*, which runs an internet site. Only *Unie otců* has received any outside financing: a small grant once from a municipality. Thus, all their activists are volunteers and they live from donations of their supporters and from their own money.

Rather than engaging in lobbying activities, the fathers' organizations—with the exception of LOM—focus on direct protest actions, as in the case of "angry fathers" groups in Poland (Korolczuk and Hryciuk in this volume). The other organizations are mostly small groups that support one-man organizations (although one has three members) that engage in confrontational activities to fight against the legal system, such as chaining themselves to the doors of court buildings and organizing demonstrations and petition drives. For example, in 2008 activists from the organization *K213* blocked the court and judges in Prague (*Dnes*, April 4, 2008, 1). They also blocked the Minister of Social Affairs in Prague. In January 2008, they also blocked the entrance of the director of the Office for International Legal Protection of Children (OILPC), Lenka Pavlová, in Brno for three working days. According to one newspaper there were five men with banners at any particular movement (*Dnes*, January 23, 2008).

When the men's groups organize protest happenings, they often do so in connection with the launching of a petition drive. For example, in June 2012, the men's organizations *Spravedlnost dětem*, *Stridavka.cz*, *Unie otců*, and other non-governmental organizations (NGOs) organized a petition drive at an event, which among other things demanded the dismissal of the minister of justice (Jiří Pospíšil).[4] The activists organized events at Václav Square in the center of Prague, as well as a demonstration in front of the Prague City Hall and in front of the Ministry of Justice. Not many people attended these events as their numbers were usually in the tens.[5] Only nine people attended the happening at the Ministry of Justice (TV NOVA, June 22, 2012, Odpolední televizní noviny). In 2010 Střídavka announced in the discussion forum that over 2,300 signed a petition demanding joint custody (Střídavka, June 13, 2010 [00:26]). These examples indicate that although the men's groups have not been able to mobilize mass support, they still have been able to engage in activities that induce non-activists to join, and they are still able to gain media attention.

These organizations—again with the exception of LOM—embrace conservative values and claim to support the "traditional family" household (see also Korolczuk and Hryciuk, Strelnyk, Höjdestrand in this volume). Thus, even though they generally have trouble forming coalitions with other groups other than men's groups, *K213*, *Stridavka.cz,* and *Unie otců* once participated in a manifestation against Prag (Gay) Pride (http://www.adikia.cz/news/nejteplejsi-den-v-roce/). Similarly, the organization *Český svaz mužů* emphasizes the notion of "traditional family" on its website: "The traditional family is today exposed to attacks from all sides. We believe that there should be more social and political support. We disagree with destroying traditional family values; children have a right to both parents and family background, which can give them the appropriate development opportunities. Our goal is to support the complete family and the efforts to preserve it" (Český svaz mužů 2007). The fact that most of the father groups claim to support "traditional" families might seem contradictory since the activists are divorced (as traditional families are not supposed to entail divorces). However, as I show in the discussion below, the activists tend to blame their ex-wives for the divorce and indicate that they wanted to keep the family together.

In addition to being openly conservative and supportive of the "traditional" family, Czech men's groups—again with the exception of LOM—often display an aggressive stance toward feminism and women's groups whom they accuse of wanting to oppress men and prevent children from seeing their fathers. For example, in fighting against the appointment of Lenka Pavlová to head the OILPC, representatives of *K213* called her "a feminist lawyer for extremist feminist associations" (*Lidové noviny*, January 24, 2008). In official press statements on their websites, representatives of *K213* described her in very rude terms, such as a "feminist cow" (K213 undated). Another example of their antifeminism is that in 2013 several leaders of father organizations were invited to a senate hearing on May 20 on the child custody issues. As one sociologist who also attended the hearing reflects,

> the speeches [of the representatives of the father organizations] were full of personal remarks and presumed injustices, some of them explicitly insulted the judge or the psychologist expert figuring in their case, mentioning her name—this was perceived and commented very negatively by the senators—organizers.[6]

This example once again shows how their aggressive stance alienates potential allies.

Understanding Fathers' Activism in the Local Context

This theoretical section begins by discussing Czech gender relations, which the father activists basically accept, and then goes on to show how concepts from the sociology of emotions can be used to explain the behavior and views of father activists.

The Family and Czech Gender Relations

Under communist rule, family policy was based on this notion that the family was the women's responsibility. Thus, under this period in addition to a six-month maternity leave based on the income-replacement principle, mothers could receive an "extended maternity leave" flat rate benefit until the child filled the age of three. Consequently, a norm developed in which the mother should stay at home until the child reached the age of three (Saxonberg, Hašková, and Mudrák, 2012). This policy was strengthened after the fall of the communist regime, when the new government added a fourth year of leave benefits and removed funding for daycare for children under three, which increased pressure on women to stay at home three or four years for each child. Nevertheless, in contrast to the male-breadwinner/female housewife model, women were still expected by policymakers to work full-time both before and after going on maternity leave.

Even though the first postcommunist government opened the benefits for men, Castle–Kanerova (1992) notes that the low-flat rate benefit level, which only pays the same low benefits to everyone regardless of income, did not encourage men to utilize this right given the fact that fathers have higher incomes than mothers in most families. In addition, only mothers had the right to get their jobs back after going on leave until 2001 (Saxonberg 2014). As a result, in 2007 only about 1 percent of those on parental leave were men (Maříková 2008, 75). Consequently, Čermáková (1997) observes that although during communist rule almost all Czech women worked, it was men that were expected to have careers, not women. This has continued after the collapse of the communist regimes, although it has been modified somewhat in that today women stay at home for longer periods on the average. To be sure, some women have become more career-oriented as the introduction of a market economy has provided them with the possibilities, for example, of starting their own companies. Men still tend to leave the general household chores to women, as they continue to perceive the household to be the woman's responsibility (International Social Survey Programme database 2002).

Thus, men—and especially fathers—benefit in many ways, also economically, from these gender arrangements. Similar to the male-breadwinner model, in the Czech model men are not expected to do much of the caring for family members or household tasks, which gives them much more time to concentrate on their careers. While female labor market participation radically decreases when children are born (the employment impact of parenthood was −32.3% in 2007—see Saxonberg 2014, 39), the labor participation rate actually increases for fathers of young children (the employment impact of parenthood was +4.5% in 2007) and they are able to advance in their careers since they do not go on leave at all when having children. Not only do men benefit from this asymmetry in gender roles, they also benefit from the fact that—in contrast to the "traditional" male-breadwinner/female housewife model—women are still expected in the Czech model to work full-time both before and after having children. Since mothers are expected to work, after divorce, fathers rarely have to pay alimony and are only responsible for paying child support.

Fathers' Activism and the Feminism Movement

A number of theorists of masculinity (e.g., Kaufman 1999) claim that feminist movements influence men's movements as they help many men realize that they too suffer from the type of "hegemonic masculinity" that dominates their particular culture. According to this interpretation, men also suffer emotionally from social expectations of masculine ideals that state that men are not supposed to show their emotions. Thus, in some countries where the first men and father groups emerged, they sympathized with the feminist movements in their countries.[7] Nevertheless, it is true that in countries such as the United States, some of the originally profeminist men's movements later became antifeminist (e.g., Messner 1998). Similarly, after profeminist men's movements emerged in the 1970s, in later years, conservative Christian men's movements also came into being (Flood 1998).

Consequently, even though much of the mobilization of fathers' rights organizations takes place as a countermobilization against a rather strong feminist movement that had made some gains (Crowley 2009), feminist movements have also acted as an impetus for many father and men's organizations in some countries and provided a set of profeminist frames that fathers' rights movements use. In Bertoia's (1998) study of Canadian men's rights activists, rather than blame feminism for their perceived discrimination in divorce proceedings, the activists blamed the *lack* of gender equality in the legal system and the continued *conservative* view of judges and lawyers as the main cause of their problems. Rather than talk about the legal system as a "feminist" machine that works against them, which is run by *female* lawyers, judges and social workers, the Canadian activists talked about conservatives; and when they mention a gender such as talking about a judge they use the masculine "he."

This impetus as well as gender equality frames have been largely absent in the Czech Republic, where the women's movement has been relatively weak and portrayed negatively in the media (Korolczuk and Saxonberg 2014). Although the media has become increasingly more open to feminism, in the first post-communist years, the mass media basically gave the impression that feminists were women who hate men and want to castrate them (e.g., Saxonberg 2014). Interviews with leaders of the father organizations indicate that this view of feminism is also shared by most of the father activists, even though its leaders do not appear to be knowledgeable about the Czech or international feminist discourse. Thus, ironically, it seems the actual weakness of the Czech feminist movement has contributed to making the father's movement more antifeminist.

Emotions as an Explanation of Behavior

Another important factor in explaining the framing of father rights activists is the role of emotions. So far, insights from the sociology of emotions have been rather neglected in the study of men's and father movements, even though scholars have shown that the contradictions between what is expected of them and the effort of repressing their feelings can help induce men to embrace the feminist movement in their country and begin criticizing the gender regime (Connell and Messerschmidt 2005; Kaufman 1999).

However, these contradictions between what is expected of men and the effort of repressing their feelings cannot explain the emotional dynamics in antifeminist men's movements and organizations that exist in most countries. Instead, to explain the rationale behind behavior of the Czech fathers' organizations, we can look at theories of emotions to explain how activists become highly motivated by hate and anger and how these emotions are gendered.

Social movement theorists have pointed out that people often join social movements because of acts of government and/or its repressive organs, such as the police, that arose strong negative emotion. They have alternatively labeled these emotions as "moral outrage" (Jasper 1997), "moral shocks" (Goodwin, Jasper, and Polletta 2001), or "anger" (Saxonberg 2001). Theorists of the sociology of emotion have tried to explain the basis for these strong emotions. Barbalet, who examines the role of emotions in shaping human behavior, argues that emotions reflect power relations. Thus, "emotions may be understood as social relationships, so that anger, for example, is the dispositional orientation to a challenge posed by another" (2001, 67). Similarly, Kemper (1990, 227) notes that anger is connected to structural power relations, because "if the other has unjustly or arbitrarily deprived one of status, one feels anger."

The state, having power over citizens, can deprive groups of people of their status. In the view of the father activists, the state through its legal system (the courts, the social workers who report to the courts, and the lawyers defending the mothers) deprive the fathers of their status by refusing to grant them custody rights. Moreover, in their view, the state is not against them because it supports a conservative gender ideology in which only women can be carers, but rather because it has come under the influence of "feminists" who want to preserve the power of women over their children. This explains the feeling of anger and desperation that echoes their organizing and induces them to choose directly contentious actions, rather than engaging in the type of professionalization that dominates among Czech women's organizations.

Emotions and the loss of status (which we can call "social status") can also be linked to masculinity theories. It is common to distinguish between the dominating "hegemonic masculinity" that men are expected to live up to, even if few are able to do so completely, and "marginalized masculinity," which is a type of masculinity ideal that dominates among marginalized groups in society (Connel and Messerschmidt 2005). As Oates-Indruchová (2012) notes, even though the communist regime glorified the working class, the hegemonic masculinity that the regime promoted was close to the Western type of middle-class masculinity that emphasizes "competitiveness, personal ambition, social responsibility, and emotional restraint" (Tolson 1987, 39 cited in Oates-Indruchová 2012). Meanwhile, the marginalized masculinity became similar to the Western-type of working class masculinity "characterized by an immediate, aggressive style of behavior [rather] than a vision of personal achievement" (Tolson 1987, 28 cited in Oates-Indruchová 2012). Šmídová (1999, 219) claims also that that the hegemonic masculinity in the country is milder and less "macho" than the typical hegemonic masculinity in many Western countries: Czech fathers are supposed to be "laborious and apt, careful, tolerant and understanding, and men in general are required to be manly(self-confident, dominant, sensible, tough), independent, competitive but also careful, mild, strong and compassionate, they should be neither romantic (feminine, oversensitive), passive, nor 'macho.'" Notably, this hegemonic masculinity is almost the direct opposite of the highly emotional and aggressive behavior of father activists, which rather approximates the marginalized masculinity. As the fathers lose status after divorces or during divorce cases, they take on a marginalized masculinity, which encourages them to act much more aggressively than the hegemonic masculinity permits.

Harris describes what this chapter calls marginalized masculinity in his discussion of post-communist Czech films. He observes that when the male characters suddenly face unemployment (which according to the sociology of emotions approach implies a loss of status), they react very negatively. The men display "anger, performing what Connell terms a 'protest masculinity,' which reveals itself in a marginal class situation, when men have limited options. Protest masculinity is a collective practice and a "pressured exaggeration of masculine conventions," which "builds on working class masculine ethic of solidarity" (Harris 2011, 458). Thus, the loss of status that plays a prominent role in bringing out anger in the sociology of emotions, which in turn can lead to mobilization, in masculinity theory can imply a demotion from belonging to the hegemonic masculine ideal to taking on a marginalized masculinity. This in turn promotes aggressive behavior and an "ethic of solidarity" that can induce fathers to mobilize when they face child custody battles and which can induce the now marginalized fathers to want to continue to have solidarity with fathers in similar positions.

If the above argument is correct, namely that most of the men who contribute to the forum are highly educated and either professionals or entrepreneurs, then they had rather high levels of status in society. When their marriages end and they lose their home and children, they can easily feel that they have had something "taken away" from them that they had built up. Rather than being the "successful" father, who did well economically and socially by getting a good job and creating a family, they are turned into failures who lose their home and family. Thus, losing custody over one's children and living without a family results in a loss of status because the man can no longer portray himself as the successful family man. In Scheff's (1990) terms, the fathers feel shame in having lost their children, their family, and having lost the legal battle over custody. This shame—as well as the loss of status that Barbelett writes about—leads to anger, which fathers display in their forum discussions and which father groups display in their protest activities.

In order to analyze the emotions that the participants of the men's forums participate in, this article focuses on their main injustice frames. As social movement scholars have noted, injustice frames are particularly important in convincing people to begin participating in collective action, because they give expression to emotive factors that induce people to participate. Injustice frames rely on the emotions that this type of framing evokes. Thus, Gameson (1992, 7) writes that the "*injustice component* [of framing] refers to the moral indignation expressed in this form of political consciousness." Nevertheless, as Snow et al. (1986, 474) note, "the development and adoption of an injustice frame is not sufficient to account for the direction of action." Rather, it is essential to externalize the responsibility for this injustice to specific actors. In the case of the forum participants, the groups that they use to externalize responsibility to are their former female partners, as well as "feminists" whom they claim control the state apparatus (especially the judges, lawyers, and social workers who make recommendations to the judges in custody cases).

Why do they externalize their feelings to this particular group with such aggressiveness? This chapter argues that in order to understand the injustice frames that have emerged among the Czech fathers' movement—including the discussion forums, which is the focus of analysis here—one must analyze the link between the emotions that come from the loss of status and their demotion to marginalized masculinity.

Exploring Injustice Frames: Analysis of the Discussion Forum

Participants in the discussion forum use three basic injustice frames in discussing their situation concerning divorces. These are (1) the antifeminist frame; (2) the blaming-women frame; (3) the fathers as capable carers frame.

The Antifeminist Frame

Generally, fathers participating in the forum uncritically accept the view of feminists as being the equivalent of radical, fanatical men-haters, who want to censor other views and want to help mothers avenge their former partners in custody cases. Feminists have become mortal enemies, and as such evoke strong feelings of anger among the male participants in the forum. According to their injustice frame, this feminist enemy, which induces the countermobilization (Crowley 2006) of the fathers, has taken over the country and especially the legal system, which it uses to destroy families and take children away from their fathers. Not only does this view of feminists as mortal enemies contrast with many other countries where some men's groups are profeminist, it also contrasts with some of the father groups that might not be overtly "feminist" but still blame the *conservative* rather than "feminist" views of judges as the cause of their ills. Thus, writing about Canadian fathers' rights activists, Bertoia (1998, 20) states, "Judges are also criticized by fathers' rightists for their traditional and conservative views on marriage and parental roles" (see also Korolczuk and Hryciuk in this volume). This is not to deny that many antifeminist father groups also exist in Canada; what it important here is that countries such as Canada have also father rights movements that are much less conservative than their Czech counterparts.

For example, the father's organization Střídavka advertises in the discussion forum that its views are superior to "feminist propaganda" (Střídavka, December 11, 2010 [00:29]): "Give to your social worker this new color flyer on alternative care that outshines feminist propaganda: http://www.stridavka.cz/stridavka.pdf." Thus, in their view feminists are spreading "propaganda" while they are providing "information" and feminists are against joint custody, although they never give examples of any groups that describe themselves as being "feminist" who are actually against joint custody.

In the view of many of the forum's participants, at the root of their problem is not patriarchy, but rather that the country now has a matriarchy with dictatorial feminists in control. When one father complained about not getting custody of his daughter, although the mother had tried to kill herself and needed to spend time in a psychiatric ward, and he cannot even see his daughter during Christmas, Lukáš (December 26, 2010 [09:29]) replies that "perhaps this is only possible in a femo-fascist state." In this situation, the father becomes marginalized, stripped of his family and thus takes on a more aggressive marginalized masculinity that rejects the more cooperative, non-confrontational hegemonic masculinity.

The belief that feminists have the goal of preventing fathers from seeing their children can be seen in many of the comments on the legal system, for example, when a discussion begins on the issue of whether contact with children is contingent on whether they are sick. A father speaks about his negative experiences with this in the city of Kolin. Then Roman (December 28, 2010 [22:15]) reacts: "I heard that Kolin is known as a center for ultra-feminists. This just supports that!" Similarly, when a father complains about not being awarded enough time with his children, Radek (December 30, 2010 [23:15]) sympathizes with him and proclaims, "It's disgusting in this state. Feminists nestled in the apparatus dealing with custody cases harm where they can." This example again shows that they attribute the belief that only mothers can be carers as something "feminist" rather than something conservative. Once again the participant uses angry language calling the antagonists "ultra-feminists" and claiming that they are "disgusting." The type of language in the above given examples typifies much more the aggressive marginal masculinity rather than the more moderate, conflict-avoiding hegemonic masculinity. The fathers become marginalized as they lose status when they no longer have custody over their children. They often see events in terms of war, in which the "femo-fascist state" it trying to repress them and destroy their family.

The Blaming-Women Frame

Participants in the Czech fathers' forum use a second, complementary injustice frame to the antifeminist one, in which they suffer from their former female partners who were the cause of breaking up the family. In addition to blaming their former partners in particular, they often blame women in general—especially those who are involved in the legal system.

One can find misogynous men in all countries, but in the Czech forum any self-reflection about the possible mistakes that the men themselves might have made or reflection about general gender relations that are not related to custody cases seems to be absent. As scholars, such as Holmgren and Hearn (2009) or Kaufman (1999), have noted, many—but not all—men's groups in countries such as Sweden and the United States focus on self-reflection and trying to make themselves into better citizens who will fight patriarchy partially by changing their own behavior. In Bertoia's (1998) study of Canadian fathers' rights groups, he finds that although the father rights activists whom he studied believe the legal system is against them, they do not blame their former partners for these problems. Even in the United States, where many of the men's groups are rather conservative and basically support separate gender roles, some of the most famous of these groups, such as the Promise Keepers, now blame the father rather than the single mother for the crisis of the family (Eldén 2002; see also Korolczuk and Hryciuk in this volume).

In the Czech case, however, forum participants generally give their former partners full blame for the divorce and also blame all aspects of the state's legal apparatus: the lawyers, psychologists, social workers, and especially judges involved in custody cases, whom they claim are always against men and always support the mothers. In this sense, they follow the ideology of "masculinism," which Blais and Dupuis-Déri (2012) find among some strains of the French-speaking Quebec men's movement. They summarize (2012, 22) that masculinism "asserts that since men are in crisis and suffering because of women in general and feminists in particular, the solution to their problems involves curbing the influence of feminism and revalorizing masculinity." Similar to the Czech case, they blame women for divorces as well and even make them responsible for "lethal domestic abuse," in the case when the ex-spouse committed suicide following his divorce.

The participants in the Czech Forum follow this masculinist type of logic and almost always use the feminine ending for everyone working in the profession, indicating that they were not just lawyers, psychologists, social workers, and judges who were against them, but rather *females* with these professions. This also contrasts with Bertoia's (1998) study of Canada, where although activists blame the legal system, they do not claim that women in system are against them, but rather the system in general—including the male participants—have a conservative view toward gender roles, which gives mothers an unfair advantage in divorce proceedings. In the view of the Czech activists, though, there is some kind of female conspiracy against them within the legal system, so the problem is that women have the real power and use it to avenge fathers. Consequently, the participants in the forum appear to be motivated by intense anger against their former partners and the legal system, to whom they assign all the blame in their injustice frames.

Honza (April 19, 2010 [18:32]) provides an example of how father rights activists display anger toward their former partners and legal system in their injustice frame. He writes about "how the Czech justice system functions tragically in everything concerning childcare" because of the female judges in the district courts and how children are "hostages to the judges and social workers and some perverse mothers." Even when the father gets custody, it is only because the mother agrees, while the judge herself is skeptical. Thus, Momo (August 6, 2010 [10:53]) calls the female judge in his case "the number one cow!"

This derogatory comparison of women with cows has been a common theme among forum participants. In their view, the mother not only leaves the father, she takes the children with her and denies him custody as a form of revenge to satisfy their egoistic desires. In Táta's (August 11, 2010 [23:36]) words: "Most women leave men, not vice versa." Matěj [January 2, 2011 [23:18]) reacts to an ongoing discussion about a child custody case: "In this state it's really disgusting. Dads who are interested in their kids and are able to care for them are systematically liquidated and immature selfish mothers are elevated to the heavens. Aren't these quite appalling cases?" Zdeněk (December 27, 2010 [15:00]) claims that female judges help mothers "so that they can satisfy their own yearning to avenge all men—fathers." In contrast to the Canadian men in Bertoia's (1998) study, the thought does not seem to occur to him that the judges might simply be caught up in harboring conservative views about gender roles rather than trying to help mothers get revenge.

Given that forum participants see women—and especially those connected to the legal system—as the enemy whom they must mobilize against, the participants in the forum often use the aggressive tone associated with marginalized masculinity by associating their conflicts with wars. For example, one person announced an upcoming court case with the nickname "za 10 dní—bitva u Kolína 201," which means "in 10 days—the battle in [the city of] Kolin 201." The choice of terms "battle" shows that the participant sees things in terms of war and is highly motivated by anger and aggressive feelings. In trying to attract supporters the participants often use highly emotionally charged language. For example, in a previous contribution under the name "za 28 dní rozsudek!" (November 9, 2010 [23:58]), which means "in 28 days verdict!" the contributor writes that it is a case of young children "whose mother dragged them away from their homes" and concludes, "Further liquidation of the beautiful relationship between young children and their loving father would satisfy the mother if confirmed in the sentence." Terms such as "liquidation" indicate a sense of desperation on the part of the father, while the charge that the mother was "dragging" away the children from their home indicates intensive feelings of anger. The mother is clearly the one to blame for the collapse of the family and a war has begun in order to defend the family against its "liquidation."

In this injustice frame, it is clear that the participants are highly motivated by feelings of anger and aggression. They use such terms as "disgusting," "systematically liquidated," "immature and selfish" to describe their "enemies" in the custody cases. In this psychological war that women are carrying out against men, the female judges want to "satisfy their own yearning to avenge all men" and the men lose their social status when their former partners and women in the legal system liquidate their family. This pushes them toward a marginalized masculinity that encourages them to break the conventions of the hegemonic masculinity and become aggressive rather than avoiding conflict.

The Capable-Carers Frame

The lack of critical reflection about gender relations in society and the unwillingness to consider feminist arguments about the need to eliminate gender roles creates a dilemma for fathers. On the one hand, since they see "feminists" as their enemy, they are not able to develop a convincing argument against the continuation of conservative gender roles, in which mothers are the primary carers. On the other hand, to claim the right to joint custody they argue that they are just as good at raising their children as the mother is. Without such a critique it is easy for the legal apparatus to continue supporting the existing gender regime, which is based on the notion that mothers should work but still remain the only carers for children. In theory, fathers could solve this dilemma by going back to conservative traditions from the 1800s in which fathers received custody after divorces, even though the male breadwinner model dominated, but nobody in the discourse refers to this or even seems to know about this historical tradition. Consequently, framing fathers as capable carers is not grounded in any general reflections concerning the gender order and appears to be contingent upon denigrating the mothers.

Two participants go so far to claim that they in fact are better carers than the mothers. Doctor (May 28, 2010 [10:44]) writes, "My daughter is fixated on me and cries, repeatedly when her maternal grandmother picks her up. Her mother spends most of her time at work and does not spend enough time with her." Thus, the mother prefers to have daughter be raised by her grandparents than by her father, which shows that she cares for her own egoistic wishes more than for the emotional comfort of the child. Similarly, Petr (September 6, 2010 [19:55]) argues strongly that he is by far the better carer:

> My wife turned her back on us and lives for herself. We with Viktorka 4 and Anna 2 live our own lives. What do you think? How did it all happen? Next week we are moving from my wife's apartment, and I'd love to immediately ask for custody, but I hope it's possible. I guess not, huh? . . . It's not about a mother as a mother. It is not about a father as a father. It's about people and the bullshit about how a mother can do more, I've been totally buried in housework this last half year. Cooking, doing the laundry, ironing, putting the children to bed, caressing the children, solving skin rashes and greasy hair, rashes and whatnot. Fortunately I am not suffering financially because I am continuing to function as the owner of a construction company. I'm a bit overwhelmed by customers, but what the hell. . . . True mother/poor father is a myth!

Not only is he a better carer than the mother, but it is the mother's fault that the family is collapsing ("she turned her back on us"). Despite this he is the one who will lose status as he must leave their place of residence and give it to the mother and he fully expects to lose custody of the children, even though "objectively" he considers himself to be the better parent. In addition, when the discussants reveal their backgrounds, they make it clear that they are well off economically, rather than belonging to poor or marginalized groups, which suggests that they would be able to take care of their children both emotionally and financially. Their strong economic situation strengthens their sense of injustice, by showing that fathers are indeed discriminated against in custody cases.

This view that they are perhaps even more capable carers than the mothers is additionally accentuated by their emotionally charged language, which reflects the fact that the fathers take on a marginalized masculinity as they lose their status as the "successful" head of a "traditional" family. Petr, who admits to owning a construction company and thus was in a high position often uses terms like "bullshit" and "hell," while ReMomo refers condescendingly to the judge as an "elderly cow."

Interestingly, similar to the Polish activists discussed by Korolczuk and Hryciuk (in this volume) the forum participants do not extend the topic of fathers' ability to take care of their children after a divorce to other issues. There is only one case in which a man took up the issue of fathers going on parental leave. In response to the woman "A," who thought that women should have sole custody, since they are the ones who give birth and breastfeed, Pavel (August 3, 2010 [20:03]) replies, "Ms. A., a lot of women are afraid or reluctant to acknowledge that fathers are able to as well and sometimes even better to nurture and love their children. Many men would be willing to replace you on maternity leave, but would you let them?" Nevertheless, this was the only case in the forum discussions in which a man wrote positively about the issue of fathers going on parental leave. The participants in the forum basically accept the patriarchal arrangements except on the issue of child custody and they blame women and feminists for depriving them of their children in an effort allegedly to increase their power over men.

Conclusion

Czech fathers active in fathers' groups and participating in online discussion forums almost exclusively concentrate on the issue of obtaining joint custody. This focus is much more narrow that the men's movements in such countries as the United States, Australia, Germany, and Sweden, which have been more open toward feminist ideals and more interested in fighting against patriarchy and gender inequality. However, this focus has some similarities with many of the more conservative men's movements in other countries, which emphasize men's suffering especially in the case of child custody cases. Nevertheless, in such countries as the United States, even the conservative men's organizations, such as the Promise Keepers, have often emphasized other issues than child custody, such as the need for men to become more responsible in order to reassume their breadwinner role.

In focusing so exclusively on the custody issue, Czech fathers create the injustice frame that notes that it is not fair to believe that only mothers can care for children since fathers can care just as well. The participants go on to create further injustice frames that lay the blame on their former partners for divorces and for allegedly wanting to destroy families and preventing the fathers from having contact with their children, while they blame the women within the legal system for supporting these mothers. The activists also go one more step in developing an injustice frame that blames "feminists" and "feminism" for their situation and claim that the state is controlled by feminists who always side with the mother in custody cases.

Since the movement activists do not develop an analysis of the patriarchal gender relations in the country, they do not put the custody issue into perspective of the institutional logic behind a system that is based on the notion that all mothers will work full-time, but also be the sole carers of children and the sole person responsible for household tasks. Under such conditions, in which mothers have been the sole carers of the children in the vast majority of cases and they have also given up much of their career for their children, it is logical for the legal system to expect this to continue even after divorces. This, however, does not fit the desires of the fathers, whose role in the family and in relation to their children abruptly changes after divorce. They react strongly to the unfairness of losing any ability to have constant contact with their children, but they do not criticize the underlying factors upon which this system is built. In other words, they want to keep all the factors that give them a competitive advantage over women in the labor market, but they want to eliminate the one main area in which they feel disadvantaged: that of child custody.

The sociology of emotions and theories of masculinity can help explain this dynamic and the activists' choice of frames. The male activists—who seem to mostly be conservatives and support the "traditional" family—lose their status as the head of a successful family when the mother of their children leaves them and asks for a divorce. Then it turns out that the legal system supports the mother and they are denied equal custody to their children—in fact, they often expect to have very little possibility of seeing their children after the divorce. Thus, even though whenever they indicate their background they show that they are rather successful in their careers (as they are professionals or entrepreneurs), they take on a marginalized masculinity because they can no longer live up to the hegemonic ideal based on heading a nuclear family. Now that the fathers abandon the careful, tolerant ideals of the hegemonic masculinity, they take on the more aggressive tone that is associated with marginalized masculinity. Marginalized masculinity also encourages the fathers to act out the aggression and anger that they feel when losing their status. Consequently, it is easier for them to openly portray custody disputes as wars, in which their former partners and the "femo-fascist" legal system is trying to liquidate their family and their relation with their children.

In a country like the Czech Republic, with a relatively weak feminist movement, it appears to be less likely that men's organizations will seriously consider feminist critiques of patriarchal power relations as a possible cause of their ills, nor are they likely to engage in self-reflection. Instead they are more likely to narrowly focus on custody as a clear case in which the legal system appears to be unfair to men, if taken out of context of gender relations in general. The Czech case also indicates that perhaps in absence of a feminist movement that challenges the notion of "traditional" gender roles, men who lose custody cases are more likely to take on a marginalized masculinity, which in turn induces them to become more angered and therefore more aggressive and confrontational in their activities.

Steven Saxonberg, Professor at the Department of European Studies and International Relations, Faculty of Social and Economic Sciences, Comenius University in Bratislava, Slovakia. He is also Professor at the Center for Social and Economic Strategies at the Charles University, Prague, Czech Republic.

Steven Saxonberg has written extensively about democratization and about gender issues, including women in parliament, women's movements, gender attitudes, and family policy from a gender perspective. His most recent books include *Gendering Family Policies in Post-Communist Europe: A Historical-Institutional Analysis* (Palgrave, 2014); *Transitions and Non-transitions from Communism: Regime Survival in China, Cuba, North Korea, and Vietnam* (Cambridge University Press, 2013), and, together with Hana Hašková, *The Development of Czech Childcare Policies* (Prague: Slon, 2013). His most recent co-edited volumes include *Social Movements in Post-Communist Europe and Russia* (Routledge, 2014) and *Beyond NGO-ization: The Development of Social Movements in Central and Eastern Europe* (Ashgate: 2013). He has published broadly in journals such as *Social Policy and Administration, Journal of European Social Policy, Social Policy and Administration, Social Politics, East European Quarterly, Marriage and Family Review, Comparative Policy Analysis, European Societies, Problems of Post-Communism, Journal of Democracy, Czech Sociological Review*, and *East European Politics and Society*.

Notes

1. For example, on February 16, 2011, at 12:10 p.m., they posted a web address where one could sign up showing support: http://www.stridavka.cz/stiznost2.php; also on June 13, 2010 at 12:26 a.m., they announced that on June 16 they would have a meeting in Karlový Vary, where people can sign their petition.

2. This information can be found at (accessed January 12, 2015) http://www.hodina.cz/rozhovor.htm and http://cs.wikipedia.org/wiki/Ale%C5%A1_Hodina.

3. An ad for the EU parliamentary elections is shown on their homepage at (accessed January 12, 2015) http://www.unie-otcu.cz/informace.html.

4. This is based on interviews with these organizations.

5. Interviews with Aleš Hodina, *Stridavka.cz* and Valentin Papazian. *Unie otců*; Fiala from *K213* mentions similar events and similar amounts of participants.

6. Personal correspondence with the researcher, June 17, 2013.

7. See Holmgren and Hearn (2009: 406) for Sweden and Flood (1998) for Australia.

Works Cited

Barbalet, J. M. 2001. *Emotion, Social Theory, and Social Structure.* Cambridge: Cambridge University Press.

Bertoia, Carl Edward. 1998. "An Interpretative Analysis of the Mediation Rhetoric of Fathers' Rightists: Privatization Versus Personalization." *Mediation Quarterly* 16 (1):15–32.

Blais, Mellissa, and Franci Dupuis-Déri. 2012. "Masculinism and the Antifeminist Countermovement." *Social Movement Studies* 11 (1):21–39.

Brossi, Lionel, María Inés Landa, and Amalia Ortíz de Zarate. 2012. "The Intersex Movement: Empowering Through New Technologies." *International Journal of Humanities and Social Science* 2 (22):64–75.

Castle–Kanerova, Mita. 1992. "Social Policy in Czechoslovakia." In *The New Eastern Europe. Social Policy Past, Present and Future*, edited by Bob Deacon, 91–117. London: SAGE.

Čermáková, Marie. 1997. "Postavení žen na trhu práce." *Sociologický časopis*, 33 (4):389–404.

Český svaz mužů [Czech Union of Men]. 2007. Accessed January 12, 2015. http://www.svaz-muzu.cz/index.php?page=onas&page1=detail_clanku&volba=7.

Connel, R. W., and James W. Messerschmidt. 2005. "Hegemonic Masculinity—Rethinking the Concept." *Gender and Society* 19:829–859.

Crowley, Jocelyn Elise. 2006. "Organizational Responses to the Fatherhood Crisis: The Case of Fathers' Rights Groups in the United States." *Marriage and Family Review* 39 (1,2):99–120.

———. 2009. "Domestic Violence and Political Countermobilization." *Social Forces* 88 (2):723–755.

Dnes Czech Daily, issues from January 23 and April 4, 2008.

Earl, Jennifer. 2010. "The Dynamics of Protest-Related Diffusion on the Web." *Information, Communication & Society* 13 (2):209–225.

Eldén, Sara. 2002. "Gender Politics in Conservative Men's Movements: Beyond Complexity, Ambiguity and Pragmatism." *NORA—Nordic Journal of Feminist and Gender Research* 10 (1):38–48.

Fairlough, Norman. 1995. *Critical Discourse Analysis*. Harlow: Longman.

Flood, Michael. 1998. "Men's Movements: What is the Men's Movement? Who Joins It, Why and What Kind of Movement Is It?" *Community Quarterly* 46:62–71.

Gameson, William A. 1992. *Talking Politics*. Cambridge: Cambridge University Press.

Goodwin, Jeff, James M. Jasper, and Francesca Polletta. 2001. "Introduction: Why Emotions Matter." In *Passionate Politics: Emotions and Social Movements*, edited by Jeff Goodwin, James M. Jasper, and Francesca Polletta. Chicago: University of Chicago Press.

Goulding, Christina. 2005. "Grounded Theory, Ethnography and Phenomenology: A Comparative Analysis of Three Qualitative Strategies for Marketing Research." *European Journal of Marketing* 39 (3,4):294–308.

Gruszczyńska, Anna. 2006. "Living La Vida Internet. Some Notes on the Cyberization of Polish LGBT Community." In *Beyond the Pink Curtain: Everyday Life of LGBT People in Eastern Europe*, edited by Roman Kuhar and Judit Takacs, 95–116. Ljubljana: Peace Institute—Politike Symposion.

Harris, Adrienne M. 2011. "'Something Like Happiness': Post-1989 Cinematic Portrayals of the Czech Industrial North." *East European Politics and Societies* 26 (3):454–468.

Holmgren, Linn Egeberg, and Jeff Hearn. 2009. "Framing 'Men in Feminism': Theoretical Locations, Local Contexts and Practical Passings in Men's Gender-Conscious Positionings on Gender Equality and Feminism." *Journal of Gender Studies* 18 (4):403–418.

Hsieh, Hsiu-Fang, and Sarah E. Shannon. 2005. "Three Approaches to Qualitative Content Analysis." *Qualitative Health Research* 15 (9):1277–1288.

International Social Survey Programme database. 2002.

Jasper, James M. 1997. *The Art of Moral Protest: Culture, Biography, and Creativity in Social Movement*. Chicago: University of Chicago Press.

K213. The Association of 213 (Club 213). Accessed January 12, 2015. http://k213.cz/start.php?act=read&art=635.

Kamplicher, Martina, Miroslava Janouskova, and Steven Saxonberg. 2013. *Local Welfare and Female Labor Market Participation in Brno*. Brno: Masaryk University Press.

Kaufman, Michael. 1999. "Men, Feminism, and Men's Contradictory Experiences of Power." In *Men and Power*, edited by Joseph A. Kuypers, 59–83. Halifax: Fernwood Books.

Kemper, Theodore D. 1990. "Social Relations and Emotions: A Structural Approach." In *Research Agendas in the Sociology of Emotions*, edited by Theodore D. Kemper, 207–237. New York: State University of New York Press.

Korolczuk, Elżbieta. 2014. "Terms of Engagement: Re-Defining Identity and Infertility On-Line." *Culture Unbound* 6:431–449.

Korolczuk, Elżbieta, and Steven Saxonberg. 2014. "Strategies of Contentious Action: A Comparative Analysis of the Women's Movements in Poland and the Czech Republic." *European Societies* 17 (4):404–422.

Maříková, Hana, and Radimská Radka. 2003. *Podpora využívání rodičovské dovolené muži* [Support for Men Taking Parental Leave]. Praha: SoÚ AV ČR.
Maříková, Hana. 2008. "The Czech Family at Present and in the Recent Past." In *Families in Eastern Europe*, edited by Mihaela Robila, 29–48. Amsterdam: Elsevier.
Messner, Michael A. 1998. "'The Male Sex Role': An Analysis of the Men's Liberation and Men's Rights Movement's Discourse." *Gender and Society* 12 (3):255–276.
Oates-Indruchová, Libora. 2012. "The Beauty and the Loser: Cultural Representations of Gender in Late State Socialism." *Signs: Journal of Women in Culture and Society* 37 (2):357–383.
Saxonberg, Steven. 2001. *The Fall: A Comparative Study of the End of Communism in Czechoslovakia, East Germany, Hungary and Poland*. Amsterdam, London: Harwood Academic/Routledge.
———. 2013. "The Influence of 'Conservative' Organizations on Family Policies in Hungary and the Czech Republic." In *Beyond NGO-ization: The Development of Social Movements in Central and Eastern Europe*, edited by Kerstin Jacobsson and Steven Saxonberg, 97–116. Surrey: Ashgate.
———. 2014. *Gendering Family Policies in Post-Communist Europe: A Historical-Institutional Analysis*. Basingstoke: Palgrave.
Saxonberg, Steven, and Dorota Szelewa. 2007. "The Continuing Legacy of the Communist Legacy." *Social Politics: International Studies in Gender, State & Society* 14 (3):351–379.
Saxonberg, Steven, Hana Hašková, and Jiří Mudrák. 2012. *The Development of Czech Childcare Policies*. Prague: Slon.
Saxonberg, Steven, and Miroslava Janoušková. 2013. "'Honor Thy Father': Men's Organizations in the Czech Republic," unpublished conference paper.
Scheff, Thomas J. 1990. *Microsociology: Emotion, Discourse, and Social Structure*. Chicago: University of Chicago Press.
Šmídová, Iva. 1999. "Men in the Czech Republic: A Few Questions and Thoughts on Studying (Some) Men." *Czech Sociological Review* 7 (2):215–222.
Snow, David A., et al. 1986. "Frame Alignment Processes, Micromobilization, and Movement Participation." *American Sociological Review* 51 (4):464–481.
Stein, Laura. 2009. "Social Movement Web Use in Theory and Practice: A Content Analysis of US Movement Websites." *New Media Society* 11 (5):749–771.
Tatove Info Forum [Fathers' Info Forum]. Accessed January 12, 2015. http://tatove.info/diskuse.html.
Theocharis, Yannis. 2012. "Cuts, Tweets, Solidarity and Mobilisation: How the Internet Shaped the Student Occupations." *Parliamentary Affairs* 65:162–194.
Van Leeuwen, Theo. 1993. "Genre and Field in Critical Discourse Analysis." *Discourse and Society* 4 (2):193–225.

8

Resisting Mandatory Vaccination in the Czech Republic

Jaroslava Hasmanová Marhánková

Introduction

Vaccination programs are among the flagship projects of preventive medicine, with over two centuries of tradition. The authorities in the field of biomedicine promote vaccination as an integral part of responsible parenting and a safe path to health not only for individuals, but for entire populations. Vaccination is held up as a shining example of medical progress that has saved millions of lives. Despite the relatively unproblematic acceptance of vaccination by the biomedical community and the broader public, and formal sanctions leveled by the state, there are still parents who refuse to have their children vaccinated. Criticism of vaccination has even become the focus of collective action. This text will discuss the antivaccination movement in the Czech Republic as an example of contemporary health-related movements. Brown et al. (2004, 52) define the health social movement as a "collective challenge to medical policy and politics, belief systems, research and practice." These new social movements focus also on issues of personal autonomy and identity. In reaction to the ever-more-fragile boundary between one's personal life and the state, the activists turn against the authorities and their power to make decisions concerning people's personal lives (Epstein 1995; Johnston et al. 1994).

Along with most postsocialist countries, Czech Republic implemented a mandatory immunization program. Although some types of vaccines are also mandatory in the "Western" countries (e.g. France, Greece), the post-socialist context, "offers an especially rich environment for investigation of vaccination refusals as a reflection of suspicion of authority, both local and international, changing social hierarchies, and worries about the status of the newly emerged states in global geopolitics" (Bazylevych 2011, 438). The vaccination refusal in those countries emerges in the context of the heritage of Soviet immunization policy that emphasized state control as opposed to individual decisions and where the relationship between an individual, health authorities, and the state was strictly hierarchical, leaving little space for articulation of individual needs. The debates concerning mandatory vaccination, therefore, provide a unique opportunity for the study of the (re)definition of responsibility for individual/children's health and of the process of erosion/formation of trust in health authorities and state.

The antivaccination movement raises issues not only in relation to the way (mis)trust is formed toward the expert systems of biomedicine, but also in relation to the question who decides what treatment is provided to those who cannot decide for themselves. Discourses that have formed around mandatory vaccination also feed into debates concerning the responsibility of parents for the health of their children and the moral imperatives depending on one's idea of what this responsibility should look like in practice. Opponents of vaccination argue that responsible parents are the ones who weigh the risks themselves and reject vaccination despite doctors' recommendations (Hobson-West 2007; Blume 2006). Meanwhile, discourses from within the system of mandatory vaccination, which is part of current Czech law, construct the responsible parents and citizens as those who obey the orders of the authorities and have their children vaccinated. This text analyzes the parents' opposition toward mandatory vaccination as an arena of negotiation over the role of the citizen in relation to one's own health, as well as the norms of proper/responsible parenting. It asks in what ways the critique of vaccination facilitates the emergence of new norms of responsible parenthood and how the question of who is responsible for the children health is incorporated into these norms.

At the same time anxieties about vaccination stimulated the emergence of various forms of collective actions based on the resistance to the dominant biomedical discourse. This chapter analyzes if and in what ways collective identity becomes articulated through the attitudes toward biomedicine and vaccination. It focuses mainly on the ways in which the specific subjectivity of parents is formed through the practice of vaccination or nonvaccination, and new forms of demands placed on themselves and on the health care system in the Czech Republic. The text shows the ways in which new forms of biosocialities are formed within the antivaccination movement on the basis of parents' stance toward vaccination of children. These parents become the embodiment of what Rose and Novas (2005) call active biological citizens, moral pioneers who raise new ethical demands. My analysis will focus on how these biosocialities are linked to a new model of "informed parents."

Vaccination Programs in the Czech Republic–Support and Controversies

The Czech Republic currently belongs among countries with a system of mandatory vaccination, where the rate of immunization coverage is around 98–99 percent of the population (UNICEF 2012). According to the current vaccination calendar, children from the ninth to the twenty-sixth week of their lives are mandatorily vaccinated against nine illnesses. If parents fail to meet this obligation, they can be fined up to ten thousand Czech crowns (ca. 365 euros).[1] Preschool facilities have the right under law to refuse to accept a child who is not vaccinated.[2] This law was recently upheld by the Constitutional Court, which in its decision (NSS 8 As 6/2011—142) rejected a complaint by parents suing the director of a preschool who refused to accept their child because the child had not the mandatory vaccinations against measles, rubella, and mumps.[3] In the eyes of the law a person who refuses to have their child vaccinated commits a civic misdemeanor and endangers the public health (Zákon 258/2000 Sb.).

Although the current Czech antivaccination movement shares some features with other such movements in Europe and the United States, its history is significantly shorter. A strict mandatory system of vaccination (that is typical also for other postsocialist countries) can be seen as a legacy of Soviet public health policy. Bazylevych (2011, 440–441) argues that immunization programs hold a prominent position in the Soviet Union. An extensive immunization schedule fit well with the ideology that stressed the concern of the collectivity. The immunization programs became a cheap way of securing the health of the labor force as well as a symbol of the success of socialist regime in its struggle for the health of their citizens (ibid). To refuse the vaccination or even to criticize it publicly was almost impossible. There have been no significant attempts to openly challenge the practice of mandatory vaccination in the Czech Republic till 2007, when the first parental organization addressing the issues of vaccination was founded. Furthermore, the relationship between the healthcare providers and clients was strictly hierarchical under state socialism. As suggested by previous empirical research, the Czech healthcare system is currently integrating the principles of consumerism and the idea of patients as active actors. However, the patients/parents who are adopting such attitudes toward healthcare services and, for example, refuse or question the recommendation of health authorities are still stigmatized and perceived as troublemakers (e.g., Hrešanová and Hasmanová Marhánková 2008; Hasmanová Marhánková 2008).

Despite the general acceptance of vaccination on the part of biomedical authorities and the broader public, and the formal sanctions leveled by the state, some Czech parents decide not to have their children vaccinated. In 2007, the civic association Rozalio was founded by parents who are critical of the vaccination program.[4] Their goal is to support the introduction of a system of voluntary vaccination and to provide information for parents about vaccination. The topic of vaccination also recently gained growing attention in the Czech media. During the last three years alone, a number of popular books that critically evaluate the benefits of vaccination have been published and they reached considerably high sales. An increasing number of parents have taken their cases to court, demanding compensation for undesirable side effects and permanent damage done to their children by vaccination or protesting against the sanctions associated with mandatory vaccination.[5] They also form coalitions, for example, with the League for Human Rights, which has become active on the issue of mandatory vaccination in the Czech Republic.[6]

(Anti)Vaccination Discourses, Biological Citizenship, and New Forms of Biosocialities

The study of the controversies surrounding the vaccination programs offers a unique space for the investigation of the tensions between different forms of knowledge, rationalities, and the relation between state authority and individual autonomy. Although vaccination programs are based on the global actions, the processes of acceptance and refusal are shaped by the local historical and social context. For instance, the massive mistrust toward vaccination in some parts of Asia and Africa are often rooted in the legacy of colonial history. The critique of the vaccination often embodies the reference to the "Western plot" to infect and control non-Western communities (for more detailed analysis, see, e.g., Feldman-Savelsberg, Ndonko, and Schmidt-Ehry 2000). Certain religions and beliefs system oppose vaccination as unethical (due to the usage of human tissue cells to create vaccines) and/or as a form of violation of the natural order. Global vaccination programs therefore often became a site of struggle for political and religious power in different regions (Clements, Greenought, and Shull 2006) and reflect a specific history and local position in the global arena. As Bazylevych (2011) suggests in her analysis of vaccination campaigns in postsocialist Ukraine, vaccination anxieties in Ukraine reflected the renegotiation of relationship between the state, healthcare providers, and patients as well as the repositioning of the postsocialist citizens in the global arena. The investigation of vaccination refusal therefore offers an opportunity to study what happens at the intersection of different forms of values, social relations, and political power.

The mandatory vaccination programs originated mainly in Europe and the United States. In the beginning, the vaccination programs were mainly criticized as a new form of obligation imposed by the state, and, due to religious objections, to an unnatural intervention against the will of God and the natural course of human life. Contemporary antivaccination movements in Europe and the United States coalesce mainly around the question of health, and the criticism of vaccination is framed specifically in terms of parents' concerns over the negative health consequences. The main objection relates to the side effects of vaccination, such as possible damage to the child's sensory-motor development, paralysis, or even death. Vaccination is also blamed for other illnesses such as allergies, atopic eczema, diabetes, or immunity disorders. Opponents of vaccination point out the unpredictability of long-term side effects. Vaccination is often described as an unnatural intervention into the human immune system that has irreversible and unpredictable consequences (Blume 2006; Senier 2008; Poltorak et al. 2005; Hobson-West 2007).

While the historical roots of the European and US antivaccination movements are located in the resistance toward mandatory vaccination as an expression of state repression or as a sin against the God's natural order, and its criticism was not necessarily connected with the protection of children's interests, today the issues around vaccination mobilize mainly parents who want to protect the health of their offspring. Some authors point to the links between the natural birth movement and current antivaccination movement, where a critical position on vaccination becomes a continual process of seeking alternative paths to caring for children's health, and an articulation of opposition to the medicalized character of prenatal, obstetric, and pediatric care (Rogerst and Pilgrim 1994). This link can be observed also in the case of the Czech Republic. The main representatives and founders of the non-governmental organization (NGO) Rozalio are also actively involved in the Movement for an Active Childbirth (MAC), which was founded in 1999. MAC represents an association that focuses on improving the Czech maternity-care system.[7] It emphasizes the need to strengthen a woman's autonomy in relation to obstetric care and criticizes the concept of Czech medicalized obstetrics care where "mothers giving birth are usually perceived by medical professionals as incompetent and powerless patients."[8] The founders of Rozalio mentioned during the interviews that the growing interest in the issues of vaccination among the members of MAC led to the foundation of Rozalio as an independent organization focused entirely on the improvement of the Czech vaccination policy.

The close connection between Rozalio and organizations focusing on the improvement of Czech birth and maternity care reflects the gendered nature of the process of decision-making concerning the children's vaccination. As Reich (2014, 680) points out, vaccine refusal is a strongly gendered process. The responsibility to make decisions concerning vaccination can be seen as another aspect of the current ideology of "intensive mothering" (Hays 1996) that extends the gendered work of mothering and places new demands on the mothers to became "guards" of their children's health (who are superior to the authority of medical professionals).[9]

This stance on vaccination and attitudes toward biomedicine as part of caring for the health of one's children become instrumental in the shaping of specific forms of collective identity and parental agency. As Lemke (2011, 98) points out, these newly arising parental patients associations or self-help groups "represent new collective subjects that remove the borders between laypeople and experts, between active researchers and the passive beneficiaries of technological progress." These forms of collective identity and self-expression through attitudes toward one's own health and biomedicine are becoming the expression of a new form of biological citizenship (Petryna 2002; Rose 2007; Rose and Novas 2005). They also give rise to "novel forums for political debate, new questions for democracy, and new styles of activism" (Rose 2007, 137).

The concept of biological citizenship illustrates the increased importance of the body in the process of constructing one's identity, and new forms of self-discipline and self-management contained in the imperative of personal responsibility for one's health and its proper management. People are governed "at a distance" through what Rose calls "will to health." As a number of other authors have pointed out (Metzl 2010; Beck and Beck-Gernsheim 2002), in today's society health becomes above all the moral responsibility of every citizen. In an individualized society it functions as an absolute value for which we should and must strive. Biopolitics managed by the authorities, as described by Foucault, transforms itself, according to Rose (2001), into a political ethic that emphasizes the individual responsibility to choose, but which must always be led by an effort to work on oneself in order to become a better/more healthy subject. However, this shift in emphasis from the paternalistic role of the state and of medicine toward individual choice cannot be interpreted as a sign of growing freedom in relation to one's own body. On the contrary, ethopolitics as the new form of biopolitics increases the demands placed on the individual and his/her self-control. Ethopolitics focuses on the individual self-enterprising and choices that individuals are obliged to make in the name of the life itself. Constant care for oneself and one's health gives rise to new forms of agency in modern society where the body becomes the key point for the construction of the self (Rose 2001).

Biological citizenship is simultaneously both individualizing and collectivizing. It individualizes through one's relationship to oneself, through the process by which "individuals shape their relations with themselves in terms of a knowledge of their somatic individuality" (Rose 2007, 134). Individuals "learn" to know and understand themselves in categories associated with biology, the body, and health. Identity becomes fundamentally somatic, and the individual body and health emerge as a space where the individual works on himself and places new ethical demands on himself. This is the space in which "somatic individuality" is formed and where the notions of whom we are and what we hope for are organized in a new way through the somatic experience (ibid).

At the same time, biological citizenship has a collectivizing potential. The biomedical categories of illness, risk groups, specific somatic experience, and genetic predisposition give rise to specific forms of collectivities—biosocialities (Rabinow 1996). The concept of biosociality refers to the collectivities "formed around a biological conception of a shared identity" (Rose 2007, 134). It is founded upon relatively detailed knowledge of one's own state of health, which also gives rise to specific forms of activism, which Rose

(2007, 135) calls right biocitizenship; it encompasses, for example, the campaigns to improve or change the healthcare system or efforts to deconstruct the stigmas connected with the categories of illness. The internet has become the high ground for the formation of biosocialities, where people share narratives about their health and illnesses, information from the field of medicine, tips for coping with situations, and describe how and on what basis they decide how to care for oneself. The internet connects individuals through the opportunity to share one's experiences and simultaneously acts as a space in which people gain access to specialized information. Given the imperatives of personal responsibility for one's own health, there is a pluralization of interpretations about the "truths" of health and illness. Individuals gain access to an enormous amount of information, and at the same time they find themselves in the position of being the ones who must responsibly evaluate it. Such an environment redefines in a significant way the relationship between lay and expert knowledge, and it gives rise to new forms of expertise, as well as controversy (Rose 2007, 140–143).

The Research Process

This analysis is based on ethnographic research focusing on social collectives formed on the basis of a critical stance toward vaccination. The research began in the spring of 2012, and it relied on various sources of qualitative data. The first key source included the web pages of associations and individuals critical of mandatory immunization. In particular, the web pages of the civic association Rozalio were analyzed. Rozalio represents the largest and most prominent organization devoted to systematic criticism of vaccination and, as the interviews showed, their web page functions as one of the key sources of information for parents. This regularly-updated website contains information dealing with the legal and medical aspects of vaccination, and it includes stories and experiences from parents who refused vaccination. Other sources besides the Rozalio website were blogs and websites established by people who are against mandatory vaccination. The analysis of the web pages was mainly used as the source of the background knowledge concerning arguments against vaccination prior to the interviews and participant observation.

Participant observations at events devoted to the issues of vaccination (organized mainly by the Rozalio association) and at local meetings of self-help groups for parents critical toward vaccination were conducted during the research process. In the summer of 2012 I also took part in several day-long meetings of families organized by Rozalio, attended by approximately 35 people. The meetings included group discussions and sharing of parents' experiences and opinions, which I was also allowed to record with the consent of those present.

A third source of data was in-depth interviews with parents who had refused all or some mandatory vaccinations for their children. A total of 23 parents were interviewed (22 women and one man). These parents were contacted mainly through a questionnaire posted on the Rozalio website and Facebook pages. Besides questions the survey also included a request for contact in case of willingness to participate in a personal interview. The response rate by parents was relatively high. Some of the contacts were gained from the parent surveys or on the basis of direct contact at events organized by Rozalio. With one exception, the participants were women. As the subsequent analysis shows, women more often initiate the decision to refuse some vaccination. The discussion on the Rozalio website, too, is frequented for the most part by women. Meetings and events about vaccination are attended by men, too, but most often with their women partners. In these cases, their opinions were recorded in the field notes. The interviewed women came from various parts of the Czech Republic. Most often they were women with university educations; their average age was 35. There were people from large cities and from small villages. Some of them had refused all vaccinations for their children, while others only refused some. Among them were cases when the parents began to refuse the vaccinations only after a certain time, and their older children were partly or fully immunized but their younger children were not at all.

The interviews lasted 45 minutes on average and began with a request for chronological mapping of the decision on vaccination of their own children with emphasis on all aspects that seemed important to the participants themselves. Only after the first phase of the interview came supplemental questions focusing on the key factors that influenced their opinions about vaccination, the process of making the decision, the reaction of doctors and others to their decision, their opinion on the practice of vaccination in the Czech Republic and their suggestions for change, and their contacts with other parents critical of vaccination or active in Rozalio. All interviews were recorded with the agreement of the participants and later transcribed verbatim. In assembling the text portion of the data I used the software Atlas.ti, which served especially for the segmentation of the data and its coding. This was done according to the principles of applied thematic analysis (MacQueen and Namey 2012).

In the next part of the chapter I use the concept of biological citizenship (Rose 2007) to analyze the experience of parents critical to the compulsory children's vaccination. Firstly, I focus on the individualizing aspect of the biological citizenship. The text maps the ways in which the critique of vaccination facilitates the emergence of new norms of responsible parenthood/citizenship. Parental attitudes toward vaccination are analyzed as part of the process of individualization of risk and self-disciplining practices embodied in the "will to health." The next part of the chapter explores the collectivizing dimensions of the biological citizenship. I analyze how the discussions concerning the compulsory vaccination give rise to a specific form of collectivities of parents that are mobilized and united by the shared conception of who should decide about the healthcare of their children and on which criteria it will be based.

"I am Responsible for My Child's Health." Individualization of Risks, Responsibility, and the Construction of the New Norms of "Good" Parenting

As Rose (2007, 134) points out, biological citizenship has individualizing and collectivizing potential. The individualizing aspect of biological citizenship concerns the process of employing the awareness of one's own body into the self-disciplinary practices that are part of taking personal responsibility for one's health. This responsibility for managing one's own health also "introduces new distinctions between good and bad subjects of ethical choice and biological susceptibility" (ibid, 134). In the case of my participants, the attitudes toward vaccination became a vehicle by which to articulate these distinctions. Moreover, vaccination emerged as a field within which boundaries were drawn between responsible and irresponsible parenthood. In their responses, taking responsibility for the health of one's child was an important criterion by which they defined their own role as a good parent. One mother explained the following:

> It's my child and I am responsible for his health, and if there's some trouble then it's going to be me who gets blamed for it anyway. And if I am responsible for his health then I'm the one who must decide, and I am prepared to do so. I know

> that this may endanger him in some way, it gives me goose bumps to think about it, but that's how it is. As for responsibility, we had a very long discussion and thought it over, because I gave birth to the little one at home, too, so we've already been through this responsibility for the life of a child, so I just don't like it, because it's my child. I don't say, if it was a threat to someone else, I simply understand that the freedom of one person ends where that of another begins, but here it doesn't threaten anyone and there's no reason why we should stick something into him about which I have only partial information, and about which the health care system and our wonderful government doesn't feel like talking about it; I simply won't make him into a guinea pig. (Viktorie, age 29)[10]

This concept of good parenthood was constructed mainly as a fulfillment of the imperative toward responsible, informed, and individual choice. The decision to refuse vaccination is presented by these parents mainly as a statement that they have taken responsibility for the health of their children, which is a commitment they feel all parents have, but not all are willing to actively meet. A sign that this commitment is being taken seriously is the gathering of information (and not just obeying the authorities).

Although women represented the majority of people attending lectures organized by Rozalio and were also more active in the various forms of discussion concerning the vaccination, vaccination was by my participants (as well as by Rozalio) not constructed as the mothers' responsibility. Most of the mothers confessed that the final decision was in their hands and that their partners played mainly a supportive role. The imperative of informed responsible choice was, however, not framed in gendered terms as the mothers' responsibility. As Hobson-West (2007) shows in his analysis of the anti-vaccination movement in Great Britain, parents critical of vaccination are not setting themselves up as the sole experts about immunization, but they are systematically calling upon other parents to educate themselves independently of medical authority. They place on themselves and on others the strong moral imperative to be informed parents. My participants often criticized parents who place unquestioning faith in their doctors as being too gullible and failing to take responsibility for every decision they make—including the decision to have limitless faith in the recommendations of their doctor.

> A lot of people say "I wouldn't take the responsibility," like for some of the issues of vaccination, birth, not to give their children antibiotics and so on, and they don't understand that it's all their responsibility, that whatever they decide, it's always their responsibility. . . . So I think that this is maybe the main problem, this excessive belief that someone will fix it for us. (Barbora, age 39)

The concept of parenthood articulated through criticism of mandatory vaccination is constructed around the individualization of responsibility and risk. These parents more or less distance themselves from the idea of collective immunity, which is basically the philosophy of mandatory mass vaccination.[11] Within such framework, mandatory vaccination is above all an instrument for the collective defense of society, which under certain circumstances can be superior to individual interests (Petrov 2011). Nevertheless, parents critical of vaccination in accordance with the imperative of personal responsibility frame the decision whether or not to inoculate without regard for the collective interest of the population, but stressing the need for the individual evaluation of risks. The following quote shows also that parents position themselves as responsible agents, while the state is perceived as avoiding any responsibility for the effects of the policies it imposes:

> Well, I am definitely against it (mandatory vaccination), because it is universal and takes no account at all of any individuality, so I am not an opponent of all vaccination; it's not that all vaccination is totally bad, definitely not. . . . We order someone to do something, but if it leads to some screw-up, we've got nothing to do with it; that's not going to work, because I am prepared to refuse; I am prepared to take the risk that it entails. If God forbid there really is some kind of screw-up and it was because the child wasn't vaccinated, then I am prepared to take all the consequences. But the state isn't prepared. The state tells us what we have to do, but doesn't say what the state has to do. For me that is totally unacceptable. (Irena, age 33)

As the interview with Irena shows, the current criticism of vaccination and lack of trust in biomedicine is to a major extent the product of an individualized society, where, in their decision making, people are supposed to rely on themselves, and they alone bear the responsibility for their decisions.

These discourses give rise to a new form of parental agency. Those parents exercise their own self-discipline through responsibility, actively seeking information and constantly weighing risks. They become the bearers of new moral imperatives directed toward themselves and others: to be an expert parent, an informed client of the healthcare system, always skeptical, and never passive. Through this concept of parenthood, the parents I talked to set themselves apart from other parents who cannot or will not accept the commitment to always weigh the risks. The vision of collective immunity underlying the discourse on mandatory vaccination is replaced by individual health as the ultimate interest. At the same time the imperative of responsible parenthood strongly empowers the parents in the process of evaluating risk since it puts them in the position of the most important actors bearing the responsibility for the health of their own children. The parents I talked to often spent hours at a time studying and seeking information about vaccination. For example, Jana (age 29) described this process in the following way:

> So more or less on Google I always typed in some key word, then in the forums with the mothers I searched for their experiences . . . Later my sister (a medical doctor) recommended to me the names of some of her classmates who deal with vaccination, so I tried to download their work. I can't say I understand it like an expert does, but at least I read up on it. . . . I put some key words in the search engine and waited to see what Google would come up with. And that takes you to other places, that's how I did it. Just on the Internet. Otherwise if I were to go see a doctor and ask him, I'm not going to do that. There wouldn't be much chance that someone would talk to you and explain anything.

As Jana's description shows, these individuals challenge the idea of medical authority as actors who should (and can) decide about the health of their children. They see this decision as something that only parents themselves can make, for they alone will bear the consequences. The health of the parents and their children has become, in their descriptions, a project on which each of them must individually work. As Barbora (age 39) puts it, "Just as the doctor cannot forbid us from doing something, it is our responsibility [to] look after our own heath ourselves."

My participants, through the norms of responsible and informed parenthood, also challenge the hierarchy between experts and lay people and promote an egalitarian vision of doctors and parents as relatively equal authorities in making decisions about children's health care. Trust in the correctness of other people's decisions was presented as weakness. As Hobson-West (2007, 212) points out, parents critical of vaccination "become the expert themselves through a difficult process of personal education and empowerment." The parents engaged in the "will to health" project become isolated warriors who can only rely upon themselves, and they must carry the heavy burden of decisions and their consequences. But as Rose (2007) points out, although current forms of biopolitics produce self-disciplining individuals committed to responsibility for their own health, biological citizenship also has a collectivizing element, giving rise to "collectivities formed around a biological conception of a shared identity" (ibid, 134). In this case this biological conception of a shared identity did not refer to genetic risks or corporeal vulnerability as underlined by Rose but to shared ideas concerning the effects of vaccination and the nature of health risks. Those parents unite through their attitudes toward vaccination and the shared conception of how the parental responsibility toward children's health should be expressed in daily life and how it should be (not) distributed among various actors. A specific attitude toward the care for the health of their children and the conception of vaccination as a form of health risk give rise to new forms of collectivities of parents. Debates over mandatory vaccination of children thus not only produce informed responsible parents, but also collectives formed around this shared approach to their children's health.

"To Give Each Other Courage." Parents United Through Opposition Toward Vaccination

Studying of the formation of new forms of biosocialities was often related to the patient associations and self-help groups concentrating on issues of health and illness (Brown et al. 2004; Landzelius 2006; McInerney 2000). As Lemke (2011, 98–99) puts it, activity in these collectives focused mainly on communicating their experiences and attracting the interest of policy makers, on improving access to health care, and on actively debating the ethical questions associated with treatment and access to it. In this section I will show how the issue of vaccination has become an important vehicle for mobilizing parents through formation of new biosocialities.

These forms of biosocialities are not established primarily through the experience of illness or belonging to an at-risk group, but through one's position on health-related issues. The parents unite through the shared conception of who and based on what information has the right to determine whether or not to intervene in the child's bodily processes and what are the right pathways to health. They do not identify and associate as patients or carriers of a certain gene, predisposition, or physical disadvantage. The axis of their biosociality is a shared concept of parenthood, which to a large extent is based on responsibility for their children's health. They focus on questions similar to those mentioned by Lemke. In the case of vaccination, one goal is to draw public attention to issues related to mandatory vaccination, and having it made voluntary, as part of the general discussion of ethical issues of informed consent and the power of the state to interfere in parents' rights to decide about the health care provided to their children.

For some of my participants, vaccination was important only at one stage in their lives, and as their children grew, this issue (and the negotiation with the medical authorities) became less and less of concern and their interest in the topic waned. For others, however, the activism against mandatory vaccination was a long-term project through which they expressed their overall stance toward biomedicine. What had mobilized these parents and drawn them together despite the varying intensity and duration of their interest in vaccination was not necessarily the need to engage in political lobbying or organized efforts aimed at reforming the healthcare system, but more what Rose (2007, 146) calls the "new informed ethics of the self—a set of techniques for managing everyday life in relation to a condition, and in relation to expert knowledge." This form of biosociality is formed primarily through the self-disciplining mechanisms contained in the shared imperative of the responsible, informed parent, including the newly (re)defined relationship between parents and biomedical authorities and a breaking down of the hierarchy between the various forms of expert knowledge that they represent. In the following part of the text I will focus in more detail on the ways in which these forms of biological citizenship are established. I will show by what means the issue of vaccination brings parents together.

As with other forms of biosocialities, parents critical of vaccination use the internet as the place to work out a unifying platform. This is made possible by the access it provides to information about immunization. The internet brings parents together to share their self-narratives related to vaccination, to share the way they went about refusing, and tips on how to behave when dealing with doctors. Parents critical of the vaccination program in the Czech Republic interact mainly through Rozalio. Its web and Facebook pages are a place to post about people's own experiences with vaccination and legal expertise, or to provide examples of how to fill out the paperwork demanded by doctors when one refuses to vaccinate the children, or how to write a statement for The Bureau of Hygiene authorized to impose fines on those who refuse to comply with mandatory vaccination. Online discussion groups of parents serve as a platform for discussing specific questions and problems. The frequency of contributions varies over different periods, but it is not uncommon for several contributions a day to be posted. For some participants, discussing the topic becomes a major part of their everyday lives.

This sharing of information and experience gives rise to new collectivities of parents. The sharing of personal narratives adds immediacy to the need to make informed decisions, and it makes "the struggle" with the biomedical authorities visible to other parents. Through these personal stories and bits of experience, a shared collective experience of suppression emerges and parents support themselves in the correctness of their decisions and actions. Barbora describes this in a following way:

> And for these people this (sharing) is very important. It's something we didn't have before. If I'm expecting my first child, suddenly I can call on thirty people for advice, and each of them does it a little different, and I can gradually share with everyone, it's just fantastic. Most of the people who live in isolated villages, or those who live in the big towns, they are all alone in this and don't have anyone to help them deal with this and give them advice, because all they have around them are those who only know the official model. So, it's terribly valuable for them, this contact with other parents. (Barbora, age 39)

The chance to share one's experiences with others and to be assured that opinions are shared played an important role in the process of forming a community of parents critical of vaccination. Meanwhile, the key to holding this biosociality together was sharing information regarding three basic areas. The first concerns practical advice on how to deal with medical and other authorities. Refusal to participate in mandatory vaccination in the Czech Republic is classified as a misdemeanor that threatens the public health. My participants were forced to defend their decision to refuse some or all mandatory vaccinations before their pediatricians and, if they were reported, also to officials at The Bureau of Hygiene and social workers. Parents shared the completed forms and statements associated with their particular cases. On the Rozalio website and in the e-mail conferences they exchanged practical advice on how to behave during such proceedings and what arguments to use. A guide step-by-step for parents refusing vaccination that presents how parents should proceed was published on the Rozalio web pages.[12] This document also provides typical forms of argumentation that parents can use while negotiating with the health authorities.[13] During the public lectures and meetings of self-help groups, parents shared not only their individual experiences and opinions but also clear strategies how to communicate with doctors, health authorities, and other family members. Through sharing of experience and instructions, parents also "learned" what to do next and how to frame their arguments. Specific subjectivities of parents who use similar language, arguments, and strategies in order to enforce their decision emerged during this process.

The second type of information shared by these parents was not necessarily related directly to the issue of vaccination. On the blogs, in the e-mail conferences, and at meetings, they also discussed healthy lifestyle tips, treatment for various health problems, or medicines. Discussions grew to include wide-ranging topics besides health, for example, the recent parliamentary or presidential elections. These topics, however, were framed in terms of the project of biological citizenship. For example, Rozalio produced an overview of the individual parties' positions on the issue of mandatory vaccination as a potential manual for parents on how to vote.

The largest amount of shared information, of course, dealt with specialized information on the issue of vaccination. It is no exaggeration to say that the majority of my participants had read more specialized texts and publications on immunization than the average pediatrician. Many of them regularly studied foreign scientific journals or had the information translated. They knew in detail the information flyers accompanying vaccinations (which most parents never even got to look at), which they were even able to compare with the flyers given out in other countries and those put out by the vaccines' manufacturers. Information of this type was shared on web pages, blogs, e-mail conferences, and occasional meetings with parents organized by Rozalio. The chance to share information also became a significant motivation for parents to become involved in these forms of communication. As Dita put it,

> So a person always gets to the information because every time someone finds something they send it to the vaccination e-mail conference so the others can learn about it, and from there it spreads to other places, and a person is able to get the important information. (Dita, age 33)

Discourses opposing vaccination challenge the dominant biomedical paradigm that stress the unmistakable benefits of vaccination programs by highlighting its risks, doubting its beneficial nature, and instead pointing out the unresolved issue of its real impact on the human organism. The contest between these divergent discourses on vaccination in many ways reflects the character of the "risk society," with the demonopolization of knowledge along with the production of new risks. Science in the context of reflexive modernization has won an exclusive position as the holder of knowledge and technologies that are able to detect invisible risks; but at the same time its power is declining sharply. As Beck observes (1992, 156), "science is becoming something more and more necessary, but at the same time less sufficient for a socially-binding definition of the truth." Risk has become something that is fundamentally mediated through argument. The latency of risk leads many to conclude it is nonexistent. Only awareness of risk brings it into existence (ibid, 27). In this sense, then, information becomes the key component of current society.

The parents' stances reflect the uncertain status of expert knowledge in current society. It is, however, the very uncertainty of the information that paradoxically became one of the glue of the collectivities of parents. The need to share and discuss information represents the main impulse for the various forms of physical and virtual gatherings. Simultaneously, the uncertainty of the information gives rise to new forms of authorities recruited within the parents themselves. Representatives of Rozalio periodically give lectures in various Czech cities. There are local self-help groups for parents who are critical to vaccination. In both cases the meetings are conducted by parents—especially mothers—that act as authorities in terms of knowledge concerning the vaccination risks and strategies of dealing with the sanctions in case of vaccination refusal. The lectures and meetings are conceptualized as an opportunity to discuss the benefits/risks of vaccination. The organizers are in the position of those who can provide an advice to other parents based on their own experience and self-education. The parents critical of vaccination challenge the dominance of biomedical knowledge and the authority of doctors. This process opens up a space for the formation of new forms of authorities and knowledge that simultaneously help to provide a steadier ground for the biosociality itself.

Accessibility of information and its dissemination among parents had a number of effects. First, it has helped to establish the norms of responsible and informed parenthood to which individuals subsequently subscribe. Through the constantly self-renewing process of informed decision-making, the idea of "us," the informed parents, who bear the positive connotations of "good" parenthood, took shape. A stance toward vaccination, which often symbolically represented the overall attitude of parents toward their children's health, has also become the vehicle for articulating who is a good parent. Other parents were judged according to these norms. The ability to take over responsibility for the health of their children, defy the medical authorities, and above all actively seek and evaluate information has become the defining features of shared model of "responsible parenthood." Parents critical of vaccination often criticized parents who do not live up to these standards of responsible parenthood. They spoke of them disparagingly as a "herd" or "sheep," two metaphors for blindly following orders instead of actively evaluating the information:

> A temperature of 37.9 and the mothers are running to the doctor saying "Doctor, doctor, what should I do? There's a tiny pimple on his face, the baby has diarrhea." And the doctors do what the parents want them to—give them medicine. I think it's mainly because people just don't want to treat themselves. All the care for their health they leave to the doctors, whom they trust and trust blindly. That's one thing. Another thing is that they don't want to be bothered by anything. My sister-in-law would be somewhat interested in the issue of vaccination, but she says, "Please, don't tell me about it, I don't want to deal with it, I would have to think about it, start seeking information, and have a hard time deciding whether yes or no." (Alena, age 41)

My participants, while characterizing themselves and other parents critical of vaccination, often referred to the shared "responsible and active stance to life" (Erika, age 42). The polarity between obedience and the resistance was often used a demarcation line between "us" and the "other" parents. To question the expert advice was depicted as a symbol of active and responsible parenthood. This hierarchy between different forms of parenthood simultaneously reinforces and masks the privileged position of my participant who has enough resources and social capital to make such decision. The imperative of active informed choice emphasized by my participants as a key feature of good parenthood ignores that not all parents are in similar position to collect and evaluate (mostly) scientific information concerning vaccination and that not all have similar resources they can mobilize while negotiating with health and state authorities. As Reich (2014) shows in her study of neoliberal discourses of mothering, the individualization of responsibility toward children health allows parents who are critical to vaccination to situate themselves as better parents by stressing how good parents always actively manage risks by questioning expert advice. Such discourse "allows mothers a vantage point from which they can critique other mothers who they see as not working to make good decisions for their children's health, without acknowledging the privilege required to do so" (ibid, 692).

The Czech case bears many similarities with antivaccination movements in other countries, but there are also some specificities stemming from the local context and postsocialist past. The vaccination debates serve as a platform where people express their attitudes concerning the relationship between individual and state and what constitutes individual rights and duties of citizens. My participants often criticized parents who "routinely" have their children vaccinated, evoking the historical tradition of Czech society and the communist era that limited the individual's ability to decide for oneself.

> I don't know anything else about medicine in other countries, but it's true that here we lived for a time in a system that controlled everything. Maybe it's a remnant of communism. Fear of those above you, fear to consult something with them, blind obedience to orders, and mainly fitting into those forms so you could get by, and fear of showing any kind of individuality, or something like that. (Darina, age 36)

In these descriptions, the parents thus break free from the mass of citizens who blindly obey authority. References to communist history, which in their eyes left its legacy in the form of fear of the authorities and blind obedience to orders, at the same time served to symbolically elevate the parents critical of vaccination as the representatives of democratically-minded civil society. As Jana (age 39) mentioned during the interview, "I think that the main reason you find no mandatory vaccination systems in western countries is that the civil society would not stand something like this." Those parents positioned themselves as the carriers of the democratic values of active and responsible citizenship challenging the legacy of communist era. Thus parents, through care for their children's health, constructed not only a picture of good (and not so good) parenthood, but also of the active (and passive) citizen. Associating within virtual or physically meeting communities allowed them to share the norms of modern citizenship and to carry them out in practice. As one participant in a group meeting of parents critical of vaccination said, "these kinds of meetings are good, because we share information and give each other courage."

Conclusions

The experiences and attitudes of parents critical of vaccination shed light on the process of destabilization of the authority of biomedical knowledge and the changing position of medicine as an institution. In many ways, parents opposing mandatory vaccination represent a challenge to the state, the system of medical expertise, and their authority. This includes not only the decision to defy official recommendations (and implicitly the idea that these institutions and authorities always act in citizens' best interests), but also the way in which parents themselves (re)interpret expert information, creating their own "scientific credibility," and define the meaning of responsibility for their own health and that of their children. In this regard, they can be seen as a symbolic expression of broader social processes defining the active approach to one's health as part of responsible citizenship.

This chapter analyzes the debates on compulsory vaccination as a field where the role of citizens with respect to their health as well as the norms of good/responsible parent are constantly negotiated. Questions concerning the parental responsibility toward children's health as well as different concepts of how this responsibility should be expressed in daily life are integral parts of the discourses on compulsory vaccination. Experiences of the interviewed parents show that the decision to refuse some or all of the compulsory vaccination is a difficult process during which individuals constantly define and evaluate risk, develop strategies how to deal with the uncertainty, and discipline themselves through the imperative of individual responsibility. Parents critical of vaccination can be seen as an expressive materialization of the "will to health" that forms an integral part of the current practices of biopolitics (e.g., Rose 2001). The critique of the vaccination should therefore be analyzed as an expression of the changes in the conceptualization of the individual responsibilities for maintaining health as well as of the changes in relationship between individuals/parents and health authorities. Despite the obviously more significant role of mothers in the process of decision making concerning vaccination, the idea of "responsible parenthood" was not framed in gendered terms. Although this concept of parenthood may in this way challenge the traditional gendered ideology of mothers as primarily caregivers, it simultaneously hides the fact that women still bear the main burden of responsibility concerning the health of their children.

Parents critical of vaccination use the process of decision making concerning the healthcare provided to their children as a basis for defining who is a "good" responsible parent. The process of decision making concerning vaccination produces new subjectivities of parents who are following specific ethical imperatives themselves and expect others to do so. Consequently, health becomes a new form of morality (Metzl 2010). This morality enables them to define themselves as responsible parents and simultaneously exclude others from this category. Vaccine refusal thus also serves as a mechanism through which educated, middle-class parents reinforce their privileged position as informed consumers with enough resources to make informed choices and successfully negotiate with health and state authorities. Simultaneously, the imperative of individual responsibility of parents enables them to distance themselves from their responsibility toward public health (see also Reich 2014). At the same time, new forms of collectivities emerge that unite parents through their critical stance toward vaccination. Those parents embody the new form of biological citizenship that involves health a key framework of one's own identity.

Jaroslava Hasmanová Marhánková, Associate Professor, Department of Sociology, University of West Bohemia, Czech Republic

Jaroslava Hasmanová Marhánková has focused on the concepts of biopolitics and issues of choice and women's experience with prenatal care. Her second main research interest is located within the sociology of aging and body. In 2008, she was awarded a "Generations in Dialogue" Social Research Fellowship by the ERSTE Foundation. Her previous project, published in the book, *Activity as a Project. Discourse of Active Ageing and Its Reflection in the Life of Seniors*, focused on disciplinary practices surrounding representation of aging. Analysis published in this chapter is part of her ongoing project "Biological Citizenship: Forms of Governance and Resistance to Biomedical Knowledge in the Czech Republic," which was founded by the Czech Science Foundation (grant no. 13-18411S) and explores the ways in which health and individual "biology" facilitate emergence of novel forms of collectivities.

Notes

1. The fine of ten thousand Czech crowns represents approximately 40% of average monthly net income in the Czech Republic (in 2013).

2. The mandatory vaccination against these illnesses does not apply only to persons with chronic counterindications; that is, health conditions that prevent the application of the vaccination materials (for example, because of neurological or immune system disorders). However, fines for failing to vaccinate children are seldom enforced. The monitoring of mandatory vaccination is in the jurisdiction of Regional Public Health Authorities. They have competence to conduct random inspections in the pediatricians' offices and check their records. Pediatricians themselves have no right to report the cases of parents who refuse vaccination. However, the parents I interviewed as well as the analysis of The League for Human Rights in the Czech Republic confirm that the pediatricians often do not respect this rule and contact Regional Public Health Authorities. The Regional Public Health Authorities can impose the financial sanction. However, in most cases (as confirmed also in interviews with my participants) the authorities hardly ever initiate such actions.

3. Children who have not received some or any of the mandatory vaccinations even though they have no counterindications cannot, according to existing rules, be accepted for public preschool education and may not take part in recreational activities at elementary school (for example, summer camp, winter ski camp, etc.). This fact is also cited by parents critical of vaccination as one of the most difficult problems of the current law. The threat that their child will not be allowed to attend state preschool or participate in activities at school is frequently mentioned by parents as the most harmful form of sanctions. It severely limits the options for combining work and family life (when a child cannot attend preschool) and the family's financial situation (if their child has to attend a private facility).

4. Accessed May 20, 2015. http://www.rozalio.cz.

5. For example, at present there is a court case brought by parents whose son became paralyzed after vaccination and who are seeking damages from a nurse who failed to inform them of the risks and alternatives (see "Chlapec ochrnuty po ockovani by mel byt odskodnen. Stat ale nechce nest odpovednost," Liga lidskýchpráv, accessed February 15, 2015, http://llp.cz/pripady/chlapec-ochrnuty-po-ockovani-by-mel-byt-odskodnen.).

6. The League for Human Rights is an influential Czech nonprofit organization that prepares analyses, publishes academic articles, officially comments on laws, and provides free-of-charge consultations and helps to people in solving the human rights litigation. Healthcare and children's rights represent two of its main areas of interest (see Liga lidských práv website, accessed September 29, 2014, http://llp.cz/en).

7. For a detailed discussion concerning the natural childbirth movement in the Czech Republic, see also the chapter by Ema Hrešanová in this volume.

8. Source: Website of the Movement for an Active Childbirth. Accessed May 9, 2014. http://www.iham.cz/about-us.

9. However, Rozalio as an organization does not define itself as a women's organization and strictly stresses that the decision-making concerning vaccination concerns all parents. The same attitude was stressed by participants in my research (although they simultaneously acknowledged that the role of men and women in the process of decision-making concerning vaccination is different).

10. Participants' names were anonymized during the analysis and any information that could lead to their identification was deleted.

11. The introduction of mandatory vaccination can be seen as part of the technique of biopolitics, through which the health of the population is cultivated (Foucault 2003). Through the individual (vaccinated) body a new form of health is established, that of collective immunity, which becomes characteristic of the population and is measurable through the indicators of vaccination coverage and the statistics on illness. The concept of collective immunity assumes that if a certain rate of vaccination among the population is achieved, the risk of contagion and spread of infection will be significantly reduced. The necessity to maintain a certain rate of immunization so that all members of society are protected (for example, even those who for health reasons cannot be vaccinated) is also one of the most prominent arguments in favor of mass vaccination.

12. Source: Rozalio website. Accessed May 15, 2015. http://www.rozalio.cz/index.php?option=com_content&task=view&id=236&Itemid=33.

13. For example, the guide published by Rozalio refers to specific terms that parents should use while communicating with health authorities; an example is that their child does not threaten the public health or that Czech Republic signed the Universal Declaration on Bioethics and Human Rights that ensures that all medical interventions can be carried out only with the free and informed consent—in other words, the state cannot order mandatory health intervention.

Works Cited

Bazylevych, Maryna. 2011. "Vaccination Campaigns in Postsocialist Ukraine: Health Care Providers Navigating Uncertainty." *Medical Anthropology Quarterly* 25 (4):463–456.

Beck, Ulrich. 1992. *Risk Society. Towards a New Modernity.* London: SAGE.

Beck, Ulrich, and Elisabeth Beck-Gernsheim. 2002. *Individualization: Institutionalized Individualism and its Social and Political Consequences.* London: SAGE.

Blume, Stuart. 2006. "Anti-Vaccination Movements and Their Interpretations." *Social Science & Medicine* 62 (3):628–642.

Brown, Phil, Stephen Zavestoski, Sabrina McCormick, Brian Mayer, Rachel Morello-Frosch, and Rebecca Gasior Altman. 2004. "Embodied Health Movements: New Approaches to Social Movements in Health." *Sociology of Health & Illness* 26 (1):50–80.

Clements, Christopher J., Paul Greenough, and Diana Shull. 2006. "How Vaccine Safety Can Become Political—The Example of Polio in Nigeria." *Current Drug Safety* 1 (1):117–119.

Epstein, Steven. 1995. "The Construction of Lay Expertise: AIDS Activism and the Forging of Credibility in the Reform of Clinical Trials." *Science, Technology & Human Values* 20 (4):408–437.

Feldman-Savelsberg, Pamela, Flavien T. Ndonko, and Bergis Schmidt-Ehry. 2000. "Sterilizing Vaccines or the Politics of the Womb: Retrospective Study of a Rumor in Cameroon." *Medical Anthropology Quarterly* 14 (2):159–179.

Foucault, Michel. 2003. *"Society Must Be Defended": Lectures at the Collége de France, 1975–1976.* New York: Picador.

Hasmanová Marhánková, Jaroslava. 2008. "Konstrukce normality, rizika a vědění o těle v těhotenství: příklad prenatálních screeningů" [Construction of Normality, Risks and the Knowledge of Pregnant Body. The Case of Genetic Screenings]. *Biograf* 47 (3):19–49.

Hays, Sharon. 1996. *Cultural Contradictions of Motherhood.* New Haven: Yale University Press.

Hobson-West, Pru. 2007. "'Trusting Blindly Can Be the Biggest Risk of All': Organized Resistance to Childhood Vaccination in the UK." *Sociology of Health & Illness* 29 (2):198–215.

Hrešanová, Ema, and Jaroslava Hasmanová Marhánková. 2008. "Nové trendy v českém porodnictví a sociální nerovnosti mezi rodičkami" [New Trends in the Czech Birthing System and Emerging Social Inequalities among Birthing Women]. *Sociologický časopis / Czech Sociological Review* 44 (1):83–112.

Johnston, Hank, Enrique Larana, and Joseph R. Gusfield. 1994. "Identities, Grievances and New Social Movements." In *New Social Movements: From Ideology to Identity,* edited by Enrique Larana, Hank Johnston, and Joseph R. Gusfield, 3–35. Philadelphia: Temple University Press.

Landzelius, Kyra. 2006. "Introduction: Patient Organization Movements and New Metamorphoses in Patienthood." *Social Science & Medicine* 62 (3):529–537.

Lemke, Thomas. 2011. *Biopolitics. An Advanced Introduction.* New York: New York University Press.

MacQueen, Kathleen M., and Emily E. Namey. 2012. *Applied Thematic Analysis*. London: SAGE.
McInerney, Fran. 2000. "'Requested Death': A New Social Movement." *Social Science & Medicine* 50 (1):137–154.
Metzl, Jonathan. 2010. "Introduction. Why Against Health?" In *Against Health: How Health Became the New Morality*, edited by Jonathan Metz and Anna Kirkland, 1–14. New York: New York University Press.
Petrov, Jan. 2011. "Povinné očkování proti jednotlivým nemocem z hlediska ústavnosti." *Zdravotnické forum* 2:10–15.
Petryna, Adriana. 2002. *Life Exposed: Biological Citizens after Chernobyl*. Princeton: Princeton University Press.
Poltorak, Mike, Melissa Leach, James Fairhead, and Jackie Cassell. 2005. "'MMR Talk' and Vaccination Choices: An Ethnographic Study in Brighton." *Social Science & Medicine* 61 (3):709–719.
Rabinow, Paul. 1996. *Essays on the Anthropology of Reason*. Princeton: Princeton University Press.
Reich, Jennifer A. 2014. "Neoliberal Mothering and Vaccine Refusal: Imagined Gated Communities and the Privilege of Choice." *Gender & Society* 28 (5):679–704.
Rogerst, Anne, and David Pilgrim. 1994. "Rational Non-Compliance with Childhood Immunisation: Personal Accounts of Parents and Primary Health Care Professionals." In *Uptake of Immunisation: Issues for Health Educators*, 1–67. London: Health Education Authority.
Rose, Nikolas. 2001. "The Politics of Life Itself." *Theory, Culture & Society* 18 (6):1–30.
———. 2007. *The Politics of Life Itself: Biomedicine, Power, and Subjectivity in the Twenty-First Century*. Princeton: Princeton University Press.
Rose, Nikolas, and Carlos Novas. 2005. "Biological Citizenship." In *Global Assemblages: Technology, Politics, and Ethics as Anthropological Problems*, edited by Aihwa Ong and Stephen J. Collier, 439–463. Oxford: Blackwell Publishing Ltd.
Senier, Laura. 2008. "'It's Your Most Precious Thing': Worst-Case Thinking, Trust, and Parental Decision Making about Vaccination." *Sociological Inquiry* 78 (2):207–229.
UNICEF. 2012. "Immunization Summary. A Statistical Reference Containing Data through 2010." Accessed May 20, 2015. http://www.childinfo.org/files/immunization_summary_en.pdf.
Zákon 258/2000 Sb. Zákon o ochraně veřejného zdraví [Act No. 258/2000 on Protection of Public Health].

9

Advocacy for Children with Intellectual Disabilities: The Case of the Baltic States

Egle Sumskiene

Introduction

"My son is my teacher and he is the main drive that enables me to move forward," states Dana Migaliova, one of the founders and a long-term leader of the Lithuanian Welfare Society for Persons with Intellectual Disabilities "Hope" (*Lietuvos sutrikusio intelekto žmonių globos bendrija "Viltis"*). This quote shows how private and public spheres are interconnected in the case of parental activism in the post-Soviet Baltic states.[1] Children with intellectual disabilities (hereafter ID) can become teachers and a driving force for their parents who then engage others and participate in the development and implementation of the state's disability policy. Consequently, parents often play an important role in influencing the development of various policies related to disabilities as they seek to improve their children's lives.[2]

International experiences show that parents' involvement may be instrumental in creating changes in various areas of social policy, such as antidiscrimination, and to establish access to social services and education, as well as influence the public's perception of both children's special needs and of disability in general (Symeonidou 2007, 164). In many cases the reform of disability policies has been achieved through organized social movements. This is also the case in the Baltic states, where over the past twenty years, parents raising children with ID have founded non-governmental organizations

(NGOs) and led the way in promoting disabled people's rights. Since the 1990s, these NGOs demanded that children with ID would not have to live in state-run residential care institutions and, instead, be included in society just like children without disabilities (Anti-Defamation League 2005).

In the Western context, social movements composed of parents of children with severe intellectual disabilities emerged in the late 1940s and early 1950s.[3] Over the succeeding decades, activists managed to achieve major attitudinal changes in the care for persons with ID and established the movements' political influence at both the national and international levels. In the Baltic states, parents' movements emerged together with the rebirth of civil society in the early 1990s, and they quickly developed into national nongovernmental umbrella organizations. These larger networks unite a number of other, smaller NGOs and groups.

Initially, the Baltic disability rights groups were focused on providing direct support to families raising children with ID, but they soon evolved into political advocacy groups. Developing community care services, as well as organizing social campaigns for equal opportunities, social inclusion, and human rights, became the main focus of their activities.[4] Hence, in some respects parental civil participation in the post-Soviet area echoed the above-mentioned trends in Western countries. There are also numerous differences between the post-Soviet Baltic states and Western disability-rights NGOs. In the post-Soviet region, parents' initiatives emerged, developed, and evolved over a much shorter period of time than in the West. In many cases the types of claims and activities, such as service provision and advocacy, overlapped with each other, whereas similar processes in the West were more gradual and differentiated according to the different types of activities.

The aim of this chapter is to analyze social activism of parents raising children with ID in the three post-Soviet Baltic states of Estonia, Latvia, and Lithuania and to explore this development in light of the most relevant social movement theories. The research question that has guided this study is the following: Which developments, both within NGOs and external circumstances, determined the trajectories leading from unstructured gatherings of "tired parents" to influential disability policy actors in each Baltic country? My analysis shows that movements of parents of children with ID are not fixed, static units. These movements define themselves, develop, and grow while responding to the needs of their members and to various external social and political circumstances. Given the complex reality and constraints that individuals with ID face in society, parents' movements promote structural changes in disability policy and encourage tolerance and solidarity within society.

Intertwined with social movement theories, I extensively rely on a close reading of the recent history of Estonia, Latvia, and Lithuania while they were part of the Soviet Union. I take into account the kinds of resources (emotional, normative, and material/time) that were mobilized during the early postcommunist period as well as the institutional structure, social norms, and family roles that the communist period left behind. I discuss the specificity of institutional and family care for individuals with ID during the time of the Soviet Union (hereafter Union of Soviet Socialist Republics, USSR) and the development of parents' movements during the Perestroika period of the 1980s as well as after the collapse of the USSR. After describing the communist-era conditions, I synthesize various theoretical approaches to explain the development of parents' movements in the three post-Soviet Baltic states. First, emotion-driven theory helps to explain the origins and incentives for the emergence of parents' groups and NGOs. Second, resource mobilization theory sheds light on how these movements gathered financial and human resources, whereas the political process theory provides insights into contextual factors, such as the openings in the political systems in the 1990s, that are decisive for the growth of the movements' political influence. Finally, new social movement theory helps to explain the most recent trends of parental involvement and the professionals' role in NGOs, as well as new organizational capabilities that have responded to political, societal, and economic challenges.

The significance of this research lies in its thematic novelty and the comparative nature of the analysis. Although social movements and development of civil society in the post-Soviet area have become popular subjects in the social sciences, the disability movements have not yet received their due attention. This chapter focuses exclusively on activism focused on ID, with ID having been ignored during Soviet times but receiving an impressive increase in attention and broader influence following the Soviet Union's collapse. The focus is intentionally broad to include three post-Soviet states to reflect the complexity of movement emergence and effectiveness from both the geographical-chronological and individual-organizational perspectives.

This chapter analyzes the emergence and development of parental movements in three countries: Estonia, Latvia, and Lithuania, known as the post-Soviet Baltic states. Due to their geographical proximity, considerable parallel developments of their modern histories, and similar size of population and territory, Estonia, Latvia, and Lithuania are usually perceived to be similar in many ways, but in fact there are many significant cultural, political, and economic differences among them. The most obvious differences concern distinct cultural, religious, and historical traditions. For example, the influence of the Lutheran religion and German culture has been significant in Latvia and Estonia (the latter has also experienced strong influence of the Scandinavian culture and ethnolinguistically is closely related to Finland), whereas Lithuania has been influenced mainly by its geographic proximity to Poland and a closer affiliation with Roman Catholicism. These geographic and cultural differences could have had an impact on the differences in care for persons with ID.

Arguably, the three states also share many similarities, most notably that they all were part of the Soviet Union and implemented the Soviet model of disability policy between the late 1940s and 1991 (Phillips 2009; Puras, Sumskiene, and Adomaityte-Subaciene 2013; Rassel and Iarskaia-Smirnova 2013). A very similar implementation has reigned across all the Soviet republics while the disability paradigm steadily changed in the West. Due to the isolation of the three Baltic states at the time, parental activism could emerge, exert its effects, and influence medial and state authorities only after the fall of the Soviet Union. Families raising children with ID in all three Baltic countries faced highly comparable challenges and implemented similar (patchwork) solutions for decades. Consequently, even though there are a number of important differences among these three countries, the focus of this analysis is on their similarities. Thus, in this analysis the post-Soviet Baltic states may appear as more homogeneous than they are.

Research Method

The analysis provided here is based on triangulation, using both qualitative and quantitative methods. First, I conducted interviews with individuals who founded the largest parents' NGOs in the three Baltic states during November and December 2013. These individuals are both experts in the field of disability policy and also work as activist-parents in the NGOs. As Michaela Pfadenhauer puts it, an expert often has comprehensive knowledge of the subject in question that enables him/her to identify and account for causes for problems and potential solutions (2009, 82–83). In the disability field, the people with the most valuable expertise are parents raising children with ID, who are responsible for the day-to-day care, which includes coping with a lot of stress, difficulties of combining work and family life, and attending to the many medical, psychological, social, and educational needs of the child. Sometimes, they become the founders and leaders of parents' NGOs. Many activist-parents become experts who engage with the development of local or state-level disability policy development and disability rights advocacy. Many contemporary Baltic parental activists have developed considerable experience in founding and managing NGOs: they negotiate and attempt to find balance between the needs of parents, the medical, social and legal professionals, and children with ID. Organizations in all three countries promote children's inclusion and integration in society and its institutions, as well as the establishment of community services to persons with ID. I have conducted interviews with the representatives of the largest and most influential ID NGOs in the Baltic countries, which are active on both the national and international levels. My aim was to approach individuals who are both activists and experts in the field. Thus, I interviewed participants who met the following set of criteria: being a close family member of an individual with an ID, having at least 10 years of experience of being a head of a parents' NGO, active participation in disability policy development, and being nationally recognized as an expert within the field. I conducted four semistructured interviews with activists in parents' NGOs from Lithuania, Latvia, and Estonia.[5] The interviews inquired about the emergence and development of the national umbrella NGOs: Lithuanian Welfare Society for Persons with ID "Hope" (*Lietuvos sutrikusio intelekto žmonių globos bendrija "Viltis"*) and its Vilnius branch, the Estonian Mentally Disabled People Support Organization "Alternatively Gifted" (*Vaimupuudega Inimeste Tugiliit "Vaimukad"*); and the Latvian group Riga City Society "Child of Care" (*Biedrība Rīgas pilsētas "Rūpju bērns"*).

The semistructured interviews were based on a questionnaire that contained inquiries concerning the activists' initial motives for establishing an NGO, the NGO's organizational goals, its developmental strategies, the political and societal challenges they have faced, and the progress of parental influence in shaping and implementing the state's disability policy. I analyzed the interviews with the qualitative data software NVivo8. The same six steps were followed with each interview: transcription, paraphrasing, development of captions, theme comparison, sociological conceptualization, and theoretical generalization (Meuser and Nagel 1989).

As a second part of the triangulation method, participant observation was also an important and integral part of the research. As an expert in the field for over 10 years, I have closely cooperated with NGOs working in the field of ID, participated in numerous meetings, conferences, and advocacy events, and I provided trainings and scientific expertise. My personal and professional knowledge along with my practical experience in the field of disability provided a good starting point in preparation for and the implementation of the abovementioned interviews. Finally, I extensively reviewed previous research and studied various official documents, analyses, and reports produced by national and international disability, mental health, and human rights NGOs.

Theoretical Perspectives for the Study of Parental Disability Movements

Social movements emerge as a result of turbulent changes within society, and in return they also stimulate further social and political change. Instead of focusing on social movements as a group, they are better defined as a social and political process (Foweraker 1995, 23). In this chapter, I adopt such a process-oriented approach to tracing the development of the post-Soviet Baltic disability movements over the twenty-five years (from about 1989 until 2014). During this period, parents managed to channel their individual grievances into collective political action and gain significant results. Four theoretical perspectives—emotions in social movements, resource mobilization theory, political process, and new social movement theory—aid the following analysis.

In the 1970s, the importance of emotions in social movements was used to explain their growth and unfolding (McCarthy and Zald 1976). This perspective gained further support in recent studies (Goodwin, Jasper, and Polletta 2004; Jasper 1998; Van Zomeren et al. 2004). Helplessness, fear of the future, exhaustion, and anger with regards to social injustice are just a few emotions that parents of children with ID experience. As discussed later in this text, at the beginning of the 1990s, these emotions resulted in a shared and increasingly public grievance and formed an important precondition for the emergence of parental NGOs in the Baltic states. Shared anger and mutual emotional support may explain group members' tendencies to take collective action to address their collective disadvantages (Van Zomeren et al. 2004).

The second theoretical approach applied in this analysis is resource mobilization, which is perhaps the most broadly accepted theory of social movements. The theory of resource mobilization argues that social movements are rational, targeted activities in organized and purposeful processes, instead of emotion-driven, unstructured collective actions (Dalton, Küchler, and Bürklin 1990). Emotions may lead to producing resources, because social movements have often few tangible resources (such as money, space, and means of publicizing) but they are strong on human resources, which many consider as the primary intangible resource of social movements (Freeman 1979). Instead of sharply separating emotions and calculated actions, observers also emphasize connections and point out the role of movements as agencies for social change (Jenkins 1983, 528). In this chapter the resource mobilization theory is used to explain how the Baltic disability social movements mobilize both tangible and intangible resources and reveal parental participation as a rational behavior based on strong emotions to protect and provide for children.

The third useful theoretical approach applied in this research is the political process framework, which concentrates on the political environment in which social movements operate, asserting that the trajectory of a given movement depends on the political dynamics, determined by the interactions between political actors (e.g., Kriesi et al. 1992; McAdam 1982; Kitschelt 1986; Tarrow 1994). Highlighting the importance of the political process that contemporary movements utilize has challenged the interpretation of social movements as "marginal and anti-institutional expressions of dysfunctions of the system" (Della Porta and Diani 2006, 17). Applied to the case of parents' movements in the Baltic states, the political process perspective allows for tracing gradual increases in their political influence and the eventual implementation of these movements' political claims.

Fourth, the New Social Movements (NSM) approach applies to this research by arguing that social movements arise as a result of the contradiction in the areas of "cultural reproduction, social integration and socialization" (Habermas 1981, 34). The cases discussed in this chapter demonstrate that parents' movements share some important characteristics often associated with NSMs, such as a focus on equality, minority rights, identity, personal autonomy, and regular self-reflection[6] (D'Anieri, Ernst, and Kier 1990; Melucci 1996; Offe 1985; Pichardo 1997).

Care for Individuals with Intellectual Disabilities in the Soviet Union

In order to fully analyze the complexities and general context that impacted the development of parental NGOs in the Baltic states, it is crucial to present the Soviet tradition of care for persons with ID.[7] It is useful, however, to introduce a number of terms and definitions first. The term "intellectual disability" is defined by the American Association on Intellectual and Developmental Disabilities (2013) as significant limitations both in intellectual functioning and in adaptive behavior that cover a number of day-to-day social and practical skills. The diagnostic criteria for establishing ID requires an IQ score of 75 or below. ID originates before the age of 18 and affects approximately 2–3 percent of the general population. The Russian equivalent of this term, which was used during Soviet times, was *умственная отсталость* (mental retardation).[8] "Residential care institution," according to Jan Pfeiffer et al. (2009), is understood as any care facility where users are isolated from the broader community and/or compelled to live together; they do not have sufficient control over their lives and over decisions that affect them, and the requirements and priorities of the institution tend to take precedence over the residents' individual needs. Such institutions, termed *Психоневрологические интернаты* (psychoneurological internats) were state-run pillars of the system of care for individuals with ID in the Soviet Union.

During Soviet times, many aspects of social diversity were not acknowledged and thus their carriers were, and often remain, marginalized. The persons with disabilities, along with the representatives of sexual minorities, political opponents, and other "deviant" individuals, were perceived as a menace to the intended homogeneity of the Soviet society. Even veterans who had physical disabilities due to injuries suffered during World War II were deported from large cities to the Valaam archipelago in the Republic of Karelia (Phillips 2009). Individuals with ID were considered unable to contribute to the building of communism in the Soviet era. Moreover, these individuals' deviations from the "norm" posed a serious threat to the myth of a healthy and productive Soviet society (Puras, Sumskiene, and Adomaityte-Subaciene 2013). Finally, as a result of isolating and marginalizing children with ID, they grew up without proper education and socialization, and thus were often unable to obtain the skills needed for meaningful participation in society. Due to these circumstances, the dominant discourses on ID were filled with stereotypes and negative attitudes toward this specific social group.

Developmental disorders in Soviet times were often diagnosed at an early age due to a strong school of the Soviet "defectology."[9] Unfortunately, early detection did not lead to provision of comprehensive early intervention services for the child and his/her family. Instead a "residential assumption" prevailed: a person diagnosed with ID would be assumed to need residential facilities simply because of the diagnosis (Skarnulis 1979, cited in Mitchel 2004, 332). Parents of such children were strongly recommended to place their offspring in state-run institutions (Carter 2001; Sammon 2001; Tobis 2000; UNICEF 2004).

Elayn Sammon (2001) notes that a widespread belief and acceptance of the notion that medical professionals know best, and that only state-run institutions can provide appropriate services for children with special needs, still exists in contemporary Russia. Reality proves the contrary: medical expert commissions often make mistakes in diagnoses and the most common diagnostic mistake is placing far too many children within the borderline category of ID in residential care institutions (Tobis 2000, 9). In most cases, a verdict at an early age affects the person's entire life.

It is important to distinguish a twofold burden that loomed over families that chose to care for children with ID at home in the Soviet Union. One part of this burden entailed the typical pressures on caregiving families in every country, and the other emerged due to the characteristics of Soviet society. A wide spectrum of medical, social, pedagogical, and psychological services is crucial for families and individuals with ID. Unfortunately, almost none of these services were available in the Soviet Union because of the widespread belief that such children should be institutionalized. Additionally, children with ID were ineligible to qualify for disability benefits as they had no previous labor experience. Until 1979, Soviet legislation defined disability as an inability to perform professional functions due to sickness or trauma. This definition excluded, and consequently did not cover under disability benefits, most children with ID (Zickel and Keefe 1991).

Due to the nonexistence of daycare services for children with ID, one of the parents (most often, and nearly exclusively, the mother) had to stay home and give up their careers. This constraint had a number of implications for individuals and their families. The absence from the labor market led to loss of many civil and social rights in the Soviet Union. Most families with children who had ID faced considerable financial constraints and were deprived of many goods and services otherwise distributed by the trade unions: from food, such as salami and mayonnaise, to goods such as a car or new apartment. Ekaterina Tchueva adds that in addition to work carrying a strong ideological importance, it was a powerful means of control and indoctrination under communism (2005, 106). Consequently, every person who refused to use the state-run childcare services was forced out not only from the labor market, but also excluded from the broader, redistributive functions of the state as well. Therefore, those who chose to care for a child with an ID became suspects in the eyes of the state. The abovementioned state-propagated suspicion and exclusion that parents had to endure substantially influenced practices of caregiving in families with children with ID.

The term "carers' burden" encompasses ongoing physical, social, psychological, and economical burdens experienced by the main caregiver for a person with disabilities. Studies show a significantly higher divorce rate and high stress levels in such families, as well as significant restrictions in their social life (Douglas et al. 2005; Honea et al. 2008; Pinquart and Sörensen 2007; Soskolne, Halevy-Levin, and Ben-Yehuda 2007). What made the situation of caregiving families even more difficult in the Soviet context was that they could not rely on institutional support provided by the state or on civil society or family and extended kin networks. Internationally, family and kin networks have been depicted as an important resource in providing emotional as well as social support (e.g., Dellve et al. 2006; Friedrich 1979; Girolametto and Tannock 1994; Shonkoff et al. 1992; Sloper and Turner 1993). However, analyses show that in the Soviet reality the contrary was quite widespread. Sammon (2001, 14) asserts that due to the overwhelming caring responsibilities and ongoing pressure from extended family members, as well as the broader society, some families decided to place their children in institutional care following several years of immense struggle.

On the macro level, caregivers were excluded from Soviet society, experiencing stigma for having a family member with a disability, consequently condemned as "unproductive citizens." On the mezzo level, these individuals did not benefit from relevant social services and faced extensive pressure by medical and pedagogical professionals to place their child in state-run institutional care. Finally, on the micro level, carers experienced persistent emotional stress, poor living conditions, financial constraints, and dramatically reduced social capital.

All the above mentioned factors need to be taken under consideration when analyzing contemporary social movements composed of parents of children with severe intellectual disabilities in the Baltic states. At the same time, however, historical determinants intertwine with contemporary influences, such as political openings and closings on the national and local levels, availability of resources, or the ways in which people construct collective identities.

Mobilizing on Behalf of Children: Parents Establishing NGOs

Many NGOs that focus on the rights of persons with ID in the Baltics emerged from small, informal parent groups that grew into movements, with the majority eventually undergoing the process of institutionalization by establishing NGOs. Some social movement NGOs emerged even before the regime change. NGOs included in this analysis are the Lithuanian NGO *Viltis*, which was founded in 1989, and *Rūpju bērns*, which was founded in Riga, Latvia, in 1990. Similar NGOs emerged in other countries in the region; for example, in 1991 a group of parents funded the *Республиканская ассоциация родителей детей-инвалидов* (Respublikanskaja associacija roditelej detej-invalidov, Republican Association of Parents Who Care for Children with Disabilities) in Belarus.

The *Djerela*, Charity Association for People with ID (Blagodijne tovaristvo dopomogi invalidam ta osobam z intelektual'noju nedostatnistju «Dzherela» *Благодійне товариство допомоги інвалідам та особам з інтелектуальною недостатністю «Джерела»*) emerged in Ukraine in 1996 as a combination of parents' initiative and Western support of similar NGOs. All of the abovementioned NGOs are active to this day, operating on national and local levels, and parents continue to play an important role in shaping the NGOs' agenda and organizing activities.

The leaders of these NGOs were often inspired and supported by Western groups. The leading activists were the first to visit various centers, programs, and services for persons with ID in Western countries. Often these visits encouraged the parents to begin speaking up, both at home and internationally, about the situation in the post-Soviet region. These activists brought new approaches to ID back to their home countries, urging their respective governments to reform disability policy and simultaneously developing and piloting new community services with financial and ideological support from international donors. These emerging leaders have considerable achievements in the field of social policy development. A joint meeting of the World Health Organization and the European Commission in 1999 heartily acknowledged the influence of parents' NGOs in post-Soviet societies.

> In many cases [mental health—author's note] reform initiatives originated from the non-governmental field, with governments either being largely indifferent or even hostile. . . . State institutions in Central and Eastern Europe are often very medicalized and thus work at the NGO level is of utmost importance. (World Health Organization 1999, 6)

NGOs established by parents raising children with ID worldwide have to face many difficulties and they tend to focus on similar issues, such as pervasive social and medical stereotypes concerning ID and a lack of adequate support for families and individuals with disabilities. Parental activists face the lack of political will and limited financial resources, which hinder development of services and prospects for reforming the existing infrastructure of institutional care (Bulić and Parker 2010; Holland 2010; Jenkins, Klein and Parker 2005; Knapp et al. 2007; Sumskiene 2014). Parental activism is very difficult in the context of post-Soviet countries, where institutional legacy and existing prejudice toward individuals with ID continue to obstruct positive reforms and further development in the respective fields.

Looking back on the last twenty-five years, it is evident that the sheer number of obstacles, as outlined above, has unexpectedly provided a significant stimulus for parents to effectively work together to achieve significant alterations in the Baltic states' disability policy. The following section discusses the development of parents' organizing for over more than twenty years and explains how the movement, which started with tumultuous meetings of "tired parents," eventually led to the establishment of influential NGOs within the policy making and service provision fields.

Explaining Social Activism of Parents of Children with ID

In the following sections I will apply the four theoretical perspectives on social movements to explain how social mobilizations of parents of children with disabilities emerged and developed. I will start with discussing the role of emotions, then move to resources and political openings. The last theoretical perspective I discuss concerns New Social Movement theory.

"All of Us—We Were Crying": Emotions of Parental Activists

In the cases presented here, having a family member with ID was the main reason for the activists to either join or establish an NGO. Most often these NGOs started as a gathering of volunteers and then an activist eventually took on the responsibility of a chairperson. I found, in all cases I analyzed, social activism was the result of a personal experience of being a mother or sibling of a person with ID. Care for an individual with ID contains a significant component of emotional involvement. Emotions such as fear, loneliness, and vulnerability can impede social activism, but they can also motivate people to act collectively to overcome them. That was the case of people engaged in the parental activism I analyze here.

Recounting the feelings of loneliness and helplessness that the parents perceived as pervasive prior to the establishment of their NGO, one of the two Lithuanian parental activists I interviewed stated, "We were on our own" (*Viltis*-2). In many cases taking care for the children with ID entailed decades of experiencing very intense emotions. These emotions were stemming not only from the burden of everyday tasks, but also from the fact that the parents who decided to take care of their children at home had to resist social and institutional pressure to place their offspring in a state-run institutional care facility. One of the two Lithuanian respondents, who had several years of experience in raising children with ID under the Soviet regime, describes the heated atmosphere at the meetings during the first days of collective action: "All of us, we were yelling, shouting, . . . and crying" (*Viltis*-1). Even the names given to NGOs carried an emotional message: "Hope" in Lithuania, "Child of Care" in Latvia, and "Alternatively Gifted" in Estonia.

The first gatherings of parents raising children with ID in the Baltic states consisted of "tired parents," as activists later recounted how they saw themselves. The first activists consisted mostly of women and several men, all aiming for institutional change while also looking for emotional support. The Perestroika period in Lithuania, Latvia, and Estonia had created opportunities to strive for policy changes for their families and to recognize their children as equal and valuable citizens. "[We wanted] to 'legalize' the lives of our children" (*Viltis*-1), recalled one of the two Lithuanian interviewees. At the same time, parents realized that they would have to become the main driving force behind the policy reform. "Go ahead and do it yourselves!" was the imperative of a young Lithuanian mental health professional who was the first person to organize Lithuanian parents and prompt them to establish a parents' NGO. The interviews with activists revealed that emotional aspects of mobilization were especially important and strong in the early 1990s, when the people had the chance to speak up about their problems and needs for the first time in their lives. The interviewees from Latvia and Estonia joined their NGOs at a later date than the early perestroika period, and they stressed not only emotional but also rational factors behind their activism. For example, the leader of the Estonian NGO *Vaimukad* stated at the time she was looking for better education for her child.

Proponents of the emotions-driven approach to social movements usually stress the importance of emotions in the initial stage of the movement, when people start to address collective disadvantages (Goodwin, Jasper, and Polletta 2004; McCarthy and Zald 1976). Interviews with representatives of parents' NGOs confirm that emotions were crucial at the founding stage of mobilization when the collective grievances were identified and expressed for the first time. When new possibilities opened up, activists' individual feelings were transformed into the basis for collective action. Participants' concern for the future of one's child was extended toward the whole group of children who suffer from discrimination or social marginalization. These testimonies highlight how such emotions can have transformative power when the political structure is open and the activist group has sufficient resources to work together.

Applying the Resource Mobilization Perspective to Baltic Parents' NGOs

Proponents of the resource mobilization approach stress the synergistic effect of joint efforts of activists and suggest that movement actions are rational in their undertaking. They also argue that formally structured movement organizations, such as NGOs, are more effective at mounting sustained challenges than informal ones. This perspective shows that strategic factors and involvement in the political processes determine the success of the movement (Jenkins 1983, 528). The present analysis does not singularly follow the rational-choice approach but rather considers both material and symbolic resources as important elements of success. Resources appear as part of a multidimensional perspective on social activism, with two main types of resources particularly relevant in this case study. As my interviewees noted, financial and human resources contributed fundamentally to their movements' success. This argument corresponds to those of Pamela Oliver and Gerald Marwell (1992), who note that movements' participants can either mobilize their financial contribution or participation (their time). Oliver and Marwell argue that these two resources follow different logics, require employing different tactics, and involve pursuing different goals. Building on this argument, the present analysis shows that the value of time and money fluctuates across different stages of organizational development of disability NGOs in the Baltic states.

According to my interviewees, the first years in the development of their NGOs were marked by extensive personal involvement and making significant time available. Highly motivated parents were willing to actively participate and support others. As one activist argued, "We were led by this enthusiasm, that there is something completely new, an opportunity to help our children, to help ourselves" (*Viltis-1*). Parents contributed much of their time to provide information about disability issues across their respective societies, they organized meetings with public officials, journalists, pedagogues and social workers, arranged trainings for health professionals, prepared programs, and raised funds. The Lithuanian respondent provided an example of how they contributed to establishing a daycare center for children with ID: "We prepared a program and approached the municipality asking for premises and we provided a very clear argument as to why we needed a home. It turned out that the location we got was in need of refurbishing, so we petitioned various foundations asking for their financial support to accomplish the reconstruction and adapt the building to its new purpose" (*Viltis-2*).

The "do-it-yourself" logic stemmed from the fact that in the early 1990s most newly established NGOs were poor, similar to the families caring for individuals with ID. According to my interviewees, the lack of finances resulted in a number of disputes and divergences within the NGOs regarding their goals and long-term mission. Some years later the financial situation of parental movements greatly improved, mostly due to the appearance of foreign donors who realized the importance of a strong and vibrant civil society in newly democratic countries and began supporting the emerging NGOs at the beginning of the 1990s. Parents' NGOs received support from the World Bank, Swedish International Development Cooperation Agency, the Open Society Foundation, as well as other international organizations. Disability organizations from Western countries also provided both financial support and organizational and managerial assistance. This material and technical support became an important stimulus for parental engagement in the movement, attracting new participants during the first years of mobilization. According to my interviewees, generous financial support, organizational help, and personal visits abroad prompted more parents to join and work in behalf of the disability NGOs.

It is important to note that international support and cooperation gradually changed the character of parents' NGOs in the post-Soviet Baltic states. Professionalization led to establishing formal partnerships, in which NGOs had to compete for funds from international donors. The professionalization has increased requirements for gaining support for the provision of services and awareness-raising projects. Entering the European Union (EU) in 2004 also substantially increased the requirements of financial accountability and the pressure toward managerial professionalization. In turn, growing professionalization resulted in a decrease in parents' interest in working for an NGO, thus reducing their time commitment. As the Estonian respondent claimed, "It is not so interesting anymore . . . there are no more fun projects, no more 'disco'" (*Vaimukad*). Thus, while initial support from international donors was essential for the establishment of parents' NGOs and expansion of the scope of their activities, in the long run it resulted in decreased parental participation and their partial replacement by professionals.

Regarding the financial resource dimension, in other words, money, increased state funding for disability services and donors' support resulted in the availability of special programs, services, and centers for individuals with ID. Thus, not only did parental involvement ("time") become less vital for the NGOs, but parents who did not belong to any NGO became less likely to contact the activists, unless they were seeking help in a crisis situation. The role of parents' groups has changed from being essential at the time of the emergence of the movement to becoming appreciated but only sporadically contacted today. As one activist argued, "Still, if something bad happens, parents call me. Of course, when they call me, they ask me why I don't do something about a problematic situation" (*Vaimukad*). The activists also stressed the change in parents' attitudes, claiming that there were many parents who expect the NGO to "do something" for them, while refusing to take on any responsibility themselves. One interviewee recounted a particular experience where, following an incident in a state-run residential care institution, she received many calls and letters from parents urging her to take action. Consequently, she arranged a meeting at the Ministry of Social Affairs and "I invited everybody and only one parent came because it was during the work week" (*Vaimukad*).

There are numerous significant conclusions that emerge from the cases of parental mobilization in the post-Soviet Baltic states. First of all, lessened parental involvement can be interpreted as an illustration to the application of resource mobilization that NGOs either mobilize people's time or financial resources. Second, lower parental activism in the NGOs can also signal that the process of NGO-ization (professionalization) can be detrimental to people's involvement. Third, the contemporary cases of parental mobilization also signal a generational change and show contemporary Baltic parents' decreased interest and ability to dedicate time for a common cause. Parental involvement remained high only during acute cases/crises and involvement in central decision-making processes in the NGOs. The Estonian interviewee regretted fellow parents' passivity and their lack of motivation: "Of course, they come [to] the meetings and I hope that they have read the emails, but, for example, if I send out some kind of new bill that I need their opinion on, it is very rare that I get an answer" (*Vaimukad*). Lack of continued parental involvement arose due to generational differences between the "young" and the "old" leaders of the movement, as the Lithuanian respondent commented. According to her, the generational divide tended to weaken parents' NGOs: "Leaders from my generation are pooped out and tired. Anyhow, they are of a respected age. But young parents don't come to work under existing conditions, because during the last ten years it has been difficult for NGOs to survive" (*Viltis-1*).

Changes in generational characteristics and professionalization influence the aims and achievements of parental movements in the post-Soviet Baltic states. Parents who have been involved in parents' NGOs from the 1990s are presently close to retirement age, whereas the attitudes, needs, and priorities of the new generation of parents differ from the ones nurtured by the "old-timers." The newer generation of parents whose children have ID are less likely to dedicate their time to the NGO, but they are eager to use the resources it provides. As an activist argued, "Parents come with different ideas. They come to receive. [They come] to require" (*Viltis-1*). The new generation of parents, whom the "old timers" consider demanding, can be considered as an effect of successfully functioning NGOs and state-run services. Parents of children with ID cannot imagine their lives without access to inclusive kindergartens, schools, daycare centers, independent living facilities, family support centers, rehabilitation and employment centers, as well as other services, developed and in many cases run by NGOs. Most NGOs' leaders have experienced an increased scope of responsibilities and pressures. After all, these parental activists were the first ones who struggled for the right to raise their children with ID during the late Soviet period. The NGO leaders were also the ones who had started parents' NGOs from scratch, both physically and ideologically. Because they were there from the beginning, these activists felt responsible for the NGOs' future and for ensuring a reliable flow of resources that are crucial for the movements' survival, in terms of money, time and the personal engagement of parents.

"Everything Had to be Changed": Applying the Political Process Perspective

Parents' NGOs in all three Baltic states had been founded shortly before Lithuania, Latvia, and Estonia officially declared their independence in 1990–1991. Parents' initiatives became part of the emerging civil society in these post-Soviet states. Other movements for freedom, independence, and democracy in the Baltic states also propelled parents' activism to fight for the rights and interests of their children. Mass mobilization to change the political regime boosted parents' endeavors to participate in the political process and advocate for the reform of disability policy.

Parents' NGOs were active members of their local civil societies from the very beginning, and according to my respondents, parents have fully understood the importance and necessity of political influence at a very early stage of their movement. Consequently, they aimed to become stakeholders in the policy formation process to play an important role in shaping and implementing the disability policy. The Estonian interviewee recalls the year 1990 when her NGO realized that they had to influence the state's social policy. To become an influential political player was an instrument to achieve the long-term goals of the movement. She stated, "At the very beginning it needed to be . . . influence on politicians to make regulations and ensure the finances for such services. So from the very beginning, before even first day care centers emerged, we started to influence the politicians and officials" (*Vaimukad*).

Activists reported that many parents joined NGOs pursuing long-term goals, not just to solve their own child's situation. These members advocated a change in the way society sees persons with ID, stressing that this is a group of people who are deprived of human rights and broader opportunities in life. Parents' NGOs planned and implemented reforms on all levels, including development of new legislation, introduction of new social services, and training of professionals. As one activist in Lithuania noted, "Everything on all levels had to be changed" (*Viltis*-1). At the time these efforts seemed to be basically successful.

The fact that in the contemporary Baltic states questions concerning disability issues are routinely discussed with representatives of these social movement NGOs is arguably one of the activists' major achievements. Today, parents' NGOs can express their concerns, initiate political debates on disability issues, and participate in political processes on different levels, starting from the local community and ending with the government ministries or parliament. The Latvian respondent stressed that his NGO gets invited to participate in the relevant political debates, and his Estonian colleague noted, "If we send an invitation, politicians will come to talk to us" *(Vaimukad)*. The Lithuanian respondent provided an overview of the milestones that marked the increase of political influence of the association *Viltis*:

> We have communicated a lot on the ministerial level, and laws have been changed; this is of the utmost importance. First of all, it was the Law on Social Integration [of the Disabled] in 1991; the Law on Special Education was a separate one, now it is integrated into the Law on Education. These were followed by the Law on Social Services and Catalogue of Social Services. Now, even the Convention on the Rights of Persons with Disabilities [was ratified]. (*Viltis-2*)

It has been a long journey from the very first parental gatherings in the 1990s to reach the current situation when parents' NGOs are active in shaping disability policy. The interviewees gave numerous examples of various strategies for expanding their political influence and for gaining society's sympathy: "a celebration of the Disability Day on the 3rd of December, public awareness campaigns, extensive collaborations with journalists and media, political lobbying as well as social performances" (*Vaimukad*).

The interviews suggested that cooperation with political parties has changed over time, depending on the situation and the views of the activists involved. Support of politicians is an important factor that determines the chances for an NGO to pursue its political goals. As a representative of the Estonian NGO explained, the targets of their initiatives are usually politicians: "We use favorable society's opinion to pressure politicians" (*Vaimukad*). At the same time, cooperation with politicians is a challenge because parliamentary majorities and coalitions of political parties are usually less stable than parents' NGOs in their commitment toward people with ID and their families. Therefore, over a long period of time, a movement's NGO must be able to enter into a dialogue with different political parties representing different ideologies and approaches. This openness and flexibility may be difficult at times for the activists; hence one of the activists used the derogatory term "political prostitution" to describe how they achieve their aims. The Lithuanian respondent used the term while describing NGOs' flexibility and willingness to cooperate with every political party: "We had to read their [political] programs, to find and make important suggestions. . . . Well, we are not a political organization and our members have different political preferences and we divide responsibilities among ourselves regarding who works with which political party" (*Viltis-2*). The Estonian and Latvian respondents were somewhat more skeptical toward their NGOs' collaboration with political parties. Especially assertive was the chairman of the Latvian NGO, who insisted that "we are not connected directly [to political parties] and none of our members or high level managers are involved in political parties and there is no direct connection between our organization and the high level decision-making position in the government or municipalities" (*Rūpju bērns*). However, later this respondent also stressed that while his NGO remains politically independent, it is open to collaboration with all political parties.

"To Be Together with Parents": The Applicability of the New Social Movements Approach

Parental activism discussed in this chapter bears a number of characteristics that have been associated with the New Social Movements (NSM): focus on equality, identity, minority rights, and self-reflexive nature of the movement. Additionally, the new social movements' framework applies to the post-Soviet Baltic parental movements because they stress the importance of the quality of life of individuals with ID and the desire to introduce a rights-based disability paradigm in public debates.

Parents' NGOs as actors in the policy development process have a double role in Lithuanian, Latvian, and Estonian societies: they nurture their political influence both by becoming an important provider of services and they persistently challenge the still lagging aspects of official disability policy. The parents' movements strive for enhancing the rights of persons with ID, and for a higher quality of life for both children with ID and their parents. The problem is that activists' understanding of rights and what they consider "desirable quality of life" often diverges from the views of state representatives. The Latvian interviewee mentioned a current conflict with the government regarding funding and the provision of social services for children with ID. Parents' NGOs understand quality of life as object of negotiation and continuous improvement, whereas the government tends to focus on maintaining the existing standard. Moreover, parents' NGOs follow the rights-based approach, and they argue their responsibility is to introduce and build up this perspective in the Baltic states, first of all by promoting and ensuring human rights and fundamental freedoms by persons with ID. These values and activism lead to conflicts with the state, and these conflicts channel social activism mainly into service provision, giving up putting on side broader advocacy activities. The Lithuanian interviewee discussed their group's desire to switch from a "charity-based" to a "rights-based" approach the society and the state should follow regarding individuals with ID.

> While drafting our NGO's bylaws, we extensively discussed whether we should aim for charity reaching every family as do all charity organizations and cry together with every mom, dad, or child. Or, should we be there together with parents and go for systemic changes. . . . Somehow we were wise enough to realize that it is important to find out why our children are not allowed to go to kindergartens or schools. We realized that we have to work on all levels. We had to examine the legal basis and to find out what hinders equality. (*Viltis-1*)

The analysis of the interviews with leading parental activists in the Baltic states shows a high level of self-reflectivity that influences the "kinds of tactic, structures and participants in New Social Movements" (Pichardo 1997, 415). This approach means that these organizations are able to adjust to new challenges and make conscious choices of structures and action, regarding processes of professionalization, bureaucratization, and participation in developing the state disability policy.

One example of how the activists respond to new challenges in a self-reflective fashion concerns the increased professionalization of the previously parents-led NGOs. Every interviewee noted the growing significance of professionals, such as social workers, psychologists, doctors, educators, lawyers, and managers in their organization, although attitudes toward this trend and strategies toward professionals' involvement differ across the countries. The Latvian movement utilizes increased participation of professionals in service delivery, whereas parents continue to dominate the decision-making level of the NGO. The Lithuanian *Viltis* association successfully invites parents to become and remain active members and participants in the functioning of the NGO. Similarly, the Estonian counterpart reported that professionals tend to be hired only on an ad hoc basis, for example, to organize a public relations campaign or to draft a new law. Thus, the Estonian NGO appears to be the most consistent of all three cases examined here, having only parents of children with ID as staff members and decision makers. At the same time, the Estonian movement has reported drawbacks to this system, arguing that parents employed by the NGO experience considerable pressure because they have to become all sorts of professionals, such as handymen, managers, social workers, lawyers, and public relations representatives.

Retrospectively analyzing the development of her NGO, the Lithuanian interviewee recalled that parents in *Viltis* were gradually replaced by professionals, even on the decision-making level in the beginning of the twenty-first century. "Everything goes to hell then," (*Viltis-1*) said the Lithuanian respondent arguing that overprofessionalization tends to narrow the movement's agenda to bureaucratic issues and results in losing personal contact with people the NGOs supposedly represent. Thus, during the last five years, *Viltis* has focused on attracting new parents as activists, which led to the renaissance of the NGO. "Currently we have only two professionals out of thirteen, and the rest are parents [on the organizations' board]. The organization is back on track again" (*Viltis-1*). The Latvian *Rūpju bērns* has chosen a path of development that differs from the Lithuanian and Estonian experience: their staff consists of professionals and they make up a significant part of the board as well. This latter trend is explained by the need for professionalism on the decision-making level. The Latvian interviewee advocated for what he considered to be the appropriate division of tasks between parents and professionals and for the right to choose one's favorite job. "We can achieve better results, better life standards when we act like professionals. When professionals are skilled in their jobs, then the parents can do their jobs how they like" (*Rūpju bērns*).

The New Social Movement approach helps to see parents' NGOs as dynamic and adaptive entities, focused on rights, equality, inclusion, and appreciation of differences. Responding to internal developments and external expectations, these NGOs continue to develop and evolve. This process of change may question the essence of parental involvement in NGOs. Parental involvement as well as professionalization varies across the disability movements in the Baltic states. Nevertheless, the NGOs associated with these movements continue to pursue their goals and remain core actors in shaping the concept of ID in Lithuanian, Latvian, and Estonian societies.

Conclusions

Research findings from the interviews, personal observations, and analysis of written materials confirm that social movements are vital factors in (re)building democratic societies in the Baltic states. Parents' NGOs contribute to these processes by promoting tolerance, inclusion, protection of rights, and dignity of this highly vulnerable segment of society. Parental NGOs have successfully challenged both previous institutional rules (such as the inhumane system of near-obligatory, state-run residential care) and prejudices (such as discriminating myths, stigma, and stereotypes) surrounding individuals with ID. Due to their active participation in public debates, the disability paradigm in the Baltic states has been reconceptualized and gradually moved from the medical to social rights-based disability model.

The development of parents' NGOs in the Baltic states has been a process in which the activists moved from an unstructured grassroots movement to at least partially professional organizations that have taken on the role of prominent political actors. The history of parental activism highlights the importance of emotions at the outset of organizational development, gradual alteration of available resources, continuing growth in response to political openings, as well as ability to keep and promote fundamental values. Consequently, Lithuanian, Latvian, and Estonian parents' NGOs have become similar to their counterparts in Western Europe, serving as exemplary models for the countries of the former Soviet Union and beyond. At the same time, these movements and their NGOs remain vulnerable and exposed to major challenges. Parental groups undergo processes of professionalization, a trend that has been amply observed in the postcommunist region (Howard 2003). Professionalization channels the movements' activities toward service provision and limits their ability to negotiate and change their focus, which may be detrimental for parental involvement in the future.

The important challenge that every interviewee notices is the decrease in parental participation and the NGOs' shift of focus toward their clientele. These developments suggest changes in parents' attitudes and reflect structural changes within NGOs, which would further affect their efficiency in advocacy, political participation and service provision. The role of parents in such NGOs is in the process of being renegotiated and redefined. Different organizations have chosen distinct paths of parents' involvement. In this process of renegotiation, in some cases parents simply become clients or can even be marginalized when professionals take over the NGO as managers. On the other hand, some parents continue to act as lobbyists and remain involved as employees of the movement NGO. A related question needing further research is to what extent can and should parents' voices be replaced by the voices of individuals with ID, who may want to speak up for themselves.

Parents' NGOs in Lithuania, Latvia, and Estonia have been working for similar changes in state policy and social attitudes, and they employed similar strategies to influence both society at large and their respective governments. Parental movements in the three Baltic states have also faced very significant difficulties and similar obstacles along the course of their development. All three NGOs were established relying on the strong motivation of parents' emotional engagement and experiences, such as love for their children, concern for the children's future, and desire to overcome discriminatory practices and discourses. Parents' focus on long-term goals and aiming for sustainable results was an important part of their efforts to ensure safe and good lives for individuals with ID.

Parents' NGOs have strong normative orientation based on respect for rights and dignity, social integration, and better quality of life for individuals with ID. This value-orientation and external opportunities (such as democratization, independence and EU membership) dictated the choice of the movements' tactics that includes nurturing of good relations with various politicians, while at the same time the activists were challenging the still faulty social and disability policies, norms, and practices. So far, parents' NGOs have managed to balance between establishing comprehensive links to political and social elites (thus gaining greater organizational impact) and maintaining political independence (thus leaving doors open for collaboration with a wide variety of political parties). However, the question of whether these movements and their respective NGOs can or wish to change their focus from service providers toward political advocacy remains open. In light of the New Social Movement theory, this kind of a conscious and caring collective action is explained by the self-reflective nature of such NGOs. Nevertheless, collective action is more than just a "qualitative leap," as identified by Alberto Melucci (1996, 76). From the emergence of parents' NGOs in the Baltic states in the early 1990s, a path emerged that includes constructive cooperation with various political partners. Paradoxically, the roots of such deliberate and rationally calculating tactics of negotiations may actually lie in the emotional nature of the parents' movements, in other words, it points to the fact that the founders of the NGOs share a collective identity of being caregivers, and the resulting emotional synergy may have led to the creation of strong and politically influential NGOs and movements.

Egle Sumskiene, Associate Professor, Social Work Department, Faculty of Philosophy, Vilnius University, Lithuania

Egle Sumskiene is a social worker, sociologist, and expert on disability, mental health, and human rights issues. She completed her PhD on the topic "From traditional to modern care: The case of persons with psychosocial disabilities." Since 2002, she has working for Vilnius University Social Work department as a lecturer, and in 2012 she became associate professor. She is actively collaborating with the Lithuanian NGO sector, focusing on mental health and human rights. As an expert, she was involved in various international and national projects focusing on the areas of human rights and disability, discrimination, mental healthcare, policy, and social integration of people with psychosocial disabilities. She is author of over twenty scientific publications covering issues of human rights and mental health.

Notes

1. The author wants to express her gratitude to Daina Zekaite, a former MA student of the Social Work Department at Vilnius University, for her help in data collection from research participants.

2. "Children" refers both to minor and adult children with ID who live with their parents.

3. By "Western" I mean countries that share similar values based on liberal democracy, human rights, personal liberty, and gender equality.

4. Any care or support provided to individuals with ID in the community.

5. Each interview was approximately sixty minutes long. They were conducted at the respondents' offices or electronically via Skype. Two of the four interviews were conducted in Lithuanian (mother tongue of both the respondents and the researcher), and two were conducted in English.

6. Collective actors' perception of an operation upon themselves (Eriksen, Fossum [eds.]2002, 39)

7. People with physical disabilities were more often part of the community, whereas people with psychosocial or intellectual disabilities were generally excluded from it or (from the very outset of the welfare state) institutionalized. Philosopher John Locke was one of the first who distinguished between intellectual and psychosocial disabilities by using the terminology of the seventeenth century, referring to one group as "idiots" and the other as "lunatics." The position of individuals with intellectual disabilities in society depends on the sociopolitical context. Only in the second part of the twentieth century has this problem begun to be discussed in terms of social inequality, human rights, integration of persons with intellectual disabilities, etc.

8. The term "mental retardation" was used worldwide instead of previous "oligofrenia" until the second half of the twentieth century. It still prevails in the Commonwealth of Independent States although new terms are being introduced, such as *психическая недостаточность* (mental deficiency), *психическое недоразвитие* (mental subnormality), *психический дефект* (mental defect), or*психическая несостоятельность* (mental disability) (Научный центр психического здоровья) (Scientific Mental Health Centre 2015).

9. Vygostkyis usually credited as the scholar establishing the fundamental principles of Soviet defectology. Based on experimental and clinical observations of children with physical

and mental disabilities, defectology was devoted to diagnosing, educating, and rehabilitating what this school called "defective children."

Works Cited

American Association on Intellectual and Developmental Disabilities. 2013. "Definition of Intellectual Disability." Accessed January 22, 2015. http://aaidd.org/intellectual-disability/definition#.VXMVoM-qqko.

Anti-Defamation League. 2005. "A Brief History of the Disability Rights Movement." Accessed December 11, 2014. http://archive.adl.org/education/curriculum_connections/fall_2005/fall_2005_lesson5_history.html.

Bulić, Ines, and Camilla Parker, eds. 2010. "Wasted Time, Wasted Money, Wasted Lives . . . A Wasted Opportunity?" European Coalition for Community Living. Accessed April 11, 2014. http://www. http://community-living.info/wp-content/uploads/2014/02/ECCL-StructuralFundsReport-final-WEB.pdf.

Carter, Richard. 2001. *Defying Prejudice, Advancing Equality 1: An Analysis of the Situation for Minority Children in Central and South Eastern Europe and the Former Soviet Union*. London: EveryChild.

Dalton, Russel, Manfred Küchler, and Wilhelm Bürklin. 1990. "The Challenge of the New Movements." In *Challenging the Political Order*, edited by Russel Dalton and Manfred Küchler, 3–20. Cambridge: Polity Press.

D'Anieri, Paul, Claire Ernst, and Elizabeth Kier. 1990. "New Social Movements in Historical Perspective." *Comparative Politics* 22:445–458. Accessed September 1, 2013. doi:10.2307/421973.

Della Porta, Donatella, and Mario Diani. 2006. *Social Movements: An Introduction*. 2nd ed. Malden, MA: Blackwell.

Dellve, Lotta, Lena Samuelsson, Andreas Tallborn, Anders Fasth, and Lillemor R. Hallberg. 2006. "Stress and Well-Being among Parents of Children with Rare Diseases: A Prospective Intervention Study." *Journal of Advanced Nursing* 53:392–402. Accessed April 4, 2014. doi:10.1111/j.1365-2648.2006.03736.x.

Douglas, Sara L., Barbara J. Daly, Carol G. Kelley, Elizabeth O'Toole, and Hugo Montenegro. 2005. "Impact of a Disease Management Program Upon Caregivers of Chronically Critically Ill Patients." *Chest* 128:3925–3936. Accessed May 5, 2014. doi:10.1378/chest.128.6.3925.

Eriksen, Oddvar E., and Erik J. Fossum. 2002. *Democracy in the European Union—Integration Through Deliberation?* New York: Routledge.

Foweraker, Joe. 1995. *Theorizing Social Movements*. London: Pluto Press.

Freeman, Jo. 1979. "Resource Mobilization and Strategy." In *The Dynamics of Social Movements*, edited by Mayer N. Zald and John M. McCarthy, 167–189. Cambridge, MA: Winthrop.

Friedrich, William N. 1979. "Predictors of the Coping Behavior of Mothers of Handicapped Children." *Journal of Consulting and Clinical Psychology* 47:1140–1141.

Girolametto, Luigi, and Rosemary Tannock. 1994. "Correlates of Directiveness in the Interactions of Fathers and Mothers of Children with Developmental Delays." *Journal of Speech and Hearing Research* 37:1178–1191.

Goodwin, Jeff, James M. Jasper, and Francesca Polletta. 2004. "Emotional Dimensions of Social Movements." In *The Blackwell Companion to Social Movements,* edited by David A. Snow, Sarah A. Soule, and Hanspeter Kriesi, 413–432. Oxford: Blackwell.

Habermas, Jürgen. 1981. *Kleine politische Schriften* [Short Political Writings] (I-IV) (1. Aufl). Suhrkamp.

Holland, Daniel. 2010. "Social Entrepreneurs and NGOs for People with Mental Disabilities in Post-Communist Europe: Implications for International Policy." *Review of Disability Studies: An International Journal* 6:7–24.

Honea, Norissa J., Ruthann Brintnall, Barbara Given, Paula Sherwood, Deirde B. Colao, Susan C. Somers, and Laurel L. Northouse. 2008. "Putting Evidence into Practice: Nursing Assessment and Interventions to Reduce Family Caregiver Strain and Burden." *Clinical Journal of Oncology Nursing* 12:507–516. doi:10.1188/08.CJON.507–516.

Howard, Marc Morjé. 2003. *The Weakness of Civil Society in Post-Communist Europe.* Cambridge: Cambridge University Press.

Jasper, James. 1998. "The Emotions of Protest: Affective and Reactive Emotions in and around Social Movements." *Sociological Forum* 13:397–424.

Jenkins, Craig J. 1983. "Resource Mobilization Theory and the Study of Social Movements." *Annual Review of Sociology* 9:527–553.

Jenkins, Rachel, Judith Klein, and Camilla Parker. 2005. "Mental Health in Post-Communist Countries." *BMJ* 7510:173–174. doi:10.1136/bmj.331.7510.173.

Kitschelt, Herbert. 1986. "Political Opportunity Structures and Political Protest: Anti-Nuclear Movements in Four Democracies." *British Journal of Political Science* 16:57–85.

Knapp, Michael, David McDaid, Elias Mossialos, and Graham Thornicroft, eds. 2007. *Mental Health Policy and Practice across Europe*. Buckingham: Open University Press.

Kriesi, Hanspeter, Ruud Koopmans, Jan W. Duyvendak, and Marco Giugni. 1992. "New Social Movements and Political Opportunities in Western Europe." *European Journal of Political Research* 22:219–244.

McAdam, Dough. 1982. *Political Process and the Development of Black Insurgency, 1930–1970.* Chicago: University of Chicago Press.

McCarthy, John D., and Mayer. N. Zald. 1976. "Resource Mobilization and Social Movements: A Partial Theory." *American Journal of Sociology* 82:1212–1241.

Melucci, Alberto. 1996. *Challenging Codes: Collective Action in the Information Age.* Cambridge: Cambridge University Press.

Meuser, Michael, and Ulrike Nagel. 1989. "Experteninterviews—vielfach erprobt, wenig bedacht: ein Beitrag zur qualitativen Methodendiskussion" [Expert Interviews—Tried on Numerous Occasions, Seldom Heeded: An Article on the Qualitative Method Discussion]. Universität Bremen, (Arbeitspapier/Sfb 186 6). PID:http://nbn-resolving.de/urn:nbn:de:0168-ssoar-57737.

Mitchell, R. David, ed. 2004. *Special Educational Needs and Inclusive Education: Assessment and Teaching Strategies.* New York: Taylor and Francis.

Offe, Claus. 1985. "New Social Movements: Challenging the Boundaries of Institutional Politics." *Social Research* 52:817–868.

Oliver, Pamela E., and Gerald Marwell. 1992. "Mobilizing Technologies for Collective Action." In *Frontiers in Social Movement Theory,* edited by Aldon D. Morris and Carol McClurg Mueller, 251–273. New Haven: Yale University Press.

Pfadenhauer, Michaela. 2009. "Auf gleicher Augenhöhe; Das Experteninterview—ein Gespräch zwischen Experte und Quasi-Experte" [At Eye-Level. The Expert Interview—A Talk between Expert and Quasi-Expert]. In *Experteninterviews, Theorien, Methoden, Anwendungsfelder. (3., grundlegend überarbeitete Auflage)*, edited by Alexander Bogner, Beate Littig, and Wolfgang Menz, 99–116. Wiesbaden: VS Verlag für Sozialwissenschaften.

Pfeiffer, Jan, Georgette Mulheir, Anne-Sophie Parent, Celine Simonin, Luc Zelderloo, Ines Bulić, Carlotta Besozzi, Ask Andersen, Gert Freyhoff, and Josee van Remoortel. 2009. *Report of the Ad Hoc Expert Group on the Transition from Institutional to Community*. European Commission: Directorate-General for Employment, Social Affairs and Equal Opportunities.

Phillips, Sarah D. 2009. "'There Are No Invalids in the USSR!': A Missing Soviet Chapter in the New Disability History." *Disability Studies Quarterly* 29. Accessed November 19, 2013. http://dsq-sds.org/article/view/936/1111.

Pichardo, Nelson A. 1997. "New Social Movements: A Critical Review." *Annual Review of Sociology* 23:411–430.

Pinquart, Mark, and Silvia Sörensen. 2007. "Correlates of Physical Health of Informal Caregivers: A Meta-Analysis." *Journals of Gerontology Series B-Psychological Sciences and Social Sciences* 62:126–137.

Puras, Dainius, Egle Sumskiene, and Ieva Adomaityte-Subaciene. 2013. "Challenges of Prolonged Transition from Totalitarian System to Liberal Democracy." *Journal of Social Policy and Social Work in Transition* 2:31–50. Accessed January 4, 2014. doi:10.1921/6104030204.

Rassell, Michael, and Elena Iarskaia-Smirnova, eds. 2013. *Disability in Eastern Europe and the Former Soviet Union: History, Policy and Everyday Life*. London: Routledge.

Sammon, Elayn. 2001. *Children and Disability in the Context of Family Breakdown in Central and South Eastern Europe and the Former Soviet Union*. UNICEF: Every Child.

Scientific Mental Health Centre (*Научный центр психического здоровья*). 2015. "Глава 2. Умственная отсталость" [Chapter 2. Mental Retardation]. Accessed June 6, 2015. http://www.psychiatry.ru/lib/54/book/36/chapter/2.

Shonkoff, Jack P., Penny Hauser-Cram, Marty W. Krauss, and Carole C. Upshur. 1992. "Development of Infants with Disabilities and Their Families: Implications for Theory and Service Delivery." *Monographs of the Society for Research in Child Development* 57:1–153.

Sloper, Patricia, and Stephen Turner. 1993. "Risk and Resistance Factors in the Adaptation of Parents of Children with Severe Physical Disability." *Journal of Child Psychology and Psychiatry* 34:167–188.

Soskolne, Varda, Sara Halevy-Levin, and Arie Ben-Yehuda. 2007. "The Context of Caregiving, Kinship Tie and Health: A Comparative Study of Caregivers and Non-caregivers." *Women Health* 45:75–94. Accessed February 12, 2014. doi:10.1300/J013v45n02_05.

Sumskiene, Egle. 2014. "Psichikos sveikatos priežiūros deinstitucionalizacija Lietuvoje: minimalūs pokyčiai "maksimalistinėse' organizacijose" [Deinstitutionalization of Mental Health Care in Lithuania: Minimal Reforms in "Maximalist" Organizations]. *STEPP: socialinė teorija, empirija, politika ir praktika* 8:89–99. Vilnius University.

Symeonidou, Simoni. 2007. "Parental Associations and Education Politics Regarding Disability: The Case of Cyprus." *International Journal about Parents in Education* 1:164–173. Accessed January 6, 2017. http://www.ernape.net/ejournal/index.php/IJPE/article/viewFile/39/29.

Tarrow, Sidney. 1994. *Power in Movement: Social Movements, Collective Action and Politics*. Cambridge: Cambridge University Press.

Tchueva, Ekaterina. 2005. "Мир после войны: жалобы как инструмент регулирования отношений между государством и инвалидами Великой отечественной войны" [World after the War: Complaints as an Instrument of Regulating the Relationships between the State and the Disabled in the Great Patriotic War]. In *Советская социальная политика: сцены идействующие лица, 1940–1985*, edited by Elena Iarskaia-Smirnova and Pavel Romanov, 96–120. Moscow: Variant.

Tobis, David. 2000. *Moving from Residential Institutions to Community-Based Social Services in Central and Eastern Europe and the Former Soviet Union*. Washington, DC: World Bank.

UNICEF. 2004. *Innocenti Social Monitor 2004: Economic Growth and Child Poverty in the CEE/CIS and Baltic States*. Florence: UNICEF Innocenti Research Centre.

Van Zomeren, Martijn, Colin W. Leach, Russel Spears, and Agneta H. Fischer. 2004. "Put Your Money Where Your Mouth Is! Explaining Collective Action Tendencies through Group-Based Anger and Efficacy." *Journal of Personality and Social Psychology* 87:649–664.

World Health Organization and European Commission. 1999. *Balancing Mental Health Promotion and Mental Health Care: A Joint World Health Organization and European Commission Meeting*, Brussels, April 22–24, 1999. Typescript. WHO, MNH/NAM/99.2. Accessed December 10, 2013. http://www.psychosocial.com/conferences/brussels.pdf.

Zickel, Raymond E., and Eugene K Keefe. 1991. *Soviet Union: A Country Study*. Washington, DC: Federal Research Division, Library of Congress. Accessed January 18, 2017. https://www.loc.gov/item/90025756/.

Transliterated Text

Biedrība Rīgas pilsētas Rūpju bērns Riga City Society "Child of Care"

Благодійне товариство допомоги інвалідам та особам з інтелектуальною недостатністю «Джерела» ("*Djerela*," Charity Association for People with Intellectual Disabilities)

Научный центр психического здоровья (Scientific Mental Health Center)

Психоневрологические интернаты (psychoneurological internats)

Республиканская ассоциация родителей детей-инвалидов (Republican Association of Parents Who Care for Children with Disabilities)

Умственная отсталость (mental retardation)

10

The Natural Childbirth Movement in the Czech Republic

Ema Hrešanová

Introduction

One of the most visible parental movements in contemporary Czech Republic that attracts a lot of attention of the wider public and media assembles around "natural childbirth." Natural childbirth is a cover term for various approaches to vaginal physiological childbirth that generally oppose the excessive, and sometimes any, use of medication and medical interventions during the birthing process, and warn against their detrimental side effects (Michaels 2014, 8; Gabriel 2011, 6–7). Presented by some activists as an essential part of active, responsible parenthood, it is also a contested term because of its link to the "nature-culture divide" that has been so frequently used in history to subjugate women (Moscucci 2003). While other terms such as "alternative" or "normal childbirth" are used as synonyms and promoted as more appropriate (Donna 2011, 1), in the Czech context, however, the adjective "natural" became the most popular (Lábusová et al. 2002, 12).

There have been similar movements around the globe that have criticized the medical model of childbirth and raised various issues related to the appropriate and sensitive provision of birth care. In different countries these have emerged at different times and raised various issues related to childbirth and birth care. Seen chronologically, the Czech natural childbirth movement (NBM) belongs to those which formed relatively late. In the Czech context childbirth was first discussed publicly in relation to the extremely low fertility rate at the end of the 1990s (Hašková 2001).[1] In comparison, in the United States and Canada, the natural or alternative birth movements had already emerged in the 1950s, becoming widespread during the 1970s and 1980s, when they converged with the feminist and consumer movements that addressed similar issues of control and decision-making vis-a-vis institutions (Daviss 2001, 71; Mathew and Zadak 1991). In North America, childbirth activism was linked predominantly to an effort to revive midwifery (Daviss 2001; see also MacDonald 2007; Bourgeault 2006; Davis-Floyd and Johnson 2006; O'Connor 1993). In Australia, a similar movement formed around the 1960s when women's groups advocated a better consumer choice in birth care, which they framed as an important aspect of "women's citizenship claims" (Reiger 2000, 312; Reiger 2001). Later it became incorporated into the wider women's health movement while converging with the aboriginal health movement, community health movements, and public health movements (Jamieson 2012). In Russia the movement dates back to the early 1980s when it mainly evolved around water birth, which was seen as the most "natural" way of giving birth (Belousova 2002). In Hungary and Poland the movements similarly appeared in the first half of the 1990s. The Hungarian childbirth movement has especially fought for the woman's right to choose the place of birth and for the availability of midwifery services for homebirth, which has been seen as a highly controversial issue. Consequently, Hungarian independent midwives face severe restrictions from the state and medical authorities and experience persecution (Fábián 2013). While this resembles somewhat the situation in the Czech Republic, it differs significantly from Poland, where homebirth and other issues related to the improvement of perinatal care have not been perceived as particularly problematic—unlike other reproductive rights such as abortion, contraception, or sexual education. The Polish childbirth movement seems to be one of the most successful, probably because it gained significant support from the national media during the period of "normalization" of society in the early 1990s, when childbirth "with dignity" was seen as part of such a process (Hryciuk and Korolczuk 2013, 58). In Portugal, the movement was started by a group of doulas in 2005 (Akrich et al. 2012), while in Slovakia similar women's groups formed around 2011 to raise their voices against obstetrical violence.

These examples demonstrate that the natural childbirth movement has become a truly global phenomenon which has, however, always been situated in a particular cultural, social, and historical context. The concept of natural childbirth often becomes the flagship of the key ideas for which these movements fight but the term itself refers to diverse ideas of various historical origins. In current research I track the different trajectories of the ideas linked to the concept of "natural childbirth" and aim at understanding how they were brought into the Czech context, how they were transformed and "domesticated," and by whom they were applied in what sense.[2] In this text I build on that part of this project which deals with the activities of particular collective and individual actors advocating approaches related to natural childbirth in the Czech Republic. In particular, I aim to answer three sets of research questions: (1) in what context/ in response to what particular circumstances did the movement emerge and what/whom did it target? (2) What forces shaped its further course and how did the movement evolve further? (3) What strategies have those who have been involved in the Czech natural childbirth movement employed and with what success? I am especially interested in how birth activists and promoters of natural childbirth have framed their demands for improving birth care and extending birth alternatives in the Czech birth care system. I pay particular attention to the civic rights discourse to which they adhere. In this regard I ask how the emergence and actual trajectory of the movement have been shaped by socialist and postsocialist legacies employed by the state and medical institutions while paying special attention to the gendered dimension of such power relations. I approach these questions from the interpretative perspectives of medical anthropology and the sociology of health and illness, which cause me to view and study Czech natural childbirth as an example of a global health-related social movement (Brown et al. 2004; Brown and Zavestoski 2005; Brown et al. 2011) that demonstrates features typical for the new social movements (Scambler and Kelleher 2006).

This analysis draws attention to the role of science and medicine in the Czech context and to the power dynamics between medical and state authorities and NBM proponents. At the same time I show how deeply gendered the nature of such power relations is. I argue that in the Czech cultural context the traditionally powerful position of doctors and medicine—related to the general scientization of a society in which midwives and women birth care users are not able to become their equal partners—is one of the biggest obstacles to the movement's success.

The first section of the paper introduces a theory on health-related social movements and new social movements. Secondly, I describe my research methods and data. The third part describes the historical and sociopolitical context of changes in maternity care since the birth of an independent Czechoslovak state in 1918. In the next section I characterize the movement and provide an outline of what led to its emergence and how the movement further evolved. Then I explore birth activists' strategies to achieve their goals. In the final section I discuss the dialectic of power relations between the medical authorities and the movement in a wider social context.

Health-Related Social Movements as New Social Movements

In the European context the concept of the "new social movement" (NSM) usually refers to those social movements that arose in the period of high/late modernity or global/disorganized capitalism at the expense of "old" class-based labor social movements (Scambler and Kelleher 2006, 220; Císař et al. 2011). According to Diani (2012, 2) new social movements are closely linked to "social movement organizations" that may display diverse organizational forms, but they often show decentralized participatory structures, protest repertoires, and even explicitly anti-institutional attitudes. New social movements are associated with a new kind of activism which, for instance, Císař et al. (2011, 138) define as "organised collective and public strategies, i.e. demonstrations and petitions, aiming to defend political claims in other ways than in participating in the polls;" originally, new repertoires of collective action, organizational models, and spontaneous participation were highlighted as significant in these new social movements, but with time they became more normalized, formalized, and professionalized. Today they mostly build on small informal nonmember advocacy groups (Císař et al. 2011, 141).

Examining new social movements in the sphere of health, Scambler and Kelleher (2006) refer to an overall "culture of challenge" that these movements generally embrace. Such a collective challenge and resistance to neoliberal regimes, and to a (partial) commodification of health systems and other social processes in healthcare taking place since the last quarter of the twentieth century, have become symptomatic of many health-related social movements.

Brown et al. (2011, 119) conceptualize health social movements as "collective challenges to medical policy and politics, belief systems, research and practice that include an array of formal and informal organizations, supporters, networks of cooperation, and media." At the same time they note that the challenges articulated by health social movements have a form of wide-scale social critique, which especially focuses on medicine, science, and politics (Brown et al. 2011, 5, 125). In relation to childbirth, Moscucci (2003) demonstrated in her historical analysis of the concept that the term "natural childbirth" is an especially apt conceptual tool for articulating such societal critique. It is not a universal value-free concept but has always served as a form of cultural and political critiques of profound societal crises in modern Western societies, caused, for example, by industrialism, capitalism, materialism, mass culture, etc. (ibid., 168).

Brown et al. (2011, 121) distinguish three ideal types of health-related social movements that, in reality, often overlap. Still, this typology provides a useful introduction to the subject. First, the *health access movements* are those that aim to enforce equitable access to health care and to improve it. Second, there are *constituency-based health movements* (CBM) that strive against health inequalities based on gender, ethnicity, race, class, sexuality, religion, belief system, etc. and aim to abolish stigmatizing practices resulting from regulations and scientific work. The third category, *embodied health movements* (EHS), deals with embodied experiences, usually related to illness and disease (Brown et al. 2011, 119–121; 2004, 52–53; Brown and Zavestoski 2005, 2). Brown et al. (2011, 120) identified three distinct features of the EHS: they address the biological body transforming individual (illness) experiences into the collective movement identities. Second, they challenge "existing medical and scientific knowledge and practice" in a more distinctive way than other social movements because they assess how scientific knowledge corresponds to their own intimate knowledge of their bodies and the health issue at hand. Third, EHMs often collaborate with scientists and health professionals to conduct research, get funding, to improve and advance treatment and care (Brown et al. 2011, 120), and to achieve credibility in the eyes of the public. The last point goes along with Akrich et al.'s (2012) argument that childbirth activist organizations prevailingly deal with scientific facts and "evidential work."

The natural childbirth movement (NBM) demonstrates all three features typical for embodied health movements. It makes the embodied experience of giving birth key to parental practices and mother and newborn health and well-being, and it challenges obstetricians' claims to define the childbirth experience solely in medical terms. Its proponents work with allied experts and health professionals to make their claims eligible in negotiations with the state authorities and in disputes with ob-gyns. But the movement also shows features typical for constituency-based health movements because it opposes obstetricians, healthcare facilities, and the state limiting women's rights to make free decisions about their prenatal and birth care. Yet, this categorization does not sufficiently explain what the driving forces behind these social movements are.

In this regard, Scambler and Kelleher argue that the most essential feature of new social movements is "what they do and how they do it" (Scambler and Kelleher 2006, 229), and claim that categorizations of social movements are not able to capture their dynamism and adaptability (ibid., 224). Instead, they propose to focus on various types of "mobilizing potentials" of such movements. Their provisional typology includes five illustrated categories of mobilizing potentials. First, there are movements aiming to achieve rights—cultural and civil. Second, mobilizing potentials realized through *users* typically have origins in "patient dissatisfaction with local or national treatment, options, as well as with medicine's functions as an institution of social control" (Scambler and Kelleher 2006, 226–227). Third, there is campaigning as a mobilizing potential which revolves around "specific interventions in civil society and public sphere." Fourth, identity potentials are linked to segments of society differentiated by gender, ethnicity, age or sexual preference (ibid., 227). In the views of the authors above, movements with these potentials are the closest to the typical definitions of NSMs. Fifth, there is politics as a mobilizing potential which is associated with "resistance to the subsystems of economy and/or state," typically with environmental concerns or also material and psychosocial forms of deprivation (ibid., 228). In this text I will show that the first two mobilizing potentials are especially relevant for the natural childbirth movement in the Czech Republic.

Research Methods and Data

Findings presented here build on a long-term ethnography of the movement, which I have been conducting since spring 2011. During its course, my position gradually changed. As characteristic for the ethnography, from being a "researcher as an outsider" I have become a "participant as observer/ observer as participant," more involved in the movement (Gold 1958, 220–221; O'Reilly 2005, 106–109). This includes several research methods. First, I conducted numerous participant observations of key public events associated with the natural childbirth movement, such as the World Week of Respect for Childbirth Festival, a public workshop on homebirth organized by the Parliamentary Board for Healthcare (March 29, 2012), midwifery conferences, and lectures and workshops organized by mothers' groups and individual birth activists on the topic. I also employed knowledge learned during informal meetings with birth activists, especially those held by the Czech Women's Lobby.

Second, from March 2012 to November 2013 I interviewed five key figures of the movement, including independent midwives and a representative of a midwifery association, whom I got to know through my ethnographic involvement in the movement. Next, I conducted nineteen narrative interviews with women who gave birth naturally. I first contacted women from a wide circle of my friends and relatives who stated that they had had a natural childbirth, or desired it, and who had given birth to their last child preferably no more than two years before the interview, as I wanted to ensure that they remembered their birth experience adequately. Other researchers (e.g., Bryant et al. 2007) apply a similar restriction of two years to ensure that women recalled adequate and accurate details about their birth experience. I applied a snowball technique to find other participants. In doing so, I tried to reach the widest diversity of women in terms of their education and socioeconomic status, age, potential birth experience, and geographical location of their residence. I talked to women from major cities as well as those living in villages in different regions of the Czech Republic. Their ages ranged from 26 to 38. Most of them were university educated; four had only secondary education.

Third, I triangulated findings drawn from the interviews and ethnographic observations with the qualitative media analysis of 77 contributions published in printed nationwide newspapers, magazines, and TV and Radio broadcasting (excluding internet sources) from January 1, 1996 to June 27, 2011, thus covering the period before the movement started to form until the present.

Fourth, I conducted a "netnography" of Czech childbirth activism, which combined the "conduct of computer-mediated ethnography with other forms of cultural research" (Kozinets 2010, 17). It seems particularly apt for studying childbirth activism, which increasingly takes part online. Dudová (2012, 132), referring to Clark and Themudo (2006), even argues that "natural childbirth" activism exemplifies "cyberactivism" while creating a virtual public space on the internet. According to Dudová it creates a typical "dotcause," that is, "political network(s), which mobilize(s) support for social causes primarily (but not necessarily exclusively) through the Internet" (Clark and Themudo 2006, 52). Fábián (2013, 77) observes similar patterns of e-mobilizations among the Hungarian home birth activists, showing that such techniques are common to childbirth activists in other parts of the region. I particularly analyzed internet sources related to natural childbirth, such as the web pages of key organizations and activists promoting natural childbirth, online forums, and open discussions, blogs, and commentaries.

The Historical and Sociopolitical Context

The independent Czechoslovak state was formed in 1918 out of northern, mostly Slav speaking territories of the quickly disintegrating Austro-Hungarian Empire. In that time babies were mostly born at home with the help of midwives. Only around 22 percent of women gave birth in maternity clinics, as only those with serious health complications were by law eligible to such care (Štembera 2004, 25). In this period obstetrics was still a surgical subdiscipline and most hospitals lacked separate obstetrical-gynecological wards; there were only sixteen ob-gyn units in the whole country, and eight out of this number were located in Prague (ibid.).

Obstetricians and gynecologists managed to found their professional association independent from surgeons as late as in 1936. In comparison, midwives established their Central Union of Midwives already in 1919 (Vránová 2007, 81). In university clinics obstetricians practiced the "active medical management of childbirth," which involved the administration of analgesics (Pařízek 2002, 29–34). The obstetrical practice, however, substantially varied across maternity clinics (Štembera 2004, 25); some hospitals performed only a few Caesarean sections per year, while in others the rate escalated up to 3 percent (ibid., 27).

The main changes in the whole healthcare system came after the Second World War. The newborn and maternal mortality rates were very high at that time, and a source of concern to women's activists. In spring 1946 in response to a parliamentary interpellation moved by the female members of the Czechoslovak National Socialist Party, the minister of health passed a resolution to establish ob-gyn and newborn units in all of 130 public hospitals that existed in Czechoslovakia. The socialist female politicians lobbied for the hospitalization of childbirths because they believed that it could prevent unnecessary deaths caused by preterm births and mothers' poor knowledge of how to care for an infant (Uhrová 2005, 94–95).

The Communist Party took over in 1948 and pushed through revolutionary reforms of the healthcare system shortly afterwards (Mášová 2005). The healthcare system was rebuilt into a centrally directed enterprise, fully controlled and funded by the state. Healthcare became free to all citizens at the point of provision and was provided to patients in outpatients' districts and regional health facilities only in a district of their residency (Heitlinger 1987, 75). The government also established a national site of district and regional health facilities, which included a site of prenatal clinics (Štembera 2004, 44). These were run by gynecologists who performed surveillance and monitored their pregnant "patients" for potential health-related, as well as social risks (ibid., 45). Biomedicine surrounding pregnancy and childbirth constituted a crucial institution of social control in the socialist state, which operated on various levels—in the sphere of scientific discourse and policy-making as well as in situ during gynecological consultations and care provision (see also Heitlinger 1987; Hrešanová 2014, 963–965).

From the 1950s gynecologists and obstetricians became the main experts in the realm of childbirth (Štembera 2004, 44–45), while an independent profession of midwifery was gradually transformed into "obstetrical nursing" subordinate to doctors in the healthcare system hierarchy. Obstetrics and gynecology in Czechoslovakia were male-dominated and masculinized disciplines (Hrešanová 2008), unlike in other countries of the Eastern bloc, for example, in Russia (Belousova 2002; Rivkin-Fish 2005, 70–76) or in Poland (Mishtal 2010). Currently, there are 45.7 percent women working in the field of obstetrics and gynecology (ÚZIS 2013b, 181).[3]

The medicalization of childbirth increased steeply after the Second World War with the move to hospitals. By the mid-1950s almost all childbirths (92.6%) took place in hospitals (Štembera 2004, 67). This trend gave rise to perinatology, a new science studying pregnancy, childbirths, and newborn health. Perinatology played a key role in the state's biopolitics and policy-making.[4] Its main successes included a substantial decline in the perinatal mortality rate, which contributed to good reputation of the Czechoslovakian state internationally (ibid., 77). But there were also many side-effects, such as the separation of newborns from their mothers (Šráčková 2007, 26) and a considerable depersonalization and unfriendliness of hospital birth care. Since the very 1950s the leading journal, *Czechoslovak Gynecology*, has periodically called attention to these aspects but without a noticeable success (Hrešanová 2014, 964–965).

In the early 1980s, criticism of the depersonalized, dehumanized, and technocratic nature of the socialist maternity and birth care grew stronger, and as a result several "niches" of birth care alternatives emerged in the birth care system. Some hospitals adopted changes in their institutional arrangements of care and relaxed their strict aseptic rules. A few of them also introduced the rooming-in arrangement in which newborn babies could stay with their mothers in the same room constantly instead of being carried away and cared for in a separate room. Similarly, some hospitals allowed fathers to accompany their birthing wives into delivery rooms (Heitlinger 1987; Petrák 1983; Mlynářová and Tošner 1995). Among those, the maternity ward in Ostrov nad Ohří, a small town in Western Bohemia, particularly became famous nationally for turning childbirth into a gentle family event.[5] And there were also a number of individual healthcare providers, especially obstetrical nurses and psychologists, who were strongly dissatisfied with the prevailing way how birthing women were treated in hospitals, and they decided to take action to change it.[6]

The 1989 Velvet Revolution brought the end of the communist regime and initiated a societal change, which was fueled by fundamental reforms. Market-driven principles were introduced into a number of sectors, including healthcare. Primary outpatient care, including gynecological care, became privatized while at the same time allowing users to choose their provider according to their will. Health care reforms further involved a shift in health insurance administration from the state to nine newly established health insurance funds that cover most of the provided care (Kinkorová and Topolčan 2012, 5). Health insurance remained compulsory and healthcare stayed free of charge until 2008, when the right-wing government introduced user fees for doctor visits, hospital stays, and prescription pharmaceuticals, as well as out-of-pocket payments into the system (ibid., 3). With a new left-wing government, fees for hospital stays were canceled and some groups of users were exempt from this duty.

In May 2004, the Czech Republic became a member of the European Union. Bringing legislation in line with Europe, Act 96/2004 Coll. set conditions for the practice of nonmedical professions (including midwives) and guaranteed midwives professional rights in the field of physiological pregnancies and childbirths. Nevertheless, in practice this right has been frequently violated, and gynecologists and obstetricians remain the prevalent providers of prenatal and birth care.

Most women, around 108 thousand per year, give birth in one of almost one hundred maternity hospitals in the country.[7] The official statistics indicating high rates of medical interventions such as episiotomy and medication (including analgesics and anesthetics) in the labor process and delivery (ÚZIS 2013a) implies that prenatal and birth care in the Czech Republic is generally highly medicalized. Moreover, the number of childbirths managed by physicians has been continuously increasing at the expense of those attended by midwives (ÚZIS 2013a, 19). Most pregnancies are subjected to close medical scrutiny, and women who refuse to comply often face moral condemnation and criticism from the side of healthcare providers (Hasmanová Marhánková 2008; Hrešanová 2010).

Such an authoritative role of medicine reflects the high social standing of physicians in Czech society. In public opinion surveys, physicians have been repeatedly marked as the most prestigious occupation, and their prestige is still increasing, while leaving scientists as the second and nurses as the third most prestigious occupations (Tuček 2013). Studies focusing on other aspects of professions also prove that physicians enjoy a high symbolic capital in Czech society. For instance, Šafr and Häuberer (2008) investigated the interactional subjective social distance to various occupational groups while building on a representative survey of the Czech population. They found that physicians enjoyed the lowest social distance from all the listed occupational categories. Moreover, a recent survey mapping citizens' opinions on healthcare indicates that patient-doctor relations are perceived as one of the least problematic spheres of the Czech healthcare system; 68 percent of respondents saw no, or only small, issues in this field (Nováková 2013, 4).

The Birth Activists: Who Are They?

The Czech natural childbirth movement includes diverse groups of individuals and organizations that intertwine in various ways, as is typical for such movements (see Daviss 2001), while generally sharing a common goal to resist the extensive medicalization of childbirth and to include more birth care alternatives into the birth care system. So far my analysis shows that it is possible to characterize such groups along two lines: first, looking at what these groups strive for and, second, how they relate to birth care (whether they are its providers or users).

Seen from the first angle, the vast majority of activists in the movement are women (and several men) supporting the idea of natural childbirth who oppose the overmedicalization of birthcare. But there is also a relatively small group of rather radical activists who try to promote homebirth as a legitimate birth alternative and strive to incorporate it into the birthcare system. The homebirth promoters include individual women—potential users of homebirth care, several independent midwives, and also individual experts from various fields, for example, psychology or law.

The second line of my analysis shows that there are two streams in the movement: one part is midwife-dominated, while the other mainly involves various prenatal and birth care user groups. The midwife-dominated section mainly strives to finish the professionalizing process of midwifery in order to establish an independent and respected midwifery profession. It is mainly led by independent midwives who have formed an important part of the movement since the beginning. Some of them already started running their own private practice in the first half of the 1990s. Some of these midwives are united in the Union of Midwives (UNIPA), which was founded in 2005 with Ivana Königsmarková as the head. It is one of three Czech midwifery professional associations. These midwives are supported by groups of women seeking nonmedicalized care in accordance with the midwifery or "social" model of birth, which typically emphasizes an active role of a birthing woman during labor and delivery. This model of birth care also highlights a physiological normalcy of most childbirths, the importance of informed choice about prenatal and birth care, and a midwife capacity to appropriately support and empower a birthing woman in various birth settings (including hospital environments) (Van Teijlingen 2005; Rooks 1999; Howell-White 1999; Hrešanová 2008, 129). Such alliances between midwives and their consumers are common in childbirth movements. For instance, Craven (2010) and Kline (2010) demonstrate how similar alliances emerged in the US context.

Besides the midwifery wing, there are very diverse groups and individuals supporting normal/natural childbirth. Many of them are past birth care users who were greatly dissatisfied with the hospital birth care they received. Some of such groups are very informal, sometimes based solely on online manifestos (e.g., *Ijinak*) or formed via virtual networks (especially chat rooms like Baby-café or E-mimino, which are the most popular) and the internet. Others are formally organized into non-governmental organizations (NGOs) working in the area of parenthood, addressing parents' needs, and trying to promote parental rights—such as the Aperio, The Society for Healthy Parenthood, or HAM (Movement for Active Motherhood)—which are the most influential. Or they focus more on women's rights and related issues, such as NESEHNUTI (*Nezávislé sociálně ekologické hnutí*, Independent Social Ecological Movement), whose agenda includes environmental-feminist issues. There are also NGOs dealing generally with civil rights issues; for instance, the League for Human Rights (*Liga lidských práv*) focuses on women's rights violations in birth care and parental rights.

This wide range of women's groups focusing on childbirth issues seems to constitute the only women's movement in the country that is truly grassroots. Dudová (2012) shares this view and states that these groups are the only really activist women's networks in the country "being able to mobilize the civil society (of women)" from below (Dudová 2012, 130). Highlighting their grassroots character, she contrasts them with highly formalized women's and feminist organizations employing professionals with gender expertise, such as the NGO Gender Studies, o.p.s., which were often initially founded, funded, and supported by international women's organizations; these NGOs mostly pursue topics like work-life balance, gender equity, or women's rights in the labor market.

While NGOs like Aperio, HAM, and UNIPA are indisputably the core engine of the natural childbirth movement, I argue that individual actors loosely associated with the movement play a crucial role. My ethnographic research points to a number of such key individuals who have influenced the course of the movement while not being particularly affiliated with any maternity organizations; for instance, Adéla Hořejší, Ivana Königsmarková's attorney; Michaela Mrowetz, a psychologist promoting mother-baby bonding in Czech maternity hospitals; or Markéta Pavlíková, a biostatistician whose expert reports have played a crucial role in negotiating with governmental representatives and in court.

But, individual "ordinary" women who sympathize with the idea of natural childbirth and the movement's goals often break the line between the "mobilized clients" and activists. As I learned from the narrative interviews with nineteen women who gave birth naturally, many of them became activists with their new birth experience.[8] However, the extent to which they are able and willing to take an active part in the movement differs (compare with Reiger 2000, 315). Some of my interviewees decided to give talks, organize public lectures, and write articles about the issue, or they started a new activist group to contribute to changes in the Czech birth care system. Other women limited their activities to cyberspace or to spreading news and advice in circles of their friends, which they also perceived as part of being an activist in the field. Some of them plan to become more active in the future when their children get older.

Looking at its gendered dimension, the movement is prevailingly a women's business. The majority of the individuals and groups, as well as employees of the NGOs involved in the movement, are women. This is consistent with observations by True (2003, 131–147), who observed that the post-1989 civil sphere in the Czech Republic became prevalently occupied by women aspiring to build a democracy from below in opposition to the highly masculinized formal politics. Czech women joined "transnational networks of non-governmental organizations (NGOs) and discourses of democracy and human rights, which have been more open to women's concerns, thus becoming a part of an emerging 'global civil society'" (True 2003, 132). Similarly, Phillips (2008) describes the post-socialist NGO sector in Ukraine as a "women's sphere." This gendered aspect, however, seems to fundamentally affect the movement's chances to succeed.

The Emergence and Trajectory of the Movement

The beginnings of childbirth activism in the Czech Republic date back to the late 1990s. But—as I outlined above—efforts to "humanize" Czech birth care are much older and go back to the beginnings of the 1980s when they were restricted by the political regime. Midwives belonged to most active promoters of change before, as well as after the fall of the communist regime.

The first informal professional networks of midwives formed in the early 1990s. Midwife Zuzana Štromerová was among the key figures who organized bus trips to Western European countries, where Czech midwives could meet their colleagues and learn from them. In 1997 a group of midwives in the front with Štromerová founded the independent professional organization called the Czech Association of Midwives (ČAPA) to advocate and promote their professional interests. A year later the Centre for Active Childbirth (CAP), run by midwives who promoted a philosophy of "natural childbirth," was opened as an independent unit of the gynecological-obstetrical clinic Bulovka in Prague. Even though the center became very popular among birthing women who knew about it from the media, it was closed down in 2000 due to disputes about operating conditions between the maternity hospital

Fig. 10.1 The demonstration "Do Not Allow Doctors to Take Over Your Childbirth: Do You Know What Is Going On Behind the Doors of The Delivery Room?" Organized by HAM on the occasion of the International Midwives's Day on May 5, 1999, at the Wenceslas Square in Prague, a traditional setting for demonstrations. Courtesy of Marie Vnoučková's archive. Photo by Ludvík Hradílek. Printed with permission of the photographer.

management (PD Čáp 2013). The midwives left but were frequently sought after by women who desired to give birth in the same way as offered at the CAP (Vnoučková 2013). Simultaneously, Štromerová founded an independent birth center *Porodní dům u Čápa* in Prague which, however, has never been successful in receiving a license to provide birth care. Since 1998 ČAPA has also organized several international conferences on natural childbirth to promote the idea further. Among those, the international conference "We Bring Babies into the World," held in February 2001 in Prague, was among the biggest and most influential; it was attended by 640 participants from twenty-six countries, including representatives of the WHO, EU, and the Czech Ministry of Health. It awakened a lot of interest among healthcare professionals, the public, and the media (Ryntová and Wallerová 2002).

In 1999 the two most important NGOs—HAM and Aperio—were founded. HAM was set up by a group of women dissatisfied with the birth care which they had received in Czech maternity hospitals. And they aimed to change it for the better. Inspired by similar organizations abroad, and by a manifest written by British childbirth educator and activist Janet Balaskas, they originally named their organization *The Movement for Active Childbirth* (HAM).[9] Intending to create "a platform to initiate changes in the Czech birth care system—to promote normal childbirth and mother-and-newborn-friendly birth care provided in compliance with the latest scientific evidence" (HAM 2012)—they became one of the key advocates of birthing women's rights in the country. HAM covered various groups of women with a range of activities and interests including doulas, nonmedical assistants accompanying birthing women throughout childbirth. In September 2001 they founded their own organization, the Czech Association of Doulas.

Half a year later, in September 1999, the Open Society Fund program Healthy Parenthood started "to support natural childbirth and related health care reforms in the Czech birth care system and in this way help to create an option of free and informed choice" (Aperio 2001). Its agenda gradually expanded into other domains related to parenthood. In April 2001 Lucie Ryntová, Eva Labusová, and Alena Frydrychová, who were involved in the program, decided to transform it into an independent NGO that adopted the name *Aperio*, Society for Healthy Parenthood. Its objectives were to enlarge the range of available birth alternatives in the Czech birth care system and to frame childbirth as a matter of concern to civil society, to educate health care providers on the issues related to birth care, to emphasize and promote citizens' rights to have information on their health, and change traditional gender roles in families, among other objectives. To meet these goals it carried out a wide scope of activities (Aperio 2001, 3–4). Among others, it started to run an information center and library, initiated research on birth care (together with sociologist Hašková), collaborated with the media, and published translated works of key international promoters of natural childbirth (Aperio 2001). But one of the most important and influential acts was the publication of *The Guide to Maternity Hospitals in the Czech Republic* (Lábusová and Frydrychová 2002), which was inspired by similar works released in Poland and Great Britain (Aperio 2001; for details see Hryciuk and Korolczuk 2013, 55–60). The book includes details of the birth care services provided in particular maternity hospitals in the country, building on questionnaires that were filled in by maternity hospital authorities. The online version accessible on Aperio's website also includes a section for women's comments and is regularly updated. It has become a crucial source of information for birthing women on where to give birth. I witnessed during my ethnographic research in two maternity hospitals (Hrešanová 2008) that healthcare providers frequently visited the online guide to find out how satisfied women were with their care.

Since 2006 various groups of birth activists, including midwives, parental organizations, and women's groups, have organized a series of collective actions to promote the idea of childbirth, and they have lobbied for a change in the birth care system. These have included cultural events (e.g., the multimedia art exhibition "The Art to Give Birth"), educational campaigns and festivals, among which the annually held World Week of Respect for Childbirth festival—brought to Prague from France—is one of the most influential; or activist events (e.g., a hike to the highest mountain in the Czech Republic, Sněžka). But they have also held several demonstrations to implement changes in the Czech birth care system. On October 21, 2008, Lucie Ryntová from Aperio explained to a *Catholic Weekly* correspondent that they usually organized such demonstrations in response to the refusal of the Ministry of Health to respond to their pleas and proposals for changes and to initiate negotiations with them.[10]

One of the biggest protest meetings took place in front of the building of the Ministry of Health in October 2008. It was organized by five key parental organizations promoting changes in the Czech birth care system. These organizations are involved in the Czech Women's Lobby (ČZL) platform, which has a special group dealing with birth care. The network of mothers' centers joined them (HAM, UNIPA, IMBCI 2008). The demonstration aimed to hand over a petition calling "for improving Czech birth care and for mother-and-baby-friendly and safe care," which pointed to a growing dissatisfaction among birthing women and their partners.[11] Around 3,000 people signed it, including prominent representatives from cultural and political life (e.g., Czech filmmaker Olga Sommerová and Zuzana Roithová, a member of the European Parliament).[12] However, the event was altogether ignored by political representatives.

In fall 2011, two special events aroused a new series of petitions, proclamations, open letters to key policy makers, protest happenings, campaigns, and demonstrations. First, it was a new legislation severely restricting health-care services for home birth, namely, the Act No. 372/2011 Coll. on health care services and conditions for their provision and its executive ordinance No. 92/2012 Coll., on the requirements for minimal technical and material equipment of health facilities and of contact workplaces for homecare. This legislation set high sanctions for those providing birth care at home without

Fig. 10.2 A demonstration for the accessibility midwifery care, a free choice of the place of childbirth, and against the trials with independent midwives; organized by activist groups with the ČZL's official support. Held on October 17, 2011, in front of the Ministry of Health in Prague. Courtesy of *IJINAK*. Photo by Jakub Mrákota. Printed with permission of the photographer.

a valid registration, while the Ministry of Health and regional authorities ceased to provide midwives with valid registrations covering such services. Second, there was the trial of leading independent midwife Ivana Königsmarková, who was sentenced to two years' imprisonment with a conditional deferral of five years, for causing damage to health and subsequent death to a newborn by her negligence during home birth; she was also mandated to pay compensation of 2.7 million Czech crowns to the health insurance company for subsequent treatment of the baby. In response to the ruling against Ivana Königsmarková new groups of women began to form to organize activities to support her, such as the initiative "The Public for Natural Childbirth" or "We Demand the Care of an Independent Midwife," who called for the Czech state to quickly harmonize the national legislation with European directive 80/155/EU. These women distributed a petition that 5,000 people signed. Inspired by the Hungarian website http://tortenetek.szules.hu/ and struck by the resemblance between Czech midwife Ivana Königsmarková and a similar trial with Hungarian midwife Ágnes Geréb, these activist groups began to release daily

Fig. 10.3 A demonstration for the accessibility of midwifery care, a free choice of the place of childbirth, and against the trials with independent midwives; organized by activist groups with the ČZL's official support. Held on October 17, 2011, in front of the Ministry of Health in Prague. Courtesy of *IJINAK*. Photo by Jakub Mrákota. Printed with permission of the photographer.

"Stories for Ivana." Since Christmas Eve 2011 a story related to Ivana's work has been published daily on a special website http://www.pribehyproivanu.cz/.

The lobbying activities of birth activists resulted in their first achievements in spring 2012 when the Minister of Health, Leoš Heger, appointed a working group of experts to discuss ways to ensure the basic rights of pregnant and birthing women in a better way. The minister—a member of the right-wing government—was obliged to find new and more cost-effective solutions for birth care, and midwives seemed to offer such low-cost care while referring to international scientific journals. However, the minister's efforts to implement such changes were spoiled by the Czech Obstetrical and Gynecological Society's representatives, who boycotted the negotiations. Refusing to participate in the working group's meetings, they proclaimed, "There is no reason to change a well-functioning system of care for pregnant and birthing women and newborns that is of world-class quality" (Vláda České republiky 2012). In this regard the obstetricians referred specifically to perinatal and early newborn mortality rates, which are among the lowest in the world, and they argue that these numbers are the result of high quality health care in the Czech Republic.[13] The minister dissolved the group in March 2013 because it was not possible to reach a consensus within the group—"especially because of the medical representatives' attitudes" (Vláda České republiky 2013, 10–11). Immediately afterwards he appointed a new one into which he nominated those medical representatives who refused to participate in the previous working group and did not include any representatives of midwives or birth care receivers (Plívová 2013).

Strategies

Birth activists have adopted a number of strategies to achieve their goals, as is partially evident from the movement's trajectory. They launched educational campaigns and published relevant literature on the issue, including translations of publications iconic for international natural childbirth activism. They organized cultural events and exhibitions that made their efforts visible in the media, while they were also able to establish close cooperation with a number of journalists. Several organizations (e.g., LLP) and individual birth activists were also actively involved in preparing legal strategies to fight controversial regulations, and they defended parents and midwives in court when their rights were violated. For instance, Adéla Hořejší defended in the European Court for Human Rights two Czech women, Dubská and Krejzová, whose rights to make free decisions about their childbirths were allegedly violated.[14] Hořejší, together with other birth activists, hopes that the Court will support women's rights in childbirth and rule in the same way as in the case of Ternovszky versus Hungary in December 2010.[15]

Besides legal actions, Czech birth activists were able to organize a number of collective events, including public demonstrations and petitions and, according to Fábián (2013, 78), in this regard the Czech natural childbirth movement would belong to those "more radical" childbirth movements in the region of Central and Eastern Europe. These activities also reveal features typical for new public activism and the "new social movements." Concerning this, Císař et al. (2011, 160) argue that most public collective events held in the Czech Republic today are organized by "new activist" organizations. However, they further point out that these organizations do not primarily focus on public collective protests, but on political consultancy and lobbying instead. Czech birth activism seems to differ from other "new" activist groups in the country in this regard. Císař et al. (2011, 156–157), with reference to Petrova and Tarrow (2007), further note that new activist organizations demonstrate a high "transaction capacity," that is to say a capacity to establish connections with other activist groups. Czech childbirth activist groups demonstrate a high transaction capacity, which is performed and demonstrated through their joint activities in the Czech Women's Lobby.

Birth activists have been lobbying among local, as well as parliamentary, politicians and, as a result, several political parties addressed the issue of home birth and changes in birth care in their agendas before the autumn elections in 2013.[16] A representative of one of the midwifery associations also told me that several political parties expressed interest in promoting changes in the birth care system and close cooperation with midwives (in-depth interview with V., February 2014). However, the most direct political involvement consisted of the participation of birth activist representatives in the expert working group established by the Minister of Health Heger. The birth activists who were members of the group heavily built on "evidential work" and presented scientific reports and facts to make their claims legitimate. Akrich et al. (2012) showed that such evidential work constituted an essential feature of childbirth activism in four organizations situated in different European countries, but as already indicated it proved to be inefficient in the Czech Republic.

Power Dialectic

Brown et al. (2011, 123) point out that "social movements are fundamentally about challenging power," while "in our modern scientized world, science and medicine have become increasingly dominant political and socioeconomic systems" (Brown and Zavestoski 2005, 2). This view is in tune with the Habermasian argument about the colonization of lifeworld by the system (i.e., economy and the state), when it is possible that the "voice of medicine" expands into the "voice of the lifeworld" (Scambler and Kelleher 2006,224). (Health) social movements, including the natural childbirth movement in the Czech Republic, increasingly oppose such a "scientization of decision-making," because people are increasingly aware of medical and scientific errors and technological failures (Hasmanová Marhánková 2014).

Brown and Zavestoski (2005, 7) note an effort to "democratize" biomedicine and see it as part of wider societal processes. In this regard Rose (2001, 19) points to emerging claims on "new rights" that are based on the simple fact of a living existence and ethopolitics in terms of an "ethos of human existence" (ibid. 18, 19); that is the politics of the life itself, in which "even choosing not to intervene in living processes becomes a kind of intervention" (Rose 2001, 19). Similarly, Plummer (2003, 6) observes that the sphere of "intimate troubles and choices," including those around infertility and giving birth, constitutes claims to new rights. These are the rights for which the Czech natural childbirth movement has been striving.

The analysis of the results of the birth activists' efforts demonstrates that for most of the time the authorities have either ignored activists' attempts to initiate a dialogue or their responses have been prevailingly hostile. For instance, in the hearing held by the Parliamentary Board for Health Affairs in March 2012, its members refuted most birth activists' arguments as unfounded and misleading. The attending obstetricians asserted that there was no wide demand for home birth services, and only a small group of extremists created a fuss and the impression that there was a need to change the Czech birth care system. For instance, Antonín Pařízek (2012), the CGPS leading obstetrician, said that obstetricians are "often attacked by a loud minority" while adding that "some midwives have hypotrophic cravings for authority." He explained, "What the problem is, and it will certainly become evident here at this symposium, is that ideology is on one hand and expertise on the other" (Pařízek 2012, verbatim transcript). The hearing reflected yet another aspect of the dispute; as most contributors fighting against home birth as a legal alternative were male physicians, the vast majority of the birth activists lobbying for this option were women. Consequently, the discourse used by the opponents of natural childbirth was heavily gendered, and the claims of the activists were dismissed as both non-scientific and grounded in strong emotions rather than rational views, which is supposedly typical to women.

Some healthcare providers also initiated counter-events. For instance, a group of healthcare rescuers initiated their own petitions in which they demanded to ban planned home births immediately; it was signed by 162 people (Poslanecká sněmovna 2013) and provoked a lot of controversy. In response, Czech childbirth activists sought to claim their civic rights related to parenthood, arguing that the current state excluding homebirth from legally available alternatives deviates from situations common in "normal civilized societies" (Viola, Normal birth e-forum, January 2013). Some birth activists interpreted the rescuers' petition as clear evidence of their paternalistic approach and a sign of a lack of democratic thinking in the Czech medical environment. For instance, Tina mentioned that obstetricians sometimes "behave like the communist totalitarian regime; that is to say that another opinion means a wrong opinion" (Tina, Normal birth e-forum, December 2012). Similar complaints about birth care providers who treat women the same as in "old socialist times" appeared in the birth narratives of other women I interviewed during my previous research (Hrešanová 2011; Hrešanová 2014; compare Benoit and Heitlinger 1998; Heitlinger 1987, 130–133). The socialist legacy becomes a moral category and forty years of communism is portrayed monolithically without regard to a number of actual shifts.

Conclusion

In this text I have described the trajectory of the natural childbirth movement as a case of parental movements emerging in the postsocialist Czech Republic. Its grassroots character seems to be unique among women's movements in the Czech context, but it is also remarkable that many birth activist organizations have started to cooperate to make their strategies more effective. In this regard, the Czech natural childbirth movement constitutes a typical example of the health social movements characterized by "the transformations of sporadic and relatively unorganized challenges into formal and institutionalized opposition" (Brown and Zavestoski 2005, 2).

The Czech natural childbirth movement is driven by two key categories of mobilizing potentials: (1) rights-based and (2) user-based. The first aims to recognize women's rights to make free decisions on where and with whom to give birth. In this respect a group of birth activists are striving to make home birth a legitimate choice. Along with women's greater autonomy in birth care, birth activists fight for the recognition of midwives' professional rights. Their claims to all these rights are framed by the civic right discourse. The second mobilizing potential manifests itself in a low satisfaction with healthcare services. Many women involved in the movement have had an unsatisfactory or even traumatic childbirth experience that drives them to improve and "humanize" the birth care system. But many birth activists raise bigger societal issues, apparently linked to broader social trends, such as the scientization of everyday life, or ethopolitics permeating even the most intimate matters of daily living. While this is common for many health social movements, historically, the concept of natural childbirth has served as an especially powerful tool to articulate such criticism.

Czech birth activists have so far had only partial success and many of their demands remain unmet. They face severe opposition from the state and medical authorities, who exercise a paternalistic attitude. These power relations have an important gendered aspect. Many birth activists read such paternalism as a postsocialist legacy in treating women, while that which is "socialist" marks all that is wrong and undesirable. Such paternalism significantly marks the state's position to women and women's topics such as childbirth and maternity. This can be an attribute of the prevalently masculinized character of the formal political power structures in the Czech Republic and the gender regime (see True 2003 above). Similarly, biomedical authorities exercise their "totalitarian" stance, not only on birthing women, but on midwives who become their competitors.

In this text I have argued that in the Czech cultural context the biggest obstacle preventing the movement from achieving its goals is the very powerful position of physicians and biomedicine. At the same time, birth activists (both midwives and birth care users) have relatively weak social and economic positions, and thus their attempts to negotiate with medical and state authorities as equal partners have mostly failed. The weak position of midwifes includes two dimensions. First, in the area of birth care provision, the rights of midwifes are frequently violated because the state authorities refuse to license them. Second, in academia, midwifes have struggled to establish an independent scientific discipline with a separate scope of research. Women as mothers or as midwifes are not considered equal partners to negotiate with the state and medical authorities; obstetricians especially oppose women's arguments as "non-experts." In the Czech social and cultural context, the elite status of science seems to be taken as more relevant and legitimate than the demand for better consumer choice. This substantially differs from, for instance, neighboring Poland, where neoliberal discourse supporting a better consumer choice in birth care successfully legitimized activists' demands (Hryciuk and Korolczuk 2013).

My analysis of the natural childbirth movement in the Czech Republic indicates that in Czech society the position of medicine, as well as scientific rationality, has not been significantly challenged. On the contrary, in tone with Scambler and Kelleher's observation (2006), I would argue that, at least in the Czech context, the colonization of the lifeworld by the expert systems prevails, and those health-related movements such as the antivaccination movement (Hasmanová Marhánková 2014) or the natural childbirth movement are (for the time being) only little "islands of resistance" against more powerful structures.

Ema Hrešanová, Assistant Professor, Department of Sociology, Faculty of Social Sciences, Charles University in Prague, Czech Republic

Ema Hrešanová is a Czech medical anthropologist and sociologist with long-term research interests in gender and health, especially women's reproductive health and childbirth. Her book, *Cultures of Two Maternity Hospitals* (2008), based on three years of ethnographic research in two maternity wards, provides insights into a changing nature of the postsocialist birth care system in the Czech Republic. In her current research project she investigates childbirth activism and other efforts to establish alternative possibilities within the Czech birth care system and the society at large. She was awarded a number of prestigious fellowships and grants (Go8 European Fellowship, Monash University, Australia; Czech Science Foundation grant for postdoctoral researchers; the Fulbright Fellowship, UNC, Chapel Hill, U.S.). She co-edited special issues on healthcare and medical anthropology in postsocialist Central and Eastern Europe of the *Anthropology of East Europe Review* (2011) and the *CARGO—Journal for Cultural and Social Anthropology* (2013). From 2013 to 2015 she served as a chair of the Sociology of Health and Illness Research Network (RN16) of the European Sociological Association.

Notes

1. In the first years of the postsocialist period the fertility rate generally declined. In 1994 population growth in the Czech Republic became negative for the first time since 1918 (Kinkorová and Topolčan 2012, 1), and it fell even lower in the late 1990s. From 2006 population growth became positive again, reaching a peak in 2008 (119,842 newborns) but since then the numbers have fallen again.

2. This research project (no. P404/11/P089), "Natural childbirth movement and feminist approaches to childbirth: systems of social action and thought," received funding from the Czech Science Foundation, to which I thank for support. My acknowledgements further go to Monash University, Australia, and the Group of Eight for awarding me the Go8 European fellowship, which allowed me to complete final revisions. Last but not least, I thank all participants of this research for their time and help.

3. This might change in the near future due to a rapid increase in the number of women among the youngest generation of ob-gyns. Still, many of them face strong gender stereotypes, according to which only men are physically and mentally fit to do obstetrics well (Hrešanová 2008, 150–152).

4. Michel Foucault defined biopolitics as an endeavor "to rationalize the problems presented to governmental practice by the phenomena characteristic of a group of living human beings constituted as a population" (Foucault 1997, 73).

5. Birth practices in this hospital followed recommendations of French obstetrician Frederick Leboyer. In his book, *Birth without violence* (1975),which earned him a worldwide fame, Leboyer argued for gentle birthing techniques that would make a baby's transition from a womb into the outside world less stressful and painful. In line with this claim newborns were immersed into a small tub of warm water right after being born and protected from sharp light and noise. It was mainly thanks to activities and enthusiasm of Dr Hana Marková, a neonatologist who led the Ostrov's maternity ward team that these ideas were implemented in practice. She was originally a medical scientist but for political reasons she was forced to leave her job at a prestigious clinic and transferred to a peripheral hospital in Ostrov nad Ohří. Dr Marková received Leboyer's book from abroad from her émigré friends and managed to overcome authorities' disapproval.

6. Figures like Marie Pečená, Pavel Čepický, and Květa Ludvíková decided to change the system through childbirth education classes, which built on a revived concept of the "psychoprophylactic method of painless childbirth" (see Hrešanová 2016).

7. There were 108,955 childbirths in the Czech Republic in 2012 (ÚZIS 2013a, 15). Only 197 newborns with a birth weight above 2,500 g were born outside of the health establishment (ibid, 107).

8. These women were usually university educated, around 30 years old and of middle class background. In many other countries natural childbirth movements were seen as a typical "middle-class" thing (see, e.g., Mathew and Zadak 1991; Moscucci 2003; O'Connor 1993). They lived in various parts of the country, but many birth activists believe that most of them are situated in Prague.

9. Accessed January 23, 2014. http://activebirthcentre.com.gridhosted.co.uk/about/active-birth-manifesto/.

10. Accessed January 23, 2014. http://www.katyd.cz/clanky/demonstrujici-matky-vratte-nam-porody.html.

11. Available online: normalniporod.cz/petice.pdf.

12. The petition was handed over to the Ministry of Health in December; up to that date around 5,300 persons signed it; 1,114 persons signed a printed version, and 4,200 signed an electronic version. Last accessed February 2014. http://baby-cafe.cz/clanky/vsevedna/pro-zdravi-i-v-nemoci/2378-kostlivci-ve-skrini-ceskeho-porodnictvi.

13. According to the Eurostat data in 2012 the infant mortality rate was 2.6 ‰ while the EU average rate was 3.8 ‰ for 28 countries and 3.3 ‰ for 16 EU countries (http://appsso.eurostat.ec.europa.eu/nui/show.do?dataset=demo_minfind&lang=en).

14. Accessed February 23, 2014. See: http://echr.coe.int/Pages/home.aspx?p=hearings&w=2885911_10092013&language=lang.

15. Accessed September 23, 2014. The verdict that recognized women's right to make free decisions about where to give birth is available online at: http://hudoc.echr.coe.int/sites/fra/pages/search.aspx?i=001-102254#{%22itemid%22:[%22001-102254%22].

16. Accessed January 20, 2014. See also http://www.vitalia.cz/clanky/domaci-porody-netrestat-rikaji-politici-to-je-ale-malo/.

Works Cited

Akrich, Madeleine, Maire Leane, Celia Roberts, and Joao Arriscado Nunes. 2012. "Practising Childbirth Activism: A Politics of Evidence." *CSI Working Papers Series*

No. 023. Centre de Sociologie De L'Innovation, Mines ParisTech. Accessed January 20, 2014. http://www.csi.ensmp.fr/working-papers/WP/WP_CSI_023.pdf.

Aperio. 2001. "Annual Report 2001" [Výroční zpráva 2001]. Accessed January 15, 2014. http://www.aperio.cz/236/vyrocni-zpravy.

Belousova, Ekaterina. 2002. "The 'Natural Childbirth' Movement in Russia: Self-Representation Strategies." *Anthropology of East Europe Review* 20:11–18.

Benoit, Cecilia, and Alena Heitlinger. 1998. "Women's Health Care Work in Comparative Perspective: Canada, Sweden and Czechoslovakia/Czech Republic as Case Examples." *Social Science and Medicine* 47:1101–1111.

Bourgeault, Ivy Lynn. 2006. *Pushing for Midwives.* Montreal and Kingston: McGill-Queen University Press.

Brown, P., R. Morello-Frosch, S. Zavestoski, L. Senier, R. Gasior Altman, E. Hoover, S. McCormick, B. Mayer, and C. Adams. 2011. "Health Social Movements: Advancing Traditional Medical Sociology Concepts." In *Handbook of the Sociology of Health, Illness, and Healing,* edited by B. Pescosolido, J. Martin, J. McLeod, and A. Rogers, 117–137. New York: Springer.

Brown, P., S. Zavestoski, S. McCormick, B. Mayer, R. Morello-Frosch, and R. Gasior Altman. 2004. "Embodied Health Movements: New Approaches to Social Movements in Health." *Sociology of Health and Illness* 26:50–80.

Brown, Phil, and Stephen Zavestoski. 2005. "Social Movements in Health: An Introduction." In *Social Movements in Health,* edited by P. Brown and S. Zavestoski, 1–16. Oxford: Wiley-Blackwell.

Bryant, Joanne, Maree Porter, Sally K. Tracy, and Elizabeth A. Sullivan. 2007. "Caesarean Birth: Consumption, Safety, Order, and Good Mothering." *Social Science and Medicine* 65:1192–1201.

Císař, Ondřej, Jiří Navrátil, and Kateřina Vráblíková. 2011. "Staří, noví, radikální: politický aktivismus v České republice očima teorie sociálních hnutí" [Old, New, Radical: Political Activism in the Czech Republic through the Prism of Social Movement Theory]. *Sociologický časopis/Czech Sociological Review* 47:137–167.

Clark, John D., and Nuno Themudo. 2006. "Linking the Web and the Street: Internet-based 'Dotcauses' and the 'Anti-globalization Movement." *World Development* 34:50–74.

Craven, Christa. 2010. *Pushing for Midwives: Homebirth Mothers and the Reproductive Rights Movement.* Philadelphia: Temple University Press.

Davis-Floyd, Robbie, and Christine B. Johnson, eds. 2006. *Mainstreaming Midwives: The Politics of Change.* London: Routledge.

Daviss, Betty-Ann. 2001. "Reforming Birth and (Re)making Midwifery in North America." In *Birth by Design: Pregnancy, Maternity Care, and Midwifery in North America and Europe,* edited by Raymond DeVries, Cecilia Benoit, Edwin R. Van Teijlingen, and Sirpa Wrede, 70–86. New York: Routledge.

Diani, Mario. 2012. "Interest Organizations in Social Movements: An Empirical Exploration." *Interest Groups and Advocacy* 1:26–47.

Donna, Sylvie. 2011. Introduction to *Promoting Normal Birth—Research, Reflections and Guidelines,* edited by Sylvie Donna. United Kingdom: Fresh Heart Publishing.

Dudová, Radka. 2012. *Interrupce v České republice: zápas o ženská těla* [*Abortion in the Czech Republic: A Struggle for Women's Bodies*]. Praha: Sociologický ústav AV ČR.

Fábián, Katalin. 2013. "Overcoming Disempowerment: The Homebirth Movement in Hungary." In *Beyond NGO-ization: The Development of Social Movements in*

Central and Eastern Europe, edited by Kerstin Jacobsson and Steven Saxonberg, 71–95. Surray: Ashgate.

Foucault, Michel. 1997. *Ethics: Subjectivity and Truth*, edited by Paul Rabinow. New York: The New Press.

Gabriel, Cynthia. 2011. *Natural Hospital Birth: The Best of Both Worlds*. Boston: The Harvard Common Press.

Gold, Raymond L. 1958. "Roles in Sociological Field Observations." *Social Forces* 36:217–233.

HAM, UNIPA, IMBCI. 2008. Press Release. "Nejde o porody doma" [It's Not about Home Births]. October 9. Accessed January 15, 2014. http://duly.cz/dokumenty/tisk.zprava_nejdeoporodydoma.doc.

HAM. 2012. "Kdo jsme" [Who We Are]. Accessed January 15, 2014. http://www.iham.cz/o-nas/kdo-jsme/.

Hašková, Hana. 2001. *Názorové diferenciace k současným změnám v českém porodnictví* [*Differences in Opinions on Contemporary Changes in Czech Birth Care*]. Praha: Sociologický ústav AV ČR.

Hasmanová Marhánková, Jaroslava. 2008. "Konstrukce normality, rizika a vědění o těle v těhotenství: příklad prenatálních screeningů" [Construction of Normality, Risk and the Knowledge of Pregnant Body: The Case of Genetic Screenings]. *Biograf* 47:19–49.

———. 2014. "Postoje rodičů odmítajících povinná očkování svých dětí: případová studie krize důvěry v biomedicínské vědění" [The Views of Parents Who Reject Compulsory Vaccination: A Case Study of the Crisis of Trust in Biomedical Knowledge]. *Sociologický časopis/Czech Sociological Review* 50:163–188. http://dx.doi.org/10.13060/00380288.2014.50.2.75.

Heitlinger, Alena. 1987. *Reproduction, Medicine and the Socialist State*. New York: St. Martin's Press.

Howell-White, Sandra. 1999. *Birth Alternatives: How Women Select Childbirth Care*. Westport, Connecticut, London: Greenwood Press.

Hrešanová, Ema. 2008. *Kultury dvou porodnic: etnografická studie* [*Cultures of Two Maternity Hospitals: An Ethnographic Study*]. Plzeň: Vydavatelství ZČU v Plzni.

———. 2010. "The Moralities of Medicine and Birth Care in the Czech Republic: The Case of Arrested Mother." *Durham Anthropology Journal* 17:65–86. Available online: http://www.dur.ac.uk/anthropology.journal/vol17/iss1.

———. 2011. "Porodní zkušenosti českých žen: kvalitativní studie" [Birth Care and the Experience of Czech Women: A Qualitative Study]. *Gender, rovné příležitosti, výzkum* 12:63–74.

———. 2014. "'Nobody in a Maternity Hospital Really Talks to You': Socialist Legacies and Consumerism in Czech Women's Childbirth Narratives." *Sociologický časopis/Czech Sociological Review* 50:961–985.

———. 2016. "The Psychoprophylactic Method of Painless Childbirth in Socialist Czechoslovakia: From State Propaganda to Activism of Enthusiasts." *Medical History* 60: 534–556. https://doi.org/10.1017/mdh.2016.59.

Hryciuk, Renata, and Elżbieta Korolczuk. 2013. "At the Intersection of Gender and Class: Social Mobilization around Mothers' Rights in Poland." In *Beyond NGO-ization: The Development of Social Movements in Central and Eastern Europe*, edited by Kerstin Jacobsson and Steven Saxonberg, 49–70. Surray: Ashgate.

Jamieson, Gwendolyn Gray. 2012. *Reaching for Health: The Australian Women's Health Movement and Public Policy.* Canberra: Australian National University E-Press.
Kinkorová, Judita, and Ondřej Topolčan. 2012. "Overview of Healthcare System in the Czech Republic." *EPMA Journal* 3:4.
Kline, Wendy. 2010. *Bodies of Knowledge: Sexuality, Reproduction, and Women's Health in the Second Wave.* Chicago: University of Chicago Press.
Kozinets, Robert. 2010. *Netnography: Doing Ethnographic Research Online.* Los Angeles: SAGE.
Lábusová, Eva, and Alena Frydrychová, eds. 2002. *Průvodce porodnicemi Česke republiky* [*A Guide to Maternity Hospitals in the Czech Republic*]. Praha: Aperio.
Leboyer, Frederick. 1975. *Birth without Violence.* New York: Random House.
MacDonald, Margaret. 2007. *At Work in the Field of Birth: Midwifery Narratives of Nature, Tradition and Home.* Nashville: Vanderbilt University Press.
Mášová, Hana. 2005. "Dva pilíře přestavby československého zdravotnictví: Nedvědův a Albertův plán. Porovnání" [Two Pillars for the Restructuring of the Czechoslovak Health Care System: Nedvěd's and Albert's Plans. A Comparison]. In *České zdravotnictví, vize a skutečnost. Složité peripetie od plánů k realizaci,* edited by Hana Mášová, Eva Křížová, and Petr Svobodný, 65–97. Praha: Univerzita Karlova v Praze.
Mathew, Joan, and Kathleen Zadak. 1991. "The Alternative Birth Movement in the United States: History and Current Status." *Women and Health* 17:39–56.
Michaels, Paula. 2014. *Lamaze: An International History.* New York: Oxford University Press.
Mishtal, Joanna. 2010. "Neoliberal Reforms and Privatisation of Reproductive Health Services in Post-socialist Poland." *Reproductive Health Matters* 18:56–66.
Mlynářová, Alice, and Jindřich Tošner. 1995. "Historie přítomnosti muže u porodu" [History of a Man's Presence at Childbirth]. *Gynekolog* 4:216–218.
Moscucci, Ornella. 2003. "Holistic Obstetrics: The Origins of 'Natural Childbirth' in Britain." *Postgraduate Medical Journal* 79:168–173.
Nováková, Jana. 2014. "Česká veřejnost o zdravotnictví—prosinec 2013" [The Czech Public Opinion on Health Care—December 2013]. Praha: CVVM, Sociologický ústav. Accessed September 15, 2014. http://cvvm.soc.cas.cz/zdravi-volny-cas/ceska-verejnost-o-zdravotnictvi-2.
O'Connor, Bonnie. 1993. "The Home Birth Movement in the United States." *The Journal of Medicine and Philosophy* 18:147–174.
O'Reilly, Karen. 2005. *Ethnographic Methods.* London and New York: Routledge.
Pařízek, Antonín. 2002. "Historický vývoj porodnické analgezie a anestezie v České republice" [Historical Development of Obstetric Analgesia and Anesthesia in the Czech Republic]. In *Porodnická analgezie a anestezie,* edited by A. Pařízek, 43–48. Praha: Grada Publishing.
———. 2012. Plánovaný domácí porod v ČR—cesta zpět [Planned Homebirth in the Czech Republic—A Retrograde Step]. Paper presented at the workshop "Homebirths—a Step Forward or Backward" for Chamber of Deputies of the Czech Republic, Board for Healthcare, Prague, March 27.
PD Čáp. 2013. "Od CAPu po Čápa. Kapitola druhá—Centrum aktivního porodu (1998–2000)" [From CAP to a Stork. Chapter Two—The Center for Active Childbirth]. Accessed January 20, 2014. www.pdcap.cz/Texty/Historie/Historie.html.

Petrák, Tomáš. 1983. "První zkušenosti s rooming-in v prostředí porodnického oddělení nemocnice I. typu" [First Experience with Rooming-In a Maternity Ward of a Type One]. *Československá gynekologie* 48:202–206.

Petrova, Tsveta, and Sidney Tarrow. 2007. "Transactional and Participatory Activism in the Emerging European Polity: The Puzzle of East Central Europe." *Comparative Political Studies* 40:74–94.

Phillips, Sarah. 2008. *Women's Social Activism in the New Ukraine: Development and the Politics of Differentiation*. Bloomington and Indianapolis: Indiana University Press.

Plívová, V. 2013. "Odpověd Ministerstva zdravotnictví na dotaz dle zákona č. 106/1999 Sb. vznesený Zuzanou Candigliota dne 29.3. 2012" [The Ministry of Health's Response to Zuzana Candigliota's Question Posed on March 29, 2012]. Ministry of Health, Department for Communication and Press. April 24. http://normalniporod.cz/.../Odpoved-MZ-zadost-o-informace-ZC-29.3.13.pdf.

Plummer, Ken. 2003. *Intimate Citizenship: Private Decisions and Public Dialogues*. Seattle, London: University of Washington Press.

Poslanecká sněmovna [Chamber of Deputies]. 2013. "Zpráva o peticích přijatých Poslaneckou sněmovnou Parlamentu ČR, dle jejich obsahu a způsobu vyřízení za období od 1. 7. 2012 do 31. 12. 2012" [Report on Petitions Received by the Chamber of Deputies of the Parliament of the Czech Republic, Sorted by Their Subject Matter and a Type of Settlement]. Accessed May, 29, 2014. http://www.psp.cz/sqw/text/orig2.sqw?idd=131206.

Reiger, Karreen. 2000. "Reconceiving Citizenship. The Challenge of Mothers as Political Activists." *Feminist Theory* 1:309–327.

———. 2001. *Our Bodies, Our Babies: The Forgotten Women's Movement*. Carlton South, Victoria: Melbourne University Press.

Rivkin-Fish, Michele. 2005. *Women's Health in Post-Soviet Russia: The Politics of Intervention*. Bloomington and Indianapolis: Indiana University Press.

Rooks, Judith. 1999. "The Midwifery Model of Care." *Journal of Nurse-Midwifery* 44:370–374.

Rose, Niklas. 2001. "The Politics of Life Itself." *Theory, Culture and Society* 18:1–30.

Ryntová, Lucie, and Radka Wallerová, eds. 2002. *Sborník textů z konference Přivádíme děti na svět* ["We Bring Babies into the World" Conference and Proceedings]. Praha: Aperio, Společnost pro zdravé rodičovství.

Šafr, Jiří, and Julia Häuberer. 2008. "Subjektivní sociální distance k profesím: existují v české společnosti subjektivní třídní hranice?" [Subjective Social Distances to Professions: Are There Subjective Class Boundaries in the Czech Society?]. *Naše společnost* 6:28–38.

Scambler, Graham, and David Kelleher. 2006. "New Social and Health Movements: Issues of Representation and Change." *Critical Public Health* 16:219–231.

Šráčková, Danuše. 2007. "Rooming In." *Praktická gynekologie* 11:26–29.

Štembera, Zdeněk. 2004. *Historie české perinatologie* [*History of Czech Perinatology*]. Praha: Jessenius Maxdorf.

True, Jacqui. 2003. *Gender, Globalization, and Postsocialism: The Czech Republic after Communism*. New York: Columbia University Press.

Tuček, Milan. 2013. "Prestiž povolání—červen 2013" [Occupational Prestige—June 2013]. Praha: CVVM, Sociologický ústav. Accessed September 15, 2014. http://cvvm.soc.cas.cz/prace-prijmy-zivotni-uroven/prestiz-povolani-cerven-2013.

Uhrová, Eva. 2005. "Národní fronta žen a Rada československých žen—dva proudy ženského hnutí v českých zemích a jejich zájem o sociální a právní postavení žen. Květen 1945 až únor 1948." In *Bolševismus, komunismus a radikální socialismus v Československu*, edited by Zdeněk Kárník and Michal Kopeček, 88–112. Praha: Ústav pro soudobé dějiny AV ČR, Dokořán.

ÚZIS. 2013a. *Rodička a novorozenec 2012* [*Mother and Newborn 2012*]. Praha: ÚZIS.

———. 2013b. *Zdravotnická ročenka České republiky 2012* [*Czech Health Statistics Yearbook 2012*]. Praha: Ústav zdravotních informací a statistiky ČR.

Van Teijlingen, Edwin. 2005. "A Critical Analysis of the Medical Model as Used in the Study of Pregnancy and Childbirth." *Sociological Research Online* 10. Accessed January 25, 2013. http://www.socresonline.org.uk/10/2/teijlingen.html.

Vláda České republiky [The Government of the Czech Republic]. 2012. "Čtvrté zasedání Pracovní skupiny pro porodnictví" [The Fourth Meeting of the Working Group for Maternity and Birth Care Services]. *Archiv zpráv pracovních a poradních orgánů vlády*, October 31. Accessed May, 29, 2014. http://www.vlada.cz/cz/ppov/zmocnenec-vlady-pro-lidska-prava/aktuality/ctvrte-zasedani-praconi-skupiny-pro-porodnictvi-100325/.

———. 2013. "Výroční zpráva o činnosti Rady vlády pro lidská práva za rok 2012" [Annual Report on Activities of the Government Council for Human Rights]. Accessed May, 29, 2014. http://www.vlada.cz/scripts/modules/fg/fulltxt.php?langid=1&locale=CZ&sort=rank&searchtext=www.vlada.cz%2Fassets%2Fppov%2Frlp%2Fcinnost...%2FII-Zprava-o-cinnosti-2012.doc.

Vnoučková, Marie. 2013. "Kulatý stůl o situaci v českém porodnictví—Dánsko příklad dobré praxe" [Round Table Discussion about the Czech Birth Care System—Denmark as an Example of Good Practice]. Paper presented at the round table meeting for the *Nesehnutí*, funded by OSF. Prague, June 21.

Vránová, Věra. 2007. *Historie babictví a současnost porodní asistence* [*The History and Present Status of Midwifery*]. Olomouc: Univerzita Palackého v Olomouci.

11

Parents Rebelling against the State in the Hungarian Home-Birth Movement

Katalin Fábián

Building on two decades of grassroots, inward-focused, and small-scale local activism among families who chose home-birth in Hungary, the country's home-birth movement finally began to command intense public attention after October 5, 2010, when one of the movement's main protagonists, Dr. Ágnes Geréb, was shackled and imprisoned for allegedly causing the death of two newborns and injuring others. The photographs of the small-framed, then 58-year-old obstetrician and independent midwife wearing leg chains and handcuffs, held as if on a leash by young minders on each side, appeared in nearly all the Hungarian news media. With this widely circulated photo of Dr. Geréb, the use of emotive images to supplement verbal arguments has emerged as a centerpiece of a parental rebellion against the state and the medical authorities. The debate about Dr. Geréb's fate and about regulating home-birth in Hungary took an unexpected turn that made the doctor's case and the associated parental movement an international cause. The movement has influenced public debates and politics, including many legal changes and modifications in health policy both domestically and internationally. The persecution of Dr. Geréb and, by implication, the development of the home-birth movement are elements of a broader struggle over competing interpretations of authority, knowledge, gender equality, rights, risk, and safety in contemporary Hungary.

How did the images produced by and of the activists of the Hungarian home-birth movement contribute to disseminating their arguments and to the movement's eventual successes in changing this symbolically and practically important health policy and public discourse? In this chapter, I describe some of the most important images produced by parental activists that played a notable part in the mobilization of the Hungarian home-birth movement. In addition to the images that activists produced to carry their message, I also rely on images that portray actions of home-birth activists to show who the activists have been and what kind of visual tactics they have applied during demonstrations. I argue that the emotionally compelling visual forms of self-representation created meaningful messages in and of themselves that significantly supported the movement's many carefully crafted texts, such as newspaper articles, petitions, blogs, and websites.

This chapter demonstrates that the Hungarian home-birth movement generated an effective set of visual self-representations that enhanced their arguments opposing the position of medical and state authorities. The movement's images served to counter the charges against Dr. Geréb and negative views on home-birth more broadly. By showing healthy, happy, and loving families, the activists challenged the dominant medical and public positions that rejected the practice of giving birth outside of hospitals and that depicted it as a dangerous practice that uninformed, potentially neglectful, and selfish mothers pursued. In particular, the images that the movement created as its own representation have simultaneously used and creatively subverted traditional gender roles by portraying actively engaged, emotionally involved, and effectively contributing fathers. The activists have frequently depicted fathers' involvement during pregnancy and child rearing, and in particular, during birth. These unusual images of Hungarian men directly engaged with and challenged traditional gender stereotypes, especially in the secluded space where birth takes place. The birth process has traditionally been an exclusively female experience, with the notable exception of contemporary obstetrician-gynecologists—who are nearly exclusively male in Hungary.

In the first part of this chapter I describe my data sources, methods, and the main theories that guided the analysis. In the second part I investigate the history of the contemporary Hungarian home-birth movement, highlighting the transnational ideational context and value orientation from which it emerged. The third segment highlights how and why the home-birth movement emerged as a transnational mobilization. The fourth segment analyzes some of the movement's best-known images and explains how they resonated both nationally and internationally. The inviting hybridity of values and their representations in images are the subjects of the conclusion.

Sources, Methods, and Applied Theories

Since 2009, I have been collecting an archive of press releases and newspaper articles about the Hungarian home-birth movement. When an article on this topic appeared in a newspaper, I systematically searched in the newspaper's online archive for previous mentions of the home-birth movement and the names of activists they interviewed or referred to. I organized the records of the movement's activities to create a chronology of events and then compared my chronology with information that the movement posted online about itself and with interview data from various activists. I selected interviewees whose names appeared in newspapers articles and on the websites associated with the movement. Some of the most influential internet sites that I regularly checked are the non-governmental organization (NGO) *Születésház*'s szules.hu (which has become an archive, split into two new sites: http://www.szuleteshaz.hu and http://www.otthonszules.hu) and FreeGereb.org, the platform for protesting against the imprisonment of Dr. Geréb.

Between 2011 and 2015, I interviewed seventeen activists who referred me to one another, including four practicing independent midwives (including one male midwife), three doulas, and ten parents who all worked with the home-birth movement for an extensive period.[1] There is an overlap between the categories of movement participants because some parents trained as doulas and midwives after a very satisfying birth experience at home. Midwives and doulas who participated in the home-birth movement tended also to be parents who actively engaged with the movement in both a personal and a professional capacity. I also had a chance to interview Dr. Geréb multiple times. With the help of the activists, I collected approximately one hundred photographs and four documentary films in addition to the textual archive, which has a sizable and diverse set of sources on the Hungarian home-birth movement. I regularly checked the websites of the movement and followed how each petition reached out to the broader public and how the movement documented itself.

Following Gillian Rose's (2001) approach, I used visual content analysis to explore the social meanings of the most important images of the home-birth movement. I first sorted the visual images in my archive by focusing on how frequently a particular image appeared. I analyzed the images that appeared most frequently. Second, I moved from the frequency of the image to examining its production. I divided the images into two groups: one with images focused on depicting the movement during actions, such as demonstrations, and the other with images the activists have produced as part of the movement's visual propaganda, such as large drawings and posters representing them. While both sets of images represent a high degree of intentionality on part of the activist-producers, the production of second group of artistic images requires even more steps in organization and reflection on the group's aims than how activists chose to appear in street protests. From the first group in my collection, I selected one image, fig. 11.1 that often appeared in social and traditional media to discuss in this essay. From the second group, I selected an image on a central NGO's site (fig. 11.2) and three prominently used posters: figs. 11.3, 11.4, and 11.5.

A Brief History of the Hungarian Home-Birth Movement

The first official event of the Hungarian home-birth movement took place in 1992 in Szeged, where Dr. Geréb organized an international conference on alternative birth practices. It was probably the first such conference on this topic not only in Hungary, but most likely in the whole postcommunist region (Nemzetközi konferencia 1992). The networking at this conference led to the establishment of the *Alternatal Alapítvány* (Alternatal Foundation), the first Hungarian NGO dedicated to "woman- and child-centric" birth practices. Alternatal became a training center, hosting many internationally known midwives and medical experts as trainers.

In 1993, the Hungarian Parliament allocated the sizeable sum of 32.6 million Hungarian forints in support of Alternatal.[2] With the support of a Soros Foundation loan, Dr. Geréb was able to start the birth house before Parliament transferred the money. However, the Hungarian Board of Obstetricians and Gynecologists refused to issue an official review of the plan, effectively and forever blocking the transfer of funds. The birth house, *Napvilág Születésház* (Daylight Birth House), was built with personal loans and considerable physical help from families whose children were born with Dr. Geréb's and other, by then independent, midwives' assistance. These families numbered over 3,000 by 2010 (Fábián 2013). Their activities converged in networking, information exchange, and an increasingly large annual birthday party that gathered the parents, children, kin, midwives, and doulas.

Dr. Geréb is to date the most prominent of the doctors who accompanied births outside of hospitals. When she won two notable Hungarian awards in 2006 and 2011, her portrait, showing a confident and smiling woman, was displayed in a large mall in the center of Budapest along with portraits of the other winners of a nationwide public opinion poll.[3] The image of Dr. Geréb in this mall appeared in various magazines, promoting the issue of home-birth in the country. Despite the growing recognition of Dr. Geréb's work and home-birth as an alternative to hospitals, the practice and the associated movement met growing medical and public opposition.

The fiasco of blocking the transfer of legislatively approved funds for the birth house in 1993 was just the first in a series of escalating conflicts between the emerging home-birth movement and the medical establishment and eventually the legal and political authorities. Instead of resorting to direct confrontation, however, Alternatal and associated NGOs, such as Mérce, started publishing guides for the women who found their way to their childbirth workshops because, beyond hearsay, there was very little information about the services in hospital obstetric departments (Mérce 2001; Mérce 1999). The trickle of news items about and associated images of the home-birth movement distributed in traditional media and increasingly online became a flood in 2010 when Dr. Geréb was imprisoned. The widely reported case of Dr. Geréb's imprisonment led to a massive parental mobilization that has pressured the Hungarian government to free and exonerate her.

The movement's other important goal was to change the highly restrictive laws on independent midwifery and the availability of medical help during birth that were in place at that time. Within mere months a diverse group of parents, grandparents, close family members of children born outside of hospitals, independent midwives, and doulas built a dense transnational network that included alternative birth proponents and human and women's rights advocates in such diverse areas as Berlin, Cape Town, London, New York, Mexico City, and Tallinn. Dr. Geréb's imprisonment and the ensuing confrontation with the Hungarian legal and medical authorities dramatically transformed the home-birth movement. From a grassroots, informal group that considered home-birth a private decision, the activists developed into a nationally and internationally known, politically engaged parental movement.

The parental rebellion against the state and medical authorities effectively created and then used emotionally laden imagery aimed at igniting righteous anger with the repressive state (which put women who help such families behind bars) and juxtaposed the state-sanctioned oppression with pictures of loving families with their healthy, happy children, including their newborns. The outreach was so successful that all Hungarian media outlets, and numerous internationally recognized newspapers—such as the UK's *The Economist* (2010, 2011) and *The Guardian* (Hill 2010; Associated Press 2012; Hill 2012), the Qatari *Al Jazeera* (2011; Heathcote 2012), the Canadian *The Star* (Porter 2012), and the Polish *Krytyka Polityczna* (Celichowski 2014)—reported on the Hungarian home-birth movement and Dr. Geréb's case. Major international organizations (such as the UN's CEDAW Committee and the European Union's Petitions Committee, headquartered in Brussels) have expressed their concern about Dr. Geréb's treatment to the Hungarian government (Igazságot Geréb Ágnesnek Mozgalom and Születésház Egyesület 2013).

The parents' movement reached out and found allies among human rights activists. Through litigation, important domestic and international policy changes ensued as a result of Hungarian parental activism. In 2010, an expectant mother named Anna Ternovszky (assisted by parental activists, among them lawyers associated with the movement and *Társaság a Szabadságjogokért*, the Hungarian Civil Liberties Union) filed an action against the government of Hungary with the European Court of Human Rights, an institution of the Council of Europe. Anna Ternovszky's legal team based her claim on the violation of her right to privacy because she was unable to legally give birth at home with Dr. Geréb in attendance due to the long-established prohibition under Hungarian law of medical personnel attending births outside of hospitals (Hungarian Board of Obstetrics and Gynecologists 2007). Anna Ternovszky won her landmark case: the Court ruled that Hungary must recognize the mother's right to choose where and how she wishes to give birth (Ternovszky 2012).

During 2010–2013, the number of the Hungarian home-birth movement's supporters grew dramatically to include many thousands of parents. The activists not only employed lobbying, litigation, and information outreach to the public, but also started to organize numerous street protests by families in Hungary. Pregnant women and mothers with very young children formed a sizeable proportion of the more than 600 people who kept a vigil outside Budapest's remand prison the day after Dr. Geréb was arrested. Two days later, a similar group of about 1,200 people made a human chain from the Budapest Municipal Court to the Parliament (fig. 11.1). Many of the

Fig. 11.1 Supporters of Dr. Geréb form a human chain from the National Parliament to the Budapest City Courthouse (October 12, 2010). Printed with the permission of Eszter Dobay (photographer, dobaye@gmail.com).

participants wore red t-shirts, which the organizers selected because the color symbolizes both love and danger, and it is the color that stops traffic.

The home-birth movement designed and orchestrated the street protests as picturesque and strongly emotive. Along with demonstrating the deep solidarity forged through the past two decades of the movement's emergence, in these street protests the parental activists have put on public display their profound care toward family and community. Juxtaposing the loving and protective emotions toward other families and Dr. Geréb, the movement showed a deep sense of hurtful rejection from the authorities and society at large.

On November 8, 2010, more than 800 of Dr. Geréb's supporters and their children participated in a torchlight procession from the Budapest City Courthouse through the center of the city. The torchlight procession itself was a novel way of representing a social cause at the time. The associations with carrying torches are twofold. First, they remind people of what is seen as "the dark ages," in terms of both the distant past and the recent restrictions on home-birth. Observers have compared the prosecutions against Dr. Geréb to witch hunts against female herbalists in the Middle Ages (Varró 2009). Second, they call to mind the show trials of the communist era (Ónody-Molnár 2012 quoting Imre Szebik), which indicates how pointedly the activists have used references to recent history to promote their cause. However, the torchlight parade can also be seen as a joyful and carnivalesque gathering, a family event. Organizing a torchlight parade accompanied by fairy-tale-like characters, fiddle music, and community singing is a peculiar, but very effective way to reverse the authorities' negative portrayal of the home-birth movement as neglectful. It is highly unusual to see streams of parents with small children out at night in peaceful protest, and immediately after this event, pictures of the procession appeared on numerous social networking sites, both in Hungary and internationally. These images showed the world the emotional warmth felt for Dr. Geréb and the midwives who assisted at the children's births as well as the parents' determination to fight for their rights and beliefs.

The fairytale-like public protests against Dr. Geréb's imprisonment contributed to the broad dissemination of visual messages of the home-birth movement depicting the cause of home-birth as good, standing against oppression as heroic, and the state/medical authorities as wicked. Public singing, traditional Hungarian fiddle music, and the principal activists' fairytale-like dress (such as medieval capes) served well the immediate practical aim of keeping the attention of the many youngsters, but they also added another meaningful layer to the self-representation of the movement as accessible and caring for all.

Extensive online parental activism and notable international media attention have resulted in a series of protests in front of Hungarian embassies in South Africa, Western and Central Europe, and North and Central America. In the course of Dr. Geréb's imprisonment of three years and four months (with continuing restrictions on her movement and suspension of her ob-gyn and midwifery licenses), this parental movement rallied around her and kept her case in the global spotlight, which led to major policy successes. The home-birth movement was probably the first one in Hungary which extensively and effectively utilized social networking sites for both domestic and especially international information dissemination, networking, and transnational coordination of activities, such as street protests, global film showings, and signature collections for petitions that were then submitted to the Hungarian authorities. The social networking sites became not only depositories of evidence of transnational protest actions, but they encouraged the development of like-minded support activities that used the same movement-produced emotionally expressive images as their trademark. In Hungary, the spark that Dr. Geréb's case ignited led directly to the 2011 regulation of home-birth, allowing for the first registered independent midwifery services (2011 No. 35).

Twenty years of grassroots activities followed the first official event of the home-birth movement in 1992, culminating in the legislation on independent midwifery in Hungary. The relations between the practitioners of the movement and the medical/legal authorities developed from benign tolerance in the late 1990s, moving to intermittent cooperation in the early 1990s, becoming outright rejection and vilification by 2000.

The Hungarian home-birth movement has emerged as the most open and dramatic conflict between a government and a movement regarding alternative birth practices in post-communist Central and Eastern Europe. There have been parallel developments with parents demanding less medicalized and more natural support during birth with the help of midwives and doulas instead of doctors in the Czech Republic, Estonia, Lithuania, Poland, and Russia (Hryciuk and Korolczuk 2013; Hresanova, chapter 11 in this volume), but in none of these countries has such a long, international, and conflict-ridden debate between the protagonists of midwifery and the medical-legal authorities ensued as in Hungary, although midwives and doctors also had to face criminal charges in other countries. The cases against Lithuania's Jurgita Svede, Russian Elena Ermakova, and Czech midwives Ivana Königsmarkova and Zuzana Stromerova did not lead to prison sentences and did not provoke extensive social mobilizations analogous to Hungary's (Tonetti 2012; Volynsky 2013). There are many reasons for such a discrepancy; one of them probably is the strength of the Hungarian medical lobby that perceived both a symbolic challenge to their authority and also an economic threat to limit the corruption that the extremely lucrative under-the-table payments create that obstetricians receive for each birth. In addition to the entrenched political and cultural position of medical doctors, the Hungarian governments may have also wanted to put a lid on emerging social movements and demonstrate their power by intimidation and producing fear when imprisoning the most visible and popular protagonist of the home-birth movement.

A Rebellion of International Proportions: The Transnationalization of the Hungarian Home-Birth Movement

The success of the Hungarian home-birth movement stems partly from the international ideational links and partly from the personal and professional connections that the parental activists have developed. Since its inception in the early 1990s, the Hungarian home-birth movement has ideationally and often personally connected to various international midwifery movements and alternative birth movements that had developed since the 1970s in North America and Western Europe. The crisis of Dr. Geréb's imprisonment prompted previous parental networks to develop a more formal existence, and these networks aptly connected with both national and international supporters of alternative birth practices and independent midwifery, as well as human and women's rights advocates.

Midwifery and natural birth movements came into vogue in the early 2000s in the United States as a personalized and often spiritual search by upper-middle-class parents to achieve what they consider to be holistic health. In the UK and other Western European countries, governments started over a decade earlier to institutionally support midwifery as a cost-cutting measure for low-risk pregnancies. While recognizing the value of contemporary medical knowledge and technology, practitioners of the movement challenge many of the biomedical routines generally used during birth in hospitals. The corresponding international alternative birth movement is explicitly diverse in its strength, types of organization, scope, achievements, and degree of confrontation with medical authorities and the state (Davis-Floyd, Barclay, Daviss, and Tritten 2009; Goer 2004).

Being part of the international network of midwifery advocacy for decades, the postcommunist Hungarian home-birth movement is also similar to and different from its Western counterparts. On the one hand, like its Western counterparts, the Hungarian parental movement has raised awareness of the benefits of home-birth as it responds to the problems of modern health care (such as excessive medicalization and corruption). In this respect it is an expression and amalgamation of both rising conservatism and nationalism, and it also shows the influence of feminism and human rights movements. On the other hand, the Hungarian movement is uniquely situated in a transitional social and political environment where the recognition of women's rights (in this case, the right to choose where and how they wish to give birth) carries the legacy of an overly powerful communist state.

These international networks provided the practitioners and supporters of the Hungarian home-birth movement not only with sympathetic ideational support but also with tangible resources. The parental movement benefited from valuable legal advice on how to reach international audiences (organizations, the broader public, and notable individuals), recent medical data to challenge the official medical interpretations, and probably most importantly, access to a wide group of members and news outlets that spread the news on Dr. Geréb's case and the Hungarian home-birth movement. The ideational resonance between midwifery movements across the globe produced actual network connectivity that produced support in the form of petitions signed and submitted to pressure the Hungarian government and bring about change in both awareness and policy regarding alternative birth practices.

Producing visual images that were extensively distributed to various domestic and international news media and online sites fundamentally connected and strengthened existing connections between local, national, and international audiences. The transnational links also qualify the Hungarian home-birth movement as a postmodern social movement, defined here as surpassing the constraints of territoriality and national borders. By reaching out to existing virtual communities (such as human rights and women's activists, international associations of midwives, birth centers), the movement established new networks and expanded previous grassroots groups that together translated into enhanced political pressure on the government and higher awareness of the practice among the broader public.

The methods of exerting pressure on the Hungarian government effectively extended the "boomerang effect" to the virtual space of the internet (Keck and Sikkink 1998). In the classic "boomerang" model the domestic activists throw a "blame-and-shame" plea for support to transnational allies who then send resources back to place pressure on the rights-abusing (authoritarian) national government. With a dense network of transnational allies, an electronic method of mobilization, and actual protest events both at home and abroad, the contemporary Hungarian home-birth movement applied a hybrid boomerang pattern of traditional social movement leverage substantially enhanced by web-based social networking.

Faced with a partially hostile public and denied access to Hungarian authorities, the home-birth movement reached out to international partners by activating the extensive international network of the alternative birth movement. Dr. Geréb's imprisonment ignited further actions and reactions from the human rights and midwifery network nodes, "jumping scales" from local (small scale), to a domestic level (mezzo scale), to large international levels and back again many times over several years (Brenner 1999, fn50). A similar back-and-forth pattern of engagement between local, national, and international circles has been observed in an increasing number of cases where social movements have attempted to change public policies (Bruszt and Holzhacker 2009).

The first step in reaching out to international supporters was to contact the various renowned medical scholars and midwives who had visited Hungary at Dr. Geréb's invitation to present at conferences and meetings. This international outreach paid dividends when Ina May Gaskin publicly called on the Hungarian government to reverse its unjust prosecution of Dr. Geréb as she accepted her "alternative Nobel prize," the Right Livelihood Award, in Stockholm, Sweden, on December 5, 2011 (Gaskin 2011).

The second step was using Facebook to disperse news and encourage activism to correct the perceived injustice against the Hungarian home-birth movement. Easily understandable and emotionally expressive images used on Facebook posts helped to gain and rally supporters both in Hungary and from abroad. Linking and multiplying the effects of the social networking site, active members and movement sympathizers reached out to their Facebook friends, asking them to inform others about the cause. The resulting networks operated online: they gathered signatures for petitions and staged and visually documented often highly creative protests, large and small, across the globe.

The third stage, the explicit integration of the domestic and international networks into social movement activism, produced a rapid exchange of successful images that used the creative arts to disseminate the Hungarian home-birth movement's political message. The Hungarian home-birth activists did not substitute their national environment for the supranational community; rather, they interweaved and hybridized these networks in part by mixing actual and virtual arenas for action and as message conduits, and in part by using expressive images that managed to link the different cultural affiliations of its audience. The images of family-and-friends-like gatherings in support of freeing Dr. Geréb in Tartu, Estonia, and Cape Town, South Africa, were just as prominently displayed on Facebook as the more traditional protests in front of Hungarian consulates and embassies in various cities.

However, not even the most carefully elaborated arguments could unilaterally dispel the prejudiced claims of the public and the medical profession that women who want to give birth outside of hospitals are either uninformed and crazy or simply selfish, putting their own comfort before the safety of their baby. The images that the movement promoted of itself directly address this assumption.

A Movement in Images

The Hungarian parental movement has extensively used the visual arts to evoke positive emotions in families of children born at home. They used images that were easy to understand without any accompanying text and carried the argument that home-birth was beneficial for mother, child, and the whole family. The movement frequently used the English phrase "Free Geréb," which served as a clear and straightforward message understood by Hungarians and internationally, pairing the words with the color white and surrounding them with figures of young children and their parents. The straightforward nature of this and other slogans (such as "to be born free is to live free") translated to an effective message that could travel easily both online and internationally. The home-birth movement frequently chose to present itself through various straightforward messages (e.g., "Free Geréb!") and transnationally easily decodable images of parenthood, both in place of and alongside extensive textual deliberations.

The motif of imprisonment is present, but not dominant and foreboding in the images that the Hungarian activists produced. Evoking solidarity and stressing the bravery of women in general and Dr. Geréb in particular, one such design appears on www.FreeGereb.org. In this image, a row of symbolic, simple, "cut-out" figures hold hands, reaching out to the single woman separated by two bars (symbolizing a prison cell, hospital room, or home) and crying "Free Ágnes Geréb!" on the lower left-hand side and "*Szabad Szülést*!" (Free birth!) on the lower right hand side (fig. 11.2). The text is in both Hungarian and English to make it accessible to a worldwide audience.

In the period following Dr. Geréb's arrest, the arguments and images presented by the home-birth movement became headline news, competing for airtime with such major topics as near-state bankruptcy and protests both for and against the policies of the ruling nationalist center-right government (Gati 2011; Nol 2012). A reflectively critical evaluation of this achievement may

Fig. 11.2 Home page banner of FreeGereb.org. Printed with the permission of Ilka Kása (designer).

claim that the home-birth movement attracted attention because it distracted people from the deep political and economic crisis that Hungary faced in 2010–2011. However, a more contextual analysis would assert that the home-birth movement won the public's attention because of its effective mobilization and use of domestic and international political opportunities.

The visuals of the home-birth movement tend to portray a wholesome and deeply caring image of mothers. Mother and child often appear closely bundled together in the Hungarian home-birth movement's materials (furthest person on fig. 11.1 and all except on the far left on fig. 11.3), which is why the movement earned the label *kendősök* ("the ones with scarves," loosely translated as "those with baby slings"). Significantly, this contemporary physical bundling does not erase the individuality of either person as is the case in many traditional, and especially religious, representations of mother-and-child—in both fig. 11.2 and fig. 11.3, the mothers appear differently dressed, with varied physical characteristics. Rather, it stresses a close emotional connection between a mother and child, counteracting the views on women who opt for home-birth as selfish, risk-prone, and potentially neglectful mothers. My interviewees noted that in addition to Dr. Geréb's portrait, the image of a woman wearing a baby on her body became the most readily recognized symbol of the home-birth movement. By using the image of the caring mother, the movement relied on the traditional gender role for women, which most seamlessly legitimizes their public actions especially in the contemporary Hungarian official political environment that promotes conservative family roles and increased procreation. At the same time, the mothers' actions as part of the Hungarian home-birth movement challenged women's subordination to the medical and legal authorities as each activist expresses her conscious rebellion against the official directives regarding giving birth.

Another visual representation of the contemporary, reinterpreted mother-and-child bond that the activists offered to inform and engage the public and

SZERINTED MI NEM VIGYÁZUNK RÁJUK UGYANÚGY, AZ ELSŐ PILLANATTÓL FOGVA?

Csak mi otthon hoztuk őket a világra.

A születés csoda.

Az otthonszülés egy lehetőség.

freegereb.org

Fig. 11.3 Poster. Top: "Do you really believe that we do not take care of them the same way from the beginning? The only difference is that we gave birth at home." Bottom: "Birth is a miracle. Home-birth is an opportunity." Printed with the permission of István Csintalan (photographer) and Stég Grafikai Stúdió (designer).

politicians was the provocative traveling public photography exhibit *A szülés valódi természete* (The true nature of birth). The Hungarian home-birth movement commissioned the exhibit, which included black-and-white photography testimonials of home-births and was on display in the center lobby of the Parliament building in December 2010. The families portrayed took considerable legal, financial, and personal risks to put themselves on display in this very personal, explicitly naked series of photographs. Such open and deeply personal images of birth had never before been on public display in Hungary. The aim of showcasing these photographs was to break down the vilification of home-birth advocates as crazy, uninformed, careless, and selfish and offer portraits that showed detailed preparations for the birth and photographs of pain and joy that everyone could relate to. The exhibit then traveled to several large cities and, in a move that became increasingly characteristic of this movement, was made accessible on YouTube and Vimeo.[4] Documenting their own activities online produced two positive outcomes: the broad accessibility made more people aware of the movement, and the ease of finding one another enhanced involvement and support, regardless of a viewer's location and ability to travel to a demonstration.

Images of the Hungarian home-birth movement represent three main themes: (1) images of pregnancy and mothers, (2) representations of birth, and (3) a happy family life that involves fathers as much as mothers. These images carry the message of righteous parental rebellion against an oppressive state.

Parents frequently used images of pregnant women in support of the movement, and such artistic renditions have often become carriers of the activists' aims during street protests. Such public representations of pregnancy are rare in Hungary, and using such images to exhort political pressure is even less common. One example of using the creative arts representing both the image of pregnant women and simultaneously bringing across the movement's aims in protest took place in front of the prison where Dr. Geréb was held. Activists created large colorful drawings of pregnant women, placed them in the protest area, and inscribed messages demanding freedom for the doctor and simultaneously promoting *Napvilág Születésház*'s (Daylight Birth House) website as an information source. One artist, Balázs Kő, used bright and warm colors to contrast with the white snow and the gray official building and to highlight the vivaciousness and possibly the irrepressibility of new life, associating these two characteristics with the future of the home-birth movement.

Similarly, in mid-December 2010, more than 1,200 people came together to sing "Happy Birthday" to Dr. Geréb in front of the prison. They hoisted a large "Merry Christmas" greeting card showing a photograph of her fragile but smiling face. The movement could have chosen a less loving and gentle message to reflect the harsh treatment Dr. Geréb experienced while in prison, but the artist activists' motivation was to portray Dr. Geréb as a symbol of love and defiance and to highlight the movement's refusal to admit defeat.

On the first anniversary of Dr. Geréb's imprisonment, about 300 people demonstrated in Budapest, and a parallel international petition drive and media outreach effectively reinforced the claims of the movement (Janecskó 2011). Women and children each laid a flower to form the words "Free Geréb" on the pavement. This action and the simple, straightforward message and white flowers echoed an earlier white-lettered public installation of the same text painted on a highly visible surface: the large dark gray cement banks of the River Danube in the center of the capital. Both of these creative and unambiguous collective actions were recorded and posted online as videos, along with the speeches delivered at the rallies.[5]

One particularly powerful image originated from Polish supporters because the case of Dr. Geréb was also widely discussed in Poland. Dariusz Paczkowski, a parental activist of the 3fala graffiti artist collective, produced a striking rendition of a woman's hands holding a newborn baby out of a prison window (fig. 11.4). Paczkowski's two children were born at home, and his motivation to create this picture stemmed from his active involvement with the Polish NGOs *Klamra* (Brace) and *Rodzić po ludzku* (The Foundation for Childbirth with Dignity), which focus on birth-related issues, mostly on the quality of the birthing process (Hryciuk and Korolczuk 2013). Paczkowski produced this painting in 2010 in various locations in Żywiec, Bielsko-Biala, and Warsaw (where it is still visible according to an email communication). In 2011, the NGO Klamra sent the picture to the Hungarian NGOs and it appeared on numerous websites as well.[6]

Paczkowski's picture follows the late-communist era Polish poster tradition in its simplicity of composition, use of starkly contrasting colors, and shockingly strong, clear message (McCoy 1988). One may associate the oppression implied in this picture also with dictatorial regimes, such as 1970s Argentina or apartheid-era South Africa. The picture's painful combination of incarceration and attempt to save a newborn challenges the authorities more than any Hungarian-made image I have thus far encountered.

Fig. 11.4 Polish graffiti of hands holding an infant out of a prison window, January 9, 2011. Printed with the permission of Dariusz Paczkowski (member of 3fala graffiti artist collective).

While the Hungarian home-birth movement relied on significantly less frontally shocking images than Paczkowski's picture, its message was similarly emotionally intensive. In Hungary, the parental movement chose to display showcasing happy, healthy, attractive, intelligent-looking mothers with their children. At the same time, the home-birth movement also addressed the (for the mother-activist) unfavorable gender hierarchy by innovatively portraying and effectively cooperating with fathers. The movement included men as prominent activists in the Hungarian home-birth movement, and it encouraged fathers to represent the movement in the media. This strategy helped the activists to successfully sidestep the popular misogynist attitude that condemns women—mothers—for not conforming to social expectations and "risking the life of her baby in exchange for their own comfort" by choosing home birth instead of giving birth in the hospital. The decision to prominently include men in the images of the movement's self-representation resulted in promoting gender neutrality.

The most representative set of posters that substantiates the simultaneity of traditional (gender-segregated) and postmodern (gender-equal) roles in the visual self-representation of the Hungarian home-birth movement is a set of attention-grabbing, serious but humorous photographs by István Csintalan. The posters show either only men or only women holding their small children. The groups are diverse in appearance, allowing the viewer to ascribe different economic status and political affiliations (by appearance, such as hairstyle and clothes) to each carrier of the message that asks the reader to consider home-birth an honorable choice. The posters representing both sets of parents have been displayed at demonstrations and appeared on the websites of the home-birth movement's central NGOs. The hundreds of comments on social network sites suggest that these images, which communicate a serious message in a light-hearted manner, resonated deeply and positively with its Hungarian audience.

The two posters of fathers and of mothers are mirror images of one another. If viewed together, they suggest a postmodern gender equality where both sexes equally care for and are equally involved in the emotional and physical well-being of their offspring. Viewed separately, traditional value orientations of exclusively female-specific care can be attributed to the mothers' claim that the only difference between them and other mothers is that "We gave birth at home." Highlighting that the movement put special emphasis on demonstrating that men are just as emotionally invested in home-birth as mothers, the poster showing the fathers includes three times as many men as there are women in the other poster. The text in the fathers' photograph argues, "Do you really believe that s/he is not our priority?! That is exactly why we decided that the baby should be born at home. Birth is a miracle. Home-birth is an opportunity."

The diversity of the parental participants in the various images highlights that the home-birth movement comprises supporters from divergent economic backgrounds and with vastly different political and religious affiliations. Regarding other indicators of diversity, one parental activist noted that the limited appearance of various minority groups is characteristic of the Hungarian context: "There are no social movements in Hungary where Roma or homosexuals would participate in large numbers, except their own, and if they are part of our movement, they do not announce that they are lesbians or Roma, and we do not ask" (Budapest, July 2014).

In addition to the cultural markers noting the diversity of the men in the poster, the most pointed message and probably the deepest symbolism can be attributed to the traditionally dressed and mustached elderly man, proudly standing in support of home-birth (fig. 11.5). His clothing (dark trousers and

Fig. 11.5 Poster. Top: "Do you really believe that s/he is not our priority?! That is exactly why we decided that the baby should be born at home." Bottom: "Birth is a miracle. Home-birth is an opportunity." Printed with the permission of István Csintalan (photographer) and Stég Grafikai Stúdió (designer).

vest with a white shirt and a hat reminiscent of the nineteenth-century style now back in fashion) symbolizes the approval of the conservative-nationalist forces. It is rare to find liberal elites (presumably represented by the other characters with their long hair, beards, and eyeglasses) and advocates of the conservative-nationalist agenda enjoying friendly, family-like relations and agreeing on cultural and political values in Hungary. Repeating the previously established image of bundling the baby close to the mother's body, this picture represents all the fathers swaddling, holding, and in established close emotional relationships with their very young children. With most Hungarian men rarely involved in the lives of young children and probably even less willing to be seen with a baby attached to their body, this poster represents the image of new (postmodern), emotionally available men who are fully and equally invested in their children's lives and who have moved beyond the confines of traditional macho expectations. This is an image of strong family values without resorting to conservative gender roles.

Although the Hungarian home-birth movement has until recently avoided explicit association with the women's movement and feminism, they have challenged one long-standing observation of the literature on political participation. Because of their physical vulnerability, pregnant women and mothers with small children constitute some of the most unlikely social movement participants. Most participants of social movements are usually the younger, childless generation and when females with children join, they tend to be older women (Basu 2010; Krook and Childs 2010). By focusing on and actively involving childbearing women and their supporters, the Hungarian home-birth movement and, more broadly, the alternative birth movement give voice to and empower this often unheard and symbolically important segment of the population.

The movement's outreach to the public presented a unique combination of traditional and postmodern images with the celebration of contemporary family love and affection at center stage. Under the banner of fighting for the right of a *háborítatlan* (undisturbed) birth, the implication of the seemingly casual photographs of parents and children was that giving birth in the safety and spiritual support of the home environment creates long-term, healthy family cohesion. At the same time, the home-birth movement's image of a mother with her young children symbolizes women's right to make strong personal choices, often against the expectations of the broader cultural and medical milieus. The photograph of the politically involved and thus empowered woman in various active roles has appeared in many kinds of protest actions: these usually educated and middle-class women formed the majority of those who participated in marches, wrote and performed songs, played musical instruments, and created photographs and drawings on paper and with chalk on pavements, and just as unexpectedly, used pottery and cookies to demand freedom for Dr. Geréb.[7]

Regarding markers of appearance, the bodies represented on posters, artistic renditions such as the traveling photography exhibit on birth, and images posted on the webpages associated with the movement are no hollow advertisements, void of depth and lived reality. On the contrary, such literally flesh-and-blood images of pregnancy and birth have never before appeared in public spaces in the country, even though Hungary (like most European countries) is saturated with images of naked female bodies being used to sell anything and everything. In contrast to these commercialized and retouched interpretations of femininity stand the images of pregnant and birthing women as the subject of artistic photograph exhibits (as noted above) and chalk drawings as part of public protests. Collectively, the images associated with the home-birth movement chip away at the social powers that silence real and actual birth as a taboo topic. While presenting pregnancy and birth in its reality, the movement skillfully interwove into its repertoire the whimsical nature of tales and the many unadulterated expressions of childhood creativity, such as drawings, while questioning the many prescribed boundaries of gender roles.

The movement's creative twist of adding an emphasis on individual rights to traditional cultural images of motherhood highlights that Hungarian mothers have a constitutionally guaranteed right to choose the conditions in which they want to give birth. But the various images of the Hungarian home-birth movement have reached far beyond an appeal to pregnant women to empower them to choose the conditions in which they give birth. This small but exceptionally artistically expressive movement has encouraged people of all backgrounds to participate in a birth-supportive and child-loving alliance that supports freedom of choice about this important realm of life.

Conclusion: Hybridizing Grassroots

Although the Hungarian home-birth movement is over twenty years old, it only recently entered the center stage of domestic and international politics.

This parental movement expeditiously transformed itself from a local and grassroots organization to raise its voice both nationally and internationally. Using emotionally laden images representing pregnancy, birth, and child-care and healthy families whose children were born at home, the movement challenged the authority of the state, the condemnation of the Hungarian medical authorities, and the negative projection of the broader public. The movement's ubiquity is greatly due to Dr. Geréb's imprisonment, which triggered mass mobilization and an artistic wave of expression to challenge what critics of home-birth frequently characterized as selfish and uninformed actions of mothers. By offering a unique mix of traditional and postmodern values in their arguments and self-representation, a few thousand parental activists managed to challenge prevailing medical regulations, resulting in new health policy guidelines regulating midwifery in Hungary. The Hungarian home-birth movement has made public a daring dispute with fundamental cultural practices as well as with the medical and political authorities. The activists developed grassroots support and put pressure on the Hungarian government with its exceptionally creative and surprisingly transnational mobilization.

Although the media frequently provide uneven or biased coverage of social movements, an effective and multitiered media outreach has often helped movements attract attention and support for their claims (McCarthy, McPhail, and Smith 1996). Indeed, the sophisticated arguments and the transnational and highly creative images and extensive professional and online networks associated with the Hungarian home-birth movement have promoted its claims at multiple venues. The parental activists' efforts invited manifold traditional and novel media coverage of their actions to inform and to pressure the political leaders to speak out in support of their cause. The apparent contradiction between the newly regulated midwifery practice and the continuing prosecution against Dr. Geréb may show that we are witnessing an initial and difficult stage of development full of birth pangs in accepting the values and practices of freedom and respect for individuals in a new democracy.

Considering even the partial accomplishments of the home-birth movement's goals, its mobilization is noteworthy in Hungary and possibly in the rest of postcommunist Central-Eastern Europe. It deserves attention not only because of the topic, but also because of the numerous creative and expressively transnational images in support of Dr. Geréb and the freedom of a woman to choose the conditions in which she gives birth. These visual representations of protests, songs, and even craft projects have been part of a greater strategy of parental activists. The underlying strategy for an easily accessible, hands-on mode of participation is that the more the movement's claims are on public display, the more people will understand them and the more likely it is that previously held assumptions may be questioned. The images of the grassroots projects of the home-birth movement invite broad audiences to positively view their case against the social and legal injustices that Dr. Geréb and mothers who chose home-birth have experienced. The home-birth movement has grown in size and importance while fitting its grievance into broader international human rights and gender considerations. Given this transnational salience, the unremitting deep emotional connections between parents and the medical support who attend home-births, and the continued unresolved nature of the movement's many claims including the continuing criminal prosecutions against Dr. Geréb, neither the movement nor the many issues that mobilized people are unlikely to disappear any time soon.

Katalin Fábián, Professor, Department of Government and Law, Lafayette College, Easton, PA, USA

Katalin Fábián studies the intersection of gender and globalization as they influence various policy processes of emerging democracies. She edited *Globalization: Perspectives from Central and Eastern Europe* (Elsevier, 2007) and served as the editor of a special issue of *Canadian-American Slavic Studies* that focuses on the changing international relations of Central and Eastern Europe. Her book, *Contemporary Women's Movements in Hungary: Globalization, Democracy, and Gender Equality* (Johns Hopkins University Press, 2009), analyzes the emergence and political significance of women's activism in Hungary. She conducted research among government officials and activists of NGOs that support victims of domestic violence in the post-Soviet Baltic countries, the Czech Republic, Hungary, Poland, Slovenia, and Slovakia. This research led her to contribute chapters to and edit *Domestic Violence in Postcommunist States: Local Activism, National Policies, and Global Forces* (Indiana University Press, 2010), which focuses on the transnational connections between the various European and Eurasian postcommunist movements against domestic violence.

Notes

1. Doulas provide nonmedical support to the birthing mother. The concept, the name, and associated training for this new profession have emerged as part of the home-birth movement in Hungary. One of the first such services started in 2010, see Holdudvar Bábaház and its list of doulas. http://holdudvar.babahaz.hu/dula_szolgalat.htm.

2. Approximately US$300,000 in 1993 prices, or about US$500,000 in 2015.

3. Dr. Geréb was one the first recipients of the Central European initiative "Promenade of Women" that honors female activists. She also won the "Favorite of the Decade" award of one of the most popular Hungarian women's magazines, *Nők Lapja*, in the category of public affairs.

4. The most extensive website of the exhibit is http://www.aszulesvaloditermeszete.eu/. The process of creating the exhibit at the House of Representatives can be seen at http://vimeo.com/26499962. The exhibit in Kecskemét was documented at http://www.youtube.com/watch?v=sjBfiNukwuI, in Szolnok at http://www.youtube.com/watch?v=-uB5quTlRCo, and in Békéscsaba (posted at the local yoga studio's site) at http://iziszjoga.com/2011/11/22/a-szules-valodi-termeszete-vandorkiallitas-bekescsaban/.

5. Accessed October 8, 2010. http://freegereb.org/home/9-magyar/166-installacio.

6. The history of the 3fala (Third Wave) graffiti artists' collective can be found at http://archiwum.grafffiti.pl/en.php. The image in Żywiec can be seen at http://www.facebook.com/photo.php?fbid=192073887473441&set=0.167283166621117&type=3&theater; in Bielsko-Biala at http://www.bb365.info/free-agnes-gereb,newsy,akcje,1711,0; and in Warsaw at http://www.facebook.com/photo.php?fbid=195880467092783&set=a.195880350426128.55784.100000124947836&type=1&ref=nf.

7. One of the most renowned Hungarian singers of Roma origin, Bea Palya, wrote and performed "How to Give Birth? Delivery Song," which became very popular: http://www.youtube.com/watch?v=IWAd6Ip_-Wc&feature=related.

Works Cited

2011 No. 35. 2011. "Kormány rendelet az intézeten kívüli szülés szakmai szabályairól, feltételeiről és kizáró okairól" [Professional Regulations, Conditions and Exclusions on Giving Birth Outside of Institutions]. *Magyar Közlöny* 29(5119). Accessed December 26, 2016. http://www.complex.hu/jr/gen/hjegy_doc.cgi?docid=A1100035.KOR.

Al Jazeera. 2011. "The Battle over Birth." March 28. Accessed December 26, 2016. http://www.aljazeera.com/programmes/birthrights/2011/02/201122214012285918.html.

Associated Press. 2012. "Hungarian Home Birth Midwife Loses Appeal Against Jail Sentence." *The Guardian*, February 10. Accessed December 26, 2016. http://www.theguardian.com/world/2012/feb/10/hungarian-home-birth-midwife-loses-appeal.

Basu, Amrita, ed. 2010. *Women's Movements in the Global Era: The Power of Local Feminisms*. Boulder, CO: Westview Press.

Brenner, Neil. 1999. "Beyond State-Centrism? Space, Territoriality, and Geographical Scale in Globalization Studies." *Theory and Society* 28 (1):39–78.

Bruszt, László, and Ronald Holzhacker, eds. 2009. *The Transnationalization of Economies, States, and Civil Societies*. New York: Springer.

Celichowski, Jerzy. 2014. "Rodzić po węgiersku." *Dziennik Opinii*, March 24. Accessed December 26, 2016. http://www.krytykapolityczna.pl/en/artykuly/ue/20140224/rodzic-po-wegiersku.

Davis-Floyd, Robbie, Lesley Barclay, Betty-Anne Daviss, and Jan Tritten, eds. 2009. *Birth Models that Work*. Berkeley: University of California Press.

The Economist. 2010. "Difficult Delivery: The Pioneer of Home Births in Hungary Faces Jail." March 11. Accessed December 26, 2016. http://www.economist.com/node/15671546.

———. 2011. "Home Births: Is There No Place Like Home?" March 31. Accessed December 26, 2016. http://www.economist.com/node/18483775.

Fábián, Katalin. 2013. "Overcoming Disempowerment: The Home-Birth Movement in Hungary." In *Beyond NGO-ization: The Development of Social Movements in Central and Eastern Europe*, edited by Kerstin Jacobsson and Steven Saxonberg, 71–95. Aldershot, UK: Ashgate.

Gaskin, Ina May. 2011. Speech at the 2011 Right Livelihood Awards. Accessed December 26, 2016. http://www.rightlivelihoodaward.org/speech/acceptance-speech-ina-may-gaskin/.

Gati, Charles. 2011. "Hungary's Backward Slide." *The New York Times*, December 12. Accessed December 26, 2016. http://www.nytimes.com/2011/12/13/opinion/hungarys-backward-slide.html?_r=1&ref=global-home.

Goer, Henci. 2004. "Humanizing Birth: A Global Grassroots Movement." *Birth* 31 (4):308–314.

Heathcote, Julie. 2012. "Hard Labour in Hungary." *Al Jazeera*, July 9. Accessed December 26, 2016. http://www.aljazeera.com/programmes/birthrights/2011/03/201132213446347184.html.

Hill, Amelia. 2010. "Hungary: Midwife Agnes Gereb Take to Court for Championing Home Births." *The Guardian*, October 22. Accessed December 26, 2016. http://www.theguardian.com/world/2010/oct/22/hungary-midwife-agnes-gereb-home-birth.

———. 2012. "Hungarian Home Births Champion to Move from House Arrest to Jail." *The Guardian*, April 27. Accessed December 26, 2016. http://www.theguardian.com/world/2012/apr/27/hungarian-home-births-jail.

Hryciuk, Renata, and Elżbieta Korolczuk. 2013. "At the Intersection of Gender and Class: Social Mobilization Around Mothers' Rights in Poland." In *Beyond NGO-ization: The Development of Social Movements in Central and Eastern Europe*, edited by Kerstin Jasobsson and Steven Saxonberg, 49–70. Farnham, UK: Ashgate.

Hungarian Board of Obstetrics and Gynecologists. 2007. "Állásfoglalása az otthon szülésről" [Statement on Home-Birth]. September 21. Accessed December 26, 2016. https://www.doki.net/tarsasag/noorvos/hirek.aspx?&nid=5284#5284.

Igazságot Geréb Ágnesnek Mozgalom (IGÁM) and Születésház Egyesület. 2013. Press Release. "Geréb Ágnes és az otthonszülés helyzetét továbbra sem tartja megnyugtatónak az ENSZ" [The UN Finds the Situation of Ágnes Geréb and Homebirth Unsettling]. March 21. Accessed December 26, 2016. https://nokert.hu/sun-03242013-1326/1058/1/gereb-agnes-es-az-otthonszules-helyzetet-tovabbra-sem-tartja-megnyugtatonak.

Janecskó, Kata. 2011. "Egy éve siratják Geréb Ágnest" [One Year of Lament for Ágnes Geréb]. *Index*, October 5. Accessed December 26, 2016. http://index.hu/belfold/2011/10/05/egy_eve_fogoly_gereb_agnes/.

Keck, Margaret, and Kathryn Sikkink. 1998. *Activists Beyond Borders: Advocacy Networks in International Politics*. Ithaca, NY: Cornell University Press.
Krook, Mona Lena, and Sarah Childs, eds. 2010. *Women, Gender, and Politics*. New York: Oxford University Press.
McCarthy, John, Clark McPhail, and Jackie Smith. 1996. "Images of Protest: Dimensions of Selection Bias in Media Coverage of Washington Demonstrations 1982 and 1991." *American Sociological Review* 61 (1):478–499.
McCoy, Katherine. 1988. "Graphic Design: Sources of Meaning in Word and Image." *Word & Image* 4 (1):116–130.
Mérce Egyesület. 1999. *Születéskalauz* [*Guide to Birth*]. Budapest: Mérce Egyesület.
———. 2001. *Születéskalauz 2* [*Guide to Birth 2*]. Budapest: Mérce Egyesület.
Nol. 2012. "Bayerék bevárták az utolsó vonulókat, egymillióig számolnak—A Fidesz a hidegtől féltette saját erődemonstrációját" [Bayer and the Other Organizers Waited for the Last Participants, They Are Counting Until the Millionth Member of the March—FIDESZ Was Concerned for Supporters because of the Cold]. *Népszabadság*, January 21. Accessed June 15, 2016. http://nol.hu/belfold/kormanyparti_tuntetes__a_koran_erkezok_is_megtoltottek_a_hosok_teret.
Ónody-Molnár, Dóra. 2012. "Az otthon szülés hazai háborúja" [The War at Home about Home-Birth]. *Népszabadság*, June 1. Accessed June 15, 2016. http://nol.hu/belfold/20120601-az_otthon_szules_hazai_haboruja.
Porter, Catherine. 2012. "Hungarian Doctor Agnes Gereb to Go to Jail for Helping with Home Births." *The Star*, March 26. Accessed June 15, 2016. http://www.thestar.com/news/gta/2012/03/26/hungarian_dr_agnes_gereb_to_go_to_jail_for_helping_with_home_births.html.
Rose, Gillian. 2001. *Visual Methodologies: An Introduction to the Interpretation of Visual Materials*. London, UK, and Thousand Oaks, CA: SAGE.
Ternovszky, Anna. 2012. Speech at Human Rights in Childbirth Conference. Accessed December 26, 2016. http://www.humanrightsinchildbirth.org/blog/2013/9/26/anna-ternovszkys-speech-at-hric-conference-2012?rq=anna-ternovszky.
Tonetti, Elena. 2012. "Imprisoned Midwifes." *Birth into Being* (blog). September 28. Accessed December 30, 2016. https://birthintobeing.wordpress.com/tag/russia/.
Varró, Szilvia. 2009. "És máglyát is raknak?—Geréb Ágnes nőgyógyász, az otthon szülés hazai népszerűsítője" [Gynecologist Ágnes Geréb: Will They Also Prepare to Burn Her at the Stake?]. *Magyar Narancs*, September 24. Accessed January 18, 2012. http://magyarnarancs.hu/belpol/es_maglyat_is_raknak_-_gereb_agnes_nogyogyasz_az_otthon_szules_hazai_nepszerusitoje-72241.
Volynsky, Masha. 2013. "Constitutional Court Decision Encourages Further Discussion on Home Births." *Radio Praha*, August 28. Accessed December 30, 2016. http://www.radio.cz/en/section/curraffrs/constitutional-court-decision-encourages-further-discussion-on-home-births.

12

Regional and Theoretical Lessons: New Perspectives on Civil Societies and Ambiguities toward the State, the West, and Gender Equality

Katalin Fábián and Elżbieta Korolczuk

Lessons from the Case Studies: Civil Society in the Local Context

The cases included in the volume demonstrate that people can and do mobilize in contemporary Central-Eastern Europe and Russia, sometimes even on a mass scale. The parental activists rebel against the state and various authorities, for example, against the medical authorities and international gender experts, claiming to act on behalf of their children, family, and the larger community. Parental activism in the region is not only increasingly visible, but also brings tangible results such as changes in law and welfare provisions, shifts in public debates on parenthood, treatment of infertility, and reconsideration of the role of the state or gender equality. Depending on the sociopolitical context, the activists opt for either degendered identity of parents or the gendered identity of fathers or mothers, to legitimize their claims and gain wide social resonance. They employ a wide array of tactics, which include petitioning the government, lobbying, service provision, and demonstrations, often combining different types of activism. The cases described in this book attest to the potential for mobilization also in seemingly apathetic and distrustful societies.

Despite the ongoing activities and wide-ranging agendas of parental mobilizations, there is no established theoretical perspective on parental activism in the postcommunist region. This collection of essays provides the beginnings of a framework for such a perspective by highlighting how the existing theoretical frameworks on civil society and social movements apply to the postcommunist context. Additionally, the contributing authors suggest how the existing theories may need to be adapted to take local and regional characteristics into account.

Although not every contributing author discusses the notion of civil society, this concept emerged as the most widely applicable theoretical framework across the case studies included in this volume. Several related but distinct conceptualizations of civil society (see Lichterman and Eliasoph 2014) closely correspond with the lessons emerging from the Central-Eastern European and Russian parental movements.

The earliest liberal accounts of civil society depict it as clearly delineated from government. In such accounts, it is a crucial actor in creating and maintaining democracy, functioning as "civil society against the state" (Arato 1981). Building on the well-established liberal interpretation, civil society in the communist and then the postcommunist context took on an additional moral dimension with Václav Hável's (1985) description of civil society as anti-politics. Continuing to rely on the antipolitics provided by the private sphere as a network of friends and family to protect against the intrusions of the contemporary state, the proto- (emerging) middle class in the postcommunist region has used parenthood as a powerful symbol to enter public deliberations on a wide range of topics. Parental activists have established networks to express solidarity against the many disruptive political and economic transformations since the end of communism (Chernova 2012). Bringing this important but long-neglected perspective into consideration along with liberal and antipolitical interpretations, the gendered conceptualization of civil society informs our analysis, highlighting the processes of inclusion and exclusion inscribed in existing definitions and practices. The application of these three perspectives leads us to stress the need for developing a more encompassing comparative perspective on "civil societies" that is devoid of privileging any class, gender, age, ability, or specific political-cultural context (Hagemann et al. 2008; Howell 2005).

Interpreting the family as an economic, political and emotional unit, civil society—as parental movements present it—stands in contrast to the neoliberal practice of individualism. Parents' social activism, as expressed in at least some of the case studies in this book, also reflects the contemporary disillusionment with democratization, consumerism, and social inequality. These disillusionments and demarcations have produced numerous similarities between parental mobilizations in the region and grassroots activism in other contexts. One important parallel with other countries and regions is that activists engage in but remain highly skeptical of political life. For example, parental movements adopt a similar approach to civil society activists in the United States in that they "disavow" politics associated with corruption, unproductive conflict, and privileged access for special interest groups (Bennett et al. 2013).

Our intended theoretical contribution was to develop a less Western-centric and more meaningfully comparative perspective on civil society by challenging the functional, normative, and ideological aspects of its Western liberal definitions (Dunn and Hann 1996; Ekiert and Kubik 2012; Jacobsson and Saxonberg 2013). The six principal observations, presented below as challenging dichotomies assumed in most existing scholarship, invite us to rethink existing positions concerning contemporary civil society and social movements in Central-Eastern Europe and Russia. The interrelated dichotomies that the case studies prompt us to discuss are (1) deficient/lacking vs. adequate/functioning civil society, (2) formalization/non-governmental organization (NGO) vs. grassroots character of organizing, (3) progressive vs. conservative ideological orientation, (4) locally embedded vs. Western-inspired norms, (5) service provider or lobbying functions, and (6) clear divisions between public and private spheres and between civil society and political society.

First, the qualitative case study analysis in this book contributes to challenging the conventional social science view that has persistently depicted social movements and civil society in Central-Eastern Europe and Russia as weak, passive, and overly professionalized. We argue that many important forms of collective action are not included in the existing canon (cf. Ekiert and Foa 2012; Ekiert and Kubik 2013; Jacobsson and Saxonberg 2013; Jacobsson and Korolczuk 2017). If we account for grassroots activism, civil society in postcommunist Europe may appear richer than many scholars have claimed: while it is diminishing in some ways, it develops and expands in others. The emergence and proliferation of parental activism in the region shows that grassroots activism embedded in everyday practices and identities tends to better correspond to what people perceive as legitimate forms of social activism than other forms of engagement, such as membership in trade unions and NGOs. While the number of grassroots activist groups is extremely difficult to reliably verify because they are not always formalized, we can reasonably assert that this form of civil society may be the most popular in political contexts where distrust in formal politics reigns supreme.

Second, the parental movements examined here also challenge the dichotomies ingrained in the existing definitions that relate to the assumed formal organizational and affiliated institutional attributes of civil society, such as the ability to apply for funding and the presumption of transparency. Many (although not all) activists openly distance themselves from professionalized NGOs for practical or ideological reasons. In this respect, the analysis of parental mobilizations in the Central-Eastern European region and Russia sheds light on how the formalized "NGO-ized," donor-responsive civil society model is challenged and reinterpreted by the activists to better fit and apply to local contexts (Jacobsson 2015). Parental activists reinterpret existing relations between citizens by claiming their role is an exemplary manifestation of true civic-mindedness organized informally.

Although not necessarily renouncing ideological or financial resource transfers from the state or international partners, the activists highlight their notion of civil society as uncorrupted by such funding. They state their opposition to what many scholars critical of the process of NGO-ization depict as alienated, Western, or state-founded, bureaucratized NGOs (e.g., Chaudry and Kapoor 2013; Ghodsee 2004). Particularly relevant in the contemporary Russian setting, but applicable elsewhere as well, the claim of being locally embedded and funded provides broad appeal. This is true not only in the case of parental movements but also in the broadly defined political sphere (Ljubownikow, Crotty, and Rogers 2013). "True civil mindedness" may appear more substantiated when movements claim local embeddedness and incorruptibility. Combining the claims of informal organization, local roots, and transparency with the self-description of apolitical engagement for the betterment of the community has provided a springboard for parental activists.

Many parental movements reorient attention from the ideological axis of progressive vs. conservative values to the transformed pair of locally embedded vs. Western-inspired norms. Within this reoriented ideological framework, the liberal underpinnings of civil society that include the promotion of individual freedoms and rights along with gender equality are replaced by incorruptibility and orientation toward the well-being of the family as a whole (cf. Fábián 2014; Kocka 2006). Some parental movements have adopted elements of a human rights framework in their rhetoric, but they employ it very selectively. For example, conservative parental groups opposing the right to abortion present embryos as human beings deserving human and civil rights while denying these rights to other groups such as sexual minorities, claiming that homosexuality is alien to local tradition and culture (Graff and Korolczuk 2017).

As Höjdestrand and Strelnyk show in chapters 1 and 2, the same logic applies to how conservative parental movements present the civic activism of LGBTQ and feminist groups. Such groups are often portrayed as inspired and financed by Western countries, in contrast to home-grown and grassroots mobilizations of "patriotic" civil society. Parental activists tend to define themselves as part of "true" civil society while applying a selective portrayal of what it means to be local.

The next important dichotomy that many of our case studies appear to undermine relates to the functional dimension of civil society. The functional definitions of civil society separate groups and organizations focusing on service provisions from lobbyists and protesters. Scholars studying social movements in the postcommunist region have recently challenged the applicability of such functional division (Fröhlich 2012; Jacobsson 2015; Korolczuk and Saxonberg 2014). The cases of conservative parental movements in Russia and Ukraine, fathers' groups in Ukraine and Poland, and the movement of parents of children with disabilities in the Baltic states also demonstrate that parental activists effectively combine both service provisions and lobbying, while also engaging in what they call community building. To some extent, such a combination of supposedly discrete civil society functions stems from practical constraints, such as limited funding and trying to achieve a sustainable, long-term existence. Cuts in welfare spending have made it necessary for many to rely on family and neighbors rather than the state. This increased reliance on family and friends also allows for new bonds between people who want to provide financial and social help and those who need such help. Aiming to avoid dependency on donors and advocating distance from the state mean that parental activists have to gather the necessary resources directly from individuals and families rather than from existing NGOs or the authorities. There are various organizational, functional, and emotional consequences of such choices, making parental movements more likely beholden to the personal interests, time and money, as well as value orientations of its continuing activists. At the same time, such self-limitations may unfavorably affect the longevity of such groups.

Making the movements' choice of financial independence viable are the emotional and social links between parents whose children go to the same schools or suffer from similar health problems or disabilities. Parental activism is deeply embedded in everyday life experiences and emotions, which can help parents to overcome any hesitation about taking part in collective action, and collaboration often starts with distributing information and acknowledging shared experiences, including not only childcare but also difficult divorce or custody proceedings. This often involves producing new types of knowledge that can establish a basis to challenge established authorities and powerful institutions as in the case of Czech antivaccination movement examined by Marhánková in chapter 8, parents of children with disabilities studied by Sumskiene in chapter 9, and the Hungarian homebirth movement examined by Fábián in chapter 11 in this volume. Providing emotional support and producing and sharing knowledge can lead to sustained mobilization and organization. Focusing on service provision may allow the parental groups to appear apolitical in environments where being overtly politically engaged is seen as suspect or may even be dangerous (Fröhlich 2012).

Finally, the definition and practice of parental activism entails the reinterpretation of the divides between the public-private spheres and civil society-political society (Hagemann 2008; Okin 1998; Scott and Keates 2004). While civil society is most often conceptualized as being linked with but conceptually separate from the family and kin networks and from political society, parental movements in the European postcommunist region highlight how negotiable and dynamic the connections between these distinctly imagined spheres are. As in women's movements, parental groups represent a hybrid form of civic activism positioned at the intersection of public and private identities and spaces. The activists come forward as parents, mothers, fathers, grandparents, or siblings to legitimize their movements' claims, concerning what had been considered private family matters such as infertility, disability, or the choice of how and where to give birth to a child. The activists' transgression of the public-private divide highlights that these movements are deeply political also in the sense that they energetically engage with decisions issued by the authorities.

At the same time, the parental movements studied in this book tend to reinforce the public-private division understood as the distinction between public and domestic spheres (Hagemann 2008, 29). Most parental activists defend the idea that domestic life should be free from the interference of the state, including a parent's right to control other family members, especially children, for example, in matters of healthcare (Marhánková in chapter 8 of this volume). Many parental movements strongly oppose the state's intervention in their children's upbringing, be it in the sphere of sex education, vaccination, or custody rights.

Putting these two perspectives together, parental movements' transgression of the public-private divide appears highly ambiguous. From the activists' perspective, the transgressing of the public-private divide appears open from their direction only to influence political decisions. The other direction is closed due to activists' aim to "protect the family" as a unit from the intervention of the state or the broader public. Adding to their already tense relationship with the public-private divide, most local parental movements avoid critically addressing power relations and inequalities within the family. The movements' strategic and ideological reasons for appearing gender-neutral and "parental" further strengthen their myopia regarding power inequalities embedded within the family.

The Civic Engagement of Parental Movements: Representing Strategic and Flexible Ambiguity in Relation to the State, the "West," and Gender Equality

In the cases of parental activism covered here, ambiguity appears as simultaneously distancing from, redefining, and engaging vis-à-vis three main areas. The first strategically employed ambiguity pertains to the relationship to politics and the state as the main institution that represents the highest stage of politics. The second ambiguity that the parental movements have highlighted relates to what is perceived as the "West" and its corresponding values of individualization. The third set has to do with the ambiguous relationship of parental movements to gender equality. We find these ambiguities informative because in contexts where the notion of the political is associated with both negative connotations and disengagement, activists have to navigate between contradictory discourses and practices in order to become engaged and to mobilize others around political issues.

Ambiguity toward the State and Political Sphere

The first and probably most prevalent ambiguity concerns the sphere of formal politics and the role of the state as the central institution of political society. Parental activism is usually not based on conventional forms of political participation, such as membership in parties, trade unions, or NGOs. Rather, parental movements spring from existing types of identification linked to the private sphere (as it is understood in the given cultural and political milieu). The activists tend to showcase their familiar and close private associations when they make their collectivist claims to the state as mothers, fathers, or people who want to become parents through reproductive technologies. Even when the activists formalize their organizations as NGOs, they tend to keep in close touch with the group they represent (see Fábián in chapter 11 and Sumskiene in chapter 9 in this volume).

The contributing authors analyze a specific type of civic activism in Central-Eastern Europe and Russia where skepticism about politics is high and the level of trust of others is very low (World Value Surveys 2008). Many parental activists also express a distrust of politics and note their skepticism of national and transnational institutions. Despite being involved in civic activism, the activists often appear cynical about the possibility of bringing about positive change (see Höjdestrand, Saxonberg, and Sumskiene in this volume). Yet, they continue to present political claims and attempt to influence political processes, often with notable success. How do they reconcile the contradiction between broadly held views on politics and their own engagement?

Researchers who study the paradox of civic activism combined with strong skepticism about and distrust in politics in the United States propose to conceptualize this trend as "disavowal of the political" that does not necessarily signal apathy or withdrawal from political life (Bennett et. al 2014). Disavowal entails distancing from institutional politics and from the negative connotations associated with it. Rejecting the negative aspects of what they consider to be the attributes of politics, the activists simultaneously engage in civic activism and identify with what they view as "a more positive ideal of public engagement and social change" (Bennett et. al 2014, 530). For example, although activists do not trust the government, they collaborate with it to solve what they consider to be public problems, trying to make the best of a bad situation.

The activists' focus on the private sphere and their informal organizations make the parental movements appear apolitical, at least in part because activists view the state and party politics as representing the interests of the elite rather than common people. Nationalist rhetoric offers an appealing option among these movements in promoting the ideal of a community that should exist independently of political and social shifts. Combining the high potential for mobilization with clear distancing from any type of formal politics produces broad social resonance and helps to overcome the apathy and distrust. The ambiguity toward politics and the state serves an effective purpose when parental movements stress their private identities as their source of legitimization and claim that they are apolitical in nature.

Informal groups are traditionally shunning formal politics. Adopting such ideological stance allows grassroots parental activists to distance themselves strategically from what they see as "dirty" party politics while making profoundly political claims. This strategy has become especially popular in the postcommunist region and is also observed, for example, among urban activists in Eastern Europe (Jacobsson 2015; Polańska 2015). The antipolitical trend of social movement activism can be interpreted as the legacy of communism, while it also pertains to the contemporary corruption crisis and lack of governmental transparency as exemplified by mass demonstrations against governments in Bulgaria in 2013, Hungary in 2014, and in Romania in 2017. Both communist-era and more recent experiences continue to produce profound distrust of what activists see as a corrupt political sphere that morally repels and alienates them.

At the same time, the antipolitical stance reflects a wider trend of postmodern disillusionment with liberal democracy characterized by a low level of state responsiveness to social movement activism. Scholars note that the activists in other contexts, such as in the United States, often stress that they are not political and that they do not see their work as political (Baiocchi et al. 2014). Such statements reflect not only the distance which exists between the state and citizens, but also a complicated relationship with political life and a desire to redefine what is political.

When parental activists stress their fundamental distrust of the state, they highlight what they see as an ever-intrusive intervention in the private sphere of the family and children's upbringing. In this context, the state is often portrayed as an all-powerful force that wishes to fulfill its own needs, rather than those of children or parents. This view resonates with the continued relevance of the derided role of the communist state, but transnational neoconservative ideas and networks also enliven and strengthen such rhetoric. The Bulgarian, Ukrainian, and Russian cases studies in this book exemplify the transnational, neoconservative, and ideological trends and personal connections as they highlight the involvement of representatives of US conservative groups and state-supported Russian experts and funding operating in the post-communist region.

Despite the activists' stated distrust of and distance from the state, it is in fact the state that remains the main addressee of these parental movements' claims. Some groups even demand more state intervention—for example, Polish fathers' rights activists demanding that mothers who do not allow fathers to have contact with their children after divorce should be imprisoned. The case of the Russian parents' movement also shows that the activists perceive the state as an institution that should protect citizens from the "corrupt West."

The cases examined in this volume show that depending on the aims and the current needs of the movement, the state and political sphere become simultaneously demonized and idealized in the narratives of parental activists. It is also important to note that the two opposing types of relationship to the state aptly highlight that politics is far from homogenous in any context. Even the relatively few alternatives available in some political regimes may offer excellent openings for parental movements to enter policy deliberations and exert considerable influence (see, for example, the shifting Ukrainian political environment examined by Strelnyk in chapter 2).

Principled distancing and direct participation of parental mobilizations in political society represent two clearly opposite approaches to the government and political parties. In this respect, some parental mobilizations, such as conservative movements in Russia and Ukraine, can be interpreted as counter-movements, which oppose recent developments in social policy and cultural changes especially in regard to gender equality. However, the case of the antivaccination movement in the Czech Republic may also belong to the postmodern, possibly anti-modernity, strand. In this case the opposition to the state is often interwoven with resistance to biotechnologies, which are seen as being imposed on citizens by state institutions in order to control the population at the expense of the people. The Bulgarian case of mobilization around reproductive technologies shows, however, that pronatalist, gendered nationalist discourse can be combined with the high valorization of technological progress in the field of biomedicine as supported by the state.

Ambiguity toward "The West"

The second set of strategic ambiguities in parental movements' relationships pertains to attitudes to "the West," a catch-all term for the European Union (EU), United Nations (UN), the UN Convention on the Rights of the Child, and other transnational institutions and treaties. In this context, the West is associated with these institutions and treaties and is also becoming equated with a set of values such as individual rights and "sexual democracy" (Fassin 2014), in particular gender equality and sexual and reproductive rights.

Reflecting the contested norms in the changing geopolitical belonging of Central-Eastern Europe and Russia, the informational materials and media appearances of many leaders of conservative parents' groups portray the West as the ultimate enemy. Yet again, in these narratives we can find echoes of the anti-Western propaganda of the communist era that overlap with anticolonial discourse, highlighting the contemporary cultural and economic hegemony of both the United States and the EU (Graff and Korolczuk 2017; cf. Morozov 2015; Zarycki 2014). Strong critiques of what is portrayed as the Western ideological stance point to the lack of "true" values and to "immoral" sexual ethics as well as individual-centeredness. Such a communitarian rejection also includes the distancing from neoliberal logic and praxis—for example, cuts in welfare benefits—that affect families. Some Central-Eastern European parental groups and networks have vehemently opposed cuts to welfare and demanded more support from the state, especially in childcare and in the healthcare sectors, as Karzabi, Strelnyk, Dimitrova, and Sumskiene highlight in this volume. This set of demarcations locates the general distrust of the West not only in the sphere of values, but also regarding the systemic economic changes introduced in the region in recent decades.

However, rejection of the West is only one possible aspect of parental movements in Central-Eastern Europe and Russia. Less emphasized but just as relevant are the many connections to the West—both material and normative-ideological—that parental movements maintain. Many parental mobilizations such as the home-birth movement in Hungary, the natural birth and antivaccination movements in the Czech Republic, and the fathers' movements in Poland, Russia, and Ukraine are part of a global phenomenon in which activist groups emerge adapted to a particular cultural, social, and historical context (Collier and Sheldon 2006; Flood 2012). There is a high degree of exchange among activists of not only knowledge but also material and financial funds, especially between EU member states. Most importantly, ideas now "travel" easily from country to country thanks to various media and social networks.

New norms and concepts mix with local, often contradictory meanings. Discussing the case of the contemporary Czech Republic, Hrešanová explains, in chapter 10, how concepts such as "natural birth" that emerged in the United States and Canada in the 1950s are often used as flagship causes for the key ideas that local movement fights for. The adopted term itself becomes transformed and "domesticated" in the process and refers to diverse ideas of various historical origins. A similar adaptation has emerged in the case of Russia, which appears relatively isolated today and where the state nurtures the local anti-Western tradition. Höjdestrand's analysis (chapter 1) of local grassroots mobilization in defense of what is described as traditional family values shows that these groups tap into a contemporary global social conservative ideoscape in which the Russian anti-sex rhetoric shows many similarities with the United States and West European neoconservative discourses.

The ambivalent relationships with both the state and the West have consequences for the ideological position of the conservative strand of parental movements. These relationships also affect practical choices concerning financing and cooperating with state institutions, political parties, and transnational NGOs. As we discussed above, some Central-Eastern European and Russian parental groups resist becoming professionalized (NGO-ized) and many of them neither ask for nor accept international support. In contemporary Russia, receiving any sort of financial support from abroad can dramatically marginalize such groups as "foreign agents," and some parental NGOs and networks in EU member countries did not receive state-sponsored or EU grants probably because they did not fit the ideological framework for issues such as gender equality, as the case of conservative Polish fathers' groups shows (Korolczuk and Hryciuk in chapter 4 of this volume). As conservative and illiberal parties have increasingly gained power since 2008 in parts of postcommunist Europe, this trend became subject to change. For example, in Poland, the new right-wing government has started to support conservative parental organizations while cutting funding for progressive groups and NGOs. Similarly, in Hungary, conservative groups do receive state funding

(Saxonberg 2013), but despite an explicit promise from the Parliament, the flagship birth center of the home-birth movement did not (see Fábián chapter 11 in this volume). Moreover, some parental movements have chosen to establish strong connections to political parties (as chapters 2 and 6 on Ukraine show), while others—such as the Russian parental movements—prefer to keep political elites at a distance. An even less popular option is to create a political party that focuses on the policy issue that the activists find difficult to accomplish as an actor in civil society, exemplified by Korolczuk and Hryciuk in chapter 4 on fathers' groups in Poland. Most parental groups and networks are grassroots mobilizations and do not represent the bureaucratized, donor-dependent civil society that the region has been often associated with.

Ambiguity toward Gender Equality

The third most notable ambiguity pertains to the field of gender equality, usually interpreted as the corresponding EU-mandated, and sometimes state-sponsored, discourses and policies that many local and international feminist movements promote. The movements countering gender equality label all these related ideas under the term of "genderism" or "gender ideology" (Graff 2014; Hankivsky and Skoryk 2014; Hodžic and Bijelic 2014; Korolczuk 2014). The opposition to gender equality overlaps with the suspicion of the West and the state. According to the parental movements aiming to counter "genderism," international treaties on children's and women's rights are a Trojan horse, or cover-up, for the "real agenda" of foreign institutions that is aimed at depopulation and (re)colonization of the region. In the recent wave of protests against legislation on gender equality (such as the Council of Europe's Istanbul Convention), gender-sensitive education at schools, and especially the rights of sexual-minority groups, gender equality has become one of the central elements of what is called an "anti-colonial" argument (Graff and Korolczuk 2017; cf. Kováts and Põim 2015). Adoption or rejection of gender equality policies has emerged as a demarcation line between what is seen as the local, "true" values and Western, alien values that are supposedly imposed on people through international institutions and complicit, corrupt state machineries and elites. The anticolonial discourse has reemerged powerfully not only in Russia and Ukraine but recently also in EU countries such as Poland and Hungary. Some versions have appeared in Western European countries as well, although it is reframed there to appeal to some of fundamentalist religious groups and immigrant communities to mobilize them against feminists and gays as "arrogant cultural colonizers" (Graff and Korolczuk 2017).

The ambivalent relationships to both gender equality and the West highlight the crucial importance of translation—both in practice (in part because the word "gender" has proven to be difficult to translate into Bulgarian, Polish, Russian, and Ukrainian) and also symbolically. Yulia Gradskova presents a similar argument when analyzing the discourses and practices of gender equality in contemporary northwestern Russia. She explains that even though some representatives of local authorities were open to negotiations with their Nordic partners as to what understanding of gender equality is valid and could be implemented on location, in most cases "the Soviet-style interpretation of women's issues as part of 'social problems' and protection of motherhood prevailed" (2015, 69), replacing the interpretation centered on the inequality of power between the two genders. Many fathers' movements behave very similarly, claiming to promote the idea of gender equality while in fact redefining it very narrowly as only relevant to postdivorce arrangements.

The cases discussed in this book demonstrate that the use of ambiguities in relation to the state, the West, and gender equality is an approach common to parental movements in the region. Their agenda appears flexible and adaptable in finding alliances and relying upon political and discursive openings in the interaction of local and transnational politics. We conceptualize the use of such flexible and adaptable ambiguities as a strategy to engage in political activism in a way that—similarly to "disavowal"—entails challenging and redefining what politics and civic engagement mean in a given sociocultural context. Here "strategy" is understood as a pattern of activity that emerges as the activist group aims to change its environment. The question of whether these choices are "strategic," in the sense of the degree to which they are elaborate, conscious, and goal-oriented, remains open (Bennett et. al 2014; Johnson and Robinson 2006). Applying a set of flexible and adaptable ambiguities enables parental activists to distance themselves from the main cleavages in politics while simultaneously engaging in political processes. Importantly, the resulting hybrid narratives and identities shape everyday practices and reach out to potential activists and the broader public through capillary systems instead of street politics or formal institutions in order to affect state policies and public attitudes. Arguably, these sets of ambiguities help to mobilize for change in environments where most people do not believe that political actions can make a difference.

The Nexus of Civil Society and Social Movement Theories with Local Empirical Analysis

At the intersection of communist-era influences and newly emergent and hegemonic discourses and practices such as capitalism, neoliberalism, at least superficial democratization and the recent wave of illiberal populism, Central-Eastern Europe and Russia provide an excellent arena in which to observe the many complexities in how transnational processes interact with local environments. Tensions are also bound to develop in this region due to the dramatically changing course of geopolitical alliances and their proclaimed norms. In the increasingly globally integrated social space of political contestation in Central-Eastern Europe and Russia, parental movements afford us also a more nuanced view of the state of civil society and social movements.

This collection of essays has aimed to bring the perspectives of theories on civil society and social movements closer to the turbulent and diverse empirical landscape in the postcommunist European region. We hope that our observations on the ways in which parental activists redefine civic activism, construct their collective identities, and employ a set of strategic, flexible, and adaptable ambiguities in relation to the state, the West, and gender equality have answered some of the questions noted in the introduction.

Our collection of essays shows that parental mobilizations have frequently emerged in the region, with many countries demonstrating multiple, persistent, and notably successful activism. Using the case studies presented here, we argue that a set of strategically used ambiguities have assisted mothers, fathers, and those thinking of becoming parents to respond to political, social, cultural, and economic challenges on a collective level. In each of the case studies, the legacies of different forms of communism as well as the varied impacts of contemporary neoliberal influences have affected the subject matter and manner of parental mobilization. The authors in this book have demonstrated the proliferation of conservative gendered nationalist imagery as an important trend emerging across the region. The spread of gendered nationalist imagery is clearly linked to the heightened contemporary political debates on what the state's priorities should be and whether democracy needs to be linked to liberal ideological orientation or not.

We find that existing social movement theories and conceptualizations of civil society only partially explain the developments of parental movements in Central-Eastern Europe and Russia. These theories need to be adapted and modified if we want to understand this phenomenon in all of its complexity. Analyzing parental movements in the postcommunist region through the lens of civil society and social movement theories, as well as analytical concepts developed in the studies on citizenship, gendered nationalism, and social policy, calls for a theory or theories that can accommodate local identities and practices while engaging with the Western liberal interpretations of civil society.

Katalin Fábián, Professor, Department of Government and Law, Lafayette College, Easton, PA, USA

Katalin Fábián studies the intersection of gender and globalization as they influence various policy processes of emerging democracies. She edited *Globalization: Perspectives from Central and Eastern Europe* (Elsevier, 2007) and served as the editor of a special issue of *Canadian-American Slavic Studies* that focuses on the changing international relations of Central and Eastern Europe. Her book, *Contemporary Women's Movements in Hungary: Globalization, Democracy, and Gender Equality* (Johns Hopkins University Press, 2009), analyzes the emergence and political significance of women's activism in Hungary. She conducted research among government officials and activists of NGOs that support victims of domestic violence in the post-Soviet Baltic countries, the Czech Republic, Hungary, Poland, Slovenia, and Slovakia. This research led her to contribute chapters to and edit *Domestic Violence in Postcommunist States: Local Activism, National Policies, and Global Forces* (Indiana University Press, 2010), which focuses on the transnational connections between the various European and Eurasian postcommunist movements against domestic violence.

Elżbieta Korolczuk, researcher, School of Culture and Education, Södertörn University, Sweden; and Lecturer of Gender Studies at Warsaw University, Poland

Elżbieta Korolczuk, PhD, is a sociologist working at Södertörn University in Sweden. She also teaches at the Gender Studies Centre at Warsaw University in Poland. Her research interests include social movements, civil society and gender (especially motherhood/fatherhood, assisted reproductive technologies, and feminism). Recently, she conducted research on parental activism and social and legal implications of assisted reproduction in Poland, and on gender and political cultures of knowledge. She co-edited (with Renata E. Hryciuk) two volumes (in Polish): *Farewell to the Polish Mother? Discourses, Practices and Representations of Motherhood in Contemporary Poland* (2012), which explores ideologies and practices of motherhood in Poland, and *Dangerous Liaisons: Motherhood, Fatherhood and Politics* (2015), which focuses on the intersection between motherhood, fatherhood, and politics in Poland and Russia. Most recent publications include an edited volume (with KerJacobsson) *Civil Society Revisited: Lessons from Poland* published by Berghahn Books in April 2017.

Works Cited

Baiocchi, Gianpaolo, Elizabeth A. Bennett, Alissa Cordner, Peter Taylor Klein, and Stephanie Savell. 2014. *The Civic Imagination: Making a Difference in American Political Life*. Boulder, CO: Paradigm Publishers.

Bennett, Elizabeth A., Alissa Cordner, Peter Taylor Klein, Stephanie Savell, and Gianpaolo Baiocchi. 2013. "Disavowing Politics: Civic Engagement in an Era of Political Scepticism." *American Journal of Sociology* 119 (2):518–548.

Bertoia, Carl, and Janice Drakich. 1993. "The Fathers' Rights Movement: Contradictions in Rhetoric and Practice." *Journal* of *Family Issues* 14 (4):592–615.

Chernova, Zhanna. 2012. "Parenthood in Russia: From the State Duty to Personal Responsibility and Mutual Cooperation." *Anthropology of East Europe Review* 30 (2):1–19.

Choudry, Aziz, and Dip Kapoor, eds. 2013. *NGOization. Complicity, Contradictions and Prospects*. London: Zed Books.

Collier, Richard, and Sally Sheldon, eds. 2006. *Fathers' Rights Activism and Law Reform in Comparative Perspective*. Oxford and Portland: Hart Publishing.

Dunn, Elizabeth, and Chris Hann, eds. 1996. *Civil Society: Challenging Western Models*. London: Routledge.

Ekiert, Grzegorz, and Roberto Foa. 2012. "The Weakness of Post-Communist Civil Societies Reassessed." *CES Papers—Open Forum 11*. Harvard University: Center for European Studies.

Ekiert, Grzegorz, and Jan Kubik. 2014. "Myths and Realities of Civil Society." *Journal of Democracy* 25 (1):46–58.

Fábián, Katalin. 2014. "Disciplining the 'Second World': The Relationship between Transnational and Local Forces in Contemporary Hungarian Women's Social Movements." *East European Politics* 30 (1):1–20.

Fassin, Éric. 2014. "Same-Sex Marriage, Nation, and Race: French Political Logics and Rhetorics." *Contemporary French Civilization* 39 (3):281–301.

Flood, Michel. 2012. "Separated Fathers and the Fathers' Rights Movement." *Journal of Family Studies* 18 (2–3):235–245.

Fröhlich, Christian. 2012. "Civil Society and the State Intertwined: The Case of Disability NGOs in Russia." *East European Politics* 28 (4):371–389.

Ghodsee, Kristen. 2004. "Feminism-by-Design: Emerging Capitalisms, Cultural Feminism, and Women's Nongovernmental Organizations in Postsocialist Eastern Europe." *Signs* 29 (3):727–754.

Gradskova, Yulia. 2015. "Translating 'Gender Equality': Northwestern Russia Meets the Global Gender Equality Agenda." *Baltic Worlds* 8 (8):1–2, 69–73.

Graff, Agnieszka, and Elżbieta Korolczuk. 2017. "'Worse Than Communism and Nazism Put Together': War on Gender in Poland." In *Anti-Gender Campaigns in Europe: Religious and Political Mobilizations against Equality*, edited by David Paternotte and Roman Kuhar, 175–194. Lanham: Rowman and Littlefield.

Hagemann, Karen, Sonya Michel, and Gunilla Budde. 2008. *Civil Society and Gender Justice: Historical and Comparative Perspectives*. New York, Oxford: Berghahn Books.

Hodžic, Amir, and Nataša Bijelić. 2014. "Neo-Conservative Threats to Sexual and Reproductive Rights in the European Union." Center for Education, Counseling and Research. Accessed October 6, 2016. http://www.cesi.hr/attach/_n/neo-conservative_threats_to_srhr_in_eu.pdf.

Howard, Marc Morjé. 2003. *The Weakness of Civil Society in Post-Communist Europe*. Cambridge: Cambridge University Press.

Howell, Jude. 2005. "Gender and Civil Society." In *Global Civil Society*, edited by Helmut K. Anheier, Mary Kaldor, and Marlies Glasius, 38–63. London: SAGE.

Jacobsson, Kerstin, and Steven Saxonberg, eds. 2013. *Beyond NGO-ization: The Development of Social Movements in Central and Eastern Europe*. Farnham: Ashgate.

Jacobsson, Kerstin, ed. 2015. *Urban Grassroots Movements in Central and Eastern Europe*. Farnham: Ashgate.

Jacobsson, Kerstin, and Elżbieta Korolczuk. 2017. *Civil Society Revisited: Lessons from Poland*. New York and Oxford: Berghahn Books.

Johnson, Elise Janet, and Jean C. Robinson, eds. 2006. *Living Gender after Communism*. Bloomington: Indiana University Press.

Kocka, Jurgen. 2006. "Civil Society from a Historical Perspective." In *Civil Society: Berlin Perspectives*, edited by John Keane, 37–50. New York and Oxford: Berghahn Books.

Korolczuk, Elżbieta, and Steven Saxonberg. 2014."Strategies of Contentious Action: A Comparative Analysis of the Women's Movements in Poland and the Czech Republic." *European Societies*, 17 (4):404–422.

Korolczuk, Elżbieta. 2014. "'The War on Gender' from a Transnational Perspective—Lessons for Feminist Strategising." In *Anti-Gender Movements on the Rise? Strategising for Gender Equality in Central and Eastern Europe* 38:43–53. Berlin: Heinrich Böll Foundation.

Kováts, Eszter, and Maari Põim, eds. 2015. *Gender as Symbolic Glue: The Position and Role of Conservative and Far Right Parties in The Anti-Gender Mobilizations in Europe*. Accessed October 5, 2016. http://www.feps-europe.eu/assets/cae464d2-f4ca-468c-a93e-5d0dad365a83/feps-gender-as-symbolic-glue-wwwpdf.pdf.

Lichterman, Paul, and Nina Eliasoph. 2014. "Civic Action." *American Journal of Sociology* 120 (3):798–863.

Ljubownikow, Sergej, Jo Crotty, and Peter W. Rogers. 2013. "The State and Civil Society in Post-Soviet Russia: The Development of a Russian Style Civil Society." *Progress in Development Studies* 13 (2):153–166.

Morozov, Viatcheslav. 2015. *Subaltern Empire in a Eurocentric World*. London: Palgrave Macmillan.

Okin, Moller Susan. 1998. "Gender, The Public and the Private." In *Feminism and Politics,* edited by Anne Philips, 116–142. Oxford, New York: Oxford University Press.

Scott, Joan W., and Diane Keates, eds. 2004. *Going Public: Feminism and the Shifting Boundaries of the Private Sphere,* Urbana and Champaign: University of Illinois Press.

World Values Surveys. 2008. *World Values Surveys 1981–84, 1990–93, 1995–97, 2000–4, 2005–7.* Ann Arbor: Inter-University Consortium for Political and Social Research.

Zarycki, Tomasz. 2014. *Ideologies of Eastness in Central and Eastern Europe.* London: Routledge.

Index

www.ingramcontent.com/pod-product-compliance
Lightning Source LLC
Chambersburg PA
CBHW071013280326
41935CB00011B/1332
* 9 7 8 0 2 5 3 0 2 6 6 7 5 *